Economics and World Power

THE POLITICAL ECONOMY
OF INTERNATIONAL CHANGE
John Gerard Ruggie, General Editor

Economics
and World Power

An Assessment
of American Diplomacy
Since 1789

Edited by
**William H. Becker and
Samuel F. Wells, Jr.**

Columbia University Press
New York
1984

Library of Congress Cataloging in Publication Data
Main entry under title:

Economics and world power.

   (The Political economy of international change)
   Includes bibliographical references and index.
   1. United States—Foreign economic relations—
Addresses, essays, lectures.   2. United States—
Territorial expansion—Addresses, essays, lectures.
3. United States—Foreign relations—Addresses, essays,
lectures.   4. United States—Economic conditions—
Addresses, essays, lectures.   I. Becker, William H.
II. Wells, Samuel F.   III. Series.
HF1455.E327   1984   327.73   83-15432
ISBN 0-231-04370-8
ISBN 0-231-04371-6 (pbk.)

Columbia University Press
New York   Guildford, Surrey

Clothbound editions of Columbia University Press Books are
Smyth-sewn and printed on permanent and durable acid-free
paper.

Contents

Notes on the Contributors

WILLIAM H. BECKER is professor of history at the George Washington University. His book *The Dynamics of Business-Government Relations: Industry and Exports, 1893–1921* (1982) won the 1983 Thomas Newcomen Prize for the best book in business history published between 1979 and 1982.

KINLEY J. BRAUER, professor of history at the University of Minnesota, has published *Cotton vs. Conscience: Massachusetts Whig Politics and Southwestern Expansion, 1843–1848* (1967). His continuing research focuses on American expansionism and imperialism.

DAVID P. CALLEO is professor of European studies at the School of Advanced International Studies, the Johns Hopkins University. An internationally known scholar, his books include *The Imperious Economy* (1982) and *The German Problem Reconsidered* (1978).

JAMES A. FIELD, JR. has written extensively on naval history and American diplomacy and is the author of, among others, *America and the Mediterranean World* (1969). He is the Clothier Professor of History at Swathmore College.

ROBERT M. HATHAWAY has taught at Middlebury College and Barnard College. He is the author of *Ambiguous Partnership: Britain and America, 1944–1947* (1981), which was co-winner of the 1980–81 Truman Book Award.

MELVYN P. LEFFLER is associate professor of history at Vanderbilt University. He has been a fellow at the Woodrow Wilson International Center for Scholars at the Smithsonian Institution and is the author of *The Elusive Quest: America's Pursuit of European Stability and French Security* (1979).

DAVID M. PLETCHER is professor of history at Indiana University. He has served as president of the Society for Historians of American Foreign Relations and is the author of *The Awkward Years: American Foreign Relations Under Garfield and Arthur* (1962) and *The Diplomacy of Annexation: Texas, Oregon, and the Mexican War* (1973).

ROBERT A. POLLARD is associate editor of the *Wilson Quarterly*. He has in press a study of foreign economic policy in the Truman years, *Economic Security and the Origins of the Cold War: The Strategic Ends of Truman's Foreign Economic Policy, 1945–1950*.

SAMUEL F. WELLS, JR. organized and administers the International Security Studies Program at the Woodrow Wilson International Center for Scholars in Washington. An historian and national security specialist, he has been on the faculty of the University of North Carolina and is a coauthor of *The Ordeal of World Power* (1975).

Preface
Economics
and World Power

THE CHANGING POSITION of the United States in the world economy has significantly influenced the conception, formulation, and implementation of American foreign policy. While most scholars and policymakers acknowledge that this is true today, there is much less agreement about the degree to which economic change influenced foreign policy decisions in the past. In this volume we have designed our collective effort to help focus thinking on this subject and perhaps bring about a greater scholarly consensus. But we have not written for our scholarly colleagues alone. Our hope is that advanced undergraduate and graduate students will find this volume helpful in their studies of the history of American foreign policy. Current attention to international economic issues should make the perspectives offered here valuable also to policymakers and the interested public.

Events of the last decade have made clear to Americans that international economic issues are indeed important to the United States. Oil prices, trade deficits, currency depreciations, and protectionist policies frequently have become stories in the daily news. Since World War II the international economy has become increasingly interdependent, and economic issues have profoundly affected United States foreign policy. The new ele-

ment in this is the increased recent public awareness of the interaction between economics and foreign policy.

We initially conceived this volume of essays as a response
to scholarly arguments over the place of economic interests in the
making of United States foreign policy. We addressed ourselves
to the problem that historical studies of American foreign relations
seemed either to underestimate or overestimate the importance of
economics to United States foreign relations. From our own scholarly work, we were convinced that changing economic conditions
were important in policymakers' formulation and conduct of foreign policy and that the magnitude and nature of economic influences on policy varied greatly depending on the structure of the
international economy and America's position in world politics.
Traditional studies of diplomatic history concentrate on political
and strategic issues and accounts of bilateral relations. At times
economic issues played a part, to be sure, but they were hardly
central to such scholarship, based as it was on the close following
of cables, notes, and negotiations among the elites that conducted
foreign affairs. In contrast, revisionist historians of the 1960s saw
the protection and fostering of long-term economic interest at the
root of American foreign policy. Unlike traditional diplomatic historians, the revisionists focused on the domestic, largely economic, origins of foreign policy. In the face of these sharply contrasting styles of interpretation, we thought it time to develop a
synthesis which assesses the position of the United States in the
international system and the importance of economic change, issues, and interests in foreign policy throughout the course of
America's national history.

The revisionists of the 1960s were not the first economic
determinists to write about United States foreign policy. Several
economic analyses of United States involvement in World War I
appeared in the 1920s and 1930s. These studies reflected the broad
public disenchantment over the outcome of the war and growing
isolationist sentiment. Most of the best-known World War I revisionists were not professional students of diplomacy, although the
most influential among them, Charles C. Tansill, was. Not all of
the early revisionist writers saw economic interests as the primary
cause of American involvement in the war, but those who did

tended to accord economic motives an excessive degree of importance in the eyes of many scholars.[1]

More influential in the long run was the work of Charles A. Beard. He moved beyond most other revisionists, who devoted themselves to World War I, by elaborating an analysis of the full history of American foreign policy. In several books in the 1930s, including the third volume of his popular text *America in Midpassage,* Beard provided a sweeping interpretation of the roots of American diplomacy. Throughout American history, Beard maintained, there were two major domestic impulses influencing foreign policy. One, the "industrialist," supported high tariffs and overseas commercial and territorial expansion. The other, the "agrarian," supported agricultural exports and free trade. Less aggressive than the first, the second was the source of America's interest in international cooperation. Until the end of the nineteenth century, Americans subordinated these vague traditions to a generally isolationist policy. The industrialist attitude became more insistent and elaborated as the public and political leaders became convinced that the United States would face economic stagnation without commercial expansion. As a result, Beard argued, America's elite pursued an expansionist foreign policy in the first three decades of the twentieth century. The depression had called a halt to that policy, and Beard advocated that America face up to its domestic crisis by abandoning the idea that overseas expansion solved problems at home. If the United States did not turn inward, the potential greatness of American civilization would not be developed.[2]

Beard's work did not go unchallenged. Scholarly critics claimed that his interpretation reduced the domestic sources of foreign policy to a simple economic determinism. Beard wrote, they asserted, without sufficient attention to the international system and overlooked the fact that American leaders reacted to the actions of foreign powers. Beard also appeared to be arguing a special case, a scholarly transgression which undermined his believability among historians. And his concern for the domestic roots of foreign policy was out of step with the current approach to the writing of diplomatic history.[3]

Beard's broad interpretation influenced few professional

practitioners of diplomatic history in the late 1940s and the 1950s. His ideas did influence a new generation of scholars in the 1960s, the "New Left" historians, as they were often called. Among diplomatic historians, William Appleman Williams and his adherents, like Beard before them, studied the domestic sources of foreign policy. The new revisionists believed that policymakers were attuned to domestic interests and were determined to ensure the long-term stability and expansion of the American capitalist system. Beard's work also appealed to these scholars because of his commitment to a cause. He believed that scholarship could help bring about reform, which was an attractive conviction to a generation of historians seeking a usable past, a historiography that would contribute to change.

Like Beard, Williams argued that American leaders tried to solve domestic economic problems, and the political and social discontent that they caused, through foreign economic expansion. The need for continued growth of markets abroad, Williams maintained, created a foreign policy dedicated to a world open to American trade and investment. Williams saw genuine humanitarian impulses in American diplomacy's desire to export its political and social institutions. But economic needs were the central concern of policymakers, especially those after World War II who created a foreign policy that assumed change—particularly revolutionary change—to be inimical to American economic interests.

Williams' work has stirred much scholarly controversy. Some reactions became quite heated in the early years after his ideas first appeared in *The Tragedy of American Diplomacy*.[4] Critics generally disagreed with the unicausal nature of Williams' interpretation, and some raised questions about the use of evidence by Williams and his colleagues.[5] In recent years, however, the dispute between the Williams school and its critics has become muted. While many scholars do not subscribe to the all-encompassing nature of Williams' interpretation, most would concede that economic interests played a larger part in American foreign policy than was generally accepted in the 1950s.

Many scholarly debates wind down in this way, with general acceptance that even the most criticized interpretations contain some truth. We believe that we need to move beyond the current standoff. The questions raised about the role of economics in the history of United States foreign policy need sharper formulations and answers than they have received. This volume is not a review of the historiographical debate. Instead, it is designed to move to new ground and to provide a synthesis that assesses more fully and more precisely than previous literature the interaction between foreign policy and economic needs and interests, and the perception of such needs and interests.

We want to emphasize that this book is not intended to revive the debate between revisionists and their critics. Far from it. We think that it is time to leave behind us the contentiousness that marked the debate about revisionism. Yet we are not satisfied with the muted conclusion that economic interests have at times influenced American foreign policy. As the 1970s moved on, we became convinced that the issues raised by the interaction between economics and foreign policy were too important to remain stifled in a simplistic black-and-white debate over economic determinism.

Beyond the component elements of economic interest and diplomatic policy, other determinants shape American behavior on the international scene. One important factor is the position of the United States in the international power structure. Obviously the young republic of 1789 could not play the global role that was open to the principal victor in 1945. The policies of any administration must be evaluated against the constraints and opportunities available in the international environment of the day. Another significant element is the broad popular concept of the nation's role in the world. Until the 1970s each generation of Americans talked about the special mission of the United States. As the nation matured, the sense of mission changed to reflect varying degrees of optimism and different concepts of international social purpose. Our analysis seeks to include insights from these and other elements of disciplines as diverse as political economy and intellectual history.

This volume seeks to bring about greater precision in thinking about the role of economic issues, interests, and structure in the formulation and conduct of American foreign relations. The volume that we have assembled covers the history of American foreign relations from 1789 to the present, assessing for each period the impact of economics on foreign policy. The chapters were written by specialists on the various periods of American diplomatic history covered here.

Essential to any joint undertaking is clarity about the questions posed. Computers are not alone in producing nonsensical answers to imprecise questions. In developing these essays we asked our contributors to address themselves to several specific questions. We wanted to avoid the disjointed quality of many such efforts which collect essays addressed to a rather broad theme. We chose scholars who have done, or were engaged in, original research in the periods that they were asked to cover here, and who in their work have shown interest in economic issues. We asked our contributors to consider the following:

1. What were the diplomatic implications of America's place in the global economy in the period covered?

2. In making important diplomatic decisions, were economic concerns more important to American leaders than political or strategic considerations?

3. Were economic concerns more important in relation to America's dealings with Europe, Asia, or Latin America? It is possible that interests in markets in Asia or Latin America did not reflect the economic importance of these areas to American commerce and finance in the period covered. Were policy makers accurately assessing America's position? Were they planning for future needs?

4. In regard to those aspects of diplomacy affected by economic considerations, how often and to what degree were diplomatists responding to pressure from businessmen or farmers and members of Congress representing such constituencies, and how often and to what degree were the diplomats themselves motivated by their own viewpoints, attitudes, or ideology? In short, were they trying to lead or were they being led?

5. To what extent was the management of foreign economic policy left in the hands of private interests or groups? Re-

lated to this question is whether or not government sought to ease the way for certain groups rather than actively supervise and manage their economic thrust abroad.

6. Obviously, America was a country with a growing economic and financial role in the world. Was financial and commercial expansion a result of policy (the tariff, commitment to the gold standard) or more simply of economic developments to which interest groups and policymakers responded? We realized that this undoubtedly important question was difficult to deal with. To answer it fully would require analyses beyond the scope of this volume. Yet, it was a question to keep in mind, since historians at times too readily accept the judgments of participants themselves about the effectiveness and importance of policy.

7. In short, were economic concerns central to the conceptualization, formulation, and practice of American diplomacy, or were they part of a larger constellation of considerations? To put it another way, were economic concerns the context in which foreign policy should be studied, or were economic changes only a part of a larger context and, if the latter, what was the larger context?

Not every question we posed applied to every period covered. While we left the organization of essays and the subjects to be discussed to each contributor, we asked our colleagues to answer these questions where appropriate. As editors and contributors, we have sought to provide coherence and clarity of purpose to this book. Since our contributors are scholars doing original research in the areas that they covered for this volume, the editors did not intend to dictate material or subjects to them. We welcomed dialogue and, to a remarkable degree in a joint project like this, we got it. Our contributors read and criticized the chapters that preceded and followed their own to assure coherence in coverage and ease in transition. This is a joint effort, as a result, that can be read as a work with a clearly focused set of issues. In the epilogue, the editors sum up the major findings of this joint effort and suggest a framework for future work that looks toward understanding the interaction among economics, diplomacy, and world power.

Notes

1. Charles E. Neu, "The Changing Interpretative Structure of American Foreign Policy," in John Braeman, Robert Bremner, and David Brady, eds., *Twentieth-Century American Foreign Policy* (Columbus: Ohio State University Press, 1971), pp. 14–15; also see Ernest R. May, "Emergence to World Power," in John Higham, ed., *The Reconstruction of American History* (New York: Humanities Press, 1962), pp. 180–96.

2. Neu, pp. 16–17; George R. Leighton, "Beard and Foreign Policy," in Howard K. Beale, ed., *Charles A. Beard: An Appraisal* (Lexington: University of Kentucky Press, 1954), pp. 161–84; Gerald Stourzh, "Charles A. Beard's Interpretations of American Foreign Policy," *World Affairs Quarterly* (1957), 28:111–48; Charles A. and Mary R. Beard, *America in Midpassage* (New York: Macmillan, 1939); and Charles A. Beard, *The Idea of National Interest: An Analytical Study in American Foreign Policy* (New York: Macmillan, 1934).

3. Neu, pp. 17–19.

4. See, for example, Oscar Handlin's review in *American Historical Review* (July 1959).

5. Robert James Maddox, *The New Left and the Origins of the Cold War* (Princeton: Princeton University Press, 1973).

Economics and World Power

1

1789–1820
All Œconomists,
All Diplomats

James A. Field, Jr.
Swarthmore College

TO THE STATESMEN of the first and second generations of independence the central importance of economics was axiomatic. Real or imagined economic difficulties had underlain both the Revolution of 1776 and that second revolution that brought the establishment of the Constitution. But despite success in both these enterprises problems remained, most notably in the area of foreign trade, on whose solution the survival of the new frame of government, and even of independence itself, seemed to depend. These problems were largely external in origin: prior to the Revolution they had been attributed to British imperial control; as time went by more generalized European pressures appeared responsible for their continuance. Quite naturally, then, the central aim of foreign policy, most notably articulated in Washington's Farewell Address and Jefferson's First Inaugural, was to extend commercial relations while avoiding political entanglement. But this, in the first thirty years under the Constitution, was to prove no easy task.

THE ESTIMATE OF THE SITUATION

In December 1793, only a few days before retiring from his position as first Secretary of State, Thomas Jefferson laid before the Congress a report on the "privileges and restrictions on the commerce of the United States in foreign countries." Regrettably, the latter far outnumbered the former: in the great emporium of Europe the export staples of America faced manifold obstacles and exclusions; in Europe's New World colonies "an order of things much harder" presented itself. Still more oppressive were the restrictions on American shipping, valuable as a branch of industry and "as a resource of defense essential." So what was bore small relation to what ought to be, and the facts of life conflicted with the dictates of reason: "the ocean, which is the common property of all, [should be] open to the industry of all"; if every country could be "employed in producing that which nature has best fitted it to produce, and each be free to exchange with others mutual surpluses for mutual wants, the greatest mass possible would then be produced of those things which contribute to human life and human happiness; the numbers of mankind would be increased and their condition bettered."

The restrictions which so exercised the Secretary of State were the product of two centuries of European history. The development of competitive overseas empires had given rise to a set of closed mercantilist systems designed to promote national strength and self-sufficiency through legislation encouraging or restraining private and sectional interests. Internally, this growth of regulation had emphasized the dominance of the state over the individual and of the metropolis over the colonies. As between empires, the view that it was better to beggar thy neighbor than to enrich thyself had led to endemic economic conflict punctuated by wars which the uncomprehending British colonists named for their sovereign of the moment. In the post-Revolutionary situation the persistence of the Europeans, and above all of the British, in policies so alien to American needs and aspirations, posed a serious threat to national survival.

In the years before the Revolution, the colonies had balanced off their imports from the mother country with a set of crucial exports. Most important economically was tobacco, which made up about a quarter of the value of the colonial export total. Most important strategically, in view of British deforestation, were masts and spars for ships. Other items of significance were rice, indigo for the dyeing of textiles, iron, furs, and ships—about a third of the prerevolutionary British merchant marine was American-built. In the immediate prewar years a growth in imports from Britain had been matched by increased shipments to the West Indies and to Mediterranean Europe.

But independence brought hard problems. A rush to replace shortages raised imports almost to their formal level, but exports remained depressed. The production of southern staples had suffered seriously from the war, American shipbuilders had lost their favored position inside the empire, and Canadian trappers were siphoning off the Northwest fur trade. The British West Indies were closed to American supplies and the trade with southern Europe, vulnerable to North African piracy, was bereft of British protection. Nor were hoped-for favors—protection in the Mediterranean and access to overseas possessions—forthcoming from France and Spain, whose governments still clung to the old mercantilistic attitudes.

Against these Old World systems of irrational discrimination and exclusive privilege, costly both to America and to humanity in general, Jefferson recommended measured steps of retaliation. His formulation of the governing imperative for such action firmly linked economics, diplomacy, and the question of national independence: if other nations could control the country's resources it "will be disarmed of its defense; . . . and its politics may be influenced by those who command its commerce."

Its concise and elegant analysis of America's economic predicament and of its implications for foreign policy makes the Report one of the most significant documents of the first years under the Constitution. In its advocacy of regional specialization, the removal of restrictions on commerce, and a perfect reciprocity of ocean trade, it posed the central questions concerning the place of economics in American foreign relations, the influence of interest groups on policy formation, and the role of government in forwarding through economic measures the condition both of the shareholders in the Great Experiment and of the human race. But the specific proposals also raised, as had the Revolution itself, the abiding paradox of American history: how to use power to destroy power, how to coerce in the cause of freedom. Not by reason and justice, as the Secretary observed, but only "by our own means of independence, and the firm will to use them" could fair and equal access to markets and a due share in the transportation of American products be assured.[1]

THE "MEANS OF INDEPENDENCE"

Three and a half years earlier, when Jefferson had reached New York to assume somewhat reluctantly the office of Secretary of State, the "means of independence" and the "firm will to use them" were still untested. The new Constitution, if it could be made to work, provided a potentially effective, although surely not a "strong" frame of government. Most importantly, this government had at last acquired the power to tax, and so to maintain itself. The virtue of this power in foreign economic relations was soon demonstrated in Hamilton's vigorous program of funding and assumption, which quickly converted the United States into an almost unique historical example of a new country with a good credit rating, and which led in the next decade to a rise in foreign investment from $60 to $96 million in this new country.[2]

Next only in importance to the taxing power, the exclusive control over commerce, the coinage, and the conduct of foreign relations conferred upon the new government promised an end to economic fragmentation and the creation of a large unified free-trading area. Access to this valuable area could be regulated by uniform tariff duties, regulations on foreign shipping, and treaties enforceable as the supreme law of the land. Although the staple producing states had managed to limit the commercial powers of government by a prohibition of export duties, the new capabilities were still such as to encourage hopes of productive negotiations with the countries of Europe, most importantly with intransigent Great Britain.

To the new powers over commerce and diplomacy the Constitution joined those to "raise and support Armies" and to "provide and maintain a Navy." Although a navy that would make the country the "arbiter of Europe in America"[3] was clearly far in the future, one for the marginal protection of commerce was at least imaginable. For the army, so important to settlers on the frontier (and which, at the inauguration of the new government, could muster a mere 46 officers and 672 enlisted personnel), much the same could be said, and early legislation provided both for the creation of a War Department and for a modest augmentation of strength. Finally, to assist the executive in his conduct of external relations, the Congress in 1789 established a Department of Foreign Affairs, shortly to be rechristened the Department of State.

The department over which Jefferson assumed control in 1790 was no more impressive than the army. To manage the diplomacy of the new nation (and to supervise the census, patents and copyrights, the mint, and a variety of other tasks) the new Secretary inherited from the old government two rooms, four clerks, and a part-time translator. Diplomacy itself was minimal and, as an attribute of European old regimes, largely undesired. Although treaties of amity and commerce existed with France, the Netherlands, Sweden, and Prussia, American representation abroad was limited to chargés at Paris and Madrid. With Great Britain, by far the most important foreign power, the country had neither treaty relations nor diplomatic representation. Although affably received by the king in 1785, John Adams had been able to accomplish little, and had returned home in 1788; and although the new President had dispatched Gouverneur Morris to make soundings in London, the Pitt government still showed no interest in sending a minister to America.

These limitations were perhaps only superficially important. Far more significant for the future than the embryo diplo-

matic and military establishments, assuming only that domestic
political problems could be solved, were the resources of the new
nation and the skills and energies of the American people. The
rapidly growing and westering population, probably the most
skilled and certainly the most literate in the world, inhabited an
undeveloped but enormously rich country which was already producing large export surpluses. If the nature of these surpluses (of
which tobacco, breadstuffs, rice, wood, and fish made up more
than three-quarters of the total value) suggested a vulnerable, mar-
ket-dependent, capital-hungry economy, there remained one
priceless additional resource: already the United States had shown
itself capable of creating an important merchant marine. Exploitation of the country's magnificent stands of timber, its numerous
east-coast shipbuilding sites, and its native skills had led to the
development of a vigorous maritime society. With the assistance
of well-calculated legislation it would also soon produce a tonnage
increase "without example, in the history of the commercial
world," and a tonnage total far greater than any country except
Great Britain.[4] In the first thirty years under the Constitution the
earnings of the merchant marine, greater than those of any single
commodity export, would convert a large import excess into so
favorable a balance of trade as to permit the maintenance of the
currency at home, reduction of the foreign debt, the attraction of
new capital, and the export of specie to the Orient.

THE IDEOLOGY OF COMMERCE

In their management of economic policy the statesmen of the first
generation were powerfully affected by a constellation of ideas
which pointed to a better future and which affected idealists and
realists alike. Reflecting the antagonism between advanced eighteenth-century thought and traditional eighteenth-century politics, the Americans had elevated their resistance to the oppressions of George III into a generalized anti-power philosophy. At

home, having fought their way clear of British rule, they succes-
sively limited the powers of the states by adopting the new Constitution, and the dangers of a new centralized government by the
Bill of Rights. In foreign affairs antagonism to Great Britain flowed
naturally into a generalized hostility to the great mercantile states
of Europe, with their oppressive trappings of monarchy, aristocracy, and state religion, and most particularly to their mercantilist
restrictions on trade.

In the development of these attitudes, ideals and self-interest happily reinforced each other. Isolationist hostility to political
connections with Europe went hand in hand with internationalist
emphasis on the expansion of commerce. This expansion seemed
doubly justified, by necessity as the key to American survival, and
by philosophy as the key to human progress: to some, indeed, an
unfettered spread of commerce promised to unite the nations and
bring about the reign of peace. Such liberal ideas, emphasized in
revolutionary propaganda and in the writings of committed activ-
ists like Tom Paine, David Humphreys, and Joel Barlow (not to
mention Jefferson himself), powerfully affected policy from the
time of the publications of *Common Sense*. Over the years they were
carried abroad by diplomatic and commercial agents, patriotic
propagandists, shipmasters, and entrepreneurs. And if the Americans did not in the early years persuade many European policy
makers, at least it seems clear that they persuaded themselves.

In the international arena the bias against power and the
state had obvious consequences. In economic diplomacy the belief
in commerce and the emphasis on liberal practices and minimal
restraints worked toward the maximum freedom for the individual
and the dissolution of the old mercantile world order. These aims
were perhaps most strikingly apparent in the Model Treaty of
1776, and in the Treaty of Amity and Commerce with France
which John Quincy Adams later described as the basis of all
American foreign policy. They were reflected in the continuing
emphasis on treaties of commerce and navigation, in the reciprocity policy on shipping, and in the preference for consular
over diplomatic representation eloquently articulated by Jefferson
to the Emperor of Morocco. Beyond economics, the anti-power

policy showed itself in attempts to put Europe at a distance, in the first instance by avoiding alliances and entanglements and by working to limit the impact of war on neutrals by treaty arrangements and the development of international law, and in time by boundary rectifications extending the "area of freedom" and measures of support for other Western Hemisphere revolutions.

At home, as well, the anti-power bias affected the country's posture in foreign relations through its restrictive shaping of the instruments of policy. For the regular army, designed to police and develop the national estate, appropriations were constitutionally limited in time and legislatively constrained by restrictive provisos. Control of the militia was divided between the general government and the states. The six-frigate bill of 1792 which created the navy also stipulated that all construction should cease upon conclusion of peace with Algiers. This same bias was reflected in the miscellany of duties cumulated upon the Department of State (and in its very name) and in visionary hopes, expressed in Congress and elsewhere, that as economic relations were rationalized diplomacy would wither away.

Like so much in America, this policy was clearly future-oriented. However eloquently asserted, the linked internationalist desire for freedom of commerce and the isolationist goal of political disengagement had in no way been achieved. Whatever the wish to divorce commercial diplomacy from political involvement, the connection existed, both at home where customs duties provided the main support of government, and abroad where economics remained an instrument of great power policy. Yet hopes persisted. If the pressures of the Revolution had impelled John Adams to write in 1780 that his duty was to study politics and war, the end to which his efforts were directed was to permit his children to study mathematics, navigation, commerce, and agriculture, and his grandchildren poetry, music, tapestry, and porcelain.[5]

PROBLEMS AND POSSIBILITIES

For the moment, however, the problems of economic survival governed the study of politics and war. In confronting these interrelated factors in the first thirty years under the Constitution, the nation found itself faced with problems in three principal theaters, two wet and one dry. Of the wet areas, those concerned with maritime trade, the most important was the North Atlantic over which moved an average of something above 60 percent of American exports and re-exports; if to this was added the exports and re-exports to the Western Hemisphere, the share of European-controlled regions totaled about nine-tenths of the whole. Beyond the North Atlantic lay a second and peripheral maritime theater, the product of the costs of separation from the British Empire and the mercantilist restrictions of France and Spain, which had necessitated the development of supplemental trades with Baltic and Mediterranean, eastern Asia, and the west coast of North America. But here too the price of independence was apparent: the important Mediterranean trade had been closed off by Barbary pirates, and efforts to find substitutes for the lost British protection had come to naught.

The third area, the American West, was at first more political and strategic than economic, involving an interconnected diplomacy with Britain, Spain, and the Indian tribes aimed at making good the boundaries of the Treaty of 1783. But even here economic considerations were present. Fur traders from across the northern border were exploiting the national domain. The western lands, a vast potential resource in the eyes of both general government and individual speculator, had to be defended if they were to sell and if the western population was to be kept loyal. Soon the growth of settlement would raise the question of export routes and markets, and link Kentucky and Tennessee, by way of the Ohio and Mississippi, with the problems of the high seas and the far shores.

With the other parties to the issues that confronted the Republic, the evolving American style brought dealings on three levels. With the smaller European states, which shared in greater or lesser degree the American commercial proclivities, consular representation appeared to suffice and diplomatic questions could be left to the ad hoc attentions of special agents. In this same consular world lay the interesting but little-known regions presided over by Turkish sultan and Chinese emperor, which, having escaped the legacies of European barbarism, could be presumed amenable to counsels of reason as to the value of expanded commerce. With the great powers of Europe, dangerous, unpredicatable, but controlling the major export markets and the sources of manufactures and capital, diplomacy seemed unfortunately unavoidable—even Jefferson was brought to agree that London as well as Paris deserved a minister—but the necessary evil of a diplomatic establishment was kept as small as possible. For such fractious groups as Indian tribes and Barbary and West Indies pirates a third category of treatment was reserved: toward these, when regrettably resistant to persuasion as to the virtues of agriculture and trade, rational force could be employed to strengthen the argument. But these levels of intercourse, like the three theaters of action, were never wholly separable. Policy on all levels carried a large didactic content, and since great powers by definition appear everywhere, in times of major crisis all levels and all areas were involved.

As Jefferson wrote in his report, a satisfactory solution to the country's problems depended on America's "own means of independence, and the firm will to use them." As the movement toward the new Constitution had made clear, the creation of a "firm will" depended on attention to the problems of all sections and of both wet and dry frontiers. Equally, in so large and diverse a country, the preservation of some unity of will among those concerned with the availability of foreign capital, those dependent on fishing rights and foreign markets, and those in need of frontier defense strengthened the bias of the age for generalized formulations. Where specific aims might divide, most could rally behind arguments for natural rights and principles "conformable to reason" or to the "law of nature," and finally, when tensions grew and minds became heated, to appeals to national honor. As to the national "means," the principal and perhaps the only weapon at the start was that on which the Secretary of State laid emphasis: the giving or withholding of commercial favor. On the level of practicality, the economic weapon gained plausibility from the testimony of eighteenth-century wars to the importance of overseas resources and familiarity from a history going back to the period of the Stamp Act. On a higher level, it benefited from the elevation of commerce in eighteenth-century thought into the great agency of civilization and human welfare. Like all societies with limited capabilities, the Americans perhaps tended to exalt their principal means of influence into an absolute weapon.

Nevertheless there was something in the argument. The appearance of an independent transatlantic political unit had revolutionized both strategy and economics. No longer could Great Britain dominate the world by a simple blockade of Europe's western approaches. Having lost political control of their North American colonies, the British, when trouble came in Europe, were faced with the task of maintaining through duties and prohibitions, the construction of international law, and the employment of the Royal Navy, the economic and strategic mastery formerly provided by the Acts of Trade. For the Americans the problem was precisely the reverse: how to maintain and expand trade and, at the same time, avoid being returned to a servile colonial situation. In this sense, both at sea and in the west, the struggle for independence was to continue throughout the first thirty years of the new government.

Yet despite the strategic revolution, there remained a large measure of symbiosis, not always fully appreciated by the policy makers. For the Americans, Great Britain offered both principal market and principal source of capital and manufactured goods; for the British, the former colonies constituted not only an important source of raw materials but a market for about a third of their total exports. If the American government moved to withhold its commerce, it damaged its own citizens; if the Royal Navy blockaded the United States, it also in important measure blockaded Great Britain.

EARLY POLICY DEVELOPMENT

So much attention has been centered on Hamilton's fiscal measures that the emphasis placed on foreign commerce during Washington's first administration has perhaps been slighted. At the
opening of the first Congress, in April 1789, Madison called both
for duties to provide revenue and for tonnage taxes to assist the
American merchant marine. In July the Congress passed a tariff
act, primarily for revenue but with a mild touch of protectionism,
which discriminated against foreign shipping by preferential duties on goods imported in American ships, gave special favors to
the trade with regions beyond the Cape of Good Hope, and placed
a small export bounty on fish. Two weeks later, again at the urging of Madison, further assistance was provided the shipping interest in the form of discriminating tonnage duties. These acts
marked the start of a forty-year governmental effort to undermine
the restrictive commercial monopolies of the European powers and
encourage freer trade and navigation. Motivated both by the practical need to capitalize on the country's comparative advantage in
shipping and by the more abstract aim of rationalizing and expanding world trade through reduced shipping costs, the policy
would ultimately enjoy considerable success. But here as elsewhere, in the years before 1815, the new nation found itself on
the defensive.

Nevertheless, the effort continued. Upon his arrival in New
York in the spring of 1790, Jefferson took up the problems of
foreign trade with a militance that gave rise to a series of notable
reports: on the Mediterranean trade and the prisoners of Algiers
(1790); on the tonnage law (1791); on the cod and whale fisheries
(1791); on the navigation of the Mississippi (1792); and in his final
Report on Commerce which, in preparation since early 1791, was
delivered in late 1793. This commercial concern also brought a
rapid expansion of the consular service: by the end of the first
Washington administration thirty consuls and six vice consuls had
been appointed.

In these years the burden, both of Jefferson's reports and

of congressional debates, was the liberation of American economic activity from foreign control. In maritime affairs the new government endeavored to eliminate the aggressions of Barbary pirates and the restrictions of the great powers; in the west it worked to remove the threats posed by British presence in the Northwest posts, Spanish control of the Mississippi, and British and Spanish satellite Indian tribes. In the employment of the rudimentary national "means" wisdom seemed to call for negotiations, payments, and expeditions against the Indians, and of negotiations, ransom, and tribute to Algiers; in both areas, nevertheless, the game of negotiation and subsidy encountered competitive European paymasters. As against these, hope existed that if reason failed the New World could "fatten on the follies of the Old"[6] through the use of its three principal assets: its economic value, as both market and source of supplies, its merchant marine, and its expanding population. For the moment, however, trade seemed the only potent weapon, to be used in peacetime by discriminatory commercial legislation and in time of crisis by auctioning American neutrality.

WAR IN EUROPE

All this was easier imagined than accomplished. In France, linked to the United States by treaties of both commerce and alliance, hoped-for new markets had failed to materialize. Although the meeting of the Estates General in the year of Washington's inauguration had seemed to write "the first chapter of the history of European liberty,"[7] the coming of the Terror darkened the picture, and in 1793 war between France and Britain overshadowed the opening of French colonial ports and led to Washington's Neutrality Proclamation. Increasingly relations with the French were complicated by the influence of old bureaucrats and new men, more concerned with power and profit and less with principle than the physiocrats of Paris, as well as by the antics of Genêt.

Although a sense of obligation continued manifest, as in governmental efforts to procure the release of LaFayette from imprisonment in Germany, the fund of revolutionary gratitude and republican sympathy had already begun to erode.

With Great Britain affairs remained unsatisfactory. Although American hints of commercial reprisal brought temporary gratification in the arrival in 1791 of George Hammond, the first British minister to the United States, it was soon apparent that he lacked authority to negotiate over either commerce or the Northwest posts. In the southwest, Spanish inducements to American settlers—which promised, in Jefferson's phrase, to bring in the Goths to the gates of Rome—offered hope for the future. But for the moment the legal case for Mississippi navigation was weak, and however decorated with learned references to Grotius, Pufendorf, and Vattel, and with elevated appeals to the law of nature "as we feel it written on the heart of man,"[8] the argument carried small conviction in Madrid. Worse was to come with failure on the frontier, and St. Clair's defeat in late 1791 was followed by renewed Indian activity throughout the West and British proposals for an Indian buffer state, all made more ominous by the Anglo-Spanish rapprochement of 1793.

For the most important of the peripheral trades, that with the Mediterranean, little more could be said. Since the traditional acceptance by southern Europe of New England fish, Middle States flour, and southern rice made access to this sea of national importance, some settlement with the Barbary states was urgent. But although the new government had provided funds for ransom and tribute in 1791, no progress had been made in negotiation and a new crisis with Algiers was about to develop.

In none of the major areas of concern had diplomacy brought progress by the time Jefferson left office. But at home regional differences over the conduct of economic foreign policy were developing between the staple-exporting South, the Middle States which combined farming for export with a growing shipping interest, and isolated New England which plowed only the sea. This tension between those emphasizing expanded markets and those dependent on foreign capital, between those who wished to use the commercial weapon and those who saw their survival dependent on the British connection, had emerged in the first Congress with the Hamiltonian defeat of Madison's effort to discriminate against countries with which no treaty of commerce existed. It resurfaced in Jefferson's Report on Commerce, described by the Secretary of the Treasury as a "FIREBRAND of discord"[9] and in the debate on Madison's implementing proposals for discrimination against British ships and goods. Soon to be exacerbated and perpetuated by the Jay Treaty debate and increasing party solidarity, it would continue through the War of 1812.

Yet despite lack of progress abroad and emerging strains at home, the first years under the new government had been encouraging. Hamilton's successful funding had brought a rise in security prices and an influx of foreign capital; exports and imports had grown; and increased customs receipts had permitted servicing the debt and expanding the army. Aided by the discriminating tariff and tonnage duties of 1789, shipping in foreign trade had grown from perhaps 200,000 to over 300,000 tons between 1789 and 1791,[10] while the stimulus of war in Europe was about to produce a new expansion, and by driving up export prices and freight rates bring joy to both farming and shipping interests. These developments, it should be noted, were national in extent. Although Massachusetts-owned tonnage exceeded the combined total of her closest competitors, New York and Pennsylvania, in rate of increase in the decade after 1790 the Bay State lagged far behind New York and Maryland, as indeed behind South Carolina and Virginia.[11] But while these years were bringing a generalized economic expansion, shown also in the doubling of tonnage in the coastal trade, the maritime basis of this prosperity provided an increasing hostage to fortune, or to Great Britain. Suddenly, in 1794, all appeared threatened.

In the summer of 1793 pressure on neutral shipping, already evidenced in intermittent French seizures, was increased by the British "provision order," aimed at neutrals carrying food to French ports and fruitlessly protested by the United States as contrary to "reason and usage." In the autumn a truce between Algiers and Portugal gave the pirates access to the Atlantic and led to the capture of eleven American ships. In November a second and secret order in council, directing the Royal Navy to bring in all neutral ships trading with French colonies, led to the seizure in the West Indies of over 250 American vessels. Reports of the loss of ships to the Algerines and rumors that the British had arranged the truce with Portugal reached Philadelphia in December. They were followed in March 1794 by news of the Caribbean captures and of an incendiary speech by Lord Dorchester to the Indians of the Northwest. Everywhere British hostility seemed apparent, in the Mediterranean, on the Atlantic, and in the West, while at home this triple diplomatic crisis was reflected in merchants' cries for redress and in the developing Whiskey Rebellion, whose leaders numbered among their complaints resentment of government inactivity in the Indian and Mississippi questions.

In this situation the old policy divisions reappeared as the Republicans, with Madison in the lead, argued for discrimination against British trade and sequestration of British debts. But again the disciples of prudence and national solvency won out. Although a temporary embargo was placed on American shipping, the "pro-French" policy was defeated and the problems were dealt with on separate levels: payment and force against Indians and pirates; negotiations with the mistress of the seas. West of the mountains Anthony Wayne was already drilling his troops; in March Congress authorized the construction of six frigates for use against Algiers; in April the Chief Justice, John Jay, sailed as special envoy to Great Britain.

THE JAY TREATY AND THE QUASI-WAR

In London Jay got a treaty which gave the first evidence that a major power would negotiate seriously with the independent United States and which, however unpopular, offered a variety of benefits. The continuation of trade and of customs collections strengthened the general government and provided funds for both the newly authorized frigates and the liberalized expenditures which, over the next two years, gained settlements with the Barbary regencies and opened the Mediterranean to American shipping. Improved conditions for trade with British India led to a growth of Indian Ocean commerce. British agreement on the Northwest posts, shortly underlined by Wayne's summer victory at Fallen Timbers and the Treaty of Greenville, was followed by a new flood of settlers into Ohio. At Madrid the news of this settlement, tension with England, and the activity of western pioneers brought the concessions of Pinckney's Treaty on the southern boundary, on Mississippi navigation and the privilege of deposit, and on restraint of the Indians, which would lead to increased trade with New Orleans and increased pressure on the Spanish holdings. For the moment all major difficulties seemed alleviated, and Washington, seizing upon this moment of tranquillity, retired to Mount Vernon while bequeathing to his countrymen his "Great Rule" for foreign relations: the extension of commerce with other nations while having with them "as little *political* connection as possible."[12]

Despite these benefits, the rapprochement with Britain that followed the Jay Treaty had its price. The arrangements for West Indies trade were unsatisfactory, and were rejected; the continued access to the Northwest Indians granted Canadian fur traders promised both economic and political costs; the right of commercial discrimination against Great Britain and the contention that the neutral flag covered belligerent non-contraband were abandoned; no concession was gained on the practice of impressment. At home these manifest defects gave rise to a corrosive debate between those who saw the world as it was and those who saw it as it ought to be, and which focused on the retreat from American principles of maritime law. In the future this retreat would bring problems in treaty negotiations with Sweden and Prussia. More immediately, it raised tensions with France expressed in French efforts to influence the election of 1796, in renewed French interest in Louisiana, in increasingly damaging seizures of shipping, and ultimately in limited maritime war.

This new crisis brought the first employment of the commerce-protecting navy. Three of the frigates authorized for use against Algiers had already been launched; the creation of a separate Navy Department and the purchase of land for navy yards gave promise of a permanent establishment; and hastened construction and conversion made possible the deployment of a respectable force. In the undeclared war of 1798–1800 the capability of this extemporized navy was shown in successful actions against French ships hovering on the coast and in the West Indies; its potential range (and the existing outreach of the merchant marine) in the cruise of *Essex* to Sunda Strait; and its economic virtue in radically lowered insurance rates and in customs duties derived from the commerce it helped to protect.

The operations against the French, indeed, were but the first of a number of occasions on which the navy proved its economic value to both citizens and government. The authorization of the first frigates for use against Algiers had stemmed from the need to open the important Mediterranean trade; following the conclusion of an Algerine treaty Washington had urged a continued building program as both necessary to the maintenance of a pool of skilled workers and helpful to employment. The quasi-war with France refuted the argument that a navy would be a sinkhole for public funds, aided the shipping interest, and gave rise to suggestions for the establishment of convoys to limit the inflationary effect of British impressment on seamen's wages. In later years the War with Tripoli would underline the navy's value in lowering insurance rates, as would its employment during the Latin American revolutions. Throughout the period its high standard of performance against the French, the Barbary Powers, the Royal Navy, and Caribbean pirates reflected credit on the new nation. By 1819 the navy would have attained an enviable and unique status as an institution at once conducive to public and private profit and to national honor.

For the moment the French Convention of 1800 liquidated the old Treaty of Alliance, established new commercial arrangements, filled out the series of post-Revolutionary treaties with the three great European powers, and showed that rational arguments could, on occasion, benefit from forcible support on the maritime as on the western frontier. But this success was also accompanied by a demonstration, perhaps insufficiently attended to, of the paradoxes in the use of power. Along with successful use of force at sea against the French had come abusive use at home, and the Federalists, in the moment of victory, found themselves swept from office.

THE FEDERALIST LEGACY

The rustication of the Federalists marked, one may say, a stage in the country's history. As President, Jefferson confronted a situation very different from that when ten years earlier he had entered on the duties of Secretary of State. In the course of the decade the population had grown from four to almost five and a half million. With the blessings of the new frame of government, the success of the Hamiltonian system, and the coming of war in Europe had come expanded economic activity. The rise in customs receipts from $1.8 to $9.6 million a year had supported, along with the costs of naval war and frontier defense, an orderly servicing of the public debt.[13] The treaties negotiated between 1794 and 1800 with European powers and Barbary states testified to greater acceptance abroad of the revolutionary republic and contributed to prosperity. By easing the problems of neutral trade and by clearing the Northwest posts, the Mississippi, and the Mediterranean, these arrangements had gone far to pacify the fractious residents of New England and the West while bringing generalized prosperity to farmers, merchants, and shipowners from Maine to Charleston. Clearly, the Federalists had left a going concern, to which not the least tribute was the peaceful transfer of executive power.

Of the economic developments of these years with significance for foreign relations, three were perhaps preeminent. The first was the extraordinary development of maritime commerce: American shipping in foreign trade, well in excess of 500,000 tons by 1800, now carried almost 90 percent of American exports and imports as compared to a mere 40 percent in the earlier years. Imports for domestic consumption had risen from $22.5 million to $52 million and domestic exports from $19.7 to $31.8 million; still more startling was the growth of the re-export trade, stimulated by wartime accessibility of the European West Indies, from a mere half-million to $39 million.[14] But these figures, however significant of prosperity and gratifying to national esteem, also excited the jealousy of British shipowners, created a demand for seamen that drained the British merchant marine, and represented an enormous commitment to the high seas, an area subject in time of crisis to British dominance.

Almost as dramatic as the rise in shipping was the appearance of a new export crop, upland cotton, destined in time to become the most important single commodity in nineteenth-century trade and to rival the merchant marine as the great resource for balancing the national accounts. At the time that he negotiated his treaty John Jay was unaware that the United States exported cotton, yet only six years later shipments had reached 59,000 bales a year.[15] Since almost 90 percent of this total went to supply the burgeoning British textile industry, the new crop acted to diminish the importance of the French connection and to strengthen symbiotic relations with the mother country. By adding importantly to the "necessities of life, or materials of manufacture" earlier noted by Jefferson as America's contribution to the economies of Europe, it also reinforced confidence in the value of America's favors.

The third significant development was a new wave of settlement stimulated by shortage of New England farmland, Virginia soil exhaustion, and the expansion of cotton growing into the Piedmont region. With the way opened by the treaties of 1794–95 and by new roads and land legislation, the westward flood of emigration was resumed, to continue until the War of 1812. In the 1790s the population of Kentucky and Tennessee tripled, rising from 109,000 to 326,500, and by 1810 it had doubled again. In 1800 there were 51,000 settlers north of the Ohio, and in 1810, 272,000, more than three times the population of Upper Can-

ada.[16] And while southern settlement lagged owing to Indian oc-
cupancy, the Choctaw cession and the opening of territory north
of Mobile Bay promised increasing pressure on West Florida.

As this new wave of pioneers passed beyond the subsist-
ence level its surplus agricultural production, almost wholly dependent upon the western rivers for access to the outer world,
reemphasized the importance of the deposit at New Orleans, where
the arrival of $1 million of upstream goods in 1799 grew to $2.6
million in 1802.[17] Requiring as it did the increased services of
eastern shipowners, this export traffic pointed up that interdependence of eastern maritime strength and the West's need for
"secure enjoyment of indispensable outlets" which Washington had
emphasized in his Farewell Address. Along with the new influx
of settlers, it also predetermined the outcome of the Mississippi
question.

Such national progress in wealth, population, and settlement, was gratifying to patriots. But nations, as eighteenth-century philosophers well knew, were artificial constructs, and growth
at home had consequences abroad extending well beyond the
questions of western borders and ocean commerce. Increasingly
the country found itself integrated into a developing worldwide
trading network, centered on the North Atlantic but with tenta-
cles reaching around the globe. By the turn of the century American merchants and commission houses had established themselves in the principal ports of Europe, in the Atlantic islands and
the Caribbean, and at Canton, a pattern replicated in the expanding consular establishment. Beyond the Cape of Good Hope the
China and East Indies trades continued and that with British India grew; beyond Cape Horn a transpacific commerce, based on
South Atlantic sealskins and West Coast sea otter, had begun.
John Jacob Astor, in himself a one-man multinational corporation,
was already a significant influence in the Montreal fur trade; in
1800 the dispatch of his first shipment of furs to China foreshadowed the audacious globe-girdling scheme that would lead to the
founding of Astoria. But for all its exotic attractions this Orient
trade was nationally of small account. In 1801 less than 2 percent
of American exports and re-exports went to Asia, as compared

with 33 percent to the Western Hemisphere and 63 percent to Europe.[18]

TRANSATLANTIC AND REGIONAL CONNECTIONS

The American dependence on the Atlantic trading economy was only one side of the coin: the New World, in its turn, still offered promise to the inhabitants of the Old. The United States provided a growing market for British manufactures; British merchants maintained branch offices in America; British subjects were large purchasers of American governmental securities and of stock in the Bank of the United States; the expansion of the American merchant marine generated a sizable and politically significant expatriation of British seamen. The lure of American lands, which led the Pulteney syndicate and the Holland Land Company to buy up most of western New York and Pennsylvania and Alexander Baring to purchase over a million acres in Maine, also affected less practical men: Coleridge and Southey had contemplated establishing their pantisocracy on the banks of the Susquehanna, and Byron in time would toy with thoughts of emigration.

These economic links between the two Atlantic shores were paralleled in other spheres as increased ease of travel and expanding trade furthered the development of a fluid and sophisticated international society. Benjamin West and Gilbert Stuart practiced their art in England, as did John Trumbull and Washington Allston. John Paul Jones and Robert Fulton hired out their special skills to European rulers. Political intellectuals like Joel Barlow and Tom Paine rallied to the cause of revolution in France. Scoundrels like Erich Bollman, Aaron Burr, and Gilbert Imlay moved back and forth between America and Europe. Jefferson nourished his well-being, his friendships, and perhaps his francophilia with a French mâitre d'hôtel and a French cook. Both Louis

Philippe and Talleyrand spent time in America. In 1803 Jérôme Bonaparte married the forward Elizabeth Patterson of Baltimore, a niece of the Secretary of State; after Waterloo his brother Joseph would find refuge at Bordentown, New Jersey. Like numerous other Americans the various Pinckneys, and William Pinkney as well, had been educated in England. A brother of Gouverneur Morris was a British general; the British Treasury official George Rose was brother-in-law to William Duer. William Vans Murray was married to an Englishwoman and John Quincy Adams found his wife in England. The Spanish minister, the Marquis of Casa Yrujo, married a daughter of the governor of Pennsylvania; two British ministers, George Hammond and David Erskine, had American wives; and so for that matter had the French diplomats Pichon and Barbé-Marbois. If some of these unions seemed of small effect in relaxing international tensions, more could perhaps be said for those of Alexander and Henry Baring (whose father was a friend of Shelburne and Barré and an opponent of Lord Sheffield on questions of commercial policy) to the Bingham sisters of Philadelphia (whose father had engaged in pamphlet warfare with Sheffield), which cemented connections between the banking houses of Philadelphia and Baltimore and the imperial financiers of London and Amsterdam with economic and political consequences extending to the Webster-Ashburton Treaty and beyond.

Yet however important the transatlantic movements of individuals and goods, the knitting up by economic bonds was hardly limited to the international context. At home, as well, growing prosperity and improved transport had their effects in furthering the regional interdependence emphasized in Washington's Farewell Address and reiterated twenty years later in Monroe's First Inaugural. Although policy disagreements continued they were no longer wholly explicable, if indeed they ever had been, in terms of a capitalist-agrarian, North-South dichotomy. The Federalist Party, now entering its decline, had been strong in the South in the early years. Madison had supported the maritime interest during the Constitutional Convention; in the first years under the Constitution both he and Jefferson had devoted their energies to the problems of foreign trade. The navy, the principal agent for

protection of commerce, was far from being a New England arti-
fact: Jefferson, whom John Adams later acknowledged as its "father," had urged its creation from the time of his residence in
France; the first three Secretaries were from Maryland and South
Carolina; its officer corps was drawn almost entirely from south
of the Hudson River.

Nor were the great merchants and their political representatives uniformly of the Federal persuasion. Samuel Smith, Baltimore shipowner, strong navy partisan, and longtime congressman
and senator, had left the Hamiltonians on the question of retaliation for the Caribbean captures to become a power in the Republican Party. If the Salem Derbys were strong Federalists, and if
some Cabots and Perkinses supported the Hartford Convention,
other merchants had other views. George Crowninshield named
his yacht the *Jefferson* and his cousin became Madison's Secretary
of the Navy. Although Joseph Peabody, the wealthiest shipowner
in Salem, opposed the move to war in 1812, when hostilities did
come he supported the government. Asa Clapp, the richest man
in Maine, backed the administration in both 1807 and 1812 and
subscribed largely to the war loans. John Jacob Astor had close
ties with both Jefferson and Madison administrations. No more
than his opposition to the Jay Treaty, or his support of Jefferson,
or his proffer of ships to the government during the War of 1812,
would Stephen Girard's choice of names for his finest vessels—
Voltaire, Rousseau, Helvetius, Montesquieu—have commended him to
the Essex Junto. William Gray, the greatest individual shipowner
in the country, left the Federalists on the Embargo question to
become Republican lieutenant governor of Massachusetts.

THE LIMITS OF ECONOMIC INFLUENCE

Although the emergence of the great merchants and entrepreneurs
was dramatic testimony to important trends in national and international economics, the political influence of these economic men

appears to have been largely limited to routine matters and marginal deals: as the British minister reported in 1807, property had small weight in a nation where all could vote. On both sides of the ocean, indeed, in times of crisis politics took precedence over economics. The Barings became the overseas fiscal agents of the American government and handled the financing of the Louisiana Purchase; in cooperation with the transnational financier David Parish and some Baltimore interests they maneuvered through both Embargo and British blockade in the great Mexican bullion export deal; but their remonstrances against the orders in council were unproductive. John Jacob Astor received Jefferson's praise for the civilizing promise of his Columbia River project, conducted a private diplomacy with Montreal fur interests and with the Russians in Alaska, breached the Embargo by the use of a synthetic Chinese mandarin, and managed some trading across the lines in 1812–14. But his efforts, in conjunction with a group of bank and insurance company presidents, to stave off the coming of war had no effect at all.

Economics, no doubt, was central, and commerce, at least theoretically, the great pacifier, but in times of trouble the politicians took charge. No more than the suffering British exporters and West Indies planters, or British investors in American lands and American securities, did the American magnates control policy. Although all three regretted the War of 1812 and hoped for an early peace, in the crisis of 1813 Girard, Astor, and Parish joined to take up the government loan that Gallatin had failed to float through normal channels.

These complications, however, were still in the future. In times of comparative relaxation, in a world where all were friends, in-laws, cousins, exporters, importers, economists, and diplomats, Jefferson could properly rearticulate Washington's Great Rule and call for "peace, commerce, and honest friendship with all nations, entangling alliances with none." For the moment, indeed, all appeared to be republicans and all federalists, and one could aim at a continuation of the Great Experiment and at a government, and indeed a world, which would leave men "free to regulate their own pursuits of industry and improvement." But the bulk of

American trade was nevertheless with Europe and with European possessions, European powers still controlled the St. Lawrence and the Mississippi, and in these areas the country found itself "engaged in commerce with nations who feel power and forget right."[19]

THE REPUBLICANS IN POWER

Naturally enough, perhaps, given their ideological distaste for the processes of diplomacy and the prosperous conditions of 1801, the Republicans for the moment remained largely passive in their dealings with the powers of Europe. Here, at least, the "temporizing" system which Hamilton had predicted for the new administration manifested itself. Some unsuccessful efforts were made to enlighten the French as to the value of the American economic connection and to deal by new legislation with British discriminating duties. Curiously, however, the new administration took no steps to anticipate the impending expiration of the commercial articles of the Jay Treaty, or to cope with either the economic consequences of the Peace of Amiens or the increased European pressures that followed the resumption of general war.

Yet the needs of 1801 differed little from those of 1794–95. The governing imperatives remained the maintenance and expansion of the vital North Atlantic trade, defense of the western frontiers and the fast-growing Mississippi River commerce, and the extension and protection of peripheral ocean opportunities. Equally, when confronted by problems in these areas, the Jeffersonians followed the precedents set by Washington and Adams: a defensive attitude coupled with negotiation and the attempted auctioning of economic favor when faced with the dangerous power of Europe; a forward policy, insofar as means permitted, with regard to Indians and pirates.

In the first weeks of the new administration the forward

policy was dramatically manifested in the question of Mediterranean commerce: here, at least, there was no temporizing. Despite the treaties of the 1790s relations with the Barbary regencies remained uncertain, and the Adams administration, faced in its closing months with new demands from Tripoli, had contemplated a Mediterranean cruise with its new naval force. For Jefferson, who both as minister to France and as Secretary of State had urged vigorous action against Algiers, the prospect was congenial. Two weeks after his inauguration, and even before he had found a Secretary of the Navy, the President decided to act, and in June a small squadron set forth with instructions to respond forcibly to any declaration of war.

In its unanticipated magnitude and duration, its administrative complexity, and its ultimate success, this transatlantic campaign was by far the most impressive initiative in support of commerce and national honor that the government had thus far attempted. In manner of conduct it was identifiably Republican. Diplomatic preparation was ignored in favor of Jeffersonian "pêle-mêle," and it seems simply to have been assumed that this armament from the New World, acting in the interest of the international trading community, would be assisted by the British at Gibraltar and Malta and by the Kingdom of Naples. Constitutional and legal scruples appeared in administration debate as to how far force could be employed in the absence of a declaration of war, and in concern lest the blockade of Tripoli infringe the rights of neutrals or American support of the Tripolitan pretender unjustly prejudice the right of self-determination. So compartmented from the great power world did the effort seem to be that the threat of France in New Orleans had no effect on naval deployment. In 1802, as the retrocession crisis developed, the Mediterranean Squadron was steadily reinforced. In the upshot the campaign contributed to both national reputation abroad and national feeling at home: in Preble, Decatur, and Eaton the country found its first heroes of the second generation. But transoceanic expeditions tend to have enduring consequences. The logistic problems of war at a distance, coupled with continuing concern for the Mediterranean trade, led to the establishment of new Mediterranean consulates and naval agencies and to the decision of 1805 to maintain a permanent Mediterranean Squadron.

While war with Tripoli continued, a major crisis was developing in the West. In May 1801 rumors of the retrocession of Louisiana to France raised the specter of real and dangerous power ensconced in New Orleans, the great western "vent," where American trade was already double that of the Spanish. For decrepit Spain to continue in control of the river mouth, as of the further exit between Florida and Cuba, was one thing; the presence of France would be quite another. By 1802 this threat, emphasized by the dispatch to San Domingo of the largest army Bonaparte had yet assembled and by autumn closure of the New Orleans deposit, had led to the development of comprehensive and coordinated policy. To ostentatious lack of support for French efforts to subdue San Domingo, the government joined rational diplomatic arguments as to the dangers of future collison with a France controlling the Mississippi, open flirtation with the British, and the wholly unprecedented idea, appropriate only to a nation of rationalists and land speculators with a history of Indian cessions, of transferring the sovereignty of territory by purchase.

At home, meanwhile, steps were taken to strengthen the American position all along the Mississippi. In January 1803, in a confidential message to Congress, Jefferson urged expedited efforts to civilize and settle the Indians who controlled the eastern bank, so as to permit by strategic colonization the "planting on the Mississippi itself the means of its own safety." These measures would be accompanied by efforts in the north to develop contacts with the Missouri country and divert its fur resources from "the trade of another nation." To the latter end the President proposed a small expedition "even to the western ocean," to explore the country and confer "with the natives on commercial intercourse."[20] But for the imminent larger crisis greater means were necessary. As compared to the $2,500 asked for Lewis and Clark, the Congress had placed $2 million at the President's disposal for New Orleans, and again a special envoy had been nominated. In March James Monroe sailed to join Livingston in Paris to attempt a solution of the Mississippi problem, either by purchase of New Orleans and the Floridas for $10 million or, as last resort, by marriage to the British fleet and nation.

The remarkable real estate transaction consummated in April by Livingston and Monroe accomplished both more and less than had been intended. By their purchase of New Orleans they had succeeded in 80 percent of their mission, if one can judge by the item values attached respectively to that "island" and to the Floridas in their instructions. As an added and unanticipated bonus, Bonaparte's sale of the great emptiness to the westward further removed the threat of Europe. Yet 20 percent of the original aim had gone unsatisfied. The Floridas remained Spanish, watching over the exit from the Gulf, blocking those smaller Mississippis leading to Mobile and Pensacola, and providing a haven for escaped slaves, hostile tribes, and British intrigue carried out under cover of the Indian trade.

In this situation the administration undertook a series of somewhat devious efforts to improve the "noble bargain" through broad construction of the Louisiana treaty, the Mobile Act of 1804, and an attempted second purchase of the Floridas. In the Northwest, by contrast, attention now focused on the trans-Mississippi region. On the assumption that commerce was "the great engine" of civilization the network of Indian factories was pressed westward to the Mississippi and beyond, Zebulon Pike was sent north to explore the sources of the river and warn off Canadian trappers, and plans were made for the extension of army posts as far as the Mandan villages so as to exclude the British from the Indian trade.

As the election of 1804 showed, the first Jefferson administration had been crowned with notable success. Acquisition of New Orleans had freed the commerce and cemented the allegiance of the West; national pride and maritime trade had benefited from the war with Tripoli. With these accomplishments it seemed possible to put diplomacy back on the shelf where it belonged. The Second Inaugural made no mention of foreign affairs, and in his message of 1806 the President looked forward to the extinction of the debt and employment of the surplus on internal improvements and education.

PROBLEMS OF A TRADING NEUTRAL

But from here on it was all downhill. War in Europe had been resumed in 1803 to the great benefit of neutral shipping. To circumvent the Royal Navy the Americans had developed and expanded the practice of "broken voyage" whereby goods from the French West Indies, "neutralized" by importation into the United States, were re-exported to Europe with duties rebated. But as this commerce grew, so did British resentment, and in contrast to the earlier years this second phase of the European wars now brought forth the full employment of British sea power. In July 1805 the admiralty court decision in the *Essex* case seemed to threaten the lucrative indirect trade. In October Nelson's victory at Trafalgar gave Great Britain monopoly power at sea, and the lawyer and publicist James Stephen published an influential pamphlet urging the restriction and taxation of neutral commerce.[21] Such measures were presently to be put into effect, while with a rising tempo of impressment the prisoners of the Royal Navy came vastly to outnumber the former prisoners of Algiers.

Despite French decrees and British orders, prosperity continued, and indeed increased. But little remained of the fine fabric of international law, while the policy of balancing off the contending powers, always vulnerable in the face of British maritime superiority, was now wholly obsolete. The Mississippi might roll unvexed to the sea, but on the Atlantic the British appeared to be successfully reestablishing their imperial control through the practice of impressment, a "relict of colonial servitude," and through commercial restrictions which struck at the "very root" of independence.[22]

Nor, in the face of overbearing Royal Navy and British cabinet, did the administration summon up the ingenuity and flexibility that it had shown during the retrocession crisis. Congressional pressure, not presidential leadership, brought forth the Non-Importation Act of 1806 and the dispatch of the now traditional special envoy to negotiate with the British. But this time the effort failed. While not commercially unattractive, the abortive Monroe-

Pinkney Treaty gained no concession on impressment, pushed the United States toward confrontation with France, and again required abandonment of the weapon of commercial retaliation. Here, as repeatedly over the next few years, British arrogance and power and American national pride and theoretical rigidity led to deadlock. Even before the attack on the *Chesapeake* brought national outrage and the prospect of war, it had become clear that the struggle for American independence was by no means over.

The resort to economic coercion that followed the *Chesapeake* affair has sometimes been attributed to southern or Republican hostility to commerce. But this seems hardly accurate. From the first movement toward the Constitution, southerners had been in the forefront of the struggle for expanded trade, on which, as staple exporters, their region so depended. What can perhaps be said is that from the beginning a tension existed between the believers in what was and the believers in what ought to be, and that their widely different attitudes toward commerce were, in a period of prolonged international crisis, brought into increasing conflict. To the great powers of Europe commerce remained, as throughout the preceding century, an instrument of state, and as the war in Europe dragged on, more and more emphasis was placed on power and less and less on right. The Federalists, by and large, saw commerce from the view of the individual shipowner or merchant, and national policy as individual interest writ large. But to Jefferson and Madison, and those who shared their fierce pride in the American experiment, it had a higher value, as a powerful weapon in the paradoxical enterprise of using power against power to free the seas and better the condition of mankind. For the British, however, who also saw themselves engaged in a struggle against power, such paradoxes had but small appeal. Whether in a time of continuing crisis the commercial weapon would prove equal to the heavy philosophical freight invested in it, remained to be seen.

News of the *Chesapeake* outrage reached Jefferson on June 25, 1807, and a week later the President closed American ports to ships of the Royal Navy. The Mediterranean Squadron was recalled and a warship dispatched to England with demands for dis-

avowal, reparations, and (once again) the abolition of impressment. But only disavowal was offered. In this situation the Non-
Importation Act of 1806, long suspended and of very limited application, was implemented in early December, and soon news of
the most oppressive of all orders in council was at hand. On December 18, possibly anticipating war, Jefferson suggested in a brief
message to Congress the virtue of "an inhibition of the departure
of our vessels"[23] as a measure of protection for the country's exposed maritime resources, some 1,500 ships, 20,000 seamen, and
$60 million of cargo. Four days later the Embargo forbade both
the clearance of American ships for foreign ports and the export
of American goods.

The enactment of the Embargo began, or perhaps more
accurately led into, the greatest of all efforts to capitalize on the
value of the American economy and to bend the Europeans by the
policy of giving or withholding favor. Yet the management was
curiously inept. With retirement impending, Jefferson had largely
abdicated his executive duties, and neither the purpose nor the
anticipated duration of the measure was made clear. Nor was explanation forthcoming as to why this move against Great Britain
required the abandonment of all overseas trades, or why, if American exports and navigation were to cease, American markets
should remain open to British cotton, woollen, and iron products,
and American harbors to British shipping. The costs of this executive paralysis in dissension at home and lost opportunity abroad
were soon to be emphasized by events to the southward.

THE SPANISH AMERICAN REVOLUTIONS

Long closed off by Spanish and Portuguese regulations, South
America was in many respects a dark continent, little known or
understood in the United States. But the wartime opening of the
Spanish colonies had led to increased contacts, and while American trade was still concentrated in Cuba and the Caribbean, a

considerable commerce had developed with Chile and the River Plate. The Adams administration had shown its interest by establishing agencies and consulates, effective although unrecognized by Spain, in New Orleans, Havana, Santiago, and LaGuayra. Popular concern had been reflected in sympathy for the revolutionary ambitions of Miranda and the ambiguous schemes of Aaron Burr. In the decade before 1806 the share of American exports taken by the Spanish colonies had increased from 3 to 12 percent of the total; with the migration of the Braganzas in 1807 Brazil was opened to trade. But the new possibilities had also attracted others. Although British shipping had been effectively excluded from the Spanish colonies, British interest in these southern regions had been evidenced by the seizures of Trinidad, Tobago, and Demerara, by expeditions to San Domingo, and most recently by invasions of the La Plata region. With the French entrance into Spain and the Spanish uprising of May 1808, the entire region fell open to British trade.

On the theoretical level the Jefferson administration seems clearly to have perceived the commercial and political opportunities offered by events in Spain. In late October 1808 a "Large Policy"—perhaps better a large concept—was formulated, and agents in Cuba and Mexico were instructed to emphasize American friendship and a presumed common interest in the exclusion of "all European influence" from the western world.[24] To diminish Europe's power and further the breakup of its closed commercial and maritime systems the United States would encourage Latin American independence movements, oppose the transfer of territory from one European power to another, and resist European commercial penetration. But while the aims of 1776 were thus extended to the larger hemisphere the practical results were negligible. Contact with these regions had been broken by the Embargo, the appointment of agents lagged, no effort was made to legislate for the new circumstances, and this inaction eased the way for Britain to marry her exports and merchant marine to the new El Dorado. The result was thus precisely what the concept had sought to avoid: the augmentation of the economic and political influence of the great maritime power against which the Embargo, with all its domestic costs, was at the same time being directed.

Despite seemingly clear appreciation of the Latin American problem in both administration and Congress, policy remained rigidly focused on the Embargo. In the end its effectiveness was considerable. If the consummation of the Louisiana purchase had shown that at last the government could govern, the Draconian enforcement of this self-blockade certainly showed that it (or at least Gallatin) could administer. At home the impact was heavy, on producers and shippers alike, and not least on the fortunes of Jefferson himself. In England, by late 1808, its effects were clearly visible. Although some rejoiced at America's self-inflicted wounds and at American withdrawal from the Latin American trade, and although the British loss of cotton imports was cushioned by large existing stocks, Gouverneur Morris and others felt that a little more persistence would surely bring results. But in economic as in other kinds of war the moral factor predominates and the crucial question is that of resolve. In the symbiotic state of relations between America and Britain, each could go only so far in damaging the other before damaging itself; to coerce Great Britain one had first to coerce at home; and here the faith in commerce as an agent corrosive of state power had unexpected vindication in Republican disarray and Federalist resurgence. Economic distress, executive passivity, and the problems of a fragmented party brought repeal of the Embargo in February 1809, at the moment when some thought it on the verge of success.

The Non-Intercourse Act, which replaced the Embargo in March, attempted to reconcile the needs of commerce with those of policy. In the interest of policy and national honor, imports and exports were closed off from both the British Empire and regions under Napoleonic control. In the interest of the domestic economy and of governmental need for customs duties, the rest of the world was opened to American trade. But only a partial prosperity was regained and the coercive effect was small. Ships which got to sea tended to stay there, and much forbidden trade went on through neutral ports, as illustrated by the enormous flow of cotton to the Azores. When hopes raised by the Erskine Agreement and dashed by its repudiation forced the Congress to cast about for new measures, economic interest triumphed over diplomacy. The spirited effort of Gallatin and Macon to open all trades while closing out British and French shipping was beaten down, and the act of May 1810 retained only the possibility of coercive action and proved merely an incitement to Napoleonic trickery.

While the divided Congress flailed about on policy toward the European belligerents, the government made some first efforts to capitalize on Latin American opportunities. In 1808 a consul was appointed for Brazil, and in the next year the dispatch of a minister gave the United States its first diplomatic representation on the southern continent. In 1810 the Madison administration sent agents for commerce and seamen—consuls without the name—to Havana and LaGuayra, and appointed the ardent and impolitic Joel Poinsett "agent" for Buenos Aires, Chile, and Peru. In 1811 Venezuela's declaration of independence (encouraged by an American agent disturbed by British commercial competition) gave rise to a House Committee on the South American colonies and a proposed statement which mingled friendship and hints of recognition with appropriate republican, commercial, and hemispheric sentiments. Early in 1812 a disastrous earthquake at Caracas elicited a $50,000 relief appropriation from a philanthropic and hopeful Congress.

These efforts were accompanied by a helpful revival of the Latin American trade, whose linkages with the Mediterranean and Far East gave it a multiplier effect. But a fundamental change had come with the arrival of the British, who speedily acquired preferential trading positions in Buenos Aires and Brazil, and American exports and re-exports to the Western Hemisphere remained well below the totals of pre-Embargo years. In this competition no help could be gained from Napoleon: the attempt of Robert Smith in 1810 to show that French commercial liberalization would be mutually helpful in undermining British economic dominance in Latin America met with no response, and no better fate awaited the diplomatic efforts of Joel Barlow. Again the efforts to play the belligerents off against each other failed, and again transatlantic economics came to frustrate hemispheric policy. The Peninsular

War had opened the Spanish and Portuguese grain markets, and by 1811 American exports and re-exports to the Iberian peninsula had risen from a small fraction of those to Latin America to three times their total. The result was diminished concern for opportunity to the southward and a growing interested sympathy for the British cause.

Such sympathy, however, was not much felt west of the mountains. There slowing population growth, the high costs of overland imports, and the problems of marketing the produce of the Ohio valley by way of New Orleans had replaced marginal prosperity with a depression which could be persuasively blamed on British closure of European markets. British Indian policy had been cautious in the years following the *Chesapeake* affair, but since Canadian fur traders continued to encourage their friends and Tecumseh remained in contact with Fort Malden, the outbreak of frontier warfare in the election year of 1810 provided another grievance. Although the Canadian fur drain from the upper Mississippi was ended in 1811 by the private diplomacy of Astor and the North West Company, this history of trespass and exploitation could still be seen as a history of British injury. In the South, despite the occupation of the region between the Mississippi and Pearl Rivers in 1810, there remained the problem of the chaotic Floridas, increasingly ungoverned by feeble Spanish garrisons and economically dominated by British traders in close contact with the Indians. Although shipowners could still profit despite orders in council, impressment, and Napoleonic decrees, for patriots in the West too much had been endured too long. Grievances largely economic in origin were transmuted into questions of national honor, and where economics had once vitiated policy, now policy came to control.

THE WAR OF 1812

By 1811 another triple crisis had developed. On the Atlantic, in the West, and in Latin America the British appeared to bar the way. Although factionalism and indecision inhibited military preparation, some things at least were done. Acting to forestall possible British designs, Madison in January gained from Congress the passage of the No-Transfer Resolution and authority, in case of attempted foreign occupation, to take temporary possession of all the Floridas. In March the Eppes Bill closed American ports to British ships and goods. This act, in time, would bring effective pressure on British manufacturers; for the moment the first skirmishes, the encounter between the *President* and *Little Belt* in May and the Battle of Tippecanoe in November, nourished the patriotic wish for action. In the spring of 1812, as the British government, tardily alert to the situation and urged on by distressed manufacturing interests, moved slowly and secretively to repeal of the orders in council, another precautionary embargo was enacted, and in June Madison confided the issue of peace or war to "the legislative department." Since his principal complaints of deeds hostile to the United States as an "independent nation"—impressment of citizens to fight British battles, the plundering of commerce, the monopolizing of navigation, and the incitement of savage warfare on the frontiers—all echoed the complaints of 1776, it seemed clear that the Americans had not yet escaped their colonial servitude.[25]

In the approach to war and in the war itself economic interests continued manifest, influencing and at times transcending national policies. The effects of "peaceful coercion" on British interest groups had by 1812 succeeded in bringing repeal of the orders in council. French spoliations of American shipping had been so serious as to threaten "prismatic or triangular war." On the western side of the Atlantic the political importance of economics was seen in continued export of flour and grain to the British armies in Spain, tolerated by the government to conciliate the Middle States, and in a booming trade between New England and the Maritime Provinces, licensed by the British to promote northeastern disaffection. The earlier expansion of Baltic commerce, the common bonds of small-navy trading states, and the "affinity between the Baltic and American ideas of maritime law"[26] were reflected in the czar's proposed mediation, which also gave inferential support to the belief that the cause of America was that of all mankind, or at least of all except the overbearing French and British.

The war itself came close to disaster. Somewhat surprisingly, the conquest of Canada did not prove a mere matter of marching. American shipping was driven from the seas. The coasts were blockaded and the capital burned. New England resistance posed a greater danger than Spanish Conspiracy, whiskey rebels, or Aaron Burr. The threat of France in New Orleans returned in more dangerous form in a British expedition against the Floridas and Louisiana. Yet all this was in considerable measure redeemed by the feats of arms of both navy and privateers, which inflicted heavy costs upon the British and wholly justified Jefferson's earlier view that American navigation was, "as a resource of defense, essential." If the treaty ending the war settled nothing in the area of policy, peace in Europe at least brought a lifting of the oppressions on American commerce, while the victories at sea, on the lakes, and at New Orleans, could be held to have "won" the Second War for Independence. At the very least they made the navy the nation's favorite institution and Andrew Jackson its favorite hero.

And even if, as between the United States and Britain, it was hard to identify a victor, it could at least be affirmed that the Indians had lost their struggle. The Battles of the Thames and Horseshoe Bend had ensured the federal authority throughout the national domain, ended the threat of European war by proxy on the frontiers, and opened the Middle West and Gulf plains to a new flood of settlement.

POSTWAR DEVELOPMENTS

The period that followed the Treaty of Ghent saw the continuation, under easier circumstances, of the basic national aims that had prevailed since 1776: the limitation of arbitrary power and the removal of obstacles "not conformable to reason" to individual activity and human progress (of which the most important had come to seem the European presence in America). With fits and starts the efforts continued to make the world approximate as nearly as possible a system that would restrain men from injuring one another and leave them otherwise free to regulate their own pursuits.

These efforts, in the postwar years, could still be ranged under the three headings that had characterized foreign relations since independence. In the important North Atlantic trades, the government relied upon domestic legislation and diplomatic negotiation to strengthen the American economy and knit together the new world of the bourgeoisie. As regards the peripheral commerce in the Mediterranean, the Madison administration acted decisively and at once: in 1815 new Algerine aggressions brought a declaration of war and the dispatch of squadrons which speedily imposed a settlement. On the North American continent there remained the issue of the St. Lawrence–Great Lakes border and its westward projection, and the ancient problem of the Floridas, now interconnecting with new peripheral opportunities in revolutionary Spanish America. But however similar the questions, the environment had changed: after twenty-two years of warfare, Europe was at last at peace. This overriding fact—together with the survival of the American experiment, the spread of liberal ideas, and the growth of trade—gradually worked to diminish the political content of diplomacy and permit, in a period of reduced international tension, the desired concentration on economic progress.

It was, of course, far from clear that Ghent represented a lasting peace: to some, like Henry Clay, the future seemed to promise an unending series of British wars. In such an atmosphere the immediate postwar years brought appropriations for coastal fortification, enlargement of the peacetime army, and a program for the navy's "gradual increase" which contemplated the construction of a dozen frigates and nine ships of the line. But if the apparatus of defense was for the moment strengthened, that of diplomacy was not. The Prussian legation, closed in 1801, was not reopened; the legation at St. Petersburg remained untenanted for three years; in 1816 an attempt to gain salaried status for consular officials failed in Congress. In 1817, when John Quincy Adams succeeded to the post of Secretary of State, he found a department still charged with supervision of the patent system, loaded with postwar spoliation claims, and faced with the newly elaborate census requirements of 1820, with its staff overworked and its records in disarray.

While the representatives of the people gave or withheld their favor with regard to these instruments of policy, the invisible hand, assisted by some positive shipping and tariff legislation, shaped the course of trade. In economic relations with the developed North Atlantic states, the transition from a war to a peace economy was eased by high wheat prices stemming from disastrous European harvests, and by the astonishing rise of the cotton export to 40 percent of the 1819 dollar total.[27] Cushioned by these developments, economic foreign policy concentrated on providing a modicum of protection for new industry and on expanding the opportunities for the merchant marine.

Through the years of Embargo, non-importation, and war, manufacturing had increased dramatically. Between 1805 and 1815 domestic consumption of cotton grew from 1,000 to 90,000 bales a year; between 1810 and 1815 factory production of woollens quintupled. The impact on these new industries of the flood of cut-rate British imports, together with the need to service the war debt, soon brought forth the Tariff of 1816, a transitional step between earlier schedules and the protectionism of the later 1820s, which raised the general average of duties, placed a special rate on textiles, and made some effort to assist the iron industry.[28] But if these infant industries needed swaddling, the merchant marine now seemed fully competitive, and here the act of March 1815 offered, on a reciprocal basis, the removal of all discriminating provisions for foreign ships carrying own-country produce.

RELATIONS WITH EUROPE

In the case of Britain, as always far the most important trading partner, the reciprocity offered by this act was embodied in the convention of July 1815, negotiated by Gallatin, Clay, and Adams, which provided for equality in the direct trades. Supplemented in 1817 by a navigation act prohibiting the importation in foreign ships of goods not the product of their own country, this arrangement gave real competitive advantage to American shipping, a development reflected in January 1818 in the inauguration of scheduled transatlantic packet service by the *James Monroe* of the Black Ball Line. Outside the direct transatlantic trade, British refusal to open British North America and the West Indies to American shipping brought the exclusion in 1818 of British ships arriving from ports closed to the United States, a measure leading to quick victory in the "plaster of Paris war" with New Brunswick and Nova Scotia and to hardship and decline in the islands.

With the other European states commercial negotiations brought varying success. Efforts to interest France and Spain in reciprocity made small progress, although Cuba, now vastly more important than the withering British sugar islands, remained open to American trade. With Portugal and her sister kingdom of Brazil, nothing was accomplished. But North European commerce was expanded by an 1816 reciprocity treaty with Sweden, by the cooperative attitude of Russia, and by the extension of reciprocity in 1818–19 to cover goods transshipped through Prussia, Hamburg, Bremen, and the Netherlands. In the Mediterranean, where a squadron was maintained following the chastisement of Algiers, a show of force was made against Naples in support of unpaid spoliation claims, while to the eastward the growing Smyrna trade and Turkish affability brought new interest in negotiations for access to the Black Sea. All in all, it could be said that in the transatlantic context the American efforts to liberate commerce were, by 1819, making good progress.

This liberation, the goal of government and citizen alike, was greatly aided by the close relationship enjoyed with the great

English banking firm of Baring Brothers, the "sixth power" of Europe and of all those powers the most economically rational. Throughout the years of crisis and war since Alexander Baring's visit to America, this connection had grown steadily closer. During the Adams administration the Barings had provided funds for negotiations with Barbary and had facilitated the procurement of arms for use against the French. In the Jefferson administration they managed the Louisiana Purchase payments and led, however ineffectively, British opposition to the orders in council. After 1815 they took over the handling of funds for American legations and consulates in Europe, for the Mediterranean Squadron, and for American agents in South America. In 1817 they became the London agents for the second Bank of the United States and provided that ailing institution with loans of badly needed specie. For two decades the firm had been the principal engine for the assembly of British capital for American investment; in the postwar years its presence in South America and beyond the Cape of Good Hope facilitated the extension of American mercantile activity.

BORDER SOLUTIONS

On the North American continent the coming of peace and the growth of western settlement brought liquidation of the issues of three decades. In the north this process was furthered by the newly complaisant British attitude: here, as in the commercial sphere, new developments and new men brought a new willingness to negotiate. On the Great Lakes in 1817 the unprecedented idea of arms limitation was embodied in the Rush-Bagot agreement. The Convention of 1818, while renewing the commercial provisions of 1815, further tidied up the situation by arrangements on the fisheries and by extending the line of 49° to the Stony Mountains. Continued British refusal of free navigation of the St. Lawrence, perhaps in reprisal for the exclusion of Canadian fur traders from upper Louisiana, proved a minor nuisance, soon to be remedied by the application of technology to policy in the construction, by the state of New York and with the help of British capital, of the Champlain and Erie Canals. But in general relations were increasingly easy, and the existence of a highly permeable border between regions of very similar populations, attitudes, and institutions goes far to explain the contrast between the simple step-by-step extension of 49° to the Pacific and the felt necessity of advancing the southern boundary, which continued from the Jay-Gardoqui negotiations to the Gadsden Purchase.

On this southern border the ancient Spanish presence, the subject of thirty years of contention, was now at last removed. West Florida had already been swallowed in two bites, but East Florida remained Spanish and no agreement existed on the trans-Mississippi west. Talks between John Quincy Adams and the Spanish minister Onís, commenced in 1817, were at first unproductive. But their ultimate outcome was hardly in doubt, given the extraordinary influx of American settlers into the Southwest, which between 1810 and 1819 increased the population of Mississippi Territory from 40,000 to 200,000.[29] In 1818, with Jackson's invasion of East Florida and a visible lack of European support for the Spanish cause, negotiations began to move. In the treaty signed on Washington's birthday 1819, the United States, while abandoning Texas, gained in East Florida new river exits to the Gulf and one side of the Florida Strait, along with the useful incidental byproduct of a Louisiana boundary running ultimately to the Pacific.

The Florida Treaty of 1819 marked the end of an epoch. With it there was completed the series of postwar settlements, political and commercial, that had begun with the signing of the Treaty of Ghent. And if these arrangements are considered as a group, and are taken in conjunction with the war-induced renewal of "national feelings and character" commented on by Gallatin,[30] there seems small wonder that the Second War for Independence came ultimately to be counted a very considerable success.

LOOKING SOUTHWARD

There remained, nevertheless, one great exception to the general pacification. Southward beyond the Floridas and Louisiana the dominions of the King of Spain, still covering most of the Americas, remained racked by revolution. Here for a decade the steady disintegration of the Spanish Empire had offered both threat and promise, danger of a new extension of European power to the hemisphere and opportunity to extend the area of freedom. In the case of the contiguous, ungoverned, unsettled, and strategically important Floridas, this danger and this opportunity had seemed to call for annexation; in the more distant and populated regions of Spanish America they called for the support of revolution. Across the Gulf and Caribbean the continuing struggles against the Spanish crown again raised hopes (emphasized, no doubt, by the postwar collapse of the Iberian trade) for the interrelated expansion of commercial opportunity, advancement of liberty, and diminution of European influence.

In the years after Waterloo, as peace descended upon Europe and as solutions were found to the problems of North America, the focus of American diplomacy shifted from Europe and the North Atlantic. Increasingly official attention came to center on the southern regions of the hemisphere. But here policy development was tentative, influenced on the one hand by republican sympathies, anti-Spanish feelings, and the interests of such worthies as Astor, Girard, and the Baltimore merchants, and on the other by fear of European intervention, the importance of the Cuban trade, some disillusion with the new revolutionary governments, and the continuing Adams-Onís negotiations.

Summer of 1815 brought the first move, as the Treasury Department opened American ports to ships flying the revolutionary flags. Permitting as it did both increased trade and revolutionary access to military supplies, this bold measure of economic diplomacy made the question of political recognition less urgent. Although disarray among the revolutionary governments and doubts as to the attitude of Europe briefly worked for caution, the

patriot successes of 1817 and the divergence of British and French
policy brought new encouragement to the friends of liberty. But
this in turn was somewhat dampened by the revisions to the neutrality laws of 1817 and 1818 (designed, as John Randolph observed, to make peace between His Catholic Majesty and the Baltimore privateers), and by the impartial rigor with which
government and navy attempted to enforce American neutral rights
against both sides.

In the waters to the southward, American shipowners
were once again experiencing the mixture of hazard and opportunity that war provides the neutral trader. From the Gulf and
Caribbean to Cape Horn and beyond, armed vessels, doubtfully
identifiable as public ships, privateers, or pirates, preyed upon
shipping: over the years from 1815 to 1823 some 3,000 cases of
piratical aggression would be reported.[31] Ironically enough, given
the earlier economically motivated migration of British sailors
which had underlain the quarrels over impressment, these vessels
were in considerable measure manned by American seamen, unemployed owing to the postwar depression. In its response to this
situation the government returned to the pattern now institutionalized by experience with France and Barbary: agents were dispatched to the theaters of conflict to preach the virtue of liberal
policies, and a redeployment of the navy was begun.

In 1816 a frigate was ordered to Cartagena to protest seizures of American shipping. In the Gulf, where the navy's gun-
boat flotilla had long been skirmishing with Baratarian pirates,
combined operations were mounted against a fort on the Appa-
lachicola in 1816; in the next year another expedition expelled the
pirates from Amelia Island on the Florida coast. In October 1817
the special agent J. B. Prevost sailed in the sloop of war *Ontario*
for the west coast of the Americas, with the dual mission of defending American shipping against contending royalist and patriot
forces and of reestablishing, pursuant to the suggestion of John
Jacob Astor, the American claim to the mouth of the Columbia
River. A few weeks later a commission headed by Caesar A. Rodney set forth in the U.S.S. *Congress* for Rio de Janiero and Buenos
Aires with instructions to gain information, cultivate friendly re-

lations, and protect commerce. In November 1818 Monroe followed up earlier protests against special privileges for the British by enunciating an American policy of equal commercial opportunity. Already the administration had sounded Britain, France, and Russia on the question of recognition of the new states, and in January 1819 it unsuccessfully proposed concerted action to Great Britain.

While recognition waited, naval support of American commerce was increased. Returning from the Columbia River, *Ontario* remained on the Chilean coast to defend American neutral rights; early in 1819 she was replaced by the frigate *Macedonian*, and from this time on a permanent force was maintained on the Pacific Station. At the same time the navy expanded its commitment to the Gulf and Caribbean. In March 1819, in response to a proliferation of uncontrolled Colombian and Venezuelan privateering, the Congress gave the navy enlarged powers in dealing with pirates. In the summer Oliver H. Perry sailed with a small squadron to Venezuela to protest the excesses of privateers and urge a policy of reciprocity, and later in the year a frigate was dispatched on a similar errand to Buenos Aires.

In addition to their primary function of commerce protection, these naval forces, both in the Caribbean and on the coasts of South America, assisted American traders by receiving and safeguarding funds, issuing bills of receipt which served as negotiable paper, and returning specie to the United States to the benefit of the distressed post-1818 economy. But the situation continued unstable, and complaints from New Orleans exporters, Havana merchants, and insurance companies brought further reinforcement. By 1822, when the West Indies Squadron was formally established, the navy had committed thirteen ships to the continuing campaign: by 1826 it had assigned more than two-thirds of its total strength to the West Indies, Brazil, and Pacific Squadrons; and this southward tilt was also reflected in the diplomatic establishment, in which Latin America accounted for seven of a total of fourteen American ministers and chargés.

Looking beyond the sentiments for liberty and the concern

for hemispheric independence of Europe, Latin American policy in these years can be seen as a continuation, in a new theater and under new circumstances, of the old struggle against British economic power. In this sense, at least, the Abbé de Pradt had been right in his 1815 prediction that Latin America would be the new European frontier against the United States. But against the British resolve that France would not get Spain "with the Indies," the American hope that these particular Indies would escape all European influence faced heavy odds.

In no sense was the United States a match for Britain in available capital, manufactured exports, or maritime strength. The years of Embargo and war had broken southern contacts and given the British a free field. Although Americans aplenty had joined the privateering effort and some had fought with the revolutionary armies, their assistance to freedom's cause seemed small when measured against the deeds of General Miller's British legion in Venezuela or of Lord Cochrane and his naval officers in Chile. Only in presumed ideological compatibility and in the weapon of political recongition did the United States have advantage. But here action was slowed by disillusion with Latin American behavior, concern about the attitude of Europe, the importance of the Cuban trade, and Spanish delay in ratifying the Florida Treaty. Yet when in 1822 recognition at last seemed feasible, the anti-British commercial motive was not the least important stimulus to Monroe's action.

Despite these continuing Latin American problems, the years after 1815 had seen a steady diminution of diplomatic tensions. Throughout the North Atlantic basin commerce was by now liberalized, or liberalizing, or at least regularized. With the new solutions to border problems in north, south, and west, Europe seemed for the moment at a sufficient distance. For all its complications, the South American situation promised some opening of new areas to trade and a new importance to the South Atlantic, hitherto primarily useful as a highway to Asia. In this happy situation relations with the powers could at last become low-keyed. Over the next generation foreign affairs would yield precedence to internal development and international dealings would increasingly be left to the interested private individuals to whom Americans believed they properly belonged.

BEYOND THE ATLANTIC

On a small but significant scale such individuals had long been active outside the Atlantic, in Baltic and Mediterranean, and beyond the Cape of Good Hope and Cape Horn. At the far end of the Mediterranean, once the European wars were over and the Barbary pirates quelled, American commerce grew steadily and American merchants established themselves in Smyrna. On the Indian Ocean route to the East the early traders had made their presence felt at Cape Town and had established entrepots at Madagascar and the Ile de France. Although American access to Japan, an outgrowth of contacts with the Dutch at Batavia, had ended in 1809, and although the trade in Indian cottons had been hard hit by the Tariff of 1816, new opportunities were developing. At Manila increasing traffic brought the appointment of a consul in 1817, while the Sumatran pepper trade expanded steadily through the twenties and beyond.

Along the Pacific track to China a similar expansion of activity was visible. The needs of the Canton market had led by way of the southern seal rookeries to the sea otter trade of Oregon and California and the exploitation of Hawaiian sandalwood. From this commerce had followed the displacement of British traders on the northwest coast, illegal contacts with Mexico and California, the imperial scheme of John Jacob Astor with its cooperative arrangements with the Russians at Sitka, and a growing penetration of the Hawaiian Islands by what a visiting British sea captain had referred to, as early as 1805, as the American "commercial hive."[32] By 1818 the islands had become the emporium of the North Pacific and contained, in addition to a number of American traders, a small population of American deserters whose skills in such practical matters as carpentry and boatbuilding commended them to King Kamehameha. At Canton, the destination of West Coast furs and Hawaiian sandalwood as of New England ginseng, Turkish opium, and South American specie, a consul had been intermittently maintained since 1786; in the postwar years the growth of American shipping threatened to rival the East India Company and furthered the development of important American trading houses.

These unofficial representatives of the Great Republic, with their missionary views on freedom, commerce, and technology, had now been joined *in partibus infidelibus* by the emissaries of the foreign missionary movement. And while this movement in theory took the world for its province, the direction of its outward thrust was necessarily influenced by available shipping connections. Guided, perhaps, by the growth of the East India trade that followed the Jay Treaty, the first American missionaries to the heathen had sailed to India and Burma in 1812. Three decades of contact with the Hawaiian Islands led in 1819 to a mission in which farmers and carpenters were joined to divines with the precept, ultimately to be fulfilled, of wholly remaking that civilization. In the same year expanded contacts with the eastern Mediterranean, concern for the sad state of the Oriental Churches, and the millennial significance of the conversion of the Jews, brought forth the first mission to the Near East.

On these far shores, as indeed everywhere abroad, the government, for all the lively activity of its citizens, remained largely passive. With the organized states of Europe it would negotiate in the interests of commerce and navigation. When the rights of citizens were infringed, whether by Indians, pirates, privateers, or hostile navies, it would respond as best it could. But where men refrained from injuring one another they were best left to their own devices, and the postwar years brought little governmental initiative in extending the maritime frontier.

Economical and theoretical restraints had kept the diplomatic establishment small, and expanded horizons were reflected only in a proliferation of navy agents and the growth of the consular service, unpaid except for those who labored in Barbary.

Despite Ottoman initiatives and mercantile interest the negotiation of a Turkish treaty lagged, and the missionaries got there first. The decline of the southern seal fisheries had produced petitions for a government exploring expedition and the annexation of the South Shetlands, but nothing was done. The annexation of Nukahiva by Captain David Porter during his Pacific cruise of 1813–14 was forgotten; his postwar proposal for the opening of Japan and Korea was ignored. Beginning in 1815 the Russians in Alaska had shown increasing interest in California and Hawaii, and Prevost, returning from his mission to the Columbia, had expressed concern for the future of the islands, but diplomatic action was not forthcoming. Nor, despite the American dominance of North Pacific commerce and the rapid growth of the Pacific whaling fleet, did ships of the Pacific Squadron venture north of Mexico, once Astoria had been regained. In 1818, when the frigate *Congress* was ordered out on the first naval voyage to China, her concern was the protection of American shipping against Chinese and Malay pirates, and both outward and homeward trips were by way of the Cape of Good Hope and the Indian Ocean.

A DIPLOMACY PURELY COMMERCIAL

The commerce-protecting voyage of *Congress* can usefully serve as paradigm, both of the basic mission of the navy and of the central thrust of American external policy from its beginning. For an explication of this policy one can perhaps best resort to John Quincy Adams, who from his arrival in Paris in 1778 had lived through it all, and who in 1817 became Secretary of State. In 1823, following the recognition of the Latin American states, Adams drew up notable and eloquent letters of instruction to the first ministers to Buenos Aires and Colombia. In these, after defining American policy—"The basis of all our intercourse with foreign powers is *reciprocity*"—he turned his attention to the future of South America. Seeing the revolutions in that continent as natural successors to that of his own country, and so as opening great prospects for the future of humanity, Adams contrasted the American system, "founded in the unalienable rights of human nature" and based on *"Civil, political, commercial,* and *religious* liberty," with the outworn systems of Europe based upon "partial rights and *exclusive privileges.*" Pointing to the preamble and the first four articles of the French Treaty of Amity and Commerce of 1778 as the external counterpart of the Declaration of Independence and the "cornerstone for all our subsequent transactions of interest with foreign nations," he urged that Colombia, in the interest of futurity,

look to *commerce* and *navigation,* and not to empire as her means of communication with the rest of the human race. These are the principles upon which *our* confederated republic is founded, and they are those upon which we hope our sisters of the southern continent will ultimately perceive it to be for their own welfare, no less than for that of the world, that they should found themelves.[33]

Such views might, at first sight, seem to come oddly from the Secretary who had only recently arranged for an Oregon "free and open" to both British and Americans, acquired the Floridas, and limited Spanish holdings on the Pacific coast, and who in the next year would press the boundary of Russian America north to 54°40′. Nevertheless, they appear to have commanded lasting agreement. In 1828 Theodore Lyman, Jr., the first historian of American foreign relations, observed that American diplomacy found its origin in commerce and that it "may be termed, altogether, of a commercial character." In 1834 both Adams and Lyman were drawn on by Jonathan Elliot for the preface to his *American Diplomatic Code,* a useful manual and compendium, the adoption of which by both State and Navy Departments worked to perpetuate these views as operating doctrine. Returning in 1878 to first principles, after the distractions of the Civil War, Robert W. Shufeldt, soon to become the opener of Korea to the West, argued the importance of the navy as the "pioneer of commerce." Eight years later the learned diplomat Eugene Schuyler published a book of detailed analysis of *American Diplomacy and the Furtherance of Commerce.*[34]

The clue to a reconciliation of these views with the remarkable extension of the national boundaries lies perhaps in Adams' conjunction of *"Civil, political, commercial,* and *religious* liberty." The sacred rights of mankind were all of a piece, and in dealings with foreign nations in accordance with Washington's Great Rule, the linked questions of commercial and political liberty led at once to the central problem of power, and emphasized the antagonism between New and Old World systems and the imperative to put Europe at a distance.

This problem and this imperative, most fundamentally, had underlain the revolutionary cause, and these, rather than land hunger, formed the basis for the first thirty years of boundary expansion. The purchase of Louisiana, unintended and unexpected, stemmed from a European threat, and the acquisition of an empire from the attempt to gain a riverbank. The conquest of Canada was attempted as means rather than end, as a way to free the seas and control the Indians rather than a method of gaining real estate. In the negotiation of the Florida treaty, the central aims were economic and strategic: the acquisition of river openings to the Gulf and the removal of Europe from the southern border. The reassertion of title to the Columbia River and Adams' restriction of Spanish and Russian claims reflected the same desire to push back European political and commercial influence that strengthened sympathy for the revolutionary movements in Spanish America.

In none of these boundary extensions was an expansionist demand for territory the dominant factor. Although patriotic poets like Philip Freneau and Timothy Dwight had early raised the vision of transcontinental expansion, in practice affairs were different. So stalwart a westerner as Thomas Hart Benton would speak in 1825 of placing "the statue of the fabled god, Terminus" at the continental divide. Concurring in this view in 1828, the historian Lyman could only foresee that settlement would "perhaps," in the course of another century, expand across the continent. As late as 1841 it appeared to the explorer Charles Wilkes, after his visit to the West Coast, that "before many years" California would separate from Mexico and join with Oregon to form an important Pacific nation.[35] Unquestionably it was hoped that respect for the "unalienable rights" would overspread the hemisphere and ultimately leap the oceans. But concepts were not limited by boundaries, and the principal mechanism for this contribution to the world's welfare, as well as to that of the Americans, was less an expanded territory than an expanded commerce. When Adams described the principles on which the "confederated republic" was founded, and when Lyman defined his country's diplomacy as "altogether, of a commercial character," it would seem, at least as regards the first thirty years, that they were very nearly right. Certainly that was the way it was supposed to be.

Notes

1. *The Writings of Thomas Jefferson*, A. A. Lipscomb and A. E. Bergh, eds., 20 vols. (Washington, D.C., 1905), 3:263–83.

2. Bureau of the Census, *Historical Statistics of the United States; Colonial Times to 1957* (Washington, D.C.: GPO, 1960), pp. 565–66.

3. Alexander Hamilton, *Federalist XI*.

4. Timothy Pitkin, *A Statistical View of the Commerce of the United States of America*, 2d ed. (New York, 1817), pp. 425, 431.

5. *Familiar Letters of John Adams and his Wife Abigail Adams, during the Revolution*, C. F. Adams, ed. (Boston, 1875), p. 381.

6. Merrill D. Peterson, *Thomas Jefferson and the New Nation* (New York: Oxford University Press, 1970), p. 398.

7. *The Papers of Thomas Jefferson*, Julian P. Boyd et al., eds. (Princeton: Princeton University Press, 1950–   ), 15:326.

8. *Writings of Jefferson*, Lipscomb and Bergh, eds., 3:176, 178–82.

9. Peterson, *Jefferson and New Nation*, p. 515.

10. Early tonnage figures are at best approximations. See Pitkin, *Statistical View*, p. 425; idem, revised edition (New Haven, 1835), 348–49, 363, 371–72; *Historical Statistics*, p. 445; J. G. B. Hutchins, *The American Maritime Industries and Public Policy, 1789–1914* (Cambridge: Harvard University Press, 1941), p. 225; National Bureau of Economic Research (NBER), *Trends in the American Economy in the Nineteenth Century* (Princeton: Princeton University Press, 1960), p. 595.

54   James A. Field, Jr.

11. Pitkin, *Statistical View*, pp. 435–36.

12. James D. Richardson, ed., *A Compilation of the Messages and Papers of the Presidents*, 10 vols. (Washington, D.C., 1899), 1:222.

13. *Historical Statistics*, pp. 7, 712; NBER, *Trends*, p. 355.

14. Hutchins, *Maritime Industries*, p. 225; Pitkin, *Statistical View*, pp. 425, 428; *Historical Statistics*, pp. 445, 538; NBER, *Trends*, pp. 590–91, 595. See note 10 above.

15. Pitkin, *Statistical View*, pp. 60, 132, 136; *Historical Statistics*, p. 547.

16. *Historical Statistics*, 13; Henry Adams, *History of the United States*, 9 vols. (New York: Scribner's, 1931), 6:316.

17. Emory R. Johnson et al., *History of Domestic and Foreign Commerce of the United States*, 2 vols. (Washington, D.C.: Carnegie Institution, 1915), 1:207, 209.

18. Pitkin, *Statistical View*, pp. 275–76.

19. Richardson, *Messages and Papers*, 1:321–23.

20. *Writings of Jefferson*, Lipscomb and Bergh, eds., 3:489–94.

21. James Stephen, *War in Disguise: or, the Frauds of the Neutral Flags* (London, 1805).

22. *The Writings of John Quincy Adams*, W. C. Ford, ed., 7 vols. (New York: Macmillan, 1913–17), 3:200, 202.

23. Richardson, *Messages and Papers*, 1:433.

24. Arthur P. Whitaker, *The United States and the Independence of Latin America, 1800–1830* (New York: Norton, 1964), p. 46.

25. Richardson, *Messages and Papers*, 1:500–4.

26. *The Writings of James Madison*, Gaillard Hunt ed., 9 vols. (New York: Putnam, 1900–10), 8:243–44.

27. *Historical Statistics*, pp. 538, 547.

28. F. W. Taussig, *The Tariff History of the United States*, 5th ed. (New York: Putnam, 1901), pp. 18, 28, 40, 50–51, 68.

29. *Historical Statistics*, p. 13.

30. *The Writings of Albert Gallatin*, Henry Adams, ed., 3 vols. (Philadelphia, 1879; reprint ed., New York: Antiquarian Press, 1960), 1:700.

31. Dudley W. Knox, *A History of the United States Navy* (New York: Putnam, 1948), p. 139.

32. H. W. Bradley, *The American Frontier in Hawaii* (Stanford: Stanford University Press, 1942), p. 25.

33. *Writings of J. Q. Adams*, 7:432, 460–61, 466, 468–69, 473.

34. Theodore Lyman, Jr., *The Diplomacy of the United States*, 2d ed., 2 vols. (Boston, 1828), 2:495; Robert W. Shufeldt, *The Relation of the Navy to the Commerce of the United States* (Washington, 1878), p. 6; Eugene Schuyler, *American Diplomacy and the Furtherance of Commerce* (New York, 1886).

35. Henry Nash Smith, *Virgin Land: The American West as Symbol and Myth* (Cambridge: Harvard University Press, 1950), p. 26; Lyman, *Diplomacy*, 2:120; Charles Wilkes, *Narrative of the United States Exploring Expedition*, 5 vols. (Philadelphia, 1845), 5:171.

2

1821–1860
Economics
and the Diplomacy
of American Expansionism

Kinley J. Brauer

University of Minnesota

A new epoch has arisen; and it becomes us deliberately to contemplate our own actual condition, and the relations which are
likely to exist between us and other parts of the world.

Henry Clay, 1820[1]

DIPLOMACY AND AMERICAN
ECONOMIC GROWTH

ECONOMIC CONSIDERATIONS PLAYED a particularly
important role in American diplomacy between 1821 and 1860.
During these years, the American economy depended heavily on
overseas commerce, and American diplomats necessarily devoted
the bulk of their energies to attempts to liberalize the terms of

Research for this chapter was facilitated by grants from the National Endowment for the
Humanities and the Graduate School and Putnam D. McMillan Fund of the University of
Minnesota.

American commerce and to open new markets around the world. These years also marked the culmination of American territorial expansion, and since expansionists often couched their appeals in terms of international economic competitive advantage, diplomats were always sensitive to economic matters in their negotiations for the acquisition of new territories and the resolution of disputed boundaries. In addition, American diplomats posted in major maritime and imperial nations realized that the economic policies of those nations could seriously affect the American economy and so were especially interested in economic affairs overseas.

Officials in Washington were equally concerned with economic questions as they related to foreign affairs, and very often controversies over domestic economic programs revolved around the effect that those programs would have on America's foreign relations. Powerful economic interest groups throughout the nation continually sought government aid in their overseas ventures, and both territorial and commercial expansionists often demanded aggressive foreign policies. As the American economy divided along regional lines, sectional leaders developed and promoted distinctive foreign policies calculated to serve the economic interests of their constituents. Thus, economic considerations played a prominent part in the construction of foreign policy as well as its implementation.

The growth of the United States between 1821 and 1860 was extraordinary. The value of farm output rose from $619 million to more than $2 billion; cotton production increased from 335,000 bales to 3,841,000 bales; and investment in manufacturing rose from $50 million to $1 billion.[2] A massive increase in population promoted this growth. Between 1820 and 1860 approximately five million immigrants entered the United States, and the population as a whole expanded from 9.6 million to 31.5 million. Despite the addition of 1.2 million square miles of virgin land to the national domain, the United States became increasingly urbanized. The number of cities with a population greater than 10,000 increased from thirteen in 1820 to ninety-three in 1860, and the percentage of urban dwellers rose from 7.7 percent in 1820 to 24.6 percent in 1860.[3] And tying the nation together was the most extensive transportation network in the world. Already blessed by an incomparable system of navigable rivers, Americans added 3,700 miles of canals by 1850 and had laid 30,600 miles of railroad track by 1860. In comparison, by 1860, Britain had laid only 14,600 miles of track and all of Western Europe only 19,700.[4]

To a considerable degree, the economic growth of the United States stemmed from its exports to Great Britain. Following the Napoleonic Wars, Britain entered a period of massive industrial expansion based largely on the phenomenal growth of its manufacture of cotton textiles. According to estimates, British manufacturers purchased over three-fourths of their cotton fiber from the United States,[5] and nearly two-thirds of all the raw cotton exported by the United States between 1820 and 1860 went to Britain. Furthermore, the manufacture of huge surpluses of cotton goods led to the enormous expansion of Britain's foreign commerce. By the mid-1840s, eager to facilitate that commerce, the British government turned toward free trade, and its repeal of the tariff on grain imports opened the British market to American farmers as well as planters. Britain thus provided the United States with a continually expanding market for cotton throughout the period and a significant, though not nearly as important, market for American foodstuffs.

Britain thus firmly established itself as the most vital overseas market of the United States. Although France, the Low Countries, and the German states also absorbed substantial American supplies, since the manufacture of cotton textiles was less central to their industrialization, they were in earlier stages of industrialization, and they were more self-sufficient in agriculture than Britain, their economic ties to the United States were considerably less important.

The significance of the foreign market for American cotton can hardly be overestimated. Raw cotton overwhelmingly dominated all American exports, accounting for 42.3 percent of total exports in 1820 and 60.8 percent in 1860. In terms of value, cotton exports rose from an annual average value of $24.6 million between 1821 and 1825 to $148.9 million between 1856 and 1860.[6] With only a small (but growing) textile industry at home, Americans exported approximately 74 percent of all the cotton they raised between 1820 and 1860. The economic well-being of planters, brokers, shippers, and countless others relied extensively upon the fortunes of British industry, and the prosperity and growth of the United States as a whole rested heavily upon the bales of cotton that filled British and Continental warehouses.

No other commodity ever challenged cotton's position as America's primary export. Most American farm products and manufactures were absorbed at home, and only occasionally during European famines and wars in the 1840s and 1850s did the former achieve some significance in America's overseas commerce. The export of foodstuffs, which increased from an annual average of $10.9 million between 1821 and 1825 and rose to $54.7 million between 1856 and 1860, accounted for only about 22 percent of all American exports and never exceeded 26 percent in any single year. Exports of manufactured goods increased in value during the same five-year periods from annual averages of $5.6 million to $33.5 million and comprised only about 12 percent of America's exports.[7]

The export of raw materials and foodstuffs, however, was more than balanced by the import of manufactured goods, and the United States had a favorable balance of trade in only twelve of the years between 1820 and 1860. As an agrarian nation, the United States was heavily dependent upon foreign manufactures—the United States was Britain's primary overseas customer and, after Britain, France's most important. Thus, while total American exports rose in value from $52 million to $316 million between 1820 and 1860, payments for imports rose from $56.4 million to $336.3 million.[8] Were it not for other sources of income and domestic sources of wealth, the balance of trade would have rendered the United States a permanently impoverished and utterly dependent economic colony of Britain.

Americans more than made up their trade deficit and acquired surplus capital for investment through shipping. In 1821, American vessels carried 90 percent of all tonnage cleared in American ports, and although that percentage declined to around 65 percent after 1855, the total cleared in American ports increased from 1.6 million tons in 1821 to 12.1 million tons in 1860.[9] American merchants thus acquired vast fortunes, which were further augmented by the carrying trade, re-exporting goods of foreign origin from the United States to Europe, Latin America, and Asia and carrying foreign goods directly between foreign ports. The American share of the carrying trade also declined before 1860, but the transshipment of certain goods at various times returned huge profits. Particularly important were the transport of British manufactured goods to Latin America in the 1820s, Turkish and later Indian opium to China in the 1820s and 1840s, Canadian wheat to Britain in the 1850s, and Chinese tea to Britain during the clipper ship era of 1848 to 1854. Between 1821 and 1860, American merchants earned an estimated $663 million in overseas commerce.[10]

Not all of the wealth acquired by merchants remained in overseas commerce. Many invested all or a major part of their profits in domestic banking, manufacturing, and transportation enterprises, thereby accelerating a shift in the American economy toward industrialization that had begun around the time of the War of 1812. The relatively rapid industrial growth and obvious potential of the United States similarly attracted foreign capitalists, who invested between $300 and $500 million in American land, state bonds, banking, manufacturing, and (after 1840) railroads between 1821 and 1860.[11]

Thus, the economic development of the United States between 1820 and 1860 was intimately tied to the massive exports of raw materials and foodstuffs, the success of the merchant marine, and substantial foreign investment in manufacturing, finance, and transportation, and American leaders were well aware of the vital relationship between American prosperity and American diplomacy. Widening old markets and opening new ones, expanding production, and promoting industry became the central concerns of American diplomats and statesmen.

There was, however, considerable disagreement on priorities and the most fruitful tactics needed to accomplish these ends. And there were some who were determined to end the dependence that the United States had on external sources for its prosperity. Despite the broad understanding of the importance of international economic relationships to national growth, prosperity, security, and mission, the unequal power exerted by special interest groups and the serious economic and regional divisions that developed within the nation prevented Americans from developing a single, national foreign economic policy.

Until the 1820s, the American economy was relatively homogeneous. Special interest groups were relatively equally dispersed throughout the nation; small-scale manufacturing existed in each of the sections; and overseas commerce flourished at ports ranging from Boston to New Orleans. Agriculture dominated the entire American economy, and although most farmers provided goods for local consumption, Northern and Western farmers and Southern planters provided export commodities in roughly equal proportion.

After the 1820s, the economies of the North, South, and West became increasingly distinctive, and certain interest groups within each of the sections acquired predominant political control. Involvement in international commerce varied from section to section, and each developed its own special overseas relationships. Each also established different hemispheric priorities upon which sectional growth, prosperity, and security were thought to depend.

As the sectional dispute intensified, regional leaders increasingly evaluated foreign policies primarily in terms of sectional advantage and their implications on sectional economies. Sectional competition began to paralyze the federal government, with the result that individuals and private agencies undertook foreign programs of their own. These activities not only complicated American foreign relations; they also further intensified the sectional conflict.

The sectionalization of American foreign policy was never complete, however. Functional groups in each section often combined to champion single policies, especially when issues involved questions of national honor or security. And Americans also remained united in the broad conception of a special American mission to remodel the external world. That conception, too, contained a significant economic component.

THE AMERICAN MISSION
AND COMMERCIAL RECIPROCITY

Although Americans remained unwilling to sacrifice political isolationism for active involvement in the domestic affairs of foreign nations, most remained committed to the vague notion that the United States possessed a "higher destiny" to serve mankind. Most, too, seemed committed to fulfilling that destiny, as John Quincy Adams put it, only by exerting "all the moral influence which we can exercise by our example."[12] Individual merchants, missionaries, and diplomats promoted the American system overseas through propaganda, and it was generally accepted that "commerce itself is one of the most powerful means of civilization and national improvement."[13] Commercial exchange, it was thought, would open the door to the exchange of ideas and provide benighted people around the world with tangible evidence of the superiority of the American political, economic, and social system. Only a relatively few individuals offered more than exhortation and moral support to foreign revolutionaries.

American officials, however, including Adams, were not content merely to wait passively for liberal world reform. They attempted to fulfill the American mission actively by breaking down traditional political and economic systems and by replacing them with progressive new ones. Adam's famous comment that America "goes not abroad in search of monsters to destroy,"[14] pertained only to direct intervention in the domestic political affairs of individual nations. As Adams realized, there were other ways to effect reform.

One of the strategies Adams and his successors employed to destroy reactionary systems and to open the world to America's moral and material influence was commercial reciprocity. Before the Civil War, the American government made no legal distinction between its citizens and aliens engaged in domestic economic activities and imposed no special restrictions, taxes, or other hardships on foreign enterprise in the United States. Similar equal treatment for nationals and aliens was generally the practice in Europe as well. Such equality was not provided in international commerce. All European nations imposed special duties on foreign ships entering their ports, reserved the re-export trade to their own nationals, and placed various other restrictions on foreign carriers that favored their own merchant marines.

From 1789 to 1815, the American government had sporadically engaged in economic retaliation to force European nations to abolish their special duties and restrictions on American carriers, and American diplomats continually fought for the broad liberalization of maritime policies. Their failure had led to the imposition by the United States of "discriminating duties" on foreign carriers entering American ports, which led the Europeans in turn to impose "countervailing duties" of their own. Because Americans exported bulky cargoes of raw materials and imported compact cargoes of finished goods, American merchants suffered from serious disadvantages.

By the end of the Napoleonic Wars in 1815, American merchants wanted these special duties abolished. They pressed the government to offer European nations the abolition of all American discriminating duties for a reciprocal abolition of their countervailing duties, restrictions in the re-export trade, and (where applicable) trade between nations and their colonies. Their pleas became urgent as the maritime powers adopted a number of new restrictive policies to rebuild their own merchant marines.

The government sympathized fully with the merchants. European policies seemed pointedly designed to weaken the United States, which depended so heavily on overseas commerce. In addition, the willingness of colonial powers to negotiate special reciprocal agreements easing mercantilist regulations among themselves deeply aroused American officials. The United States was implicitly excluded from these arrangements since it lacked overseas colonies. It, therefore, could not make similar bargains or benefit from traditional most-favored-nation clauses. All the United States could do was demand totally unrestricted trade. Commercial reciprocity thus became a means of breaking into the European colonial system. But to demand that colonial commerce be opened equally to all nations was to attack one of the essential purposes of colonies. The reciprocity program, as developed by the United States, was thus integrated into the anticolonial program.

Initial attempts to secure full commercial reciprocity failed. In exchange for the abolition of discriminating duties, European states gradually did abolish their countervailing duties and, eventually, American merchants acquired equal rights to re-export goods from European ports. None of the major colonial powers, however, was willing to open their colonies to Americans on terms equal to those provided their own citizens.

Attempts by the United States to subvert the European colonial system through reciprocity and commercial warfare failed altogether. In 1830, after fifteen years of bitter and costly controversy with Britain over the West Indian trade, the United States capitulated by accepting the principle of imperial preference, and far from giving up their existing colonies, Britain and France expanded their colonial empires in Asia and the Pacific. Even Russia joined in this colonial expansion, acquiring extensive territories in northern China. Americans, expanding themselves, became nervous that the revival of traditional colonialism would close areas that were perceived to be important to future American economic growth. The government continued to promote reciprocity in the hope, as George Bancroft, the American minister to Britain, put it, that an Anglo-American reciprocity agreement "would be the requiem of the old Colonial System; and in its consequences would be followed by all other nations."[15]

Other Americans, however, such as diplomats Peter Parker, David Gregg, and Ephraim D. Squier, Commodore Matthew C. Perry, and entrepreneur-propagandists Jane and William Cazneau, insisted that the United States ought to respond with an overseas colonial policy of its own. Parker suggested that the

United States seize Formosa; Gregg negotiated for the annexation of Hawaii; Squier sought the acquisition of an island off the coast of Nicaragua; Perry called for the possession of Okinawa, the Bonin Islands, or Formosa; and the Cazneaus promoted the American acquisition of Santo Domingo. In addition, Young Americans in the 1850s called for the purchase of either the island of Rhodes or the principality of Monaco in the Mediterranean.

These efforts never attracted popular support. Most Americans more likely agreed with Secretary of State William Marcy, who argued "Remote colonies are not a source of strength to any Government, but of positive weakness, in the cost of their defense, and in the complications of policy which they impose to the prejudice of home-interests. Their supposed advantage to the mother-country, is the commercial monopoly, secured by such connection."[16] Commercial monopoly was an anathema to Americans and the very antithesis of the open door sought through commercial reciprocity. And Americans still considered colonialism incompatible with the American political and ideological system. But certainly by the 1840s, sectional politics presented insuperable obstacles to colonial expansion.

American diplomats were similarly frustrated in their attempts to universalize the principle of laissez-faire. They did succeed in securing most-favored-nation treatment for the United States from nations outside of Europe, but most of those nations had little interest in providing aliens with unrestricted economic privileges within their borders. Only in a few nations in Latin America did America acquire both economic equality and perfect commercial reciprocity, but even there, American principles did not take root.

Much as Americans rejected colonialism, they also generally rejected special interest legislation comparable to that provided by foreign governments to their subjects. The few exceptions were invariably limited in time and scope and always justified in terms of national security. Rather, Americans preferred to convince others that progress depended upon economic freedom, equal competition, and open doors. Economic benefit and liberal reform had merged and become inseparable: reciprocity offered the prospect of unhindered commercial expansion and the fulfillment of the American liberal mission to destroy colonialism and to remodel the world.

Thus, far from turning their backs to the outer world and well before the twentieth century, Americans actively promoted a liberal world order based upon economic and political self-determination, representative and limited government, freedom of the seas, and personal liberty.

ECONOMICS AND NATIONAL SECURITY

Unlike the major powers in Europe, the United States had weak neighbors and was reasonably secure from invasion, a condition reconfirmed during the War of 1812. But that war and its antecedents also demonstrated that the United States was by no means safe from external threats. Its heavy reliance on overseas markets and foreign manufactured goods, its dependence on foreign credit, and the ever-increasing size and range of its foreign commerce rendered the United States highly vulnerable to forces beyond its control. Furthermore, as John Quincy Adams and others pointed out, future European wars would likely involve Britain and spread to the Atlantic, where neutral trade would again suffer. American security concerns, therefore, centered primarily on the protection of America's economic interests.

The United States Navy offered little security for American ships on the high seas and in distant ports. Generally kept at about seventy ships (not all seaworthy at any given time), it could barely meet America's peacetime needs. But rather than commit the United States to expensive naval programs, the government relied on privateering and the construction of commercial steamers that could be converted quickly into warships in wartime. Unfortunately, advances in naval technology suggested that privateering was rapidly becoming obsolete, and naval experts doubted that converted steamers would be of much use. These programs therefore provided little confidence that the United States would be able to protect itself adequately during another war on the high seas.

The government chose to place primary emphasis on international law for the protection of its merchant marine. Diplomats consistently sought agreement to American principles of neutral rights in their commercial treaties, and they were usually successful with small nations and weak maritime states. The great powers, and particularly Britain, showed scant interest in adopting the American position.

When, however, following the Crimean War, the great powers adopted a program of neutral rights that was consistent with the traditional American position, the United States ironically refused to become a party to it. The Declaration of Paris of 1856 provided, among other things, for the abolition of privateering, and Secretary of State William Marcy explained that before the United States could agree to forego privateering, it required the broadest guarantees for neutral trade, including the exemption of *all* private property, belligerent as well as neutral, ships as well as cargoes, from attack and seizure on the high seas. Since Britain and France would not agree, the United States remained outside the agreement. International law thus provided little grounds for complacency.

One of the other strategies suggested primarily by merchants for reducing the inherent dangers of relying on the British and North European trade was to develop alternative markets outside the Atlantic. Expanded commerce in neutral areas, it was argued, would make American shipping less likely to collide with belligerent maritime powers. Partly for this reason, beginning in the Jackson administration, the United States negotiated commercial agreements with the Ottoman Empire (1830), Greece (1837), Sardinia (1838), and the Two Sicilies (1845) in the Mediterranean; and with Muscat (1833), Siam (1833), China (1844), Japan (1854), Lew Chew (1854), and Persia (1856), along the crescent of Asia.

The attempt to reduce American traffic in the North Atlantic largely failed. Britain continued to dominate American foreign trade throughout the period, purchasing about half of all American exports. In fact, Britain and northern Europe together increased their share of American exports from 65.3 percent in 1821 to 74.8 percent in 1860, and they provided the United States with about two-thirds of its imports.[17] Although American merchants had begun to export increased quantities of manufactured goods, they could not break the transatlantic connection. American vulnerability and reliance on Anglo-American peace and harmony continued, and merchants insisted that the United States avoid programs and policies that would antagonize the British.

In the 1820s, a number of Americans perceived new dangers and sought a different defensive strategy. Insisting that economic nationalism and residual mercantilism in Europe and British and European commercial and colonial expansion into the nonindustrialized world required a major alteration in the American economy, they advocated the development of a home market. They insisted that both American security and prosperity would be enhanced by reduced reliance on traditional foreign markets, the determined promotion of domestic industry and internal channels of trade, and only later the exploitation of new markets on more favorable terms.

THE ANGLO-AMERICAN RELATIONSHIP

Merchants and advocates of a home market presented two substantially different schemes for the protection of the United States, and to a considerable degree, these programs involved Britain. Merchants depended upon and welcomed Britain's good will and support; others insisted that reliance on Britain was a source of weakness. And many Americans regarded Britain as a positively hostile power determined to destroy the American economy by closing colonial markets and securing special privileges in new ones.

It was well understood that Britain depended upon the United States for sufficient sources of raw cotton and that the

United States depended upon Britain for a market for its huge surpluses. But different perceptions of Anglo-American interdependency largely determined the character of discussions about relations with Britain. Those who believed that British dependence on the United States was greater generally promoted policies and programs that were aimed at maintaining American dominance. Those who took the opposite view promoted programs aimed at securing economic independence. The former thus advocated free trade and territorial expansion and tended to be cavalier and belligerent toward Britain; the latter adovocated protectionism and, sensitive to the financial wealth of Britain and the power of the British navy and aware that American development would be an extended process, were generally more dedicated to harmonious relations with Britain.

During the 1830s, differences in attitudes toward the Anglo-American connection took on a sectional character. Generally, hostility toward Britain dissipated among the upper classes in the Northeast while it increased broadly in the South and West. Much of this shift had economic roots. Merchants such as Thomas Handasyd Perkins, Patrick Tracy Jackson, Henry Lee, Jonathan Russell, Ralph Forbes, William and Russell Sturgis, and Nathaniel Silsbee, whose ships plied the Pacific and Indian Oceans and the Baltic and Mediterranean, of course, benefitted greatly from the growth of Anglo-American harmony. They relied on British bills of exchange and letters of credit and the services of British agents in distant and exotic ports. Hong Kong, Singapore, and Capetown became important ports-of-call, and American merchants welcomed the familiar customs and language and the protection that British officials and the British navy often provided. Moreover, as the American diplomat William B. Reed noted, "wherever English enterprise goes, ours is quickly along side of it . . . every dollar Great Britain spends on its postal service or in maintaining its naval force is for our benefit."[18]

Northeastern manufacturers and transportation entrepreneurs also had close connections with the British. British engineers continually contributed to the improvement of the American textile industry. America's leading textile manufacturer, Abbott

Lawrence, established a not uncommon practice when he switched from the distribution of British cloth in the United States to manufacturing after the War of 1812. Many other American enterprises were established after the war by British emigrés who similarly shifted from distribution to production and who carefully preserved their British heritage and connections while becoming prosperous and prominent Americans. Jeremiah Thompson, for example, originally a retailer of British cloth, became one of America's most successful shipbuilders in the 1820s and later dominated in the transport of British and Irish immigrants to the United States. Railroad entrepreneurs Cornelius Vanderbilt, William Apinwall, and James Murray Forbes often visited England in search of British capital for their transportation schemes, and manufacturers appreciated British investment in their businesses and in American banks and state bond issues which, among other things, helped finance canals and railroads, vital for the domestic market.

It was in Anglo-American finance that particularly strong ties developed. Among the great merchant banking houses in England devoted largely to Anglo-American trade before the Civil War, several had especially close connections with American firms that went beyond mere economic convenience. Brown Brothers was founded by an immigrant from Northern Ireland and was headed by his three sons, two of whom maintained offices in Baltimore and Philadelphia. The other established a branch in Liverpool, became a British subject, and ultimately served as a member of Parliament. George Peabody and Company, founded by a native of Massachusetts who emigrated to London in 1837, was taken over in 1854 by Junius Spencer Morgan, also of Massachusetts, who in 1860 appointed as his New York agent his more famous son, J. Pierpont Morgan. The two senior partners of Baring Brothers, which financed the lion's share of Anglo-American trade, each had married daughters of a prominent Philadelphia merchant, and two of the Baring brothers' successors as senior partners, Joshua Bates and Russell Sturgis, were New Englanders. Finally, the American agent of the London and Paris branches of the Rothschilds was August Belmont, who arrived in the United States in 1837, became a wealthy and prominent American financier, and married a daughter of Commodore Matthew Perry and niece of Louisiana politician-diplomat John Slidell. Familial as well as economic ties thus secured bonds among the wealthy and powerful of both nations.

Economic and family associations extended easily into the development of extensive social relationships among the elites. Americans regularly traveled to Britain for business and pleasure and were regaled by British society, and they provided American scholars, artists, clergymen, and politicians with access to prominent Britons. William Henry Seward, for example, toured England and the Continent in 1859 with an array of letters of introduction and a letter of credit for £1,000 from Baring Brothers. (Vanderbilt provided Seward with an attractive berth on one of his transatlantic steamers.) Scholar-politician-diplomats Edward Everett and George Bancroft were well known in England, as was Abbott Lawrence, long before they were appointed ministers to the Court of St. James's.

Spreading through the elites and into the middle classes was Anglo-American involvement in various religious, humanitarian, and philanthropic causes. British radicals, including Jeremy Bentham, John Bright, and Richard Cobden (who had invested heavily in the Illinois Central Railroad) regularly raised the American example in promoting reform at home, and the latter two maintained a lively correspondence with American reformers. Clergymen of various Protestant denominations on both sides of the Atlantic discussed and debated matters of doctrine and administration and sent delegates to each other's meetings. William Ellery Channing and Theodore Parker were highly regarded by British Unitarians. British social reformers traveled to the United States to examine first-hand American advances in penology and techniques of aid to the handicapped, and Robert Owen met frequently with American labor reformers during his American sojourn. Temperance and pacificism functioned as truly Anglo-American movements.

Each of these joint or parallel efforts strengthened and broadened Anglo-American goodwill. Most of this association, however, was restricted to the Northeast where conditions as well as connections were closest and the upper Ohio Valley which was largely settled by New Englanders. Southerners and Westerners also particpated in various of these reform movements, but not in the most notable Anglo-American humanitarian crusade of the era, abolitionism, and most British visitors to the United States were openly hostile to America's "peculiar institution." In fact, a major part of the development of Southern antipathy toward Britain stemmed from Britain's assault on slavery and the slave trade.

Southerners regarded the British Emancipation Act of 1833 as an indirect attack on Southern slavery, and Britain's unrelenting attempts to end the slave trade and to bring about emancipation in Cuba and Brazil confirmed that view. In the 1840s, Southern leaders argued that British abolitionism was little more than an attempt to weaken the Southern economy so that Britain's tropical colonies would become competitive. They expressed the same idea with regard to British opposition to American territorial expansion. These views more than balanced the friendly attitudes that initially had been based upon the important economic connection between the South and Britain, Britain's adoption of free trade, and the supposed cultural harmony between Southern planters and the British landed aristocracy.

An additional source of Southern ill will toward Britain stemmed from the activity of British investors in Southern state bonds following the Panic of 1837. When several Southern states defaulted, these investors enlisted the aid of Northern Whigs in lobbying for federal assumption of the states' debts. Many Southerners perceived a conspiracy in which British and American capitalists were determined to control the South and to maintain it as an economic colony. This conspiratorial view also became popular among Westerners, who similarly blamed Britain and Northern Whigs for their distress—and Westerners also resented British resistance to their territorial ambitions.

Finally, in the Northeast, Irish immigrants provided a large, growing, and politically important population utterly hostile to Britain. Although there had continued to be a sizable emigration from Britain to the United States after 1820, its numbers never approached the number of Irish who fled to American shores following the potato famine in the late 1840s. Between 1820 and 1860, emigration from Britain totaled nearly 800,000; emigration from Ireland totaled nearly two million.[19] Irish laborers may have had little else in common with Southern planters and Western farmers, but were even more committed and eager to "twist the lion's tail." The Southern and Western coalition in the Democratic party found Anglophobia a useful means for attracting Irish votes in Northeastern cities.

Southerners, confident that their virtual monopoly of cotton made Britain dependent on the United States and therefore unable to take serious offense, and Westerners, who had negligible economic relations with Britain until the 1840s, advanced policies that continually threatened conflict. Northeastern Whig merchants and manufacturers, who depended on Britain and had close and friendly relations with British merchants and financiers, promoted those most likely to ensure peace.

PROTECTIONISM AND LATIN AMERICA

Widespread and serious economic difficulties plagued the United States in the early 1820s. The postwar boom in foreign trade had led to an overextension of credit and massive speculation in Western land, which in 1819 led to a panic, followed by a severe depression. Contributing to the American economic collapse was a sharp price decline in world markets and reduction in the demand for American foodstuffs as the nations of Europe revived their own production and adopted nationalistic economic programs. The combination of unwise domestic policies and contraction in world commerce made recovery in the United States difficult and lengthy.

Many Americans were convinced that the panic and depression stemmed primarily from calculated policies of foreign manufacturers and their governments, who were determined to stifle American growth. Manufacturers in the Northeast struggled against the intense competition provided by British industry; merchants suffered from British and French mercantile restrictions; and Western farmers were all but driven out of foreign markets by the imposition of new taxes, duties, and tariffs in Europe. Southern cotton planters, hurt by the precipitous drop in the price of cotton in the European market, were perhaps more fatalistic than the representatives of other economic interests, but they too faced European taxes on imports of American cotton.

Different judgments on the external causes of America's distress led to different suggestions for recovery. Generally, Southern planters suggested that the current economic problems were merely transitory and would pass as the world economy stabilized. They, themselves, planned to make up their losses from the decline in cotton prices simply by expanding production, and they expected that increased exports of cotton would alleviate the merchants' distress and promote broad, national recovery. Merchants agreed, but they also tended to blame most of America's troubles on European mercantile policies, especially Britain's decision to close the West Indies to American shippers and France's imposition of protective tariffs. Less willing than planters to wait passively, merchants demanded the reciprocal abolition of all port duties, and if that failed, economic retaliation. The contraction of world trade, they argued, had aggravated America's economic distress; commercial expansion and liberalization would restore America's health and vitality. And in their cause, the merchants received the determined support of John Quincy Adams, Secretary of State between 1817 and 1825 and President from 1825 to 1829.

Manufacturers and those Westerners who had been engaged in international commerce proposed significantly more far-ranging remedies. The former believed that Britain was determined to destroy American manufacturing and to control the American economy, and the latter judged that the foreign market for American foodstuffs and raw materials (including cotton) had simply entered a permanent decline. Led by Henry Clay, these individuals called for protective tariffs and federally funded internal improvements, which together, they argued, would lead to the creation of a safe, secure, and continuously expanding home market. In 1820, Charles Kinsey of New Jersey declared that the purpose of protectionism was "to make this country independent of the world, to lay the foundation of its future greatness on the solid basis of its internal strength . . . [and to] become what we ought to be, a nation truly American."[20] Four years later, Clay elaborated on this idea and developed his "American System": a nationalistic program that aimed at integrating the American economy and providing Americans with independent control of their economic growth and development. He carefully distinguished his American System from what he called a "foreign system" in which America's future depended upon overseas commerce and the whims of foreign governments.

Protectionists did not conceive their program as commercially isolationist; in fact, they justified economic diversification behind effective tariff barriers as an essential strategy for aggressive commercial expansionism and for dynamic diplomatic initiatives around the world. Their general argument was well-constructed and persuasive. As long as the United States lacked an industrial base and relied on the export of raw materials to Britain, they contended, American commerce would be restricted to the North Atlantic. Meanwhile, Britain (and France) would penetrate and control the rest of the world's markets. Even more disconcerting, by exercising effective control of American production through various regulations, these nations would be able to develop competitive sources of raw materials in their colonies and client states. The ultimate consequences of free trade, Clay warned, would be increased debts as foreign markets for American goods declined, the destruction of American manufacturing, commercial and agricultural stagnation, and increased dependency on foreign manufactures, all of which would "lead substantially to the recolonization of these states under the commercial dominion of Great Britain."[21] Political independence would then disappear as the United States itself became either a client state or a formal colony.

Protectionism was the panacea. By protecting domestic industry, American manufacturers would absorb and stimulate domestic raw material production, domestic labor would provide an ever-growing market for foodstuffs, and by manufacturing surplus goods for export, the United States would be able to compete with Britain and other nations in all markets. Americans would thus be able to prevent the monopolization of third markets and the erection of competitive monocultures. Economic independence would allow diplomats to press Britain and France to relax their commercial restrictions and to open their colonies. In this sense, protectionists presented high tariffs as "bold measures, designed to compel the most powerful nations of Europe to give up their favorite systems of commercial and colonial policy."[22]

The third markets upon which protectionists focused their attention were in Latin America, and it is not surprising that Clay was the most eloquent and consistent champion of the Latin American cause in the early 1820s. Clay regarded close economic ties with the independent states of Latin American as an essential part of his American System. "From the character of our population," he suggested in 1820,

we must take the lead in the prosecution of commerce and manufactures. Imagine the vast power of the two countries [i.e., the United States and South America], and the value of the intercourse between them, when we have a population of forty millions, and they of seventy millions! In relation to South America, the people of the United States will occupy the same position as the people of New England do to the rest of the United States.[23]

Latin America, thus, would provide a vast market for the surplus products of American industry, which in turn would require correspondingly vast quantities of domestic raw materials. And, due to the proximity of Latin America and the abundance of resources in the United States, Americans would be able easily to undersell the British and French. While Clay was by no means oblivious to the strategic importance of Latin America and the Caribbean or unconcerned with the expansion of American ideals and institutions there, economic concerns provided both the means and ends of his policy.

Merchants strenuously objected to protectionism. They feared that in retaliation Britain and France would tighten their mercantile restrictions and shift a major portion of their commerce to low-tariff areas in which their manufactures could be more profitably sold. The consequence would be a substantial reduction in Anglo-American trade and depression in the shipping industry.

Merchants also opposed vigorous official support for Latin American independence. They doubted that increased trade with the Latin American nations would compensate for the reduction of British markets. Reflecting the merchant point of view, John Quincy Adams commented that "there was no basis for much traffic between [the Latin American nations and the United States]. They want none of our productions, and we could afford to purchase very few of theirs."[24] Finally, merchants worried that support for Latin American rebels could cause Spain to put an end to America's substantial trade with Cuba and might stimulate European efforts to reestablish Spanish authority throughout the Americas.

Southerners argued that high American tariffs would cause Britain to develop a market for its manufactured goods in Latin America, which would have disastrous consequences for the United States. They predicted that Britain would promote the widespread cultivation of cotton in Latin America in order to provide Latin Americans with the means to purchase their goods and cargoes for the return voyage. The Latin American nations would be turned into economic colonies of Britain, and the United States would lose its cotton monopoly. Free trade, Southerners insisted, was essential in order both to preserve American control of the British market and to insure general American prosperity.

Southerners also opposed protectionism for more immediate reasons. As consumers, they disliked the prospect of paying higher prices for manufactured goods. As Southerners, they opposed the promotion of Northern industry at the expense of Southern (and Western) agrarian interests.

President Monroe was primarily worried about European intervention in Latin America in retaliation against official American support for the rebels, but he was also determined to promote the triumph of republicanism in the former Spanish colonies. Faced with a dilemma in which either action or inaction could lead to different but equally dissatisfying results, the President followed a middle course, in which the United States assumed a position of benevolent neutrality toward the revolutionaries, postponed formal recognition, and permitted trade with both belligerents. He thus established a policy of caution, moderation, and restraint and was prepared only to provide moral support for the cause of Latin American freedom.

Fear of armed intervention by Europe increased after 1818 when French forces crossed the Pyrenees to suppress a liberal revolution in Spain and seemed determined to continue across the Atlantic to Latin America. British opposition to the French intervention in Spain had been unsuccessful, and when British Foreign Minister George Canning suggested that the United States and Britain issue a joint statement opposing French intervention in Latin America, Monroe and Secretary of War John C. Calhoun were sympathetic. Monroe welcomed the opportunity to defend the cause of republicanism against the reactionary Holy Alliance; Calhoun was chiefly worried that France would compromise the geographical isolation and security of the United States by acquiring a new base of operations in the western hemisphere. Thus, Monroe and Calhoun, one for ideological and the other for strategic reasons, were inclined to accept the British proposal.

Within Monroe's cabinet, only Adams opposed joining Britain. Believing that the independence of the Latin American colonies was inevitable and reasoning correctly that Britain had too much to gain commercially from the breakdown of the Spanish mercantile system to allow France to intervene on Spain's behalf, Adams discounted the threat of France's armed intervention. Except for a momentary fear that Spain might be obliged or willing to cede Cuba to Britain in compensation for British protection, which led Adams to warn Britain and Spain that the United States would not tolerate the transfer of the island to any other power, Adams dismissed Calhoun's strategic concerns. Adams also disagreed with Monroe about the prospect of republicanism in Latin America, but he joined the President in opposing the establishment of monarchies in the new states. His reasons, however, were based not on political liberalism, but on economic ideology.

Adams' economic views paralleled those of the merchants, but unlike many of them he was motivated less by considerations of profit than by the commitment to the principle of open doors and competitive equality in all foreign markets. His diplomatic program, therefore, aimed at the destruction of British and European colonialism and the removal of all barriers to American commercial expansion. With regard to Latin America, Adams was concerned that the newly created nations would develop close ties with the continental powers, providing them not with political *control*, but with great political *influence* that would lead to the establishment of special commercial privileges.

Adams made this position explicit in his instructions to Caesar Augustus Rodney and Richard C. Anderson, the American ministers-designate to Buenos Aires and Colombia in May 1823. The United States objected to the installation of petty princes in the Americas, he wrote Rodney, because "they are always connected with systems of subserviency to *European* interests—to projects of political and commercial *preferences* to that European nation from whose stock of royalty that precious scion is to be engrafted," and to Anderson, Adams added, "The political systems of Europe are all founded upon partial rights and *exclusive privileges*. The colonial system has no other basis."[25] Adams urged both diplomats to be on guard against proposals European agents "will continue to make in the furtherance of their monarchical and monopolizing contemplations."[26]

Britain presented a special problem. Between 1810 and 1823, British influence in Latin America had grown steadily. British merchants and commercial agents had acquired a number of exclusive commercial benefits and, as Adams informed Anderson, were "feeling their way" for more. Britain, Adams believed, adhered to a reactionary, monopolistic commercial system itself, already evident in its attempt to seal off the British West Indies from American merchants (against which Adams was already fighting), and he was convinced that the British were likely to expand those benefits in Latin America. "To us," he wrote Anderson, "the only object which we shall have much at heart . . . will be the sanction by solemn compact of the broad and liberal principles of *independence, equal favors,* and *reciprocity.*"[27]

Thus, perceiving Britain as much, if not more, of a menace to America's interests in Latin America as France, Adams insisted that the United States reject Canning's offer of joint action and instead adopt an independent, unilateral position clearly distinguishable from the British. Adams' views prevailed, and in December 1823, Monroe issued what came to be known as the Monroe Doctrine. Monroe announced that the United States would "consider any attempt on [Europe's] part to extend their system to any portion of this hemisphere as dangerous to our peace and safety."[28] The statement was sufficiently broad to encompass the concerns of both Monroe and Calhoun. It also won full support from Clay and the protectionists.

Clay and Adams presented different, but not mutually exclusive, remedies for the depression and economic stagnation of the 1820s, and although they were often in direct dispute, much of their disagreement was more form than substance. Both aspired to the presidency and, of course, each functioned in a different political arena. By Adams' inauguration in 1825, each had accepted the basic propositions of the other; that is, Adams committed himself to the American System, and Clay (successful in his campaign for a protective tariff in 1824) was willing to devote his attention to commercial reciprocity. As Adams' Secretary of State, Clay secured a treaty with the short-lived Central American Republic that contained full reciprocity and all the advanced liberal principles Adams had been seeking. Clay noted that the reciprocity provisions provided "perfect freedom of navigation," and he commented, "We can conceive of no privilege beyond it. All the shackles which the selfishness or contracted policy of nations had contrived, are broken and destroyed by this broad provision of universal liberality. The President is most anxious to see it adopted by all nations."[29] The Central American treaty thus served as a model for all American commercial negotiations before the Civil War, and although the United States was not as successful with other nations in Latin America or elsewhere, the thrust of America's commercial diplomacy was well established.

Protectionism suffered a different fate. Merchants and Southern planters, who had joined to defeat a tariff bill in 1820, failed in 1824 when Northeastern manufacturers and Western farmers won a narrow victory. In regional terms, the South maintained its hostility to protectionism (as it was to do throughout the period before the Civil War); the West overwhelmingly favored it; and the Northeast divided. Merchants and some manufacturers voted against the bill; most manufacturers supported it. Tipping the scales in favor of protectionism were the manufacturers who acquired dominant political control in the Northeast and committed that section firmly to protectionism. Significantly, the West lost interest in protectionism as farmers turned to the supply of local needs and then established close economic and political relations with the South. The consequence of the South-West association was that after passage of the excessively high and notorious Tariff of Abominations in 1828, which greatly intensified sectional hostilities, tariffs were gradually reduced, the only exception occurring between 1842 and 1846.

The consensus among economic historians is that the tariff had little effect on the development of the American economy as a whole and only moderately constrained American overseas commerce. Anglo-American trade continued to flourish throughout the period during years of high tariffs as well as low. Spokesmen for and against protectionism in the 1820s had not anticipated the continued expansion of the British textile industry or the astounding increase in Southern production. Neither had they foreseen the great demand for American wheat and flour in the 1840s and 1850s. Henry Clay, for example, in a collossal misjudgment, argued in 1820 that the United States had "reached the maximum of our foreign demand for our three great staples, cotton, tobacco, and flour. . . ."[30] Such was clearly not the case. Insatiable British demand and the expansion and efficiency of the Southern cotton culture, rather than tariff reduction, preserved Southern domination of the production of raw cotton. Moreover, cotton exports,

supplemented later by wheat and flour exports, continued to enrich merchants and to provide the bulk of the capital necessary for
industrialization. There is little compelling evidence to suggest that
domestic manufacturing depended upon the limited protection it
received for survival or would have grown faster with greater protection.

The establishment of political and commercial relations with
the new nations of Latin America also had little effect on the
American economy. The American government had secured competitive equality, to be sure, but while American merchants did
win a large share of the carrying trade, they were unable to over-
take British merchants. Part of this failure stemmed from the inability of American manufacturers to compete effectively with their
British and European counterparts or to disaccustom Latin Americans from their European tastes. The independent Latin American nations absorbed only about 5 percent of America's exports
and provided less than 10 percent of its imports. Britain dominated Latin American commerce until late in the century.[31]

Even without the Latin American trade, between 1820 and
1836, American overseas commerce revived and grew slowly but
steadily. Total foreign trade increased by 108.8 percent, but the
excess of imports over exports continued. Imports rose in value
by 181.1 percent and exports by 106.2 percent.[32] Although American merchants vied with the British in Latin America and sailed
the globe in search of new markets, nearly half of America's exports remained raw cotton and over half of America's imports continued to consist of British (and some French) manufactured goods.
Specific federal policies had had less effect than the general recovery from the depression.

The central debate in the 1820s had been over the best
means of acquiring economic independence and reviving the
American economy. Without the adoption of Clay's American
System, the United States industrialized, maintained its leadership in the production of vital raw materials, and developed a home
market more important than the foreign market. But the cost was
high. The 1820s ended with the full revival of bitter partisan pol-

itics and the development of intense sectional hostilities. These, as well as the continued growth of the American economy, had a profound effect on American diplomacy over the next thirty years.

POLITICAL AND ECONOMIC SECTIONALISM

By 1830, the increasingly distinctive economies of the Northeast, South, and West had generated special domestic and foreign interests that found expression in new political alignments. Manufacturers captured control of Northeastern politics and generally supported the American System of Adams and Clay; planters continued to dominate politics in the South and promoted states' rights, domestic laissez-faire, and free trade. Farmers and entrepreneurs controlled Western politics, and that section divided its loyalties between Clay, associated with the Northeast, and Andrew Jackson, associated with the South.

Between the mid-1820s and the mid-1850s, the South and West maintained a tenuous alliance. The South became the major domestic market for Western foodstuffs after the mid-1820s, and people in both sections regarded protectionism as a tax primarily for the benefit of the Northeast. Planters, farmers, and Western entrepreneurs also chafed at the conservative financial policies of Northeastern bankers, and political leaders resented the increasing power of the Northeast in Congress.

In 1834, these economic and sectional interests found expression in politics. Northeastern manufacturers gained control of the Whig party, and Southern planters and Western farmers dominated the Democratic party, both of which took on a distinctly sectional character. But both parties continually sought to win national support. Whigs won support from Southern and Western nationalists during the Nullification controversy, and the Whig program of internal improvements attracted many Westerners, especially those who were involved in supplying Northeastern and foreign, rather than Southern, markets. Similarly, Democrats had substantial support in the Northeast among laborers and small businessmen who resented the power of the manufacturer elite.

The regional specialization of the American economy and emergence of sectionally dominated parties contributed to a division among Americans on the strategy of American expansion. Whigs promoted rapid commercial diversification and expansion, and while not opposed to territorial expansion per se, they preferred that it be accomplished peacefully and gradually. Democrats argued that territorial expansion had to be accomplished first: more land for the cultivation of cotton and foodstuffs would guarantee subsequent commercial expansion while preserving the cotton monopoly and securing for the United States commercially strategic areas. This disagreement was merely over priorities, not purposes, but it was complicated by the attempts by both parties to capture the political support of commercial interests.

Merchants provided the critical group whose support was most sought by Whigs and Democrats. Associated with the planters in opposition to Clay during the tariff battles of the 1820s and hostile to Adams because of his belligerence toward Britain and France, the merchants supported Jackson in 1828 (despite his early support for protectionism). Agreement on free trade and close economic association made political alliance natural. Between 1828 and 1834, however, the merchants generally shifted their allegiance to the Whigs. Personal relationships, hostility toward Jacksonian egalitarianism, substantial investment in manufacturing, banking, and transportation enterprises in the North, and the attraction of a strong central government all combined to cause the merchants to put aside their objections to Whig protectionism and to change their political association.

Between 1834 and 1854, the Democrats consistently sought to recapture the merchants' support. Democratic leaders maintained their opposition to high tariffs and were responsible for tariff reductions in 1833 and 1846. In addition, Democrats pursued an aggressive commercial diplomacy around the world, and they demanded the acquisiton of strategic ports and territory in the Caribbean and the Pacific. Democratic administrations sent emissaries to South and Southeast Asia, Africa, and Latin America; they justified the acquisition of Oregon and California in terms of commercial advantage in the Pacific, and they spearheaded efforts in Central America for American control of interoceanic transit routes.

Despite this effort, the merchants remained constant in their support for the Whig party. Merchants understood that Whigs were as committed to global commercial expansion as the Democrats and, in several cases, provided initiatives that were later carried through by the Democrats. Also, Democratic motives were often transparent and their strategies dangerous. Western Democratic demands for the acquisition of extensive territory west of the Rockies even at the risk of war with Britain substantially reduced the merchants' enthusiasm for the early acquisition of Pacific ports. Similarly, Democratic support for the acquisition of Cuba, Nicaragua, ports in Santo Domingo, and exclusive transportation rights across Central America, all of which led to Anglo-American diplomatic controversy and the specter of war, worried the merchants. However desirable these programs, they were not worth the likely price.

By the 1850s, Southern Democrats began to lose interest in winning the merchants over to their side. The slavery question had reached a critical stage, Western economic and political relations with the North were growing stronger, and Southern power in Congress was weakening. In the mid-1850s, Southern lack of interest in merchant support was symbolized by Southern Democratic opposition to the maintenance of subsidies to Northern merchant firms. By that time, merchants had joined other Whigs in the new Republican party.

The courtship of American merchants by both political parties had important effects on American commercial expansion. The federal government provided consistent aid and comfort. Nevertheless, individual effort and private initiative were chiefly responsible for American commercial expansion between 1830 and 1860; nowhere was this more clearly evident than in American commerce with East Asia.

EXPANSION INTO EAST ASIA

Following the onset of another depression in 1836, American commerce entered a decade of stagnation. Although the volume of cotton exports continued to increase, a sharp decline in cotton prices reduced its value. Overall, between 1836 and 1846, imports declined 30.7 percent and exports 4.6 percent.[33] Merchants began seeking new outlets for American goods, and manufacturers and Western farmers, whose surplus production had only begun but who anticipated great expansion, joined them.

No area so captured the American imagination as a potential market as China. American trade there had begun with the voyage of the *Empress of China* in 1784, and for the following sixty years continued without benefit of diplomatic relations or any formal bilateral commercial agreements. Owing to the high costs of trading in China, the danger of the voyage, and the difficulty in dealing with the Chinese, the China trade was small and restricted to a few Northeastern merchant houses, the most important of which was the Boston firm of Russell and Company. This company watched over all American interests in China, appointed and funded America's consuls, and established informal arrangements with British and Chinese officials and merchants.

Russell and Company was formed by the consolidation of several Boston merchant companies all associated in the China trade. This formal business association was facilitated by considerable intermarriage, which had tied together several of Boston's wealthiest and most prominent families whose members maintained solid relationships with British financiers, American politicians, journalists, and others, all of which benefitted their business activities. Bates and Sturgis of Baring Brothers were members of this group. The Sturgis family fortune stemmed from the China Trade, in which William Sturgis was a pioneer; Bates' wife was Russell Sturgis' niece. Other members of the families participated in state politics. Nathaniel Silsbee served in the United States Senate, and Caleb Cushing served in the federal House of Representatives and was appointed Attorney General by Franklin Pierce.

Cushing negotiated America's first treaty with China. More typically, this merchant elite supported powerful editors and propagandists, contributed to the campaigns of leading politicians, and in the case of Daniel Webster, a notorious spendthrift, provided him with private funds. They and their associates sent petitions to Congress, arranged for the publication of propaganda, and sometimes applied direct pressure on politicans when they felt the need for official action in their behalf.

Until 1839, the China merchants had little interest in official involvement in their activities. They were prospering and secure and perceived little advantage to be gained from formal diplomatic relations. On the contrary, they did not welcome the prospect of a potential confrontation between the Chinese and American governments or the possible extension of Anglo-American disputes to China, which could jeopardize their beneficial and friendly relations with the powerful British. Thus, when President Jackson, in an effort to maintain and to broaden his support among New England merchants, dispatched Edmund Roberts to Canton in 1832 to negotiate a commercial agreement, the China merchants were not concerned when the Chinese turned Roberts away.

The China merchants' attitudes changed following the eruption of the Anglo-Chinese Opium War in 1839. The war endangered American lives and property, and the peace agreement of 1842 provided the British with extensive new commercial advantages, including the acquisition of Hong Kong and right to trade at four ports in addition to Canton, which until then had been the sole port open to Western merchants. At the beginning of hostilities, the China merchants petitioned Congress to provide naval protection in China and later to negotiate a formal commercial treaty with China guaranteeing most-favored-nation treatment. These petitions received a ready response in Washington chiefly because of the domestic political situation and the efforts of Daniel Webster.

In 1843, Webster was in serious political difficulties. Appointed Secretary of State by William Henry Harrison, Webster alone had remained in the cabinet after Harrison's death and the subsequent Whig repudiation of Harrison's successor, John Tyler, a former states-rights Democrat who opposed many Whig programs. Webster's decision to remain in the cabinet had led to his denunciation by other Whigs and ostracism by the manufacturer wing of the Massachusetts Whig party. Although Webster had shifted from free trade to protectionism in 1828, he had retained close ties with powerful merchant leaders, and he was particularly receptive to their concerns about China.

In an effort to salvage his political future, Webster supported the appointment of a mission to China to negotiate a commercial treaty and to establish formal diplomatic relations. And not wishing to return to a cold reception in Massachusetts, he concocted a scheme whereby Edward Everett, his protégé and minister to Britain, would be appointed commissioner to China, with himself replacing Everett in London. Since Webster had been well received in England on an earlier visit and had recently concluded the Webster-Ashburton treaty (Ashburton was a Baring; Webster was Baring Brothers' chief legal agent in the United States), he was sure to receive a warm welcome. Chinese affairs would be in safe hands, since Everett was also close to the China merchant families. When Everett declined the appointment, Webster chose Cushing for the mission and sent his son along as Cushing's private secretary. Webster, himself, was forced into an unhappy, but only temporary, retirement.

Cushing's mission was a great success. In less than two weeks of negotiation, Cushing secured all the commercial privileges that had been granted British merchants and a number of additional provisions. Much of his success stemmed from the Chinese determination to maintain equality among all Western merchants. The Chinese calculated that the Westerners' jealousy of each other would prevent any single Western nation from attempting to conquer China or to establish extensive control over Chinese affairs.

The American merchants were wholly satisfied with Cushing's treaty, and between 1844 and 1849, they prospered. Americans sent more vessels to China's ports than any other nation except Britain (and during the brief clipper-ship era, they dominated the carrying trade between China and England). By the mid-1850s, Americans controlled about a third of the carriage trade between China and Europe and handled almost half the trade at Shanghai, which became the residence of the American commissioner and rapidly replaced Canton as the major Chinese entrepot.[34]

Having satisfied the demands of the China merchants for commercial equality in China, the American government withdrew from active involvement. Both the Tyler and Polk administrations were far more interested in continental expansion than in an aggressive commercial policy in China, and thus American commissioners in China received few specific instructions. Although Cushing had acquired the right for the United States to establish consulates in the treaty ports, no consuls were sent to China until the mid-1850s, and even then their appointment stemmed from a broad reform of the consular service rather than from any special interest in China.

The merchants continued to take care of their own interests and had few complaints until Chinese affairs became chaotic in 1850. Chinese resentment toward Western intrusion and the patent weakness of the Chinese government to prevent it burst out in the great Taiping Rebellion, a quasi-religious, zenophobic movement, which threatened all Western interests and raised the specter of massive European intervention and the partition of China. American diplomats in China and the China merchants appealed to the government for aid and protection, though they disagreed among themselves on the nature of the aid sought. Most of the merchants urged the American government to ally itself closely with the British by adopting parallel policies and joint naval action. Several of the diplomats agreed. Commissioner William B. Reed wrote home, "I am more and more impressed every hour, by the identity or rather community of the commercial interests of the West, and that nothing is more likely to defeat the true aims of American Statesmanship here than a distempered jealousy of English or French progress. . . ."[35] Missionary-diplomat Peter Parker also recommended harmony with Britain, though others, most importantly Commissioner Humphrey Marshall, suggested that Britain was determined to conquer a part of

China and to secure exclusive commercial privileges in the rest. Marshall recommended a unilateral policy and close relations with the Chinese imperial government.

Initially, the American government had justified its passive policy toward China by reference to the balance of power in China among the European nations: ". . . should any European Power entertain unjust and ambitious designs of aggrandisement or conquest against China," Secretary of State James Buchanan wrote, "the representatives of other rival powers would be on the spot, ready to sound the alarm to their respective Governments. And the very knowledge that such must be the result would probably prevent the attempt from being made. . . ."[36] Aggressive European reaction to the Taiping depredations and imperial ineffectiveness did not inspire the government in Washington to alter its policy of noninvolvement. In 1856, Secretary of State Marcy instructed American diplomats to maintain cordial relations with British and French officials but to avoid close cooperation, a policy that Parker described as "a 'concurrent' policy with England and France in China, not an *alliance*, but independent and distinct action yet similar, harmonious, and simultaneous. . . ."[37]

Whig interest in China was substantially greater than Democratic, but Whig political leaders offered no serious alternative to Democratic policy, and they generally supported the Democratic program of independent action in harmony with Britain. Despite their private attitudes toward close association with Britain, they had to be careful not to appear too friendly. But the Whigs were clearly more interested in facilitating commercial expansion in China through active diplomacy. The election of Zachary Taylor in 1848 provided them with the opportunity. Much as Whigs in the Harrison administration were responsible for America's first treaty with China, the Whig administration of Taylor and Fillmore was responsible for America's first treaty with Japan.

During the 1830s and 1840s, the United States had made several attempts to open relations with Japan, but all had been half-hearted and easily repulsed by the Japanese, who were determined to remain in isolation. The acquisition of California, rise of Shanghai, and development of steam transport, however, greatly increased the strategic importance of Japan. Ships traveling the circle route from the Pacific Coast passed through Japanese waters, and merchants were eager to secure an enroute coaling station—it was rumored that Japan had an abundance of coal—and protection for shipwrecked sailors.

In response to petitions from merchants (and whalers who had extended their activities to the North Pacific), Taylor ordered preparations made for an impressive naval expedition to Japan, which ultimately was put under the command of the experienced and tough Commodore Matthew C. Perry. Perry received intrucions to secure the opening of one or more Japanese ports, the ability to purchase coal and supplies, and a shipwreck convention. In accord with general Whig policies toward international trade, the government informed other nations "that we contemplate no advantages exclusively for ourselves, but that if we succeed in opening the ports of Japan to a liberal intercourse, it will be for the common benefit of the civilized world."[38]

Perry reached Japan in 1853 and presented America's demands. After departing to give the Japanese time to consider, he hastily returned, primarily out of concern that the French and Russians were about to make a similar effort on less liberal terms. In 1854, Perry concluded negotiations for Japan's first modern treaty with a Western nation. Perry's treaty satisfied America's demands, but it was highly limited, and even Perry regarded it as only "a preliminary . . . step, in advance of a commercial arrangement. . . ."[39]

Unfortunately for the merchants, well before Perry completed his negotiations, the Democrats had returned to the White House. Consistent with their lack of interest in China, they neglected American interests in Japan. The Pierce administration delayed appointing a consul to Japan until 1855, when it chose Townsend Harris, a New York China merchant, for the post. Harris arrived in Japan a year later with full power to negotiate a new commercial treaty but with few instructions and no naval or other support. Working virtually alone and overcoming tremendous obstacles, Harris succeeded in concluding a consular agreement in 1857 and a full commercial treaty in 1858. His success, however, did little to arouse the American government or to intensify popular interest in East Asia. The Buchanan administration was chiefly concerned with a serious diplomatic crisis in the Caribbean, and most American attention was directed toward the critical domestic questions of slavery and territorial organization.

Although American overseas commerce expanded tremendously after 1846, the China trade contributed only a small fraction to that expansion. China absorbed less than 2 percent of America's exports and supplied less than ½ percent of its imports. The myth of the China market, then as later, was far more important than the reality.[40]

Between 1846 and 1860, the revival of the domestic American economy and world trade as a whole carried American overseas commerce to unprecedented heights. The value of both exports of domestic goods and imports each more than tripled, the former from $101.7 million to $316.2 million and the latter from $110.0 million to $336.3 million, and Britain and northern Europe continued to be America's major trading partners.[41] Cotton remained the primary American export to Britain, but gaining in importance was the export of grain and flour, made available by the expanding cultivation of the West and development of rail links to the East Coast and made possible by continuing British industrialization, famines in Europe, and the Crimean War. The last increased demand in Britain and France while cutting off supplies from Central Europe. The repeal of the British Corn Laws in 1846 permitted American merchants to take over the transport of American grain and flour to Britain, which previously had been transported through Canada, enriching British merchants and expanding British overseas commerce.

Americans continued to purchase a large share of their manufactured goods from Britain and northern Europe, but as American industrialization gained momentum, imports of these goods declined in relation to imports of industrial raw materials, particularly iron and steel for railroad construction. Domestic sources of iron and other minerals were still not accessible in sufficient quantities. Thus, for all the efforts of the government to promote commerce in new areas, Americans in 1860 still remained heavily committed to the North Atlantic.

Official policies facilitated American commercial expansion between 1830 and 1860, but they were of only secondary importance. The federal government, to be sure, provided general support in the form of harbor improvements, maritime and coastal surveys, subsidies to steamship companies, and the expansion of the consular service; diplomats worked assiduously around the world to remove barriers and impediments to American commerce; and the British helped by adopting free trade in 1849. But far more important to American overseas commercial growth was domestic economic development in the private sector. The discovery of gold in California in 1848 and Colorado in 1859 contributed to a general rise in world prices, thereby increasing merchants' wealth and providing them with additional investment capital. The expansion of the American transportation system, the rapid growth of population, and the beginning of the agricultural revolution in the West were also more decisive than federal policies, which merely provided Americans with the ability to capitalize on newly opening opportunities in the domestic and world economy.

Americans remained committed to the notion that the economic activities of Americans overseas were private matters to be determined by individual initiative and natural economic laws. It was assumed that merely by securing an open door for American goods and competitive equality, the United States would prosper and flourish. In 1833, Aaron Vail, the American *chargé d'affaires* in London, wrote: "The superiority of our merchant marine and mercantile skill is brought home . . . whenever anything like fair and equal terms are extended to us."[42] In the late 1850s, Secretary of State Lewis Cass, in rejecting pleas from the China merchants for special political aid, responded, "We go [to China] to engage in trade, but under suitable guarantees for its protection, the extension of our commercial relations must be the work of individual enterprise, and to this element of our national character we may safely leave it."[43] And when British Foreign Minister Lord Palmerston hinted that the British and American governments ought to join in surveying the route for an interoceanic canal in Central America, American minister Abbott Lawrence replied, "There can be no doubt, I think, that the best interests of mankind will be subserved if the combined enterprise and wealth of the world at large build this as well as the other work, unassisted by Government aid farther [sic] than in the guarantee of its safety and neutrality." [44]

Open-doorism, anticolonialism, and reciprocity were built upon these notions, which themselves rested comfortably upon assumptions that the liberalism of American institutions, the vigor and imagination of the free American people, and the unlimited natural resources of the United States and their eventual exploitation guaranteed American world economic leadership.

EXPANSION TO THE PACIFIC: TEXAS AND OREGON

Americans believed that the economic success of the United States depended substantially on continental expansion, but American officials preferred to apply laissez-faire to that growth also. It was assumed that the creation of a continental empire was inevitable and would be accomplished through a gradual, peaceful, and orderly process. Shortly before the annexation of Texas, John C. Calhoun wrote, "It is our policy to increase by growing and spreading out into unoccupied regions, assimilating all we incorporate. In a word, to increase by accretion, and not through conquest. . . ." [45] Some new territories would be added to the Union as American expatriates in contiguous territories applied for annexation; other territories would be acquired through purchase. And as the United States grew and flourished under its free and liberal institutions, many Americans expected that Canadians, Mexicans, Cubans, and Central Americans themselves would apply for annexation. The federal government merely had to wait for nature to take its course.

These assumptions permitted federal officials to adopt a relatively casual attitude toward territorial expansion until the mid-1840s and to accept Mexico's continual refusal to sell Texas and Britain's unwillingness to accept American claims to Oregon south of the forty-ninth parallel. The American government merely announced in 1823 in the Monroe Doctrine that the western hemisphere was closed to further European expansion. But it clearly was not closed to American expansion, a point made clear when the United States rejected several British attempts to secure pledges that it would not annex Cuba. Except for a few impatient malcontents and ambitious politicians, Americans generally supported this passive program.

Several developments in the 1830s and 1840s, however, weakened the American commitment to peaceful expansion. Contrary to expectations, American migration beyond the national frontiers was neither gradual, orderly, nor peaceful. During the depressions of the early 1820s and late 1830s, thousands of Americans crossed the Sabine River into the Mexican province of Texas or moved along the Oregon Trail into the lush Willamette Valley in the disputed Oregon territory. In 1835, the Americans in Texas declared their independence, established a government of their own, and over the resistance of Mexico applied for admission into the United States. In 1843, the American settlers in Oregon similarly demanded protection from the American government and the formal annexation of the entire Oregon territory from the southern boundary of Russian America at 54°40′ to the northern boundary of Mexican California at 42°.

These appeals inaugurated a period of sectional and partisan turmoil that altered the entire thrust of American territorial expansion. Demands from the periphery won immediate support in the South and West and from Democrats generally. Southerners were particularly interested in the acquisition of Texas, which offered fresh land for cotton cultivation and an opportunity to increase their regional political power. Westerners perceived Oregon more in national terms. Oregon had been a source of controversy with Britain for nearly twenty-five years, and the American settlement provided the means for resolving that diplomatic problem once and for all in America's favor. Democrats welcomed the ability to increase the power of agrarian interests and to capture a great popular issue, and with regard to Oregon, to attract merchant support. Oregon provided excellent harbors, and as Alexander Duncan of Ohio suggested in 1845, "the nation that possesses Oregon will not only control the navigation of the Pacific, the trade of the Pacific and Sandwich Islands, but the trade of China itself on the Pacific. . . ."[46] When the Democrats merged the Texas and Oregon issues into a single program and enveloped it in nationalistic rhetoric and anglophobia, the domestic battle lines were clearly drawn.

Northeastern Whigs were generally unsympathetic to this expansionism. Manufacturers opposed the "premature" acquisition of new territories for fear that they would increase the drain of labor from the east and, by elevating the political power of agrarian interests, would render more difficult if not impossible the passage of Whig legislation, including increased tariffs, in Congress. They were joined by antislavery groups both in and out of the Whig party who regarded the Texas movement as a slaveholders' conspiracy to extend and to perpetuate the institution of slavery. Antislavery forces were less opposed to the acquisition of Oregon, in which slavery was not a question, but they were not much interested in it either. Merchants were equally uninterested in Texas, but highly attracted to Oregon, though only to its harbor facilities. It was the vehemently anti-British character of both the Texas and Oregon movements that antagonized the Whig merchants and helped to preserve party unity in the Northeast.

The growing concentration on Texas and Oregon and the Whig desire for friendly relations with Britain accounted for the lack of American interest in the annexation of Canada during the Canadian rebellions of the late 1830s. With the United States in a serious depression, most American attention was directed inward. But also, Southerners opposed policies that would threaten the Anglo-American cotton trade and Westerners relied on Canadian outlets for their wheat, which entered Canada duty free under provisions of an imperial act of 1831. Even if annexation could have been peacefully accomplished, Southerners would likely have resisted the admission of vociferously antislavery Canadians into the Union, and Westerners would not have welcomed competition from Canadian farmers in addition to the loss of their backdoor entry into the British home market.

Thus, the Democratic Van Buren administration rigorously enforced American neutrality legislation, a policy opposed only by some residents along the Canadian-American border. When Webster became Secretary of State in the succeeding Whig administration, he quickly negotiated a broad agreement with Lord Ashburton that resolved problems created by the rebellion and settled several Anglo-American boundary disputes. Americans were prepared to wait for Canadians to seek annexation themselves, something in which most were plainly not interested in the 1830s. Some Americans, such as then-Governor William Henry Seward of New York, came to believe that Canadian desire for annexation and an American welcome awaited only the return of prosperity in the United States and the abolition of American slavery.

The Van Buren and Harrison-Tyler administrations followed a quite different policy with regard to the concurrent Texas revolution, which of course did not involve Britain at that point but did involve a population that overwhelmingly supported annexation. While the government maintained official neutrality, it ignored widespread violations of American statutes. Whig opposition to annexation, antislavery hostility to the Texas cause, and Western disinterestedness, however, as well as domestic economic problems and fear of an inconvenient war with Mexico contributed to Van Buren's decision to reject a formal Texan appeal for annexation in 1837. For six years, the Texas question remained dormant.

To a considerable degree, the revival of the Texas issue in 1843 stemmed from the political ambition of President Tyler. Tyler, repudiated by the Whig party and unaccepted by the Democrats for his earlier apostasy, sought to restore his political power and to secure his nomination for the presidency in 1844 by leading a great, popular expansionist crusade. At one point, he nearly drew

Webster, who had strong presidential ambitions of his own, into a scheme for creating a new political coalition. At Tyler's request, Webster sounded out Mexico for a deal in which Mexico would accept the American annexation of Texas and sell enough of California to include San Francisco to the United States in exchange for the cancellation of Mexico's large debt to the United States. At the same time, Webster proposed to Ashburton that if Britain pressured Mexico to accept the offer and Mexico agreed, the United States would accept British claims in Oregon. Success in this effort, Tyler and Webster apparently hoped, would win them the support of both Southern expansionsists and Northeastern merchants and might appease some Westerners. The attempt failed when neither Mexico nor Britain showed any interest in it. Tyler then turned toward the tactic of arousing national support for the annexation of Texas by playing upon fears that Britain was interfering in domestic Texan affairs and most importantly sponsoring abolitionism.

The failure of Tyler's tripartite scheme and appeal to Anglophobia, and Tyler's implicit defense of slavery in Texas, isolated Webster in the cabinet, and in May 1843, Webster resigned. Tyler replaced him with Abel Upshur of Virginia, a slaveholder and annexationist. The President thus cleared the way for a renewed effort at annexation and planned to capitalize on the growing concern that the independent Republic of Texas posed a threat to the South and the American nation.

The argument that Texan independence was a threat to national security was ably developed by John C. Calhoun, one of the most brilliant and articulate champions of Southern interests. Calhoun, who had succeeded Upshur as Secretary of State following the latter's accidental death in 1844, completed negotiations for a treaty of annexation with Texas that Upshur had begun. Calhoun contended that Britain was interfering in Texan affairs in order to weaken the American economy and to revive British political and commercial power in the Caribbean. He argued that Britain, by applying pressure on Mexico to recognize Texan independence, offering to defend Texas from foreign aggression, and hinting at the prospect of generous financial support if Texas abolished slavery, planned to convert Texas into an economic colony and to maintain it as a barrier against American expansion into lands suitable for the cotton culture. If Britain succeeded, Calhoun explained, soil exhaustion would reduce American production, causing a general rise in cotton prices and making it possible for Britain to develop alternate sources of supply in its client states and colonies. If slavery, upon which the efficient production of cotton rested, were abolished in Texas, it would be doomed in the United States.

The destruction of the Southern cotton monopoly and American slavery, Calhoun continued, would have national consequences. Cotton exports provided the United States with its chief source of wealth. British abolitionism was merely a "pretext" for increasing British world "power and monopoly." Since British leaders had realized that emancipation in the West Indies had been a mistake in that it had raised production costs far above those of their slave-labor competitors, Britain now sought new colonies where labor was plentiful and cheap, such as India and Africa, and promoted abolition in Brazil, Spanish Cuba, and the United States. Success would "give [Britain] a monopoly in the productions of the great tropical staples and the command of the commerce, navigation, and manufactures of the world, with an established naval ascendency and political preponderance."[47]

Whatever appeal Calhoun's anti-British justification may have had, his defense of slavery deeply offended Northerners. Antislavery Whigs and abolitionists maintained a constant rhetorical barrage against annexation and succeeded in frustrating attempts by others to elevate the British menace into the primary concern. With an election approaching and Southern Whigs embarrassed by Calhoun's position, other Northern Whigs attempted to underplay the slavery question and denied that annexation was an economic necessity or that Britain was engaged in an anti-American conspiracy. Henry Clay, the Whig candidate for President, sought to avoid the issue altogether by coming out against immediate annexation. His Democratic opponent, James Knox Polk, favored it, however, and the issue remained alive. The Senate rejected Calhoun's treaty in a partisan vote of 35–16, but the

question persisted in the campaign of 1844, when it became tied
to the Oregon question.

Advocates of the acquisition of all Oregon attempted to
broaden their appeal by concentrating on the value of Oregon as
a commercial outlet to China and its necessity for American merchants in their competition with Britain. But since only a small
part of the merchant community was immediately interested in
Oregon and there was little sense in presenting Oregon farmland
as essential to the national economy, promoters of Oregon developed an elaborate rationale based upon the "manifest destiny" of
the United States. They used the concept to justify the acquisition of territory far north of American settlement and hoped
thereby to win massive popular support on ideological and nationalistic lines.

Whig merchants were not attracted to the Democratic campaign plank calling for "the re-occupation of Oregon and re-annex-
ation of Texas at the earliest practicable period."[48] They were not
convinced that Texas was vital to American commercial growth,
and they had already begun to shift their attention from the Oregon coast to California. More important, they worried that expansion would irreparably divide the nation, and they were especially
disturbed by Democratic appeals to Anglophobia. Although Polk
narrowly won the election, his support remained primarily Southern and Western, and it is likely that few Whigs voted Democratic
because of the expansion issue. Whigs, in fact, suffered more from
the loss of votes to the antislavery Liberty party, which explicitly
opposed the annexation of Texas.

Following the election of 1844, the United States concluded its acquisiton of Texas and Oregon. Tyler succeeded in
annexing Texas by a Joint Resolution of Congress; Polk won Oregon through a compromise settlement with Britain. The latter
proved more difficult to accomplish since Democratic belligerence
toward Britain during the campaign and suspicion in both nations
impeded diplomatic negotiations, and Polk's inexperience and in-
tractibility complicated matters further. Resolution of the issue
was delayed nearly two years, much longer than was necessary.

The Oregon settlement was facilitated by a number of economic considerations. First, the Hudson's Bay Company, which effectively governed the Oregon territory and had previously insisted upon the maintenance of British claims north of the Columbia River, shifted its base of operations northward to Vancouver Island and finally agreed to a compromise boundary at the forty-ninth parallel, which Americans had suggested many years earlier. The company insisted only on British possession of all of Vancouver Island and the right to transport goods down the Columbia River to the coast. Second, British repeal of its Corn Laws won considerable appreciation from American free traders and was useful to Democrats in their successful battle for reduced tariffs in 1846, though it did not win similar appreciation from Western farmers, who realized that repeal also opened the British market to Central Europe, where farm labor was cheaper, distances to Britain were shorter, and transportation was readily available. As Edward Everett had pointed out, the highly liberal and preferential Canada Corn Act gave "our farmers a great advantage, which they would lose under a uniform free trade in corn, in competition of the North of Europe."[49] Third, and most important, the revival of Anglo-American trade after 1843 made conflict between the two nations anathema to powerful economic agencies on both sides of the Atlantic. Western Democrats strenuously objected to compromise, but they were outvoted by a coalition of Whigs and Southern Democrats.

Ultimately, however, the resolution of the Oregon issue stemmed from other factors. Southern expansionists were satisfied in 1845 by the annexation of Texas and had lost interest in Oregon, and by 1846, the political value of the Oregon question had evaporated. Western Democratic expansionists had become virtually isolated. In addition, the United States had entered into war with Mexico, and expansionists' interests now turned toward northern Mexico and California.

CALIFORNIA

Interest in California had risen steadily during the 1820s and 1830s. Initially, the safe harbors of California had attracted whalers, and later merchants regularly visited the area to acquire hides for the New England boot and shoe industry. As involvement in China increased, so too did the desire for permanent and secure ports-of-call in California and the Pacific. New England China merchants petitioned the government to survey the entire Pacific basin, and the Department of the Navy responded by sending Lieutenant Charles Wilkes on such a mission in 1838. Wilkes was enormously impressed with the commercial potential of California and went beyond mere description in his final report. He wrote, "Upper California may boast one of the finest, if not the very best harbour in the world,—that of San Francisco. . . . Few are more extensive or could be as readily defended as it. . . ." Wilkes emphasized the commercial potential of San Francisco which, with the Straits of Juan de Fuca, would facilitate a steady "intercourse with the whole of Polynesia, as well as the countries of South America on the one side [of the Pacific], and China, the Philippines, New Holland, and New Zealand, on the other."[50]

Wilkes' report, published in 1845, and similar views expressed by a number of others earlier, combined with popular acceptance of the importance of the China market, and awareness that Mexican control of California was weak, gave credence to rumors that Britain and France were interested in acquiring the province. Thus, when Polk attempted to reestablish relations with Mexico, broken after the annexation of Texas, he instructed James Slidell to investigate rumors that Mexico planned to cede California to Britain or France. Polk noted, "The possession of the Bay and harbor of San Francisco is all important to the United States. The advantages to us of its acquisition are so striking, that it would be a waste of time to enumerate them here. If all these should be turned against our country, by the cession of California to Great Britain, our principle commercial rival, the consequences would be most disastrous."[51]

Polk authorized Slidell to offer a substantial sum for northern California from the Oregon border southward to include San Francisco and as far farther south as San Diego. Meanwhile, Polk engaged in other actions aimed at American acquisition. When the Slidell mission collapsed and war erupted between Mexico and the United States, the Americans were well prepared for conquest. Within nine months, American military and naval forces controlled all of California from a line just south of San Diego to Oregon—Polk and the Democrats did not consider returning any part of it to Mexico.

There was considerable domestic opposition to the Mexican War. Whigs denounced the war as unconstitutional, unjustified, unnecessary, and unwise, and they used the issue to castigate Polk and the Democrats. Abolitionists and antislavery Whigs condemned the war as yet another thrust of the "aggressive slavocracy," a position that conservative Northern Whigs tried to suppress for the sake of national party unity. When Pennsylvania Representative David Wilmot, an antislavery Democrat, introduced a proviso to an army appropriations bill that would have prohibited slavery in any territory acquired from Mexico, antislavery Whigs gave Wilmot their full support. Northern Whig manufacturers then became concerned that the acquisition of any territory would intensify the sectional debate over slavery and thereby endanger the Union. Thus they joined with Southern Whigs in establishing as official Whig policy the opposition to the acquisition of any territory from Mexico. Merchant Whigs, however, were unsympathetic to this policy. They were too much attracted to the acquisition of Pacific ports, although they did join their political colleagues in opposing the demands of Western Democrats for the annexation of all Mexico. In 1848, the merchants were satisfied—the Senate approved the Treaty of Guadalupe-Hidalgo securing all of Upper California for the United States. The United States had effectively completed the construction of its transcontinental empire, but as the other conservative Whigs had feared, the acquisition of California and other Mexican territory provoked a bitter and protracted debate between the North and the South on slavery that ended in civil war.

Britain and France had opposed American expansion in Texas and California, but both were unwilling to commit themselves to the containment of the United States. The Anglo-French "entente cordiale" of 1843 had not ended suspicion and rivalry between the two nations, and each worried that deep involvement in American affairs would free the other for aggression elsewhere in the world. Thus the British and French chose only to attempt to work out a compromise between Mexico and Texas, which Texans did not want, and later to provide moral support to Mexico, which Mexico found of little value. Furthermore, commercial interests in both nations opposed confrontation with the United States, and British and French officials well understood that their nations were too dependent on American cotton and the American market to risk hostilities over so distant and peripheral a problem. Allegations that the British had conspired to abolish slavery in Texas in order to wreck the American economy or had planned to add California to British Empire, which had so worried Southerners and Westerners, were groundless.

BRITISH NORTH AMERICA

If British and French opposition to American expansion southward was weak and ineffectual, Britain's attempts to preserve its North American colonies were determined and successful. The repeal of the Corn Laws in 1846 had seriously hurt the Canadian economy, and a number of Canadians had begun to advocate separation from Britain and annexation to the United States. Lord Elgin, the Governor General of Canada, reported that Canadians' discontent was "due mainly to commercial causes," and he added that it was widely believed "that under the present circumstances of our commercial condition the Colonists pay a heavy pecuniary fine for their fidelity to Great Britain."[52]

In 1854 the British government dispatched Elgin to Washington to negotiate the settlement of a number of long-standing problems dealing with the fisheries and reciprocity. His visit was a success. Within two weeks after his arrival, Elgin and Secretary of State William Marcy concluded a treaty that provided reciprocal free trade for a number of goods and the liberalization of fishing and navigation rights. Although it aroused the anger of a few Canadians and led to the reduction of Canadian exports to Britain, it also facilitated Canadian-American trade and so helped greatly to revive the Canadian economy. John Crampton, the British minister to the United States, judged that the treaty removed "the only disadvantage under which the Colonies labour in consequence of not being members of the American Union, and thus [took] away every motive for annexation."[53]

Americans were divided on the treaty. A large number of Westerners opposed it on economic grounds, while Southerners and many Northern manufacturers feared that reciprocity would lead to the integration of the Canadian and American economies and eventual annexation—Southerners had no interest in absorbing a population notorious for its abolitionism; manufacturers had no wish to add to the power of agrarian interests. Most Americans, however, supported the treaty chiefly *because* they believed that it would lead to annexation. Not a few in the North, Seward among them, believed that peaceful, voluntary annexation now awaited only the abolition of slavery.

CENTRAL AMERICA AND THE CARIBBEAN

British interests in Central America and the Caribbean were ancient and important, and British officials were determined to secure their position and to delay American expansion in that area as long as possible. That Americans would ultimately occupy Central America, and all the territory in between, was commonly accepted by the early 1850s. "No one can doubt," wrote Lord Clarendon, the British foreign minister throughout most of the 1850s, "what will be the issue of the juxtaposition between the

Anglo Saxon race and the feeble mongrel races which now occupy Latin America." Referring to himself as "a firm believer in the manifest destiny doctrine," Clarendon argued that while "it is not our business to accelerate that natural progress of events . . . it is no part of our duty to embroil ourselves in a vain endeavor to arrest them." He thought that Britain "should desist from *the policy* of *police* which we hitherto pursued, and not endeavor to thwart the Americans in their natural process of expansion."[54] His views paralleled those of many British capitalists who held Mexican and Central American bonds and who welcomed American order and stability in Latin America. Even British abolitionists believed that Americans would end the slave trade and "mitigate the severity of Slave labour."[55] These ideas, however, were a bit premature.

Lord Palmerston agreed that American expansion into Mexico and Central America was inevitable, but he wanted to restrain that expansion as long as possible. By 1855, he was convinced that "a dissolution of [the American] Union sooner or later, later more likely than sooner, is not beyond Probability, and will become the more probable the more the Race extends itself Southward," and later he added, "it is for our Interest that [the expansion of the Anglo-Saxon race] should not happen until the Swarms are prepared to Separate from the Parent Hive."[56] Palmerston feared that American expansion into Mexico and Central America would threaten Britain's West Indian colonies and provide a base for an invasion of Cuba. Since many in Britain opposed the British naval guarantee to Spain in Cuba, Palmerston was determined to forestall a crisis. Failure to support Spain would embarrass Britain, increase French influence in Spain (which Palmerston had long contested), and seriously disturb Palmerston's European diplomacy.

Palmerston was particularly worried that Americans would seize control of transit routes across Central America, build a canal, secure the protection of the American government, and reserve the canal exclusively for American merchants. In order to prevent such a sequence of events, Palmerston extended British authority down the Mosquito Coast of Nicaragua in 1847 and established the port of Greytown at the mouth of the San Juan River, the likely eastern terminus of a canal. Palmerston's preemptive policy, based loosely on an ancient protectorate over the Mosquito Indians, first embroiled Britain in a controversy with Nicaragua and then, when Nicaragua won the support of the American government, with the United States.

Americans had long been interested in developing rapid transit across Central America, and that interest deepened as American merchants, missionaries, and propagandists began their campaign for an extended American role in the Pacific. By the mid-1840s, the opening of China and growing agitation for Oregon and California made Central America an area of major strategic importance. Travel between the Atlantic and Pacific coasts around Cape Horn was long and dangerous, and since the distance from Liverpool to Cape Horn was roughly the same as from New York, Boston, and even New Orleans, Americans had no geographic advantage in their competition with the British. A Central American canal would not only greatly shorten the travel time and reduce transportation expenses, but by eliminating the need to circumnavigate the Brazilian bulge eastward into the Atlantic, it would also provide Americans with a distinct and permanent advantage in Pacific commerce. The settlement of the Oregon question in 1846, the acquisition of California in 1848, and especially the beginning of the gold rush in 1849 made transit across Central America an urgent concern and an area of special attraction to American entrepreneurs.

American efforts to open a transit facility between the oceans began in 1848 when William H. Aspinwall, a prominent New York merchant banker, secured a concession from New Granada for the construction of a railroad across Panama. Aspinwall, whose Pacific Mail Steamship Company was heavily subsidized by the American government, was well-known and highly regarded in Britain, and his project attracted considerable British capital. British officials were only concerned about a treaty negotiated in late 1846 by American chargé Benjamin Bidlack in which New Granada provided the United States with the right of transit in exchange for a guarantee of New Granada's sovereign authority over Panama. British officials considered Aspinwall safe and impartial, but they worried that Bidlack's treaty provided the basis for American intervention, permanent occupation, and eventual annexation.

Even more worrisome, however, was a rival and more ambitious scheme developed by Cornelius Vanderbilt, who enlisted the aid of the United States government in securing an exclusive contract to build a canal across Nicaragua. While Vanderbilt and his partner, former Whig congressman Joseph White, appealed directly to the Taylor administration, Vanderbilt dispatched White's brother, David White, to Nicaragua to work with Nicaraguan officials. Vanderbilt was successful. Secretary of State John M. Clayton instructed the new American chargé, Ephraim G. Squier, to work closely with David White in Nicaragua, and in August 1849, Squier and White secured a highly liberal and exclusive contract for Vanderbilt's Atlantic and Pacific Ship Canal Company. A week later, Squier negotiated a general commercial treaty with Nicaragua, similar in its provisions to Clay's old treaty with the defunct Central American Republic, but which also explicitly confirmed Vanderbilt's contract.

Squier's success stemmed less from his negotiating skill than from Nicaragua's fear of Britain and hostility toward British policy on the Mosquito Coast. In late June 1849, the Nicaraguans had contacted Squier's predecessor, Elijah Hise, and concluded a "secret" treaty providing the United States with exclusive control over any canal built in Nicaragua in exchange for an American guarantee of Nicaraguan sovereignty over all of its territory, including the Mosquito Coast and Greytown. In their negotiations, Hise and Squier had responded to Nicaraguan initiatives and had exceeded their instructions. Both were motivated by Anglophobia, a strong sense of the American Mission, and the concept of America's manifest destiny. The British were fully informed of the details of the treaties negotiated by Hise and Squier and were determined, so long as Vanderbilt's project seemed feasible, to hold on to Greytown. As the United States and Britain maneuvered for position, Anglo-American relations became seriously strained.

The Taylor administration had no wish to prolong the dispute and sought a speedy compromise with the British. Clayton informed Palmerston that the United States preferred that any canal built in Central America be "a combined effort, and for the general benefit of mankind,"[57] and the new American minister to Britain, Abbott Lawrence, suggested that both governments negotiate a treaty neutralizing the area. When Palmerston agreed, Clayton facilitated the negotiation by reprimanding Squier for his anti-British policies and excessive involvement on Vanderbilt's behalf. Taylor withheld Squier's treaty (and Hise's) from the Senate.

Clayton's efforts resulted in the Clayton-Bulwer treaty of 1850, which eliminated and prevented the future acquisition of exclusive transit privileges and provided for the neutrality, nonfortification, and joint protection of any canal or railroad constructed anywhere across Central America. Both nations also pledged not to colonize any part of the area. This agreement wholly satisfied Vanderbilt and Aspinwall. In fact, while Vanderbilt traveled to Britain in search of investors in his company, Joseph White lobbied in Washington for the draft treaty. Bulwer informed Palmerston that White "smoothed over a variety of difficulties with this Government, which I should have found it hard, without his assistance, to deal with."[58] Because Whig power in the United States was tenuous, Palmerston remained unwilling to retreat from the British beachhead on the San Juan River, and he was far from reassured when the Democrats returned to the White House in 1853. Southern Democrats had roundly condemned the treaty as a cowardly capitulation to Britain and an unnecessary obstacle to the fulfillment of America's manifest destiny.

Following Pierce's inauguration, Anglo-American relations in Central America deteriorated. Vanderbilt's company became involved in a series of conflicts with Britain's clients on the Mosquito Coast and the Nicaraguan government, and American naval captains came to Vanderbilt's aid, in one case by bombarding Greytown.

Even more serious was Vanderbilt's involvement with an American filibuster, William Walker. With Vanderbilt's encouragement, an antigovernment faction invited Walker and his private army to Nicaragua to participate in a civil war and to help reform the government. Although Vanderbilt had provided Walker and his army with transportation to Nicaragua, when Walker seized control of the Nicaraguan government, he joined Vanderbilt's rivals and participated in a scheme to take control of the company away from his benefactor. Vanderbilt, in Europe at the time, returned to the United States determined to regain control of his company and to destroy Walker.

The American government disavowed any connection with Walker and attempted with scant success to convince the British that neither Walker nor Vanderbilt were official agents of the United States. While the government was determined to prevent British infringement on Vanderbilt's property, and so justified its use of naval power in Nicaragua, it was not prepared to embark on a colonial policy or to add yet another issue to the already highly charged domestic sectional and partisan battlefield.

That British officials dismissed American disclaimers is not surprising. The Southern and Western press made Walker into a great national hero, emphasizing his contribution to the fulfillment of America's manifest destiny and the American Mission in Central America. Meanwhile, the American government seemed ready to accept Walker's control as a fait accompli and to recognize his government. Walker's conquest convinced British officials that the Southern-dominated Pierce administration was plotting to colonize Nicaragua and to seize control of both the Mosquito Coast and Greytown, all in violation of the Clayton-Bulwer Treaty. Perhaps even more upsetting was the conviction that Americans planned to use Nicaragua as a base for the invasion of Cuba, a prospect that had not escaped the attention of Southern expansionists.

Americans had long expected that Cuba would ultimately become a part of the United States. Cuba's strategic importance had dominated American interest, but trade relations were also important. During the 1820s, Spain opened Cuba to American merchants, and American trade was greater with Cuba than with all the rest of Latin America combined. The profitability of Cuban-American trade muted American interest in acquisition—John

Quincy Adams even advised against promoting a revolution on the island early in the decade—and American officials continued to tolerate Spanish control until the 1840s. Nevertheless, Americans were encouraged when Cuban dissidents rose against inept Spanish rule. They expected that Cubans would request annexation to the United States immediately after they had won their independence.

During the 1850s, American interest in the acquisition of Cuba divided along sectional lines. Southerners sought Cuba in order to increase Southern power in Congress and to strengthen the Southern economy. Cuba was large, lush, populous, and unquestionably suitable for slave labor, unlike (it was thought) much of the territory acquired from Mexico. Since Cuba's population was sufficient to support the creation of several slave states, annexation would shift the sectional balance in the Senate in favor of the South. Northerners objected to acquisition just for these reasons and for the same moral reasons that had been raised over the annexation of Texas.

Annexationists turned to filibustering when it became apparent that traditional methods for the acquisition of Cuba would be fruitless. When Polk offered Spain $100 million for Cuba, Spanish officials announced that they would not sell the island at any price, and Northern antislavery groups firmly opposed aggressive diplomacy or intervention on behalf of revolutionaries in Cuba who favored annexation to the United States. When government officials harrassed filibusters planning invasions of Cuba from American ports, some Southerners decided that filibustering could best be carried out from areas beyond the control of the American government. Nicaragua had seemed a likely place.

The prospect of using Nicaragua as a base for filibustering operations against Cuba and the complications created by Walker's seizure of the Nicaraguan government ended in 1857. The other Central American nations had amassed an army against the new Nicaraguan government, and Vanderbilt, having recaptured control of his company, isolated Walker, who was driven from the nation. By that time as well, Vanderbilt's project had collapsed.

When Palmerston realized that no canal would be constructed across Nicaragua, he decided to come to terms with the United States. The economic basis of his policy in Central America became clear in 1856 when he wrote,

> Grey Town was an important Point when there was a likelihood of a Canal across the Isthmus, if we had not got hold of Grey Town & the Canal had been made, the Yankees and their Proteges of nicaragua would have had it all their own way. . . . But now that it has been ascertained that a Canal is impossible, & that the passage from sea to sea is only a road to & from California and not a road for our Commerce to China, Australia &c Grey Town has lost almost all its Importance to us. . . .[59]

The moral component of Palmerston's policy became equally evident when Britain refused to retreat from its commitment to protect the Mosquito Indians. Since the United States remained committed to Nicaragua and Nicaragua demanded total control over all its citizens and territory, the problem lingered on in Anglo-American relations and was resolved only in 1860, well after the British had decided to end their opposition to American territorial expansion.

The settlements of the Maine, Minnesota, and Oregon boundaries and the acquisition of California and the northern provinces of Mexico essentially marked the end of American continental expansion. In only a few years, the United States had added 1,204,741 square miles to its domain and increased its size by two-thirds. The newly acquired territories included such immensely valuable and diverse resources as the iron ranges of Minnesota, the oil fields of Texas, and the rich deposits of precious metals of Colorado, Nevada, and California, all of which would be developed fully in succeeding generations. And in addition, the United States gained control of magnificent ports on the Pacific. Throughout this process, expansionists had based their appeals for support on arguments derived from economic advantage and necessity, national honor and pride, ideology, and security, all combined in an inseparable amalgam.

The acquisition of these territories, however, created enormous problems for the American government in its domestic affairs, partly because the purposes behind American expansionism were so disparate. Ironically, just as Britain had decided to accept continued American territorial expansion, domestic divisions provided a brake that was never wholly released. Although the United States purchased a strip of wasteland from Mexico for a railroad route in 1854 and with difficulty purchased Alaska from Russia in 1867, the only other acquisitions were Caribbean and Pacific islands at the end of the century. Canada, Cuba, Mexico, and the republics of Central America preserved their national identities.

CONCLUSION

During the last fifteen or so years before the Civil War, the expansion of America's overseas commerce continued. Cotton exports continued to be important, and additional wealth stemmed from surges in the grain and flour trade with Britain. Exports of the latter soared from 80,000 bushels in 1845 to 34.4 million bushels in 1847, and after a drop rose again to 24.8 million bushels in 1856. The British market, however, was erratic, and after the Crimean War, Russia (which in 1846 had been the first nation to capitalize on the repeal of the Corn Laws and had exported 76.0 million bushels of grain and flour to Britain) reestablished its primacy in the British market.[60] Nevertheless, the steady expansion of American farm production set the stage for American dominance in the British grain market after the Civil War and firmly revived Western interest in international markets.

This commercial growth had important effects on the domestic American economy. Western farm production, coupled with British demand, stimulated investment in rail connections between the developing West and Northeastern ports, and merchant capital increasingly entered domestic transportation and related industries. James Murray Forbes, for example, shifted his operations from the China trade to railroads, and by 1860 Cornelius Vanderbilt ended his direct involvement in overseas commerce and began to build his railroad empire.

By 1860, the United States was far less dependent on foreign trade and investment than it had been earlier. The nation had entered its "take-off" into sustained industrial growth, and, according to Douglass C. North, had established itself as "an industrial nation second only to Britain in manufacturing."[61] By that date, the United States had developed a national economy.

American foreign policy between 1821 and 1860 contributed substantially to that result. Since a crucial part of American prosperity and growth stemmed from international trade, since nature and history had dictated that America's primary relations with the other nations would be economic, economic considerations provided the fundamental framework for American foreign relations during this period. To be sure, partisan politics, personal ambition, ideological commitments, and the like were also at work, but even many of these contained a major economic component. Political appeals were often made to functional economic groups on the basis of real or potential economic advantage; personal ambition often found its outlet in economic enterprise; and much of American ideology rested upon economic conceptions. Economic policies often provided the best available means for fulfilling America's "higher destiny."

Ironically, while economic considerations provided much of the basis for America's diplomatic activities between 1820 and 1860, diplomacy and federal support for Americans engaged in overseas economic enterprise played a relatively minor and continually decreasing role in the actual economic growth of the United States before 1860. Although the most important diplomatic activities of Americans in the "new epoch" dealt with the protection, revival, and expansion of America's international commerce and the acquisition of new territories suitable for development and useful in commercial expansion, Americans were committed to the notion that while the federal government ought to support American economic interests broadly, it ought to interfere as little as possible in the specific economic affairs of its citizens.

Thus, the government invariably justified diplomatic activities in support of special interests on the basis of national interest. The federal government provided aid to Vanderbilt in Nicaragua in order to prevent Britain from acquiring control of interoceanic transit. It provided generous subsidies to steamship companies so that the companies would be able to provide the United States with steamers easily convertible to warships. The government argued in the former case that aid was necessary to make American enterprise competitive with foreign companies, which had extensive support from their governments. It excused the latter on the grounds of national defense.

But such involvement was exceptional, cautious, continually under attack. When Squier's aid to Vanderbilt went beyond normal "good offices" to collusion, the government rebuked Squier and retreated. Southern objections to mail subsidies to Aspinwall's Pacific Mail Steamship Company and George Law's United States Steamship Company, the Atlantic counterpart, and to E. K. Collins' United States Mail Steamship Line struck a responsive chord nationally and led to reductions in 1858 which contributed greatly to the failure of Collins line. Arguments based upon nationalism, which never quite overrode deeper commitments to laissez-faire, became even less compelling as sectionalism reached its apogee.

Sectionalism virtually paralyzed the government in its foreign relations after 1848. Britain, France, and Spain prepared a major intervention in Mexico, and although the British were cautious to appease American suspicions, French and Spanish officials paid the United States scant regard. Spain also prepared to reestablish its colonial rule in Santo Domingo. American officials attempted several times to invigorate national sentiments and to divert attention from domestic problems, but they failed—the domestic crisis was too serious.

Private groups either suffered in frustration at America's weakness or seized the initiative in foreign affairs. Businessmen involved in foreign operations often attempted to hide their nationality, while adventurers, such as William Walker, continued their private efforts to fulfill America's manifest destiny and mission. Sectional leaders and some capitalists provided the filibusters with both moral and material support. More important, Southern extremists began their campaign for secession and the inauguration of an independent foreign policy.

Southerners became convinced that their economic security and advancement would best be promoted by political independence and the construction of a great Caribbean empire, comprising Cuba, northern Mexico, and portions of Central America. Lincoln's election in 1860 was decisive in rallying Southerners to this cause. Northerners were equally determined, however, to preserve the American System and to engage in an even more aggressive program of commercial expansion. And William Henry Seward, now a powerful Republican leader, insisted that the containment and gradual abolition of slavery would prepare the way for continued territorial expansion both northward and southward. The divisions of the 1820s had reappeared in a new and far more dangerous form, and the stage was thus set for civil war, reconstruction, and eventually a more vigorous world role for the United States.

Notes

1. *The Papers of Henry Clay,* James P. Hopkins and Mary W. M. Hargreaves, eds., 5 vols. (Lexington: University of Kentucky Press, 1959–), 2:826.

2. U.S. Bureau of the Census, *Historical Statistics of the United States: Colonial Times to 1957* (Washington, D.C.: GPO, 1960), pp. 284, 300, hereafter cited as *Historical Statistics;* Paul A. Varg, *United States Foreign Relations, 1820–1860* (East Lansing: Michigan State University Press, 1979), p. 24.

3. *Historical Statistics,* pp. 7, 14.

4. George Rogers Taylor, *The Transportation Revolution, 1815–1860* (New York: Holt, Rinehart, and Winston, 1951; reprint ed., New York: Harper and Row, 1968), p. 79; B. R. Mitchell, *European Historical Statistics, 1750–1970* (London: Macmillan, 1975; abridged reprint ed., New York: Columbia University Press, 1978), pp. 581–82. See also *Historical Statistics,* p. 428.

5. *Historical Statistics,* pp. 545, 547; J. Potter, "Atlantic Economy, 1815–1860: The U.S.A. and the Industrial Revolution in Britain," in *Essays in American Economic History,* A. W. Coats and Ross M. Robertson, eds. (London: Arnold, 1969), pp. 14–48.

6. *Historical Statistics*, pp. 302, 545, 547; Taylor, p. 451.

7. *Historical Statistics*, pp. 545, 547; Taylor, p. 451.

8. *Historical Statistics*, p. 538; Taylor, p. 445.

9. Taylor, pp. 440–41.

10. *Ibid.*, pp. 178–82, 202–6.

11. *Ibid.*, p. 206; Stuart Bruchey, *The Roots of American Economic Growth, 1607–1861: An Essay in Social Causation* (New York: Harper & Row, 1965), pp. 133–34; Varg, pp. 25–26.

12. Adams to Richard C. Anderson, Washington, D.C., May 27, 1823, in *Writings of John Quincy Adams*, Worthington C. Ford, ed., 7 vols. (New York: Macmillan, 1913–1917), 7:467.

13. Lewis Cass to William B. Reed, Washington, D.C., May 30, 1857 (no. 2), United States Department of State, Diplomatic Instructions (hereafter cited as USDS, DI): China, vol. 1 (National Archives Microfilm 77/Roll 38; hereafter cited as NA M/R).

14. Quoted in *John Quincy Adams and American Continental Empire: Letters, Papers, and Speeches*, Walter LaFeber, ed. (Chicago: Quadrangle Books, 1965), p. 45.

15. Bancroft to James Buchanan, London, Feb. 23, 1849 (no. 122), United States Department of State, Diplomatic Dispatches (hereafter cited as USDS, DD): Great Britain, vol. 59 (NA M30/R55).

16. Marcy to Augustus Dodge, Washington, D.C., May 1, 1855 (no. 1), USDS, DI: Spain, vol. 15 (NA M77/R143).

17. Taylor, pp. 449–52.

18. Reed to Cass, Shanghai, Nov. 9, 1858 (no. 36), USDS, DD: China, vol. 17 (NA M92/R18).

19. *Historical Statistics*, p. 57.

20. *Annals of Congress*, 16th Cong., 1st sess., 2:2150.

21. Henry Clay, *Speech of Henry Clay in Defense of the American System Against the British Colonial System* (Washington, D.C., 1832), p. 11, also quoted in *The Life, Correspondence, and Speeches of Henry Clay*, Calvin Colton, ed., 6 vols. (New York, 1864), 2:190.

22. *Annals of Congress*, 16th Cong., 1st sess., 2:1928.

23. *Papers of Clay*, 2:857.

24. *Memoirs of John Quincy Adams*, Charles Francis Adams, ed., 12 vols. (Philadelphia, 1874–77), 5:325.

25. Adams to Rodney, Washington, D.C., May 17, 1823 and Adams to Anderson, May 27, 1823 in *Writings of Adams*, 7:431–32 and 473.

26. Adams to Anderson, *ibid.*, 7:453.

27. *Ibid.*, 7:460.

28. *A Compilation of the Messages and Papers of the Presidents*, James D. Richardson, comp., 20 vols. (New York, 1897–1917), 2:778, 787.

29. Clay to William Tudor, Washington, D.C., March 28, 1828, quoted in Vernon G. Setser, *The Commercial Reciprocity Policy of the United States, 1774–1829* (Philadelphia: University of Pennsylvania Press, 1937), p. 247.

30. *Life, Correspondence, and Speeches of Clay*, 5:227.

31. Taylor, pp. 449–52; J. Fred Rippy, *Rivalry of the United States and Great Britain over Latin America (1808–1830)* (Baltimore: Johns Hopkins University Press, 1929; reprint ed., New York: Octagon, 1964), pp. 303–15.

32. Taylor, pp. 444–45.

33. *Ibid.*

34. Warren I. Cohen, *America's Response to China: An Interpretative History of Sino-American Relations* (New York: Wiley, 1971), pp. 14–15; Charles O. Paullin, *Diplomatic Negotiations of American Naval Officers, 1778–1883* (Baltimore: Johns Hopkins University Press, 1912; reprint ed., Gloucester, Mass.: Peter Smith, 1967), pp. 213–14.

35. Reed to Cass, Shanghai, Nov. 9, 1858 (no. 36), USDS, DD: China, vol. 17 (NA M92/R18).

36. Buchanan to Alexander H. Everett, Washington, D.C., Apr. 15, 1845 (no. 2), USDS, DI: China, vol. 1 (NA M77/R38).

37. Parker to William Marcy, Macao, Dec. 12, 1856 (no. 34), USDS, DD: China, vol. 13 (NA M92/R14).

38. See, for example, (Secretary of State) Edward Everett to Neill Brown, Washington, D.C., Feb. 23, 1853 (no. 15), USDS, DI: Russia, vol. 14 (NA M77/R136).

39. Quoted in Payson J. Treat, *Diplomatic Relations Between the United States and Japan*, 3 vols. (Stanford: Stanford University Press, 1938; reprint ed., Gloucester, Mass.: Peter Smith, 1963), 1(1853–1895):26.

40. *Historical Statistics*, pp. 551, 553.

41. Taylor, pp. 444–45.

42. Vail to Edward Livingston, London, Feb. 27, 1833, quoted in Varg, p. 75.

43. Cass to Reed, Washington, D.C., May 30, 1857 (no. 2), USDS, DI: China, vol. 1 (NA M77/R38).

44. Lawrence to Palmerston, London, Nov. 22, 1849, Foreign Office 5/506 (Public Record Office, Kew, England).

45. Calhoun to William King, Washington, D.C., Aug. 12, 1844 (no. 4), USDS, DI: France, vol. 15 (NA M77/R55).

46. Quoted in Norman Graebner, *Empire on the Pacific: A Study in American Continental Expansion* (New York: Ronald, 1955), p. 38.

47. Calhoun to King, Washington, D.C., Aug. 12, 1844 (no. 4), USDS, DI: France, vol. 15 (NA M77/R55).

48. *National Party Platforms, 1840–1972*, Donald Bruce Johnson and Kirk H. Porter, comps. (Urbana: University of Illinois Press, 1973), p. 4.

49. Everett to James Buchanan, London, May 19, 1845 (no. 320), USDS, DD: GB, vol. 55 (NA M30/R51).

50. Quoted in *Manifest Destiny*, Norman Graebner, ed. (Indianapolis: Bobbs-Merrill, 1968), pp. 36–37.

51. Quoted in Frederick Merk, *The Monroe Doctrine and American Expansionism, 1843–1849* (New York: Knopf, 1966), p. 117.

52. Lord Elgin to Lord John Russell, n.p., Dec. 10, 1849, quoted in Wilbur Devereux Jones, *The American Problem in British Diplomacy, 1841–1861* (London: Macmillan, 1974), pp. 79–80.

53. John Crampton to the Earl of Clarendon, Washington, D.C., June 12, 1854, Clarendon MSS, Deposit C-24 (Bodleian Library, Oxford). Quotations from the Clarendon MSS by permission of the Earl of Clarendon.

54. Clarendon to Lord Napier, [London], May 8, July 3, 1857, Clarendon MSS, Dep. C-138 and C-139.

55. Napier to Clarendon, Washington, D.C., June 14, 1857 (private), Clarendon MSS, Dep. C-81.

56. Palmerston to Clarendon, Broadlands, Dec. 26, 1855, and (London), July 4, 1857, Clarendon MSS, Dep. C-31 and C-69.

57. Crampton to Palmerston, Washington, D.C., Oct. 1, 1849 (no. 85, confidential), FO 5/501.

58. Bulwer to Palmerston, Washington, D.C., July 1, 1850 (private), FO 5/513.

59. Palmerston to Clarendon, London, June 4, 1856, Clarendon MSS, Dep. C-49.

60. Potter, "Atlantic Economy," p. 23.

61. Douglass C. North, *The Economic Growth of the United States, 1790–1860* (Englewood Cliffs, N.J.: Prentice-Hall, 1961), p. 214.

3

1861–1898
Economic Growth
and Diplomatic Adjustment

David M. Pletcher

Indiana University

"WE ARE GREAT and rapidly—I was about to say fearfully—growing." So spoke John C. Calhoun in 1817.[1] If he had been living during the two generations after the Civil War, he would have used stronger language. To be sure, as the last essay has shown, unprecedented growth of the American economy had begun during his lifetime, and by the Civil War the United States already ranked high among economic powers.

The four-year war powerfully stimulated the economy, although historians disagree concerning the unanswerable question of how much expansion would have occurred anyway. During the first year of the war shortages of raw materials, especially cotton, the loss of Southern trade, and the uncertain future caused many mills and factories to close and paralyzed foreign commerce. By

Part of the research for this essay was made possible by a grant from the National Archives, Washington D.C. The author would like to acknowledge also the kind assistance of Irene D. Neu.

1862 poor crops in Europe were attracting unprecedented exports of grain, meats, and other farm products. Government orders and their "ripple effect" on the economy brought a great boom in established industries during 1863 and 1864 and raised to prominence minor or hitherto nonexistent industries such as boots and shoes and petroleum.

After the war was over, the growth continued apace. Between 1865 and 1898 the population of the United States more than doubled, and its gross national product (measured in terms of 1958 prices) nearly trebled. The mounting production of staple crops, raw materials, and basic manufactures gives more detailed evidence of rapid expansion: Wheat, 256 percent, corn, 222 percent, refined sugar, 460 percent, coal, 800 percent, and steel rails, 523 percent. In the textile industry the number of spindles more than quadrupled. The "estimated true value" of taxable property increased by over 446 percent. Investment in railroad securities, most of it European in origin, rose by over 470 percent and miles of track in operation by over 567 percent. In newer industries the growth, starting from near zero, was so great as to make percentages meaningless. Thus the production of crude petroleum rose from about 3,000,000 barrels in 1865 to over 55,000,000 barrels in 1898 and that of steel ingots and castings from less than 20,000 long tons to nearly 9,000,000 long tons.[2]

Such rapid growth inevitably created problems: crowded cities, labor disputes, cutthroat competition, and monopolies, to name only a few. These would have appeared even if the increase had been reasonably steady, but the problems of unpredictability were added to those of rapid growth, as the economy veered up and down between prosperity and hard times. The period included two deep depressions, in the 1870s and 1890s, and a somewhat less serious one in the mid-1880s, with several smaller dips along the way. A dramatic recovery in 1879 and 1880 raised American morale after the first great depression, but the writings of the 1880s were full of forebodings, especially as the economy slid downward again. Finally, the four-year hard times of the mid-1890s, perhaps the most painful so far in American history, compelled a thorough reexamination of American political, economic, and social values.

The American people could not deal with expansion and fluctuation as isolated problems, for between 1861 and 1898 the world economy continued to be dominated by the overwhelming power of Great Britain. Exploiting an early start through the Industrial Revolution and the removal of most governmental restrictions on business between 1815 and the 1840s, British manufacturing, foreign trade and investment, shipping, and banking expanded rapidly through most of the nineteenth century. To be sure, the island-bound United Kingdom imported large amounts of American wheat, provisions, cotton, and other agricultural products. But in 1880 Britain outranked the United States in the export of iron and steel, machinery, and textiles by the proportion of 23.5 to 1.[3] Put another way, in 1883 Britain supplied 37.1 percent of the whole world trade in manufactures, the United States only 3.4 percent—ranking fifth behind Britain, Germany, France, and Belgium. During the 1880s and even more during the 1890s American factories expanded and diversified, but in 1899 the United States' figure had risen only to 9.8 percent, and it still ranked only fourth among manufacturing countries.[4]

British commercial dominance was associated with supremacy in other areas as well. Economists have variously estimated British foreign investments from 1870 to 1912 at around two or three billion pounds (ten or fifteen billion dollars); the American figure, much less intensively studied, could not have been more than one tenth as large.[5] The managers of British-owned railroads, mines, factories, plantations tended to use British products and sell to British buyers. As the period progressed, they consigned cargoes increasingly in British ships. In 1870 the British merchant marine was 3.7 times as large as the American in total tonnage and 5.5 times as large in steam tonnage, the cargo vessels of the future.[6] American shipping continued to decline, until by 1898 nearly all American exports left United States ports in foreign ships, mostly British. In many world markets the lack of a direct, cheap, efficient national merchant marine placed American trade at a heavy disadvantage. Besides widespread foreign investment and plentiful shipping, Britain controlled credit and exchange through the power of its banks, with branches all over the. world, offering favorable terms and ease of payment that the

Americans could not match. Merchants desiring insurance, wholesaling, brokerage, and other collateral services of international trade generally turned to the British.

For most of the nineteenth century, therefore, London was not only the political capital of the British Empire but the business capital of an "informal empire" that included most of Latin America and the Far East. It also included the United States itself, for British investors continued to buy and hold American land and business securities that had done much to encourage American economic growth. During the 1880s and 1890s British expansion slowed down, as it began to meet the competition of Germany and the United States. In a few areas, such as Canada, Mexico, the Caribbean, and Hawaii, where Americans enjoyed the advantage of nearness, they could sometimes drive out British competitors, but elsewhere they had to bend their plans and policies to accommodate British power. Publicists in England, especially during the 1890s, took alarm at the increasing commercial rivalry, but their fears remained largely unsubstantial until after 1900.

The area of closest and most prolonged contact between American economics and diplomacy between 1861 and 1898 was foreign trade, for even at the end of the century American investments abroad were still moderate and localized, and foreign investment in the United states, though still large, seldom claimed the attention of the State Department. The total value of this foreign trade kept pace with most other economic indices of the period, for between 1865 and 1898 exports increased from $281 million to $1,231 million, imports from $239 million to $616 million. At the beginning of the period grains, especially wheat, led American exports, but before long cotton was alternating in first place with cereals. During the latter half of the period meat and meat products came to rank third, iron and steel products fourth, and refined petroleum fifth among exports, as American manufactures gradually pushed aside raw materials. At the same time the import of finished manufactured goods gradually declined, from 39.8 percent in 1870 to 23.9 percent in 1900. (But foodstuffs not grown in the United States—coffee, tea, and the like—retained their position and even rose in percentage for a time.) The leading import was sugar, advancing from $55.7 million in 1870 to $100.3 million in 1900. The value of imported sugar was usually at least twice as large as that of any other single category of imported products.[7]

Foreign trade of the late nineteenth century was even more important to the national economy than these figures might suggest and more important than many persons realized at the time. Not only did it supply industry with critical raw materials and consumers with necessities or luxuries they could not obtain at home, but the export trade also disposed of a crucial percentage of American production that otherwise would have remained in the domestic market to depress prices further during a period already characterized by general deflation. This function was especially important to the American farmer, whose prosperity had long depended in part on sales of wheat, cotton, beef, and other staples to Britain and Europe. Between 1861 and 1898 farmers and stock raisers faced increased competition from areas such as Canada, Argentina, Russia, and Australia, whose production they could neither control nor even accurately forecast. The agricultural woes that lay behind the Granger and Populist movements were caused in part by problems of international trade.

This being the case, it is not surprising that an increased number of producers, whether agricultural or industrial, and their allies in the government and the press emphasized the importance of extending foreign trade. Historians have called these men both "commercial expansionists" and "market expansionists," and the terms will be used interchangeably in this essay, although the former is more inclusive, referring to both the export and the import trades. American market expansionists, frustrated by economic cycles and foreign competition, formed exaggerated notions concerning the potentialities facing the nation's foreign trade. The most prominent of these was the theory of overproduction or glut. Briefly stated, this theory declared that America's fertile soil, its many other resources, and the energy and ingenuity of its people had become a drag on progress. The country was producing all it could consume and more. As the economist David A. Wells put it succinctly, if we do not find or create additional markets, "we are certain to be smothered in our own grease."[8] The alarm first appeared among Western farmers, and after the panic of 1873 agricultural interests took it up all over the country: Give us foreign markets and the cheap transportation necessary to reach them at a profit.

Some industrialists had arrived at the same conclusions. One was Edward Atkinson, a textile mill owner and a prolific publicist on many subjects. He told the New England Cotton Manufacturers Association in 1876: "If we can secure an export equal to one-fourteenth that of Great Britain, our immediate prosperity as cotton spinners may be assured."[9] The depression period of the 1890s gave even greater intensity and variety to the manufacturers' push for foreign makets, which was associated with what came to be called Andrew Carnegie's Law of Surplus. Carnegie believed that cheap manufacture depended on running factories at full capacity and that foreign markets, even at low prices, were necessary to keep factories running at all in hard times and to hold domestic customers in good times. (It is worth noting that although he sought foreign markets, he did not support market expansion at all costs.)

Long before the 1890s political leaders had joined the chorus. Secretary of State William H. Seward, a transition figure between territorial and commercial expansionism, died before the fear of surplus production filled men's minds, but as early as 1850 he foresaw a time when "with a powerful economy outproducing and outselling the world, naval and coaling stations at strategic points on the globe, and domination of the monetary systems of the world, the United States would be in truth the greatest of nations."[10] James G. Blaine, the best-known Republican politician of his generation, urged government support for foreign trade—as much, to be sure, for vote-getting as for sales—and favored an economic-oriented inter-American conference, steamship subsidies, and later commercial reciprocity and other measures to gain foreign markets.

Other leaders tied increased exports more closely to the fear of overproduction. When Secretary of State William M. Evarts surveyed foreign trade in 1880, he declared: "We have advanced in manufactures, as in agriculture, until we are being forced outward by the irresistible pressure of our internal development."[11] During the depression of the mid-1880s, Secretary of the Treasury Hugh McCulloch predicted even harder times unless Americans could "share in the trade which is monopolized by European nations."[12] Six years later Senator Chauncey M. Depew of New York, a pillar of the business establishment, added another justification—that expanded markets would enable the nation to absorb its European-held securities and thus prevent a sudden contraction during a business panic.[13]

A group of historians led by William A. Williams, working back from 1898 to explain the Spanish American War and ensuing imperialism, have seized upon expressions of the glut theory and elevated them into a thesis on which to hang much of late nineteenth-century American foreign policy. As one of them put it, the business community, policy makers, and, indeed, "almost all Americans" in the 1890s agreed "that additional foreign markets would solve the economic, social, and political problems created by the industrial revolution."[14] Eschewing political domination except for a few small strategic areas (for example, Hawaii), economic expansionists would have the United States create an "informal empire" of trade and investment modeled on that of Britain and release American business from reliance on British financial power, merchant marine, and trade facilities.

Opponents of this way of thinking have branded these historians economic determinists.[15] To be sure, newspapers and the *Congressional Record* of the late 1880s and the 1890s show that publicists in these years were much exercised about the expansion of foreign trade. Anglophobia, endemic since at least the American Revolution, both stimulated this commercial expansionism and was stimulated by it. Several diplomatic episodes of these years—the Samoan crisis of 1889, the inter-American conference of 1889–90, the *Baltimore* affair of 1891, and the Hawaiian revolution of 1893, to mention the best-known—bore evidences of economic motivation or concern. But to take the rhetoric of glut at face value overlooks or unduly minimizes several factors which call into question the existence of a deliberate, consistent policy, at least before the mid-1890s.

For one thing, the fear of overproduction was not constant;

it usually appeared most prominently during hard times—the mid-1870s, the mid-1880s, and the mid-1890s. American consuls abroad repeatedly complained that their country's manufacturers and shippers sought foreign customers only when they could find none at home, and insisted that if they wished to develop reliable foreign markets, they must cultivate them in good times as well as bad.

Second, even when business was slow, a majority of industrialists and merchants placed their chief reliance on the American home market, citing population and industrial growth to justify their confidence that whatever the momentary setbacks of the present, the future would bring increased domestic demand for both producer and consumer goods. Practically the whole Republican party and a significant bloc of Democrats stubbornly supported protective tariffs, a serious obstacle to increased foreign trade; and even low-tariff Democrats used many economic and social arguments other than the need for increased exports to defend their policy. The epitome of protectionist opposition to the glut theory was voiced by Senator Justin S. Morrill, for seventeen years chairman of the Senate Finance Committee, a key position in which to dominate commercial policy: "The time is long past when nations can be enormously enriched by any excessive profits upon foreign trade. . . . National wealth must now and hereafter be mainly created by labor at home; and the home market is the only one of value over which any nation now has absolute control."[16]

A third reason for questioning the automatic nature of commercial expansionism in the late nineteenth century is the fact that many big business leaders looked to other expedients, most notably the creation of combinations or monopolies, as more direct and immediate ways to increase sales and profits. Alarmed at the cutthroat competition produced by improved technology and transportation, industrialists and railroadmen developed "gentlemen's agreements," pools, trusts, and, when these proved ineffective, holding companies or mergers. Manufacturers were more likely to enter the export trade when they possessed economic advantages such as efficient technology and organization than as a last-ditch expedient against competition or depression. Related to this reliance on their own tactics of business strategy was a fourth reason. Although the business community was strongly patriotic, many of its members mistrusted government, convinced that it should not try to bend "fixed and immutable" natural laws but confine itself to a few functions that individuals could not exercise, such as protecting life and property and administering justice.

Finally, as will be seen in more detail later in this essay, the record of foreign economic policy between 1861 and 1898 does not support the existence of a determined, consistent push for expanded markets during this period or even in the 1890s. Instead, hesitation and contradiction were the order of the day. In Cuba, where both trade and investments were large by the 1880s, a favorable commercial treaty failed to gain Senate approval in 1884 and a similar agreement lasted only two years in the 1890s. In Hawaii the even more advantageous reciprocity treaty of 1875 was subject to heavy protectionist fire for nearly two decades; and outright annexation desired by some commercial expansionists remained in limbo for five years in the midst of the 1890s depression. At the same time the United States undertook policies of confrontation and then cooperation with Britain and Germany, the two most dynamic imperialists of the day, for a share in the control of Samoa, an island group where American trade interests were practically nonexistent and prospects at best speculative. Market-seeking impulses and rhetoric were plentiful, but before 1898 they had not coalesced into an official policy.

GOVERNMENT AID TO ECONOMIC EXPANSION—ACTUAL AND POSSIBLE

Nevertheless, during the nineteenth century the American government did respond half-heartedly to some cries of businessmen and journalists for aid in developing American trade and investments abroad. Perhaps the most immediate form of such aid was improvement of the diplomatic and consular services, whose members were in the best position to advise on foreign markets and make contacts with foreign governments. In 1856 Congress had reorganized the services, but spoils politics defeated the purpose of the law. Also during the whole period from 1861 to 1898 the diplomats and consuls remained completely dependent on annual congressional appropriations, involving carping debates, party deals, and an occasional halfhearted attempt at reform.

In the mid-1880s the United States had no ambassadors, 31 ministers (of whom a dozen doubled as consuls general), 170 salaried consuls general and consuls, 96 consuls paid so little (if at all) that they were allowed to engage in trade, and 418 lesser agents, usually native merchants. These men often had considerable responsibility in defending American commerce and shipping against unfair local exactions and reporting trade conditions. Special circumstances imposed other duties too. On the Mexican border consular officials had to guard against smuggling and watch Indian movements, while in the Far East some of them conducted consular courts, maintained jails, and served as postmaster for American residents. The consul general at Havana was virtually a diplomatic official, more important than half of the American ministers.

Positions like these deserved first-rate men, but the entire diplomatic and consular services were open to spoils politics. From 1884 to 1896 the presidency changed parties every four years, causing wholesale replacements. To be sure, in 1895 Grover Cleveland issued an order establishing a merit system, but William McKinley abandoned it, and the old disorder remained until Elihu Root finally overhauled the whole State Department in 1906.

Once the victorious office-seeker arrived at his post, he found that he could hardly support his family on his salary, let alone entertain modestly. The American legation or consulate was usually the shabbiest in town—a poor advertisement for a country whose businessmen sought new foreign customers. Still worse, since many consular officials depended on fees for much of their pay or were allowed to keep up their own businesses, they had every incentive to overcharge American merchants and shippers or use their official position to crowd them out of the market.

These conditions made for mediocre diplomatic and consular services. A few American representatives abroad were outright swindlers like one minister to Brazil, James Watson Webb, whose extortions and briberies inspired Congress to vote remuneration to that country, or men of pliable scruples like General Robert C. Schenck, minister to Britain, who allowed his name to be used to entice foreign investors into a wildcat mining company. When a diligent consul general on the Mexican border inspected his district, he found that one of his agents, a crotchety old recluse, had alienated everyone with whom he dealt, another was living openly with a prostitute, and a third was apparently engaged in smuggling.

Not all American diplomats were rogues or incompetents. A few ministers, indeed, like George Bancroft, James Russell Lowell, and John L. Motley, were men of real distinction. Some others, like John W. Foster and John A. Bingham, originally patronage appointees, proved able negotiators. There were consuls too, such as Warner P. Sutton at Matamoros, Edward L. Baker at Buenos Aires, and Frank H. Mason at Basel and later Frankfurt am Main, who remained many years at their posts, sending home detailed reports full of useful advice to manufacturers, shippers, and the State Department. Nevertheless, xenophobes and economizers exaggerated the flaws in the system and, like some in the early national period, maintained that the diplomatic and consular services were largely unnecessary. The State Department, said one, "is the dress parade part of the Govt. Real diplomacy . . . will soon be obsolete with us for the whole world is anxious to be at peace with us."[17] Some would leave only consuls to handle business matters and recall all ministers, except perhaps one at Paris to carry on relations with all Europe.

Undoubtedly many critics would have moderated their attacks if diplomats and consuls had acted energetically to increase American trade opportunities abroad, but until the mid-1890s the State Department closely restricted this aid. In 1875, for example, the Grant administration stated as a long-established principle that neither ministers nor consuls were duty bound to attend to the business of private persons. Secretary of State Hamilton Fish believed that ministers should not even present claims unless for a violation of international law, but Secretary Frederick T. Frelinghuysen conceded that a minister might act as claims agent with the Department's permission. Consuls had more latitude, for they might present claims in return for expenses and fees and give advice in controversies if these activities did not interfere with their official duties.

In the ticklish matter of recommending American merchants or promoters to a foreign government, the Department followed an uncertain policy, especially in the Far East, where great hopes of future trade and investments conflicted with fears of political involvement. After the collapse of a partly fraudulent railroad project in China during 1886, Secretary Thomas F. Bayard decided that the American minister must not officially vouch for an American company until the Department had determined its respectability. The semantic difference between officially vouching for a company and informally introducing its agent to Chinese officials caused so much trouble that during the race for concessions following the Sino-Japanese War of 1894–95 Secretary Richard Olney revised the instructions in more liberal but still cautious language. The minister must not officially guarantee American enterprises, but he should use personal and official influence to help "reputable representatives of such concerns" obtain the same hearing as foreign rivals. "Broadly speaking," he should "employ all proper methods for the extension of American commercial interests in China," but without favoring one firm exclusively.[18]

Although the State Department was often reluctant to intervene abroad on behalf of the American businessman, it willingly furnished him whatever information it could about foreign market and investment conditions. Since the early nineteenth century consuls had made irregular reports which the Department occasionally sent to Congress. After reorganizing the diplomatic and consular services in 1856, Congress issued an annual publication on commercial matters, drawing on all kinds of sources. In

1869 this assumed the standard title *Commercial Relations of the United States*, and gradually its contents became more systematic.

During the depressed 1870s trade organizations all over the country, led by the New York Chamber of Commerce, besieged the government for more information than could be provided in the annual *Commercial Relations*. Accordingly, in October 1880 the State Department initiated the monthly volumes of published *Consular Reports*. Usually these excerpted statistics and descriptions from agents all over the world; but occasionally special volumes appeared, devoted to one commodity or region; and the tables of statistics became ever longer and more impressive. Originally each issue cost the government about $20,000 for 10,000 copies, of which 6,000 went to Congressmen and consular officials and the rest to trade organizations and individuals. Hampered by lack of funds, the Department considered cutbacks during the depression of the 1880s. Instead, the rising demand for foreign trade during the depression of the 1890s resulted in the publication of "advance sheets" of up-to-date information, and on January 1, 1898, the Department inaugurated *Daily Consular Reports*.

Another device for spreading information and encouraging foreign trade was to send exhibits to foreign expositions or to organize international expositions in the United States itself. Such expositions took place at Paris in 1867, 1878, and 1889, at Vienna in 1873, at Antwerp in 1884, and at Brussels, Barcelona, and Melbourne in 1888. Usually when the Department received an invitation, it went to Congress, which shied at the appropriation required, shelved the invitation, and tried to forget about it. No thanks to Congress, the United States sometimes made an excellent showing. At the Paris and Vienna Expositions of 1867 and 1873 it had a large commission and several hundred displays, most of them privately subsidized. In 1878, again at Paris, the Americans outdid themselves, with 1,229 displays, 140 gold medals, and 8 grand prizes to Thomas A. Edison, Cyrus H. McCormick, and others less well known.

The two greatest American expositions of the period, the Philadelphia Centennial of 1876 and the Columbian Exposition of 1893 in Chicago, are best remembered as patriotic celebrations or entertainments for the American people, but foreigners too came to marvel at American machinery and samples of wheat, cotton, and dozens of other products. Throughout the period foreign delegations, usually of officials gathered to discuss international peace or some other matter of moment, were taken on tours of the Northeast and Middle West which invariably led through one factory after another. In 1889, when Latin American delegates on such a tour visited the great Wanamaker department store in Philadelphia, its owner (who was then Postmaster General in the Benjamin Harrison administration) passed out to every visitor a magnificently printed catalogue of his wares.

Not content with consular reports and international expositions, promoters of foreign trade, working through both the Executive and Congress, tried to shape major economic policies to serve their ends. Perhaps the most important of these policies—and certainly the most argued over—was the tariff. Just as the Civil War was beginning, the Morrill act of 1861 ended nearly a generation of low tariffs. Wartime financial needs, the withdrawal of the Southern low-tariff bloc from Congress, and strong protectionist pressure from some Northern manufacturers combined to force the rates upward in a series of tariff acts. Between 1860 and 1866 average *ad valorem* rates on dutiable goods rose from 19.67 percent to 48.35 percent.[19] At the same time the government levied internal taxes on nearly every conceivable article of trade.

With wartime needs removed in 1865, internal taxes soon largely disappeared, but the protective tariff remained, for wartime industrial production had raised a clutch of lobbyists determined to maintain the new profits. Among their opponents, who wanted to lower tariffs now that the war was over, the ablest by far was David A. Wells, a Harvard-trained New England journalist whom Andrew Johnson appointed special commissioner of revenue. In his annual report for 1869 Wells described the lobbyists' activities and tried to convince labor and the farmers that the lopsided tariffs held little or nothing for them. Alarmed at Western demands for tariff reform, Congress lowered duties on some manufactures in 1870, only to restore them in a few years. Meanwhile

Grant abolished Wells' government post. The nation's sails were set for protection.

It will be useful to summarize the principal high- and low-tariff arguments, especially those affecting foreign trade. Philosophical protectionists, such as Henry C. Carey and Horace Greeley, saw the system as an early form of social planning, designed to spread benefits among nearly all interest groups. High tariffs would guarantee a profitable home market for the manufacturer; this market would enable him to raise wages; and the increased purchasing power of labor would enlarge consumption of both manufactured goods and farm products. Some argued that high tariffs also actually increased foreign trade in the long run by maturing American industries and enabling them to create a better product, which alone could successfully compete abroad. Others, like Senator Morrill, pooh-poohed the value of foreign trade. Britain served protectionists in two contradictory ways—as a bogey which would overrun an unprotected American market with its cheap goods and as a horrible example of the ills of free trade. To be sure, not all high-tariff supporters were extremists. Some distinguished, for example, between the iron and steel tariff, which protected a growing industry, and the raw sugar tariff, which did not. Others conceded by the late 1880s that the Treasury surplus made some reductions necessary, if only to save appearances.

Moderate tariff reformers and free traders, whose arguments often overlapped, pointed out repeatedly that under the high-tariff system the American farmer must buy in a protected market while selling in a free one. By raising the cost of railroad supplies, high tariffs also prevented cheap transportation to market. Tariffs on raw materials hurt many industrialists, who wanted to see them put on the free list. By the 1890s reformers were arguing that American industries, no longer "infants," were outproducing the American demand and that high tariffs, being a type of special privilege, encouraged selfishness, parasitism, and monopoly. The *Nation* calculated in 1888 that tariffs cost the consumer $300 million a year—as much as all state and municipal taxes.

Low-tariff and free-trade men of the 1880s and 1890s linked tariff reform with a vast program of improvements intended to make the United States a major power: expanding foreign trade, an interoceanic canal, a stronger navy, development of the Mississippi valley, education, and labor reform. Senator John T. Morgan of Alabama, who spoke often on the subject, denounced high tariffs as wasteful and monopolistic. Setting forth the theory of overproduction, he declared that all American manufacturers needed was "a fair opportunity to visit the nations that are purchasers of goods, with better and cheaper productions than any other nation."[20] Where protectionists rejoiced at every British setback, free traders constantly extolled British commercial power as a triumph for their doctrine and warned that higher tariffs would lead only to European retaliation. Worthington C. Ford, chief of the State Department's Bureau of Statistics, believed that lower tariffs might also encouraged Americans to invest their surplus capital abroad, instead of cramming it into domestic industry.

Both protectionists and tariff reformers overstated their cases, and neither could resist occasional smears and rumor-mongering. Thus reformers put on a moral cloak and compared protectionists to ante-bellum slaveholders; and protectionists returned the compliment by identifying free trade with secession and treason (since it was strongest in the Democratic party). Southerners thought that Northern free traders had set out to cripple their growing factories. Some protectionists saw in the opposition an enormous conspiracy, supported by British gold and the Cobden Club's free-trade pamphlets. Greeley's successor as publisher of the *New York Tribune*, Whitelaw Reid, declared that free traders were using the *Consular Reports* to spread their nefarious doctrines at the taxpayer's expense.

The invective and turgidity of tariff arguments were unfortunate, for the question was complex enough to challenge the strongest mind. Reforms were difficult even when one party controlled both houses of Congress (which seldom happened), for the members were often hypersensitive about suggestions from outside "experts." Also local interests predominated, especially in the House of Representatives, so that in tariff construction vote-trading ("logrolling") was commonplace. Tariffs were divided into two main types, specific and *ad valorem* (i.e., levied according to item or to percentage of value), and these could be cunningly shifted so as to disguise raised rates. Another tariff complication was the perennial rivalry between the producers of raw materials and the manufacturers who converted them into finished products.

As soon as tariff reformers realized that they faced a daunting series of assaults against strongly entrenched opponents and across a quagmire of technicalities, some of them tried to bypass Congress and the lobbies with reciprocity treaties. Probably the original inspiration for these treaties was the *Zollverein* (customs union) of German states in the 1830s. But the treaties were more modest bilateral agreements by which the United States and some other country would reduce or abolish duties on certain of each other's products so as to promote trade and economic development.[21] At one time or other between 1860 and 1898 almost a dozen reciprocity treaties or executive agreements were in operation, affecting as much as 36 percent of American imports.

Generally speaking, the United States did not try to negotiate reciprocity treaties with Europe because of the chronic European tariff wars beginning in the 1870s. Instead, it sought to use reciprocity as a means for expanding trade within the western hemisphere and in the Pacific. The first effort, a treaty with Britain covering Canada, lasted ten years, from 1855 to 1865. The second, with Hawaii, lasted from 1875 to annexation in 1898. Treaties with Latin America either failed or survived only a few years. Wool would probably have been the best bargaining counter for southern South America, but the wool lobby resisted any concessions with vigilance and vigor. Sugar-producing interests in the United States were weak and the powerful sugar refiners favored cheap raw (or partly refined) sugar. Hence the supporters of reciprocity focused their attention on Mexico and the Caribbean.

Like all compromise measures, reciprocity suffered attacks from every side. Many free traders objected to it as a placebo, which would satisfy the urge for tariff reform without accomplishing anything of value. The high priest of protection, Senator Morrill, regarded it as "a hodge podge of free trade, undermining all stable protective tariffs." The chief iron and steel lobbyist called it a "dickering, huckstering and compromising policy"—as if he had never struck a bargain himself.[22] Others declared that it was unconstitutional, an Executive intrusion into Congressional control over the purse strings.

One serious objection to reciprocity particularly troubled diplomats. Many countries included in their commercial treaties a "most-favored-nation" clause, promising that they would extend to the other signatory any privileges they might grant to a third party. If the United States bargained for tariff concessions from a Latin American country, that country sometimes turned around and extended the same treatment to Britain or Germany—when the principal American purpose in negotiating the treaty had been to displace the British or German competitors. The State Department solemnly proclaimed the principle of "conditional most-favored-nation treatment"—that concessions granted in a reciprocity treaty must not be extended to another nation unless that nation granted an equivalent in return. The Supreme Court backed up the State Department in a decision to which Europe paid little attention. Not until the 1920s did the United States give up the struggle and accept the European or "unconditional" view of most-favored-nation clauses.

Since the Republicans controlled the Presidency and at least one house of Congress almost throughout the period from 1861 to 1898, it is not surprising that protection was the dominant tariff policy. The spread of free-trade doctrines during the depression of the 1870s induced Congress to investigate the tariff question in 1882, but the only result was a "mongrel" tariff, so badly written that it required constant tinkering. When Cleveland became President in 1885, he tried in vain to lower duties. Returning to power in 1889, the Republicans put through the McKinley tariff, with higher duties and a few sops to reformers, such as free sugar (which also pleased the refiners) and a very limited provision for reciprocity agreements. The 1890s brought two new tariffs, one Democratic (the Wilson-Gorman act of 1894) and one Republican (the Dingley act of 1897). Both disturbed business conditions with rumors and readjustments; neither yielded much to tariff reformers or greatly encouraged foreign trade.

Closely intertwined with the tariff was another problem of foreign policy in which advocates of increased exports saw an important relationship between economics and diplomacy. This was the currency question. The international exchange rate, especially between dollars and pounds sterling, seemed to exercise controlling influence over American debts and foreign trade. Some felt that the adoption of a silver currency would give the United States an advantage in selling to other silver nations, above all in Latin America and the Far East.

Businessmen interested in commercial expansion held varying views on the currency question. Orthodox merchants and bankers, as well as liberals who followed British free-trade doctrines, tended to regard monometallic gold currency as "natural" and to oppose government manipulation of the value of money. Importers and wholesalers complained that currency inflation and unstable exchange rates raised the prices of both imports and domestic goods and interfered with planning. After the Civil War a newer group of industrialists and merchants, led by the protectionist Henry C. Carey, favored a moderately devalued currency precisely in order to reduce the wartime import of British manufactures and encourage the home producer, who might then export any surplus. Later, when the silver crusade got under way, this group supported bimetallism, which to them represented controlled inflation. But Edward Atkinson and David A. Wells, who opposed them also on the tariff question, denounced bimetallism as "a violation of the natural laws of supply and demand, and an attempt to provide for the survival of the unfittest."[23]

Even before the Civil War representatives from Europe and the United States had discussed an international currency as part of a broad plan to encourage trade and free it from artificial restrictions. In 1867 an international monetary conference met at Paris, to which the Johnson administration sent Samuel Ruggles, a monometallist and commercial expansionist who saw in currency unification a "golden chain binding in one common monetary civilization the out-spread lands."[24] But British and French monometallists refused to consider any currency except gold as standard; silverites could not accept this; and the conference ended in futility after explicitly rejecting bimetallism.

During the 1870s American bimetallists continued working for an international currency agreement with no more success. Many in Europe favored setting a fixed ratio between gold and silver currencies, if only to stabilize exchange rates. Most European policy makers, however, opposed any formal establishment of bimetallism, apparently in large part because they feared that Americans would use the system for speculation and make international exchange even more unstable. Although the Bland-Allison Act of 1878 seemed a mild compromise to most Americans, European monometallists regarded it as the first hole in the dike. American representatives attended monetary conferences at Paris in 1878 and 1881 but could not convince the Europeans that the United States government intended to restrain the "wild" American silverites.

Throughout the 1880s and 1890s Republicans and Democrats alike followed the pattern of their predecessors, keeping a commissioner (usually a bimetallist) wandering around Europe to "make contacts" and sending delegates to every monetary conference in the hope of working out some lucky formula to stabilize international exchange. Perhaps Cleveland might have been able to extract concessions during the late 1880s, when for a time the European gold drain was serious and the American gold reserve high, but he preferred to push for tariff reform. James G. Blaine's inter-American conference of 1889–90 seriously discussed a common silver coin for the western hemisphere, and there was even some talk that this idea might be extended to Europe.

After the repeal of the Sherman Act, the European attitude toward international bimetallism seemed to improve until the crescendo of free-silver agitation, leading to the presidential campaign of 1896, temporarily silenced all talk. William McKinley, following a campaign pledge, sent a commission to sound out British and French opinion regarding an international monetary agreement, but the new high Dingley tariff of 1897 antagonized the Europeans and silverites were, as usual, a minority in Britain, so the commission came home empty-handed. During the same year new gold discoveries in the Yukon and South Africa increased the money supply, so the currency question lost much of its urgency.

Another problem, which, like the currency, was closely related to the tariff question, was the decline of the American merchant marine. On the eve of the Civil War over 65 percent of American trade was carried in ships flying the American flag, but by 1898 this figure had fallen to less than 10 percent. In 1884, when an American inquired at Valparaiso about American steamship departures to Rio de Janeiro, the Chilean clerk replied: "American steamers? I didn't know the Americans had any steamers. I never saw one."[25] By that time American sailing ships as well had declined nearly two-thirds since 1870. Even the North Atlantic trade employed few regularly scheduled American ships.

The causes of this precipitous decline in American shipping were many and varied. During the 1840s and 1850s iron-hulled, steam-driven ships became economically feasible, giving Britain a considerable advantage with its well-developed iron industry, its cheap coal, and its advanced technology. Americans allowed the gap to widen by reacting slowly to the changes. The Civil War caused the great transatlantic cotton trade to collapse long enough to cripple American shipowners, while Confederate raiders drove them to seek the protection of other flags. After the war a number of factors prevented recovery. American manufacturing industries competed increasingly for the capital formerly employed in shipbuilding and shipping. Rising petroleum production killed off the Pacific whaling industry. Although the California wheat trade employed many American ships for a time, they lost ground to the British beginning in the mid-1880s.

Many of these factors were irreversible, but others reflected unprogressive government and business policies. The cost of American shipbuilding rose sharply after the Civil War, thanks in part to the high prices of heavily protected iron plating, machine parts, and other components. Congress sought to compensate shipbuilders by retaining the old Navigation Laws, which denied American registry (and thus participation in the coasting trade) to ships built abroad, foreign-owned, or officered by foreigners; and the government also refused to readmit American ships whose registry had been changed during the war. By the end of the period Americans controlled nearly as many foreign-built as American-built ships, but these had to fly other flags, and if they entered one American port, they had to go to Canada or the West Indies before they could call at another. In other respects—corporate organization, low pay, and bad working conditions—shipping had difficulty competing with other industries for the capital and labor it needed.

For a time the United States government tried to offset these crippling handicaps to American shipping by granting mail subsidies—a form of aid long since extended by European governments. Before the Civil War the government spent about $14 million in this manner, but only one of the subsidized companies continued beyond the war. This was the Pacific Mail Steamship Company, which had survived the cut-throat competition of the Central American trade during the 1850s and, at the end of the war, was preparing to enter the transpacific field. In 1866 it was awarded an annual subsidy of $500,000 for monthly service to the Far East, and six years later the amount was doubled in return for additional service. Unfortunately opponents, enlivened by the Grant scandals, soon discovered that the company had bribed Congressmen to vote for the second subsidy. Not only did Pacific Mail lose all its financial aid; the whole question of ship subsidies became to liberals a symbol of corruption and privilege.

As a result, the American shipping industry suffered from stalemate for the rest of the period. Protectionists insisted on retaining high tariffs on shipbuilding supplies and, for good measure, the restrictive Navigation Laws; reformers usually continued to oppose subsidies. To many it seemed inconceivable that the nation that had given millions of dollars and acres to the Western railroads should do nothing for the shipping companies that would control the sea-lanes in wartime. In 1882–83 Representative Nelson Dingley, Jr., of Maine (later author of the Dingley tariff bill), introduced a reform measure at the same time as the "mongrel" tariff. It was passed, but only after its most controversial portions had been shorn away. In 1890 Senator William P. Frye of Maine introduced two bills to encourage American steamship lines, of which one, granting modest mail subsidies, survived strong Congressional opposition. The subsidies, however, proved too small to overcome European competition.

Occasional efforts were also made to secure government financial support for oceanic cables, with even less success. The most that the United States would do for transatlantic lines was to take a stand against European monopolies by refusing landing privileges for French cables unless the French government would guarantee similar privileges for future American companies. In the Pacific several Presidents recommended that Congress foster cable construction to Hawaii and the Far East, and the question aroused hot debate in the mid-1890s, but again the only action was essentially defensive—opposition to a Hawaiian cable station for a Canadian-Australian line.

Although commercial expansionists made little progress in obtaining government aid for shipping or cables, they did exert considerable influence on the revival of the American Navy. From the Civil War to the mid-1880s the Navy was allowed to disintegrate, but during the next fifteen years reforms set in, until by 1898, although still small, it had become once more efficient. An important argument in favor of increased naval appropriations was the natural alliance between the Navy and commerce. In the words of one navalist: "Every ship should become a commercial agent and [disseminate] information about the resources of the country, the prices and value of our commodities, [and] the advantages inuring to foreign merchants of dealing with us."[26]

Between 1878 and 1880 the Navy dramatized this concept with a leisurely round-the-world voyage by U.S.S. *Ticonderoga*, which called at many African and Asiatic ports to "show the flag" and enable her commander to report on conditions. This man, Commodore Robert W. Shufeldt, a onetime merchant marine officer and consul general at Havana, was convinced of the need to expand foreign trade. Before his departure Shufeldt wrote an open letter on the subject at the request of a Congressman, saying among other things: "The man-of-war precedes the merchantman and impresses rude people with the sense of the power of the flag which covers the one and the other."[27] The argument caught on, and commerce became part of the naval ideology which Captain (later Admiral) Alfred T. Mahan popularized all over America and Europe during the 1890s. In Mahan's thinking trade was usually secondary to security and military strategy, but, especially in his later writings, it is often difficult to say where one rationalization ends and another begins. In a generation increasingly impressed with military glory, Shufeldt and Mahan were valuable allies for the commercial expansionists.

A final problem of late-nineteenth-century foreign affairs—this one with economic overtones but little direct relationship to trade expansion—was immigration. Since both businessmen and publicists realized that cheap labor was a prerequisite for the continued growth of the American economy, they made little effort to restrict that from Europe. The question, however, assumed a different aspect on the Pacific coast, where, as early as the 1850s, race-proud whites resented the alien culture and the low wages of Chinese laborers. During the 1860s the Civil War and the need for labor in constructing the transcontinental railroads temporarily damped prejudice; but during the 1870s, after the railroad was completed, an exclusionist movement grew rapidly. In 1867 William H. Seward had included—ill advisedly, as it turned out—a provision for free immigration in a treaty with China; thirteen years later the Hayes administration had to obtain its modification. Through the 1880s and 1890s negotiations continued, as Congress passed one act after another, excluding some Chinese laborers and subjecting others to onerous supervision. In 1894 the Chinese government, alleging treaty violation and American bad faith, threatened to retaliate against American residents and trade, although Chinese merchants and the common people do not seem to have shared the resentment of Chinese officials. The Sino-Japanese War intervened, and Peking dropped the matter.

This survey of American governmental policies affecting foreign trade and investment, which has included consular reform, tariff, currency, shipping, immigration, and other issues, leads to a few preliminary generalizations. While followers of the "glut thesis" and other economic expansionists sought to help businessmen develop foreign markets and later fields of investment, they faced strong opposition from others who were convinced that trade and investment, like charity, should begin at home—and, indeed, stay there. The resulting arguments between those who looked outward and inward filled Congress and the press from the 1870s on and foreshadowed the even more general "great debates" between internationalists and isolationists during the twentieth century.

PRINCIPAL EXECUTIVE LEADERS
IN FOREIGN RELATIONS

Although the late nineteenth century was not a period of strong Executive leadership, it is necessary to characterize briefly the principal policy makers who helped to determine the relationship between economics and diplomacy. From the death of Lincoln to the Spanish American War, American Presidents were a generally passive lot, with little desire to initiate bold policies, especially in foreign relations, about which they were not often well informed. Andrew Johnson was nearly overwhelmed by problems of Reconstruction. Ulysses S. Grant, influenced by shady business promoters and other advisers, set out to annex the Dominican Republic, partly to further economic as well as territorial expansion, and, in failing, discredited annexation for a generation. By his interest in the isthmian transit problem and his initiative in having the principal routes surveyed, however, he considerably influenced American policy in the Caribbean for the rest of the century.

Rutherford B. Hayes, James A. Garfield, and Chester A. Arthur undertook a few initiatives in foreign affairs. Grover Cleveland brought to the White House a sense of moral responsibility which, combined with a dislike of foreign involvement, worked against commercial expansionism in several instances—notably in withdrawing Caribbean reciprocity treaties and later in preventing for a time Hawaiian annexation. Both Benjamin Harrison and William McKinley favored expanding American political and economic influence, but except for Harrison's support of Hawaiian annexation, it is difficult to distinguish their work from that of the State Department.

The Secretaries of State, usually appointed for political reasons, sometimes reflected the passiveness of their chiefs, but a few took initiatives for trade expansion. William H. Seward was both a territorial and commercial expansionist. In his speeches and writings he expressed the Manifest Destiny spirit of the 1840s and 1850s; and he not only took the lead in acquiring Alaska from Russia but also tried in vain to bring about the purchase of some Caribbean island base, such as the Danish West Indies or Samaná Bay in the Dominican Republic. But he also believed in the attractive power of commerce—what one historian has called Seward's Law of Imperial Gravity or, as Seward himself put it, that "political supremacy follows commercial ascendency."[28] His territorial annexationism was always partly based on economic considerations, and he was chronically eager to expand trade across the reaches of the Pacific into the Far East, where territorial annexation was obviously filled with obstacles or out of the question.

A second Secretary whose name has often been identified with commercial expansionism is James G. Blaine. In his case the evidence is both fragmentary and contradictory, and, at least through the 1880s, it is open to the suspicion that, like most of Blaine's actions, his advocacy of measures to favor trade was mainly intended to further his political ambitions. Throughout his career he was a staunch protectionist. Following his nine-month occupation of the State Department in 1881, he declared that the establishment of new foreign markets had been a cardinal goal of the Garfield administration, but neither his writings nor his actions while Secretary furnish much supporting evidence. After sniping at reciprocity from his private life, he ran for the Presidency in 1884 on a platform that included a proposal for a hemispheric *Zollverein* or customs union to keep out British competition—obviously an effort to reconcile reciprocity and protectionism. When he returned to the State Department under Harrison, he used the inter-American conference of 1889–90 to expand American economic influence in the hemisphere, and after the Latin Americans rejected his *Zollverein*, he finally embraced reciprocity. During the next two years he ended his career by signing several short-lived reciprocity agreements with Latin American nations.

Other Secretaries of the 1870s and 1880s played more modest roles. Hamilton Fish built an impressive career in the State Department, but his greatest achievements were not economic— the settlement of the "Alabama" claims and related Anglo-American disputes and the avoidance of a confrontation with Spain over Cuba. Neither he nor Grant can assume much responsibility for the Hawaiian reciprocity treaty, the most notable economic measure of the administration's foreign relations. William M. Evarts made more contributions to trade expansion by encouraging and publishing consular reports than by initiating policy. Frederick T. Frelinghuysen negotiated several reciprocity treaties for the Caribbean area on the model of those with Canada and Hawaii, but Congress refused to execute them.

Cleveland's first Secretary of State, Thomas F. Bayard, generally followed his chief's policy of noninvolvement in foreign quarrels. To be sure, he widened American participation in the contest over Samoa, but from his writings on the subject it does not appear that he was motivated by any strong conviction that Samoa represented an area or a means for extensive trade development.

Taken together, the Secretaries of the mid-1890s were aware of the increased interest in expanding foreign trade that most historians have noted in those years. John W. Foster, whom Harrison appointed after illness forced Blaine's retirement in 1892, carried out policies already begun but showed some economic initiative in handling relations with Hawaii before and after the revolution of 1893. The first Secretary of Cleveland's second administration, Walter Q. Gresham, apparently favored more conventional diplomacy but was led by events into statements or actions that seemed intended to advance American trade interests, as in the case of the Brazilian naval revolution of 1893. His successor, Richard Olney, who had been a corporation lawyer, supported the movement for increased American trade and investment abroad, especially in the Far East but was restrained from more extensive action by the rising unpopularity of the administration and Cleveland's efforts to avoid involvement in the Cuban revolution of 1895. McKinley's first Secretary, John Sherman, initiated few new policies and, like Olney, was hampered by the mounting Cuban crisis.

A REGIONAL SURVEY
OF ECONOMIC DIPLOMACY

A survey by areas of diplomatic activity in economic matters will show the irregular correlation during the period between America's economic stake and America's diplomatic concern. Between 1860 and 1898 Europe accounted for by far the largest of American exports and imports. In 1898 the European percentages stood at 79.1 and 49.7 percent respectively. (For Britain alone percentages were 43.9 and 17.7 percent, respectively, of the world total.) These might be compared with percentages of 6.8 and 5.2 percent for Canada; 7.3 and 24.5 percent for Latin America; and 2.4 and 7.3 percent for China and Japan. In the field of direct investments Latin America replaced Europe at the top of the list, with 48.6 percent. (Mexico alone attracted 31.6 percent.) Canada received 25.1 percent of direct American investments abroad and Europe 22.2 percent. As in the case of trade, the Asian share of investments was insignificant, 3.8 percent.[29] (Most investments abroad were made during the late 1880s or the 1890s.)

Whereas Europe dominated the foreign trade of the United States and received nearly one-fourth of its foreign direct investments, American-European diplomatic relations caused fewer major problems and occupied less space in the *Congressional Record* and the press than Latin America, the Far East, or the Pacific basin. The greater American diplomatic involvement in underdeveloped areas may be partly explained by the bromide "Hope springs eternal in the human breast." Although year after year produced disappointing trade and investment statistics for South America or China, the varied resources of the former and the 400,000,000 customers of the latter seemed to promise a golden future just over the horizon. Another explanation may lie in the fact that, whereas European governments were usually stable and European commercial law relatively familiar to Americans, instability, unfamiliar customs, and inadequate commercial law posed problems in Latin America and the Far East that required diplomatic intervention or produced crises.

In the case of Europe, too, Americans were almost always engaged in activities that brought them into direct competition with Europeans, first in selling their goods, later in manufacturing or assembling them. Their rivals often already enjoyed the active support of European governments, whether in outright subsidies, tariffs, or other favorable legislation or in preferential administration or court decisions. Without effective military or naval strength or the ability to organize boycotts of European exports, American protests could not be much more than breath or paper. Indeed, by arousing European nationalists, they might do more harm than good, so American businessmen in Britain or on the Continent generally resorted to diplomats for routine or purely ceremonial matters.

The only serious American-European diplomatic problem of the period arising from economic causes illustrates these points. During the early 1880s France and Germany forbade the import of American pork and pork products, ostensibly for fear of trichinae in American shipments resulting from inadequate inspection but actually in large measure to protect their own agrarians. Other nations followed suit, and for the rest of the decade American diplomats protested, while American meat packers blocked effective regulatory legislation. Diplomatic ineptitude worsened the dispute with Germany, the most serious of them all. Finally in 1890 the stubborn Chancellor Otto von Bismarck retired from office. At the same time in the United States the McKinley tariff act empowered the President to levy a retaliatory duty on German beet sugar, and Congress passed adequate laws for meat inspection. The two governments quickly drew up an agreement by which Germany would admit American pork (after payment of a tariff duty) and the United States kept German sugar on the free list. At about the same time the United States also came to terms with France. Nevertheless, other European restrictions on American meats, cattle, and other products continued through the 1890s to exacerbate relations.

Economic relations between the United States and Canada were complicated by the rival attractions of American economic strength and Canadian loyalty to Britain and also by a long, zigzag border from the Atlantic to Lake Superior, which increased both interdependence and petty bickering. Canada's railroad system was supported in part by American capital and connected at many points with the American rail network. Even the Canadian Pacific, initiated by nationalists to reduce dependence on the United States and unifying the sprawling provinces, combined rivalry and cooperation with American lines after its completion. In most countries issues such as canal tolls along the border and bonded imports crossing a neighbor's territory were routine matters, but in American-Canadian relations they sometimes became problems of high diplomacy.

Late nineteenth century economic relations between the United States and Canada had their beginning in the Marcy-Elgin reciprocity treaty of 1854, the first of its kind in American history. The treaty stimulated trade, as was intended, but nationalists in each country thought that their interests had been slighted, and Confederate activities in Canada during the Civil War gave American protectionists a special argument with which they induced Congress to abrogate the treaty in 1865. Thereafter trade expansionists in both countries, but especially in Canada (which needed markets even more than the United States), repeatedly tried to reintroduce reciprocity. One chronic weakness of their campaigns was that some saw reciprocity as a prelude to Canadian entrance into the American Union, others as a substitute for annexation.

Gradually during the 1870s and early 1880s advocacy of reciprocity gave way to a broader reform, Commercial Union, a localized *Zollverein* under which Canada and the United States would remove customs houses along their border, adopt a common set of duties against the rest of the world, and divide the receipts *pro rata*. Debated seriously during the late 1880s, the movement won a variety of supporters in both countries: some American protectionists, especially those with lumber or mineral interests in Canada, trade expansionists, and many who favored political union. But many American protectionists belittled the Canadian market; and both Canadian nationalists and Imperial Federalists feared that Commercial Union would reduce the dominion to an American province. The McKinley tariff of 1890 dealt a death blow to the movement by raising the American tariff wall; its limited provision for reciprocity was aimed at Latin America, not Canada.

Canadian-American commercial relations were complicated by the fisheries question. This was a monument to the inordinate power of a well-placed minority, for in 1886, at the height of the controversy, fresh fish amounted to only 3½ percent of all American-Canadian trade; the United States imported almost as many eggs as fish from Canada. The New England fishing industry, which was overcapitalized and inefficient, wanted to retain and expand its access to fishing grounds off Newfoundland (enjoyed almost continuously since Independence), while shutting out Canadian fish from the American market. Since a clique of New England Republicans enjoyed seniority and power in the Senate and two seats on the foreign Relations Committee, they could make the fisheries a heavy bargaining counter in all negotiations. Twice during the period, in 1871 and 1888, treaties granted both fishing rights to Americans and admission of some Canadian fish. On the second occasion the Senate, dominated by the New Englanders, rejected the treaty, and for the rest of the period temporary stop-gap arrangements preserved an uneasy truce.

In American-Mexican relations railroads played an even more important role than in the case of Canada. As the Civil War and the French intervention ended (in 1865 and 1867 respectively), Mexico broke relations with the principal European countries and strengthened its ties with the United States. A group of Mexican liberals prepared to push for much needed public works with the aid of foreign (i.e., American) capital. Early projects collapsed because of Mexican disagreements on terms, the outbreak of border troubles along the Texas frontier, and the depression of the 1870s. In 1880, after what amounted to a thinly disguised official invitation to American investors, the Mexican government granted generous concessions for two long railroad lines from the Rio Grande to Mexico City. During the 1880s a spate of railroad, mining, and land concessions brought millions of dollars into northern Mexico, and although the government resumed diplomatic relations with some European nations at this time, the country had slipped out of the British orbit.

Considering the amount of capital involved (even though American-Mexican trade rose more slowly than investments), one would expect an American government supposedly obsessed by economic expansionism to have paid more attention to Mexico. Actually, aside from smoothing out the Texan border disturbances of the 1870s, the only positive support offered was a reiprocity treaty of 1883, whereby the United States would have placed Mexican sugar, tobacco, and a few other products, mainly tropical, on the free list, in return for similar Mexican treatment (or lower tariffs) for a long list of American goods, mainly manufactures. The Senate narrowly approved the treaty, but an alliance of protectionists, Southern sugar interests, and tobacco Congressmen in the House repeatedly voted down implementing legislation. In 1889 the Harrison administration further affronted Mexico by sharply raising the duty on silver-lead ores, an important product of the northern mines. (This action had the unexpected effect of drawing American capital into new smelters in Mexico.) In contrast to the noncooperation of the American government, Mexico, seeking new capital, bent its concession laws so far that a later revolutionary generation, after 1910, produced an international cataclysm when it tried to revise them and retain more benefits for Mexicans.

Although Central America eventually became known as a producer of tropical fruit, its significance to the United States between 1860 and 1898 rested almost entirely on its control of the shortest transit route between the Caribbean and Pacific. Imme-

diately after the Mexican War, the California gold rush of 1849
proved the economic importance of the Central American location, as the traffic to the goldfields called into being a half dozen
competing steamer lines and land connections in Tehuantepec
(Mexico), Nicaragua, and Panama. American capitalists inaugurated the Panama Railroad in 1855—the first outstandingly successful American investment abroad, which for the next fifteen
years paid annual dividends ranging from 12 percent to 44 percent
on a capital of $5,000,000 (later raised to $7,000,000). By the time
of the Civil War the Panama Railroad and the connecting Pacific-
Mail Steamship line controlled traffic between the east coast and
California. Even after the opening of the first transcontinental railroad in 1869, the two related concerns continued profitable operations.

Before 1865 the United States government took little action
concerning the transisthmian routes except to issue corporate
charters and agree with Britain (in the Clayton-Bulwer treaty of
1850) that neither country would dominate Central America politically or dig a canal there without the participation of the other.
After the Civil War, the Johnson and Grant administrations began
to make overtures to Central American governments and Colombia, which controlled Panama, concerning canal concessions. Neither then nor later, until after the turn of the century, did government leaders in the State Department or in Congress seriously
imagine that the United States would construct or operate a canal
itself. Expansionists, however, especially in the Executive branch,
realized that American capitalists would probably need encouragement before undertaking such a large-scale or speculative venture.
Thus, in the mid-1870s, Grant sent engineers to examine and ap-
praise the rival routes and virtually committed the United States
to preferring a relatively long canal across Nicaragua. But neither
American capital nor American technology was equal to the task,
especially at the end of a long depression.

The project would probably have gone no further at this
point, if a French engineer, Ferdinand de Lesseps, the redoubta-
ble builder of the Suez Canal, had not announced plans in 1879
for a waterway through the isthmus of Panama. President Hayes

immediately proclaimed that "the policy of this country is a canal under American control."[30] With government blessings but no direct aid a group of American businessmen affiliated with ex-President Grant formed a company to dig a Nicaraguan canal. (Also another short-lived company appeared with a proposal for an even more visionary ship-railway across the Isthmus of Tehuantepec.) The State Department engaged Britain in a long futile argument aimed at abrogating the Clayton-Bulwer treaty, so Britain would not take part in regulating the completed canal. Finally, in 1884, the State Department negotiated with Nicaragua for a canal zone protectorate across the country on terms resembling but somewhat more generous than those agreed on with Panama in 1903. Unfortunately, at that point Cleveland entered the White House and withdrew the protectorate treaty from the Senate.

From 1885 to 1898 isthmian transit enthusiasts produced much rhetoric but made little progress toward solving the problem. The Nicaragua canal company went into bankruptcy, but so did de Lesseps' French Company, thereby removing pressure from the Americans. During the 1890s the Nicaragua company came to life again and started a campaign in Congress for a government guarantee of a fixed return on canal securities to encourage investment. Despite support from trade expansionists, led by Senator John T. Morgan of the New South, the various bills made little progress. Nevertheless, although government, press, and people could not agree on the amount of financial aid to be given the canal project, a large number of them now looked on Nicaragua as a sphere in which American influence ought to be exclusive. In 1894 and 1895, when Britain sent small forces to the Nicaraguan coasts in routine exercises to protect minor interests, the outcry in the United States was astonishing. On the eve of the Spanish American War the isthmian canal project was still in its cocoon, but the period of dormacy was ending.

The American economic stake in the Caribbean long antedated the Civil War, for the thirteen colonies had imported sugar from Cuba, and during the first half of the nineteenth century this trade grew very rapidly. Cuba supplied a large part of the American market at the end of the Civil War. During a decade-long

Cuban revolutionary effort from 1868 to 1878 American expansionists combined with Cuban refugees to campaign for American intervention. (Most of the former assumed annexation would follow.) Although Grant was tempted, Secretary Fish managed to restrain him. Instead, after the decade of guerrilla warfare had bankrupted planters and devasted the island, most of the best sugar plantations passed into the hands of Americans or American companies, which had the necessary capital to modernize the industry against the threatening competition of European beet sugar. Also during the 1880s Americans began to work Cuban iron deposits and systematize the marketing of Cuban tobacco (although they did not generally buy up tobacco plantations). While the United States had not annexed Cuba, the island had become an economic satellite.

Since Spain, the political overlord of Cuba, maintained high tariffs against American flour, meats, and manufacturers, some followers of the "glut theory" urged the State Department to negotiate an agreement by which the United States might pay for its great imports of Cuban sugar with its own products instead of having to acquire European exchange. The Arthur administration negotiated a reciprocity treaty to this effect in 1884, but the Senate refused to approve it during the "lame duck" period following Cleveland's victory, and the new President preferred general tariff reform to reciprocity. Under the McKinley tariff act of 1890 Blaine negotiated an executive agreement with Spain which increased American exports to the island, while the free sugar provision of the McKinley act raised profits in the sugar industry (often received by American landowners in Cuba) and encouraged a speculative expansion of cultivation. When the Wilson-Gorman tariff act of 1894 suddenly imposed a 40 percent duty on raw and partly-refined sugar, it combined with other factors (for example, a bumper crop of sugar and bad weather) to ruin the sugar industry, spread unemployment, and bring a new revolutionary movement to the flash point.

In other islands of the Caribbean the basis of American interest combined a hope of future profitable economic development and increasing emphasis by naval expansionists on the strategic importance of the Caribbean. This latter concern usually focused on trade lanes, for few persons imagined that Britain or Germany could invade the United States by way of Cuba or Mexico, and even after the isthmian transit route became a focus of American defense, its enormous potential commercial value outweighed all its other advantages. Indeed, when the Civil War first called to American attention the usefulness of Caribbean naval bases, it was Confederate trade through the Union blockade and Confederate depredations on Union merchantmen that caused the principal concern.

Between 1865 and 1898 every effort for an island base failed. Immediately after the Civil War Secretary of State William H. Seward made overtures to acquire the Danish West Indies or a strategic harbor in the Dominican Republic, but a "backlash" from his earlier purchase of Alaska and the impeachment of President Johnson brought his plans to nothing. Grant's abortive effort in 1870 to annex the Dominican Republic rested partly on the strategic value of its Samaná Bay and partly on the speculative development projects of several shady promoters who managed to gain the support of a few reputable businessmen whom Grant admired. Thereafter the United States rebuffed occasional Caribbean overtures for naval bases until 1889, when Harrison's State Department under Blaine and his Navy Department under Benjamin F. Tracy pressed the president of Haiti to lease Môle St. Nicolas for a base. Again the foundation of the plan was partly economic, for the American negotiator offered trade and economic development in return, and an enthusiastic supporter of the administration was William P. Clyde, owner of a growing Caribbean steamer line.

A more notorious episode suggesting Caribbean expansionism in the 1890s was the Venezuelan crisis of 1895 between the United States and Britain. On this occasion Secretary Olney proclaimed American guardianship over Venezuelan interests in the Orinoco valley, at the southeast corner of the Caribbean, in an explosively exaggerated effort to bring about arbitration of a boundary controversy. Americans had no stake in the disputed territory except for the unimportant activities of a struggling development company, and the motives of Cleveland and Olney remain unclear. Some have suggested that they sought to keep Britain out of a river valley possibly containing great resources for future American exploitation, others that they hoped, by reasserting the Monroe Doctrine, to improve American chances of expanding Latin American markets. Whatever their intentions, American press reactions to the crisis certainly kept Latin America in the public mind and, in a way, prepared it for close attention to the immediately ensuing Cuban revolution.

American merchants and investors encountered more serious obstacles to expansion in southern South America. Before the days of the airplane and the Panama Canal, the whole southeast and west coasts of the continent lay as close to London as to New York. Also during the first half of the century Britain established solid commercial and financial connections with producers and customers of the ABC countries and their smaller neighbors. The United States might have partly offset these connections during the 1870s and 1880s, as many consuls urged, by subsidizing hemispheric steamship lines to compete with those from Britain and the Continent, but, as has been seen, the subsidy question remained stalemated after the Pacific Mail scandal of 1874. American steamer connections with South America were limited to one line, usually making about one trip a month each way between New York and Rio de Janeiro. Despite this handicap, the United States imported large amounts of coffee from Brazil, which usually came direct in British steamers or sailing vessels. Whatever flour, lard, or lumber American exporters managed to sell in Brazil, Argentina, or on the Pacific coast often had to cross the Atlantic twice, traveling on British steamers via London or Liverpool. Passengers usually followed the same route both ways.

During the 1870s the Grant and Hayes administrations began to reconnoiter for trade opportunities through inquiries of resident consuls and special envoys. In 1881 Secretary Blaine issued invitations for a hemispheric conference at Washington, ostensibly to consider ways of helping Chile and Peru to end the War of the Pacific but (as Blaine explained somewhat later) actually intended to encourage hemispheric trade. Since he did not issue the invitations until his chief, Garfield, was dead and he had agreed to leave office, one may well suspect that his chief purpose was to curry favor with market-seeking businessmen for the presidential campaign of 1884. In any case Arthur and Frelinghuysen, unwilling to attempt a hemispheric program, withdrew the invitations and concentrated their efforts on reciprocity in the Caribbean and support for the isthmian canal project.

The only effort of the Arthur administration to improve economic relations with southern South America was an investigating commission to determine the possible value of a hemispheric conference. Although appointed too late in the administration to have any immediate consequence, the commission's voluminous reports aroused much interest among trade expansionists and gave greater precision to their discussion of Latin American markets. Bipartisan support for a hemispheric conference grew in Congress during the first Cleveland administration, although the President himself was never enthusiastic about a proposal identified with Blaine and the Republicans. Nevertheless, he approved an enabling bill just before leaving office, with the result that when Blaine returned to the State Department in 1889, he found his conference plan just where he had left it in 1881—invitations issued and advance publicity begun in the American press.

The inter-American conference of 1889–90 was a partial success, no thanks to the subtlety or diplomatic skill of Americans. Blaine made its commercial orientation immediately apparent by appointing mainly businessmen to the American delegation and by subjecting the Latin American diplomats to an exhausting six-week tour of American cities, replete with factory visits and banquet eulogies. When the meetings finally began, the Secretary discovered that he had to face the determined opposition of Argentina and Chile, two countries whose economies and culture were interlocked with Europe and whose representatives resented American pretensions to hemispheric leadership.

As a result, the conference accomplished less than Blaine had hoped. The American delegation proposed a *Zollverein* but had to settle for a vague resolution recommending reciprocity agreements. The plan for a common silver coin divided the American delegation itself into monometallic and bimetallic factions. The Argentines would not even approve a resolution recommending common use of the metric system, although they and most other hemispheric nations had long ago adopted it. In the end, the Americans obtained approval for a plan to construct an inter-American railroad (never completed) and, more important, for the establishment of a permanent "International Union of the American Republics," with headquarters at Washington, to issue information and publicity and prepare for a possible future conference. This was the germ of the Pan-American Union and later the Organization of American States.

A powerful reason for Latin American suspicions at the conference was the simultaneous ill-timed Congressional debate over the protectionist McKinley tariff. As has been seen, through the power to impose retaliatory duties Congress gave Harrison and Blaine limited leverage for reciprocity negotiations. One of the most important resulting agreements was one with Brazil, which encouraged American exports during its brief life. Blaine did not manage to negotiate an agreement with any other nation of southern South America. What little good the conference and the Brazilian reciprocity agreement did for the inter-American trade relations was largely offset by an American confrontation with Chile in 1891 over the killing of two American sailors on shore leave from the visiting cruiser *Baltimore*. The wholly unnecessary crisis that resulted reestablished the American image as *"el coloso del Norte."* While the early work of the Bureau of American Republics in the 1890s offered promise for the future, American trade with South America continued to lag far behind that of Britain.

As in the case of Latin America, the consistency and success of American economic policies in the Pacific basin varied in inverse proportion to the distance of their application from American shores. Despite the unpopularity of the Johnson administration and the pressure of Reconstruction problems, Seward was able, in 1867, to take advantage of a Russian offer to sell Alaska, thereby extending American territorial control along the "great circle" route to Asia, which had figured prominently in his rhetoric of economic expansion during the preceding two decades.

Among the battery of arguments that he, Charles Sumner, and other supporters used in the purchase debates, trade with the Golden East and the untapped resources of Alaska itself figured prominently. Since the newly acquired territory lay far from the arenas of international power struggles and the United States was not yet prepared to develop it, the purchase of Alaska did not involve much further diplomacy. Nevertheless the persistent, if awkward, American attack on Canadian pelagic sealing in the Bering Sea during the late 1880s and the 1890s demonstrated that the United States would maintain a strong diplomatic position in the Northwest as it began to exploit Alaskan resources.

The American government and people used other expedients to establish politico-economic influence in the Hawaiian Islands. Like Alaska these formed a noncontiguous outpost on the mid-nineteenth-century American horizon. By the 1860s a colony of American missionaries and small businessmen inhabited the principal islands, advising the easy-going native government (and sometimes holding office in it) and carrying on a varied trade with other islands and California. During and immediately after the Civil War sugar culture got a hold on the Hawaiian economy, and Americans were numbered among the planters. Entrepreneurs both in the islands and on the mainland realized the opportunities to be created by a reciprocity treaty, which would guarantee a market in California for Hawaiian sugar while further Americanizing the islands through the import of manufactures from the east coast. Overcoming protectionist objections with arguments that combined trade, strategy, and an early notion of "informal empire," the supporters of reciprocity obtained the adoption in 1875 of a treaty similar in provisions to the later ones with Mexico and Spain that have already been described.

The effects of the Hawaiian reciprocity treaty were immediate and startling—a sharp increase in sugar culture on the islands, in American land ownership, and in trade with the United States. The chief beneficiary was a German-American merchant, Claus Spreckels, who bought up fertile but undeveloped Hawaiian estates, irrigated and planted them, and organized a merchandising network, with refineries in California and a steamship line to connect the parts of his "empire." His success and the chronic opposition of protectionists in the United States stimulated almost unceasing attacks on the 1875 treaty, but the Cleveland administration managed to obtain its renewal in 1887, with the additional reluctant Hawaiian concession (added to win votes in the Senate) that the United States might create a coaling station for its warships in the protected lagoons at the mouth of the Pearl River, near Honolulu. (However, the Navy did not remove the coral reef at the entrance to Pearl Harbor until after 1898.)

The climax of a half-century trend toward ever closer relations was the Hawaiian revolution of 1893. When a newly crowned nationalist queen tried to reverse course into anti-Americanism and increased dependence on European advisers, an already organized clique of American-born annexationists, most of them businessmen or landowners, overthrew the royal regime, founded a republic on American lines, and proposed to join the Union. The Harrison administration, which had been following Hawaiian affairs closely for years and had given tacit encouragement to the annexationists, gladly negotiated a treaty of admission but had to leave office before the Senate could approve it. As he had in 1885 with Arthur's reciprocity and canal treaties, Cleveland now withdrew the annexation treaty from the Senate and, suspecting the contrived nature of the revolution, left the Hawaiian Republic in limbo. There it remained until 1898, when the events of the Spanish American War emphasized the value of the islands and enabled McKinley to carry through Hawaiian annexation.

While the increase of American trade and investments in Hawaii contributed to eventual annexation, the same was not true for territories in the south and west Pacific. After the Pacific Mail scandal of 1874 it was difficult even to maintain regular steamer connections. The staple product of most islands, copra, found little demand in the United States, and although the people of Australia and New Zealand were receptive to American products, the merchants of New York, Boston, and Philadelphia did not think it worthwhile to develop such a distant market. Thus, for example, when the prime minister of New South Wales visited the

United States in 1882 to drum up interest in a steamship subsidy and a reciprocity treaty, he obtained only a polite hearing.

Nevertheless, and for reasons that defy a rational explanation, the United States became involved in an international power contest for influence in the Samoan islands, two thousand miles south of Hawaii, that lasted from the mid-1870s to 1899. It is true that an American trading company with some government connections tried to publicize Samoan opportunities in the early 1870s, but it was no more reputable than the just-exposed Dominican venture and soon disappeared from the scene. It is also true that American Navy officers came to value the protected anchorage of Pago Pago as a coaling station, but it lay far from the direct or even commonly traveled routes to the Far East, and after obtaining a lease to the ground around the harbor, the Navy seldom sent a ship there.

Whether from national pride, momentum, or merely absence of mind, five successive administrations participated more and more closely in Samoan affairs. First the State Department allowed American consuls to compete with those of Britain and Germany in backing rival native cliques. In the late 1880s all three powers sent naval detachments to outface each other, and when most of these were destroyed by a hurricane, the chastened powers set up a condominium or joint protectorate to introduce the natives to the machinery of civilization. American supporters of the government's Samoan policies meanwhile defended them with rhetoric which unintentionally parodied the rationalization of economic expansionism elsewhere. Finally, in 1899, all else having failed, the United States and Germany divided the islands, Britain received compensation elsewhere, and American Samoa sank into near-oblivion.

It was, of course, the unquenchable hope for large-scale trade with the Far East that drew American ships and merchants into the vast reaches of the Pacific beyond Honolulu. The lure of the golden Orient also figured prominently in the motives for transcontinental railroad building. As an export journalist put it in 1881: "No greater field for commercial enterprise can be found than that offered in the vast and undeveloped markets of China for our manufacturers and farmers. . . . The spirit of the age has entered this vast empire, and it stands upon the threshold of the New World and offers to America the greater share of a trade which has enriched every community which has been able to command it."[31] Publicists calculated the potential Chinese customers at 400,000,000, overlooking the facts that many lived in the inaccessible interior and few had much purchasing power. During the 1870s and 1880s a dynamic Japanese market was added to the Chinese, and railroad and other promoters began to draw up development projects in East Asia for which they proposed to use American capital.

These optimistic expectations were not wholly without factual basis, for during the middle decades of the nineteenth century a number of American commission houses had done a flourishing trade in the principal Chinese ports against the competition of more powerful British firms. For a brief time American ships had even dominated the oriental carrying trade until the decline of the merchant marine during the 1860s and 1870s. Also, the generally xenophobic Chinese seemed to regard Americans with more favor than other foreigners because they had little or no ambition for political rule in Asia.

Nevertheless, the obstacles to large-scale trade were always greater than expansionists realized: Chinese reluctance to adopt new ways and products, communication over long distances, the attractiveness of markets closer to home, and the familiar competition of the well-organized British, with their financial strength, their merchant marine, and their reliable government support. American missionaries proved a mixed blessing to trade, for, while they introduced the Chinese to American comforts and served as interpreters, they also infuriated Chinese conservatives by their cultural challenge. Against these and other hindrances American merchants managed to establish growing markets for kerosene, a few types of cheap cotton cloth, and other less important exports, receiving in return mainly tea and silk. The same was true for Japan. As in the case of most Latin America, the United States consistently imported more from the Far East than it exported thence and thereby complicated its world exchange problems.

Before the 1890s the United States government did little to support its merchants in the Far East. From the beginning of relations with China and Japan, American policymakers had favored cooperation with Britain and other foreign governments to maintain equal access to oriental markets (later called the "open door" policy). Since the United States was unwilling to maintain a strong naval detachment off the Asiatic coast, it had to rely on British power in a crisis, and when the Chinese government overtaxed foreign trade or Chinese xenophobes maltreated foreign residents, some American protests were mere echoes. Because Chinese and Japanese officials usually respected American integrity, a skilled minister or consul might improve the position of his countrymen or of foreigners in general by well-placed advice. However, the only important overt American action in support of trade between 1865 and the early 1890s was a mission to negotiate a commercial treaty with Korea in 1882 and open that country to Western trade.

During the 1890s several factors began to change these unpromising circumstances. In the Sino-Japanese War of 1894–95 China suffered an unexpectedly humiliating defeat. As a result, the Chinese government became somewhat more receptive to Western plans for modernization. At the same time the European Powers whose lands bordered China or whose merchants had invaded the Chinese market—Russia, France, Germany, and Britain—laid out "spheres of influence," where their trade and investments would be uppermost, in the expectation that when the Chinese Empire collapsed altogether, they would establish some form of political rule in these spheres. At the same time the intensification of American economic expansionism during and after the depression years of the mid-1890s produced a series of railroad and other investment projects intended to develop backward China and a noticeable increase in American exports to China and Japan from about $8,000,000 in 1890 to about $30,000,000 in 1898.[32]

Thus, at the moment of China's greatest apparent danger, the American stake in the Far East seemed to be expanding. By chance, the American minister at Peking during and after the Sino-Japanese War was Charles Denby, a one-time lawyer for American railroad companies and an enthusiastic economic expansionist who hoped to see Americans assume their rightful position in Chinese trade and development and thus retard or prevent the breakup of the Empire. As has been seen, during Cleveland's second administration the State Department relaxed its restrictions on diplomatic activity enough to allow Denby to give cautious support to the newly arrived promoters. Unfortunately Americans did not yet command sufficient capital backing to compete on equal terms with the Europeans; by 1898 they had won only one important concession. Also the McKinley administration replaced Denby with a more conventional minister.

At the outbreak of the Spanish American War American relations with the Far East seemed faltering and disorganized. Actually, however, the bases of traditional American policy remained as strong as ever. This policy was to cooperate with the European Powers (and now too Japan) in maintaining equal commercial access to the Chinese market and a reasonable amount of Chinese independence from foreign political control—but without becoming militarily involved. In February 1898, Britain, much concerned about rival spheres of influence in China, put out a private overture for renewed cooperation to maintain free access. Pressed by the Cuban crisis, McKinley had to decline, but he did not reject the general principle. After the war was over, the British suggestion fused with earlier American policy in the open-door notes of John Hay.

In the remainder of the settled world, the Near East, India, and Africa, America's trade and investments were insignificant, and so, for the most part, was its diplomacy, overshadowed by European imperialism. In Turkey and Persia the duties of American ministers and consuls were generally limited to securing protection for American residents or registering damage claims. Along the hundreds of miles of African coastline Yankee merchants continued the prosperous trade they had begun early in the nineteenth century, selling a great variety of exports. During the 1870s and 1880s they developed a considerable market for kerosene, and in Zanzibar and Madagascar cotton goods also sold well through most of the century—in the latter case until France established a colony and tariff walls in the mid-1890s. The best market on the continent proved to be that of South Africa, where a white population and booming mines created trade opportunities rather like those of Canada or the American West. Nevertheless, American exports to Cape Colony and the interior Boer republics ran a distant second to those of Britain.

Despite Commodore Robert W. Shufeldt's promising commercial reconnaissance of 1878–80, the State Department showed little interest in encouraging trade with Africa during the period. An exception was its brief involvement in the Congo question between 1883 and 1885, resulting largely from the deft publicity of the Anglo-American explorer Henry M. Stanley, who put together missionary zeal and commercial profits in an enticing mixture. The Arthur administration even sent a delegation to participate in the Berlin West African Conference of 1884, which laid down international policies for trade and navigation in the Congo basin, but thereafter the United States remained a distant observer. A few Americans were interested in Liberia—not so much for its trade as for sympathy with the transplanted American blacks who had organized its government and society—and the State Department occasionally reflected this interest by tactfully warning Britain and France not to encroach on the young nation's borders. But even the trade opportunities of South Africa elicited no active diplomacy except a brief flurry over the arrest of American mining engineers for involvement in the Jameson raid of 1895–96.

This regional survey of American economic interests and diplomacy between 1860 and 1898 is enough to demonstrate that motivations arising from trade and investment—or the hope of either—were rarely absent from American foreign relations. At the same time it suggests that they did not frequently dominate the decisions of policy makers. Opportunities for economic expansion existed; on occasion, as in Hawaii, Americans seized and fulfilled them. But even in the 1890s the prerequisites for consistent, pervasive expansionism did not yet exist. The United States economy had not developed to a point at which it produced a large surplus of industrial products others wanted. Except in a few cases it lacked the financial, shipping, and distribution networks necessary for major overseas sales. Finally, the political climate in the

United States did not favor the commitment to a larger global role
which Americans would begin to accept by World War I.

THE ECONOMIC BACKGROUND OF THE
SPANISH AMERICAN WAR

No account of the period from 1861 to 1898 would be complete
without at least brief consideration of the role played by economics among the varied causes of the Spanish American War. Evidence already presented establishes that a growing interest in foreign markets during the late 1880s and 1890s created a background
or atmosphere—pronounced if not uniform or consistent—which
encouraged Americans to play a greater role in international affairs, especially in those of the western hemisphere. Beyond this
general influence, how did economic considerations help to shape
events and decisions between the outbreak of the Cuban revolution in 1895 and the declaration of war against Spain in April
1898?

     One sector of relevant economic opinion pertained to those
with property, investments, or trade in Cuba. Some owners of
sugar lands, led by one of the largest, Edwin Atkins, despised the
rebels as riffraff, warned the State Department against recognizing their belligerency, and urged support or at least understanding
for Spain, which, they hoped, would protect their property and
restore peace. Not all Americans in Cuba shared this unfavorable
view of the rebels, and some engaged in sugar growing, tobacco
marketing, and iron mining criticized the Spanish government for
restricting their efforts to carry on business as usual. As the months
passed, the neutralism of Atkins and his associates became converted into a general desire for American intervention, provided
that it led to annexation, not independence. The last thing most
Americans wanted was government by radical riffraff.

     Outside Cuba itself some Americans had a direct economic
stake in the revolution rising from other sources. The most inter-

esting of these was a New York syndicate founded by John J. McCook, a corporation lawyer (who had already gone concession-hunting in China with little success), and Samuel M. Janney, partner of a Wall Street banking firm. This syndicate signed a contract with Tomás Estrada Palma of the Cuban revolutionary junta in New York to market 150,000,000 Cuban pesos worth of 4 percent bonds of the Cuban Republic, to be secured by customs receipts and (it was hoped) serviced under the trusteeship of the United States government. McCook and Janney tried to interest McKinley in this sponsorship and in a plan for purchasing the independence of Cuba, but without success. Their interest in American intervention is clearer than their influence.

Historians have disagreed most widely concerning the attitude of the majority of American businessmen, who had no direct interest in Cuban property, trade, or finance but who were anxious for the continued recovery of the American economy from the hard times of the mid-1890s and who may have had other, non-economic reasons for favoring or opposing intervention. Left-wing writers of the late 1920s and early 1930s tended to use the war as an illustration of the Marxist-described imperialist phase of capitalism and assumed that "monolithic" business opinion favored intervention throughout. In 1936, however, Julius Pratt demonstrated that the stock market and other indices of business conditions usually declined at every rumor of approaching war. He concluded not only that businessmen with direct interests in Cuba were divided but that "the overwhelming preponderance of general business opinion" opposed intervention.[33]

Further research since the appearance of Pratt's judgment has disclosed so many opinions on intervention and war as to suggest that business was never "monolithic" on the subject at any time before the declaration of war. As early as 1896 Collis P. Huntington, Chauncey M. Depew, Alonzo B. Hepburn, a variety of commercial clubs, and other leaders and associations expressed sympathy for the Cuban rebels. Edward F. Cragin, promoter of the recently organized Nicaragua Canal Company, urged support for them. In May 1897, almost a year before the decision for war, about three hundred merchants, steamship lines, and related businessmen petitioned the McKinley administration for action of some sort, pointing out that in two years the annual American-Cuban trade had dwindled from over $100,000,000 to about $37,000,000. While this evidence does not prove the existence of an unmistakable push for war, it surely establishes an impatience with the situation that had developed.

This impatience grew rapidly into a public desire for intervention during the winter and early spring of 1897–98. In January rioting in Havana showed that Spain was losing its grip; then an insulting letter from the Spanish minister, Enrique Dupuy De Lôme, well publicized in the United States, suggested that Spain's gestures toward reform were merely a cynical sham. The sinking of the battleship *Maine* in Havana harbor under mysterious circumstances impossible to clarify immediately raised a fire storm of American rage. Finally, an eyewitness report by a conservative Senator, Redfield Proctor, on conditions in Cuba impressed on Americans the hopelessness of the stalemate.

Without actually contradicting Julius Pratt, Walter LaFeber has offered a plausible explanation of business reactions to these events. While conceding a continuing strong current of antiwar opinion in the New York commercial journals, LaFeber feels that they spoke for the less important members of the business community. Those with interests in Cuban trade were faced with ruin. Annexationists were convinced that Spain would not surrender her sovereignty on American terms without war. Most important, to major business leaders the everlasting Cuban rebellion was no longer merely a chronic nuisance but an active threat to the American economy, now recovering from the depression of the mid-1890s. As always, the health of that economy depended to a large degree on private business decisions and was highly susceptible to uncertainty. For years business leaders had feared the disruptions that war would create. Now these were beginning to seem less dangerous than indefinite suspense.

By the third week of March pressure for an American solution to the Cuban question was becoming hard to resist. Henry Cabot Lodge reported that according to "the most conservative classes" in Massachusetts, "one shock and then the end was better than a succession of spasms" as the rebellion continued. Finally, on March 25, W. C. Reick, city editor of the *New York Herald* and "a trusted political adviser" of McKinley, telegraphed the President: "Big corporations here now believe we will have war. Believe all would welcome it as a relief to suspense." This, says LaFeber, was "perhaps the most influential note the President received that week." Two days later he presented an ultimatum to Spain, and on April 11, after two weeks of further hardening, he sent a war message to Congress.[34]

In other words, McKinley acted, not in response to an overwhelming business demand for intervention but after hearing a few well-placed words reporting a conservative feeling that "enough was enough"—and all the more impressive for being on the right wing of business sentiment. These well-placed words served to remove a constraint upon McKinley, who, as most agree, would have undertaken nothing of which business leaders openly disapproved. Knowing that these leaders did not oppose intervention, he could then make up his mind on the basis of all the political, economic, social, and humanitarian factors involved.

This interpretation does not deny the strength of other forces working on McKinley: humanitarian sympathy with the Cubans' plight, outrage at the sinking of the *Maine*, public (as distinguished from business) demand for action, and the danger of a party split in the fall elections. It does suggest a noncommittal answer to the question of economic causes of the war. If it was not a "businessman's war," neither was it a war that the most important business leaders opposed.

The effects of the Spanish-American War have caused almost as much argument among historians as its causes. In general, writers are divided between those who emphasize the continuity of established policies and those who regard the war primarily as the point of departure for new policies.[35] This review of the period between 1861 and 1898 would seem to suggest that the most reasonable interpretation is a compromise between the two. By the late 1890s American trade had expanded in many parts of the world, and Americans had invested hundreds of millions of dollars in Canada, Cuba, Mexico, and Hawaii. A series of diplomatic episodes in the 1890s had been tied to these business ventures by publicists with arguments of varying plausibility, and expansionist Congressmen and journalists were preparing the public for further economic-inspired commitments in such areas as Central America and Hawaii.

It is impossible to believe that this extension of trade and investments would not have continued without the war. How fast and where it would have led Americans and their government will never be known. What the war did was to accelerate and somewhat redirect the process. In the Caribbean the conquest of Cuba and the annexation of Puerto Rico eventually helped to encourage outright protectorates over other nations, while speeding the construction of an isthmian canal. In the Far East the acquisition of the Philippines stimulated a desire for commerce and increased strategic and humanitarian concerns. Thus the war altered the course of American economic expansion, but in a larger sense it was also the climax of a long if uneven process begun much earlier in the century.

Notes

1. Quoted in Charles M. Wiltse, *John C. Calhoun, Nationalist, 1782–1823* (Indianapolis: Bobbs-Merrill, 1944), p. 133.

2. Percentages are compiled from statistics in U.S. Bureau of the Census, *Historical Statistics of the United States, Colonial Times to 1970,* 2 vols. (Washington, D.C.: GPO, 1975), 1:8, 224, 512, 590, 592–94; 2:693–94; and Edward G. Kirkland, *Industry Comes of Age: Business, Labor, and Public Policy, 1860–1897* (New York: Holt, 1961), pp. 52, 164, 400.

3. Computed from statistics in Ross J. S. Hoffman, *Great Britain and the German Trade Rivalry, 1875–1914* (Philadelphia: University of Pennsylvania Press, 1933), p. 7. The statistics come from British official sources.

4. W. Arthur Lewis, "International Economics: International Competition in Manufactures," *American Economic Review* (May 1957), 47:579.

5. The various estimates are cited and discussed in P. L. Cottrell, *British Overseas Investment in the Nineteenth Century* (London: Humanities Press, 1975), pp. 11–15. For estimates of American investments see Cleona Lewis, *America's Stake in International Investments* (Washington, D.C., 1938; reprint, Arno, 1976), Appendix D.

6. Computed from statistics in Hoffman, *Britain and the German Trade Rivalry*, p. 10, n. 16.

7. *Historical Statistics*, 2:903–04, 906–07. Emory R. Johnson et al., *History of Domestic and Foreign Commerce of the United States*, 2 vols. (Washington, D.C., 1915), 2:66–68, 76–78.

8. David A. Wells, *Freer Trade Essential to Future National Prosperity and Development* (New York, 1882), p. 28.

9. Edward Atkinson, *Address . . . on the Export of Cotton Goods, at the Meeting of the New England Cotton Manufacturers Association, April 26, 1876* (n.p., 1876), p. 11.

10. Quoted in Ernest N. Paolino, *The Foundations of the American Empire: William Henry Seward and U.S. Foreign Poilcy* (Ithaca, N.Y.: Cornell University Press, 1973), p. 40. For other examples of Seward's rhetoric see ch. 2 and *passim*.

11. U.S. Department of State, *Commercial Relations of the United States with Foreign Countries* (Washington, D.C.: GPO, 1856–1914), *1879–1880*, 1:193.

12. McCulloch is quoted in William Appleman Williams, *The Roots of the Modern American Empire: A Study of the Growth and Shaping of Social Consciousness in a Marketplace Society* (New York: Random House, 1969), p. 250.

13. *Boston Journal*, November 21, 1890, reprinted in *Public Opinion*, 10:173.

14. Walter LaFeber, *The New Empire: An Interpretation of American Expansion, 1860–1898* (Ithaca, N.Y.: Cornell University Press, 1963), p. 412. See also William A. Williams, *The Tragedy of American Diplomacy*, rev. ed. (New York: World, 1962) pp. 18–28, and *The Roots of the Modern American Empire*.

15. Paul S. Holbo, "Economics, Emotion, and Expansion: An Emerging Foreign Policy," in H. Wayne Morgan, ed., *The Gilded Age*, rev. ed. (Syracuse: Syracuse University Press, 1970), pp. 200–01.

16. *Congressional Record*, 48th Cong., 2d sess., 16:509.

17. Quoted in Edward L. Younger, *John A. Kasson: Politics and Diplomacy from Lincoln to McKinley* (Iowa City: University of Iowa Press, 1955), pp. 281–82.

18. Richard Olney to Charles Denby, December 19, 1896. No. 1376. U.S. *Papers Relating to the Foreign Relations of the United States* (Washington, D.C., 1862–), 1897, p. 56.

19. Edward Stanwood, *American Tariff Controversies in the Nineteenth Century*, 2 vols. (Boston: Houghton, Mifflin, 1903; reprint; New York, Russell and Russell, 1967), 2:132.

20. *Congressional Record*, 47th Cong., 1st sess., 13:2106–7, 2110.

21. The term "reciprocity" as applied in the last half of the nineteenth century should be distinguished from its earlier use, mentioned in the preceding essay. When publicists of the 1820s and 1830s wrote of reciprocity, they meant a general abstention by two countries from discriminatory acts or measures against each other's commerce and navigation.

22. Justin S. Morrill to [C. W.] Sheldon, November 27, 1884. Draft in Justin S. Morrill papers, 34. Library of Congress. James M. Swank is quoted in *Bradstreet's* (January 3, 1885), 11:1.

23. Quoted in Walter T. K. Nugent, *Money and American Society, 1856–1880* (New York: Free Press, 1968), p. 190.

24. Quoted in *ibid.*, p. 74.

25. U.S., 49th Cong., 1st sess., *Senate Report 941*, p. 64.

26. James Douglas Jerrold Kelley, *The Question of Ships: The Navy and the Merchant Marine* (New York, 1884), p. 109.

27. Robert W. Shufeldt, *The Relation of the Navy to the Commerce of the United States, March 23, 1878* (Washington, D. C., 1878), p. 6.

28. Quoted in Paolino, *Foundations of the American Empire*, p. 27.

29. Trade percentages computed from figures in *Historical Statistics*, 2:903, 906. Investment percentages computed from statistics in Lewis, *America's Stake in International Investments*, p. 606.

30. James D. Richardson, *A Compilation of the Messages and Papers of the President, 1789–1897*, 10 vols. (Washington D.C., 1898), 7:585.

31. *American Exporter* (May 1881), 7:37.

32. *Historical Statistics*, 2:903–04.

33. Julius W. Pratt, *Expansionists of 1898: The Acquisition of Hawaii and the Spanish Islands* (Baltimore: Johns Hopkins University Press, 1936), p. 252.

34. LaFeber, *The New Empire*, pp. 383–93, 403–06.

35. A few historians belong to neither group, such as those who set the beginning of the "new" American foreign relations at about 1890. See, for example, Robert Beisner, *From the Old Diplomacy to the New, 1865–1900* (New York: Harlan Davidson, 1975).

1899–1920
America Adjusts
to World Power

William H. Becker

George Washington University

BETWEEN 1899 AND 1920 American diplomacy faced two major adjustments. After the Spanish-American War, the United States expanded its role in international affairs, and after World War I the United States needed to take greater responsibility for the international balance of power and the management of the international economy.

The goals of United States diplomacy in the nineteenth century had been relatively clear cut: minimizing the influence of foreign powers near the United States and the expansion of American sovereignty over the continent. American means to achieve these goals were limited. But small diplomatic and military establishments served American purposes well enough because the United States was protected by its oceans and the relative effectiveness of the European balance-of-power system.

The Spanish-American War, and especially the acquisition of the Philippines, forced American foreign policy into new channels. The United States involved itself in the politics of Asia, a guerrilla war, and colonial administration all in the matter of a few years. Enhanced foreign responsibilites provided further arguments in support of professionalizing and expanding the Department of State and the diplomatic and consular service abroad. Mismanagement of the war with Spain led to studies of the organization of the Department of War. The resulting reorganization in the early years of the century enhanced America's ability to plan for military contingencies.[1]

During these same years, American industrial corporations and banks continued to expand their activities abroad. By 1914 American exports of manufactured goods and direct investment capital affected foreign competitors and, at times, foreign economies and even governments. While a few major corporations dominated the field for foreign sales and investments, interest in expanding foreign markets agitated vocal and well-organized groups of smaller businessmen too.

Significant diplomatic and bureaucratic changes were thus occurring simultaneously in the first two decades of this century. Economic change interacted with, and influenced and was influenced by, these other developments. What, then, was the role of economics in American diplomacy between 1899 and 1920? In what ways did economic change affect how policy makers conceived American interests abroad; how did economic changes influence the conduct of American diplomacy; and to what extent did industrialists and bankers influence American policy-making bureaucracies?

Economic considerations influenced McKinley, Roosevelt, Taft, and Wilson in both the conception of the national interest and in the tactics that they used to protect what they saw to be American interests. In these years, manufacturers and bankers increased contacts with Congressional committees and govermental departments charged with responsibility for issues affecting foreign economic policy. Yet at the highest policy-making levels economic interests were not generally the primary consideration in the conduct of foreign policy. Economic concerns were only part of a larger diplomatic and domestic political context that influenced the conception, formulation, and conduct of American diplomacy. To be sure, some administrators gave more time to economic considerations than others. But even the "dollar diplomatists," William Howard Taft and Philander Knox, thought of economic interests and tactics as part of a larger strategic and political context.

Private business interest groups and economic considerations had a greater impact on the middle-level bureaucracy concerned with American foreign activities. Indeed, bureaucrats in the Departments of State, Treasury, and Commerce exhibited the most sustained and systematic interest in promoting American trade and investment abroad. The same could be said of officials at the Federal Trade Commission and the U.S. Shipping Board. After the world war middle-level bureaucrats (assistant secretaries and the like) were among those Americans with the clearest understanding of America's new international economic responsibilities. The war had weakened Britain's dominant position in the world economy. It loosened the control her banks, insurance firms, shipping companies, and commercial middlemen had on the international economic system. These American officials, joined by some members of Congress and some of America's leading industrialists and bankers, advocated foreign economic policies that would have allowed the United States to take up where Britain no longer seemed able to manage alone.

BUSINESS, GOVERNMENT, AND FOREIGN MARKETS

To assess the impact of economic change on American diplomacy between 1899 and 1920, one needs to understand the extent and importance of American economic activity abroad, as well as which businessmen and bankers were most involved in foreign economic activity. Who, in short, was engaged in foreign markets? What were the divisions in business opinion about foreign markets, and what were businessmen's general attitudes toward increasing government assistance to gain foreign sales and investments?

Clearly, the United States was becoming more important

economically in the 1890s. By 1913 America alone accounted for one-third of the world's industrial production. In the mid-1890s the United States enlarged its role in world commerce, as American businessmen began to increase exports of manufactured products. In 1890 the United States had only 3.9 percent of the world's trade in manufactures. By 1898 it had jumped to 9.8, increasing to 11.0 percent in 1913.[2]

The growth of American manufactured exports was confined to several leading industry groups, some of which had captured significant proportions of the world market for their products. In 1913, 69 percent of America's manufactured exports were made up of manufactures of processed food, metals, and machinery. In that same year, the United States accounted for about 25 percent of the international sales of metals; about 25 percent of machinery sales; and 20 percent of transportation equipment. As impressive as American performance was, these three industrial areas were nevertheless the fastest growing industries in world exports of manufactured goods. American producers of these goods, in short, were part of a significant international expansion of industrial activity.[3]

The American manufactured export expansion was directed toward a few geographical areas. American businesses' goods were exported primarily into Western Europe and Canada, with 69 percent of American manufactured exports going to these traditional American markets between 1910 and 1914. Only 13 percent of manufactured exports found their way to Latin America, most to Mexico.[4]

Before 1914 government played little part in the export expansion of that relatively small number of industrial groups dominating American export of manufactures. During the conflict war-related government policies inevitably influenced, even at times determined, foreign trade and investment decisions. Nevertheless the most successful manufacturers had gained their overseas markets before the war and, in large part, because of economic advantages based on the mastery of new technology and the creation of extensive overseas marketing systems.

The manufacturers who dominated overseas sales were those who had most profited from the dynamism of the domestic

American market. Indeed the growth of overseas trade and investment was surpassed by advances in the domestic economy. The vast American market grew as the gross national product (GNP) increased, per capita income rose, and rates of capital formation accelerated between 1865 and 1914. A telling example of the strength of the American economy is that the years of rapid export expansion were also years in which imports were declining. As a percentage of the consumption of manufactured goods, imports fell from 14.0 percent in 1869 to 5.9 percent in 1909.[5]

Many of these firms had developed mass production and mass distribution techniques to take advantage of America's growing economy. The largest stake in manufactured export markets rested with giant firms, the big businesses of the day. Markets were also developed by smaller producers who manufactured highly specialized goods, especially machinery. Not every large firm, however, moved easily into the international economy. The successful firms were the ones that were able to devote resources to large marketing operations overseas, as well as to high speed, capital intensive manufacturing domestically, investments which gave them great cost advantages. In many cases, too, these firms had made technological breakthroughs which led to new products that readily dominated sales in overseas markets. Giant firms like Westinghouse, General Electric, International Harvester, American Standard, Singer Sewing Machine, U. S. Steel, Baldwin Locomotive, Allis Chalmers, Kodak, Standard Oil, and others easily gained entrance to markets abroad. Their largest markets were in Europe and Canada, in economies similar to America's in terms of income and demand structure. Some smaller producers—such as the makers of machine tools and shoe, textile, and print machinery—found ready markets for their specialized equipment there too. In 1913, 81 percent of manufactured exports come from industry groups (processed foods, metals manufacture, machinery, petroleum, textiles, chemicals, transport equipment) that, with the exception of textiles, were marked by the highest levels of concentration or oligopoly in American industry. These industry groups had, on the basis of 1909 assets, 67 of the 100 largest corporations in America.[6]

These economic advantages made it unlikely the largest

firms would turn to government for assistance. For the most part the largest firms relied on their own marketing staffs abroad to represent them and to provide home offices with information about changing political conditions, new markets, and potential competition. They built assembly plants and factories abroad in order to circumvent foreign tariffs. Often they blunted foreign nationalistic criticisms of American firms by staffing sales operations with foreign nationals. Similarly, they were as apt to resolve foreign disputes by dealing directly with foreign officials as to turn to American consular officers as intermediaries.[7]

Nevertheless, government policy affected their businesses and the largest producers formed a National Foreign Trade Council in 1913 to make their views known to government, especially about what they saw as hindrances in the antitrust laws and the faltering American merchant marine.[8]

Most smaller producers who sought foreign markets were without the substantial technological, capital, or marketing advantages of the largest corporations. Nevertheless, during the depression of the 1890s many of these producers had concluded that foreign markets would serve as a safety valve against the loss of sales during a depression. To others, export markets would be a permanent solution to what they perceived as a long-term problem of surplus production, at acceptable prices, of a glutted market for their goods. The producers of textiles, clothing, hardware, cordage, paper, enamelware, wallpaper, etc. found it difficult to sell abroad. Their homogeneous goods resembled fairly cheap and similar products made in other industrial countries, especially Germany and Britain. Until the depression of the 1890s, most of these American producers could not sell abroad because of lower British and German prices. The American economic crisis of the 1890s, however, opened foreign markets because of unusually depressed prices in the United States. With the return of prosperity, prices rose, domestic demand returned, and those smaller firms which sold abroad either dropped out of foreign markets or reduced their efforts considerably.

Thus, in good times when prices and demand were increasing, most of these smaller producers could not compete with

European producers in their home territories, as some of the largest American manufacturers could. Smaller manufacturers looked toward Latin America as a promising market, since transportation costs from the United States could at times somewhat offset the American price disadvantage with European producers. Others saw the vast China market as an excellent possibility.

The smallest producers showed the liveliest interest in government assistance. They wanted information about foreign markets and policies to help attain and protect them. Although economically less significant than the major producers, market-seeking smaller manufacturers were more numerous and hence potentially more significant electorally than the big business corporations. They organized into vocal and at times effective lobbying groups. Such trade associations of smaller producers as the National Association of Manufacturers, American Manufacturers Export Association, and the Chamber of Commerce, as well as special interest groups devoted to one issue (reciprocity tariff agreements, consular reform, improvement of the merchant marine), were able to make their views known in Washington, although getting appropriate legislation was difficult. There were numerous conflicting interests, and the Congress itself, while paying lip-service to rhetoric about market expansion was not willing to incur the political costs of adopting policies some of the market-seeking producers wanted. The Congress resisted changes in the tariff because conventional political wisdom taught that tariff debates only lost votes. Congressmen refused to bring the consular service into the Civil Service for fear of losing patronage slots. Likewise, changes in merchant marine and antitrust laws were "no-win" from the point of view of many members of Congress. Improvements in the merchant marine would have required unpopular subsidies. Easing the antitrust laws—even to help smaller manufacturers to combine to sell abroad—appeared politically dangerous in the face of public hostility to business combinations.

But the market-seeking smaller producers were vocal and persistent. They gained some support in the Congress and the bureaucracy for their ideas of what policies needed alteration. Changes did not come easily, but market-seeking producers were able to influence legislation toward the Department of State's consular service, although it took a presidential executive order in 1906 to take consular appointments out of the patronage system. Foreign branch banking was allowed in the Federal Reserve legislation of 1913, and as amended in 1916. But the tariff was never in this period altered to their satisfaction, and changes in merchant marine policy and the antitrust laws (Webb-Pomerene, 1916) occurred only during World War I when they could be tied to important wartime goals.[9]

Despite difficulties in getting legislation from Congress, the bureaucracy was more cooperative. The Department of State responded positively to those businessmen interested in trade expansion. Since the 1870s State had provided information about foreign conditions and foreign commerce. By 1900 the department's informational services had expanded markedly. The need for information about trade possibilities and economic conditions abroad focused attention on the department's consular officials. The consular service was almost as old as the Republic, traditionally providing information about foreign health conditions, military preparations, emigrants, and the like. By mid-century they spent much time posting reports about American ships and looking after the interests of American seamen. In the later nineteenth century, their significance grew as revenues from the tariff became the major source of public funds. As late as 1895 consuls themselves saw their role in certifying cargoes—which then determined the amount of duty paid on entering the American market—as their most important function. Nevertheless, as interest in trade and investment abroad increased, consuls became more concerned about trade expansion.

An energetic chief and later director of the consular branch, Wilbur J. Carr, worked to improve services to businessmen. The department culled information from consular reports about fairly specific opportunities to help a particular industry find new markets abroad. Similarly, letters that consuls received and sent were edited and distributed with information about foreign economic opportunities.

The service, however, provided more than information

about foreign conditions. At many times, consuls were called on to assist American businessmen, especially those without foreign marketing staffs. They were asked to represent American businessmen in disagreements with local officials over duties and taxes, conflicting interpretations of foreign trademark and patent laws, disputes over payment, and complaints about packing.

On a broader and more traditional level, the State Department negotiated commercial agreements and treaties of interest to businessmen. Department officials also sought to protect Americans against discriminatory trade practices abroad, as well as the unwarranted application of health regulations against American products.[10]

The Department of State was not the only agency of the federal government assisting American business. The Department of Commerce and Labor (divided in 1913 into two departments) also provided information; it sent out its own corps of special commercial agents and attachés to study foreign conditions and markets. The department's Bureau of Foreign and Domestic Commerce worked assiduously on behalf of American manufacturers and investors abroad seeking out opportunities.[11]

Business seeking foreign trade and investment built closer ties to the bureaucracy than to the Congress. Indeed, the support of market-seeking producers provided a genuine political benefit, especially to the Department of State, but also to the Department of Commerce and Labor. Officials throughout the Department of State's bureaucracy became interested in trade expansion because it gave the department a constituency to appeal to for assistance when Congress cut the department's budget or "interfered" in what State Department officials thought were internal organizational issues.

This is not to suggest, however, that the department was supporting business expansion merely out of self-interest. Group motivation is a tricky puzzle, to be sure. There were many at the highest and middle levels of the bureaucracy who believed that the United States had to expand its foreign commerce in order to take care of surplus production. They too saw the world as a competitive place, and they worried that foreign governments, especially Germany's, provided much greater assistance to their business communities than did the American government. But there were those like Wilbur Carr, who served in several important positions and who often represented the department before the committees of the Congress, who believed that the political support of the business community was essential to the State Department.[12]

Indeed the bureaucracy at the Departments of State and Commerce had a more sustained interest in trade expansion than did many of the smaller producers whose interest in overseas sales depended heavily on conditions in the domestic market. The bureaucrats thus became more consistently interested in the need to expand trade abroad than some of the people they most wanted to serve.

Supporting trade expansion and seeking to minimize foreign discrimination against American business were popular positions to take. But the Departments of State and Commerce were less vigorous in their support of other business activity abroad. The rapid increase in American foreign investment in these years created problems that led to ambiguous responses. Investment was of several kinds: direct in marketing and manufacturing facilities, direct in developing raw materials, and portfolio investments in foreign stocks and bonds. The relationship between government and foreign investment depended much on the particular firm or industry, but especially on the area in which investment occurred. Direct investment by major firms in European and Canadian marketing networks, assembling plants, and branch factories was generally carried out without the substantial involvement of the American government. Making investments in raw materials in Latin American countries, however, was more apt to bring requests for assistance from American officials, although not in every case. American firms at times asked for assistance to protect investments already made.

The American government's position on investment was more ambivalent, however, than on commercial matters. Generally, there were fewer problems with portfolio investment—money put into stocks and bonds—than with direct foreign investment. By 1914, however, approximately two-thirds of American investment abroad was direct investment by American companies in marketing, distribution, assembling, and manufacturing facilities. The Department of State had decidedly mixed feelings about American firms that assembled or manufactured their products abroad. To bureaucrats and policy makers interested in expanding American trade to help the domestic economy, branch factories appeared to drain jobs from America. Yet the investors were American nationals who would expect the cooperation of their government if their investments were jeopardized by foreign governments. As a result, the department generally sought to give "correct" assistance. But there was little enthusiasm for such investments, and the ambivalence on whether to support the building of branch factories lasted throughout the 1920s. Overall, however, once made, these manufacturing investments did not give American officials trouble because by 1914 over 95 percent were in relatively stable places, Europe and Canada especially.[13]

As direct investment increased in less stable areas, businessmen called on the State Department to protect their investments, especially in areas where they were threatened by foreign revolution. Some members of the department were reluctant, however, to defend business and banking interests abroad. Secretary Bryan (and later Hughes) believed that foreign disturbances were one of the risks to be considered before making direct investments. They questioned the propriety of the American government stepping in to help. But businessmen expected, and increasingly the department agreed, that property owned by Americans should be protected against unfair seizure without adequate compensation. This was clearly the view of Secretaries of State Knox and Lansing.[14]

The most notable threat to American investment occurred in Mexico. It appeared to be so serious that several large firms hired former State Department counselor Chandler Anderson to represent them before his former colleagues. Anderson encouraged the department to defend American investments against a wholesale attack on foreign economic activity in Mexico. President Wilson believed that businessmen were in part at fault for problems with Mexico. Eventually the administration—after prodding by Lansing—defended business interests, although not so force-fully as either Anderson or his clients wanted. Anderson's defense of some of the major business interests in Mexico pointed up the development of another important channel of influence between business and government: the former government official working for business and representing business before his former col-leagues. Anderson was perhaps the best known, but in these years several other one-time Department of State officials went into law practices or to work for businesses, using their contacts to repre-sent the interests of business before the government.[15]

As Americans became more involved in the international economy, the potential constituencies concerned with American diplomacy grew. American businessmen and bankers were willy-nilly drawn into more and more contact with the American gov-ernment, especially the Department of State, but also frequently with the Commerce Department.

The most sustained contacts developed between business-men and officials at the middle level of the bureaucracy as well as with members of Congress. Bureaucrats needed a sympathetic public and Congressmen did not want to ignore well-organized business groups. At times, to be sure, the views of the National Association of Manufacturers or the National Foreign Trade Council made their way to the top levels of government policy makers—to the President, Secretaries of State, and chairmen of the most important congressional committees. But the top-level officials had so many other considerations to ponder that the views of a particular business group could not usually influence the di-rection of American policy. This is not to say, however, that eco-nomic considerations did not play a part in top-level decision-making. Indeed investment and trade at times were used as part of the tactics to achieve strategic goals.

STRATEGIC GOALS AND ECONOMIC TACTICS

Of the four Presidents between 1899 and 1920, William McKinley identified himself more than the others with the viewpoints of smaller market-seeking manufacturers. As with most Presidents, domestic political circumstances influenced McKinley's foreign policy as much as an analysis of international power relationships. McKinley had established his political reputation by his knowledge of the tariff, an issue requiring an understanding as much of politics as of economics. Committed as ever to protection, he nevertheless thought it important to accommodate manufacturers who wanted to gain foreign markets. At the 1895 organizing convention of the National Association of Manufacturers (NAM), convened by prominent Cincinnati manufacturers, Governor William McKinley delivered the keynote address. The future President brought the assembly to its feet with a speech supporting what the convention endorsed. "We want a foreign market," McKinley said, "for our surplus products which will not surrender our markets and will not degrade our labor. . . ."[16] To obtain such markets, McKinley advocated "reciprocity." That is, in return for lowered foreign tariff rates on particular items the United States would lower its own rates on specific foreign goods. As President, McKinley supported the 1897 Dingley tariff, which expanded the notion of reciprocal rate reduction to include European as well as Latin American nations.

McKinley, a more than usually enigmatic practitioner of the political art, has left scattered evidence for historians to track fully his growing support of market expansionism. Did he really believe that expanding markets were necessary to relieve a glutted American economy, or was he responding prudently to the political pressures of well-organized groups of businessmen? Whatever the depth of his own convictions on the matter, he had risked the wrath of uncompromising protectionists in order to satisfy a vocal, but nevertheless small group of market-seeking manufacturers. Most protectionists feared reciprocal rate reduction would lose more than it would gain, opening up the rich American market in exchange for poorer markets abroad.

Be that as it may, the 1897 Dingley tariff provided for the negotiation of reciprocity treaties, and McKinley appointed John Kasson, an experienced and able former Congressman-turned-diplomat, to negotiate treaties with, among others, France for a mutual reduction of tariff rates on specific articles. The most controversial Kasson treaties did not come to the Senate until after McKinley's death. When they did, the treaties stirred up controversy, as some manufacturers argued that their interests in a protected American market were sacrificed to the desire of others for expanded sales abroad. In the face of such dissension over the always politically troublesome tariff, President Roosevelt allowed the treaties to die in the Senate.[17]

McKinley's support of businessmen's market-seeking aspirations nevertheless became useful politically. He justified several policy maneuvers as beneficial to the interests of small businessmen already engaged abroad or seeking to cultivate foreign markets. He used the perceived need for markets to defend foreign policies that were not necessarily or primarily conceived to achieve economic benefits. America's acquisition of the Philippines was the result of the military strategy of the Spanish-American War. To return them to Spain was unthinkable; to free them invited capture by a major European power, most likely Germany. Keeping the islands, however, provoked a spirited American debate over imperialism. In the face of domestic criticism of American policy, McKinley at times defended retention in economic terms. The islands could serve as a market themselves and as a way station for American commerce moving into China, yet McKinley and his defenders argued most frequently that the islands were taken as a result of duty, honor, and simple necessity.[18]

McKinley also employed economic arguments to win support for his negotiations with the British about an isthmian canal. In fact, strategic considerations played the major role in the President's thinking. He wanted to protect the Caribbean and keep out foreign bases, goals more easily achieved with a canal that allowed quick deployment of naval vessels from one ocean to another.[19]

McKinley looked to his receptive audience among market-seeking businessmen when defending his policies in the Caribbean and Asia. The President wanted to assure stability in Cuba, ultimately to limit pretexts that foreign powers might have for intervention there or, for that matter, in any other country in the Caribbean area. But businessmen seeking markets approved the need for stability, and the President was aware of their interests and needs. In Asia, smarting over accusations that the goverment had violated deep American principles by taking the Philippines, McKinley and Secretary of State Hay issued the Open Door Notes, documents released as much to silence domestic critics as to impress European foreign offices. McKinley's attempt to postpone the final division of China by the imperialistic Europeans and Japanese won the support of businessmen seeking foreign markets.

There were limits, to be sure, to the use of such economic arguments. Domestic political considerations limited McKinley's support of policies advocated by some market-seeking business-men. He avoided the perennial and politically hopeless debate on improving the American merchant marine. Similarly, the President disappointed businessmen who wanted to remove the State Department's consular service from the spoils system. Too many patronage slots had already been lost to civil service lists, and McKinley's responsibility as party leader dictated holding on to those appointments he still had. The consular service of the Department of State, during the McKinley years, continued to be a refuge for the party faithful. He promised to appoint only good men, but they would have to be drawn from among loyal members of the party.

Roosevelt followed the lead established by McKinley. In the Caribbean he sought to minimize foreign influence and in Asia to prevent a permanent division of China. But Roosevelt had to flesh out the skeletal policy taken by the assassinated President. Bolder and less reticent in public than McKinley, Roosevelt nevertheless followed a cautious foreign policy with close attention to the limits of American power. Roosevelt was less identified than McKinley with the aspirations of the smaller manufacturers who had wanted to expand markets abroad. Indeed, the new President was to make an important distinction between good and bad "trusts," realizing that the size of many trusts was the result of efficiency and economic advantage. He understood that some giant firms gained markets at home and abroad because of efficiency— economic advantage—and not because of unfair dealing.[20]

Of the four Presidents between 1899 and 1920, Theodore

Roosevelt had thought most systematically about America's world role. Roosevelt's central concern was power. As such, the United States needed a foreign policy oriented to considerations of the balance of power, to the relations among the primary "civilized" states. Economic considerations fit into his basic considerations to the extent that a great state's power was made up of military might, industrial strength, and social order. To Roosevelt, moreover, growing American economic power at home and abroad was a fact in 1901, not a goal to be promoted by foreign policy. As a result, his ideas on America's foreign economic needs were vaguer than his comparatively clear notions of strategic interests. America's strategic goals were still to be achieved, while her economic advancement was well under way by private initiative.

Beyond considerations of power balances, Roosevelt was interested in the uses of power: to annex territory in order to protect the western hemisphere and to ensure routes to ports for American commerce in the Orient. Yet he was concerned too with peace and order in Europe and the Far East; he believed it necessary for the civilized powers to expand to bring order. Such expansion of influence and territory would lead to world peace when the world was under the rule of the major civilized Western powers.

Despite variations on the major theme of power, and musings about its benefits for civilization, Theodore Roosevelt invariably returned to the military-strategic conceptions of national interest. He saw America's greatest potential threats to be in Germany and Japan. Japan's strength posed the specter of conflicting interests over Hawaii and China. Germany became a threat primarily in that she might seek bases in the western hemisphere. Roosevelt's concern for the navy stemmed from considerations of German and Japanese power. And while he defended territorial expansion in terms of civilization and, at times, economic advantage, his first concern was for bases. Hawaii in the Pacific would protect merchant and naval ships, and control in the Caribbean would deny bases to potential enemies.

Unlike his predecessor, who used military power reluctantly in Cuba, Roosevelt was prepared to use it, and said so. He thought that peace was assured, so long as the other great powers realized that the United States would fight if necessary. He put this view in personal terms when he asserted that "an unmanly desire to avoid a quarrel is often the surest way to precipitate one: and utter unreadiness to fight is even surer."[21]

As President, Roosevelt translated his ideas about power into policies that formed the basic outlines of American foreign relations until Woodrow Wilson added extensive moral considerations. He tried to flesh out McKinley's skeletal policy toward security in the Caribbean and Asia. Roosevelt proved a cautious practitioner of foreign policy, despite occasional unsettling rhetorical indulgences. He set for his administration no less than an adjustment to a new world role marked by the Spanish-American War. America was to play a part he saw befitting a great new power. In the process, Roosevelt defined for his two successors carefully circumscribed goals for American diplomacy. He wanted to keep foreign powers out of the Caribbean, maintain a balance of power in Europe, and establish a role for the United States in Asia.

Economic tactics were to play a part in the achievement of each of these goals. But the acquisition of new markets for American goods and capital were not, in Roosevelt's mind, the reason he set the strategic goals that he had. He and his successors sought to gain predominance in the Caribbean, a base of power from which Roosevelt could keep foreign military power out of the hemisphere. Taft and Wilson followed Roosevelt's initiatives and tried to keep American influence there strong. Basically, all three wanted to keep foreign powers out of the Caribbean and to protect the Panama Canal.

The McKinley administration had begun to assert the United States' presence in the Caribbean, most obviously in Cuba, but elsewhere as well. Theodore Roosevelt's task thus was to clarify and follow through on a policy already initiated. Leading policy makers in both administrations concluded that the United States needed unquestioned authority in the Caribbean to ensure American safety in the rest of the hemisphere. McKinley and Roosevelt were careful to distinguish between control in the

Caribbean and influence in the rest of Latin America. American control was to rest on possession of bases in the Caribbean or, if not that, prevention of such bases to non-hemispheric countries.

To justify America's increased role in the Caribbean both McKinley and Roosevelt appealed to the economic self-interest of Americans doing business in the western hemisphere. McKinley took more seriously than Roosevelt the justification of Caribbean stability to trade and investment; Roosevelt was less concerned with the economic benefits to businessmen and bankers than with the strategic importance to America's position. But, like McKinley, Roosevelt had to appeal to America's economic self-interest to gain congressional support and blunt criticism of those who saw America's moves in the Caribbean as further evidence of militarism. At the same time, Roosevelt, like the other Presidents between 1899 and 1920, publicly defended the rights of Americans to trade and invest abroad, and he advocated equal treatment of Americans doing business overseas. Increased American business at times alarmed important foreign businessmen. British, German, and Japanese merchants had to compete with Americans in markets that they had become accustomed to calling their own in Asia, Latin America, Australia, India, and Canada. As a result, during Roosevelt's administration the United States government took part in numerous negotiations to assure that American businessmen were not injured by unfair foreign regulations as to fisheries, patents, trademarks, sanitary standards for food, and the like.[22]

Roosevelt first applied his ideas in Cuba. The new President had really only to implement policy worked out for McKinley by Roosevelt's good friend Elihu Root, Secretary of War. Root had ensured America a sphere of influence in the strategically located island, although the United States was not to have direct control over Cuba. Whatever imperialist expansionist sentiment there was after the Spanish-American War was no match for opposing opinion. Bloody fighting in the Philippines brought a sense of perspective to most observers, as did an increasing realization of Cuba's economic backwardness and social problems.

Root fashioned a policy designed to give the United States

maximum influence with limited direct political involvement. Working with men like Orville H. Platt, Senator from Connecticut, Root engineered an amendment to the army appropriation act in March 1901. The Platt Amendment tied the return of civil government in Cuba to assurances that American strategic interests would be protected. Thus, Cuba could not make agreements that would give territory to a foreign power or in any other way impair her sovereignty. The United States also required that the public debt in Cuba not exceed the government's ability to pay, in order to avoid a pretext for foreign intervention. The United States reserved to itself the right to invervene if Cuban independence were threatened. Root also assured that America would have the right to purchase or lease coaling and naval bases.

Cuban leaders were not enthusiastic over these terms for ending American military government in Cuba. Roosevelt had to exercise diplomatic skill to win final Cuban acceptance of the American settlement. The Cubans accepted Root's solution in a treaty signed in May 1903, but not until securing assurances that the United States would intervene only in the face of total public disorder or direct foreign attack. The Americans made as clear as possible that they sought no protectorate or colony in Cuba, although foreign governments at the time, to say nothing of later observers, recognized that the United States had imposed important restrictions on Cuban sovereignty.

The Roosevelt administration soon exercised the rights acquired in the Cuban treaty. The United States negotiated a fair-minded commercial treaty with the Cubans and quickly arranged for the lease of two naval bases. As the years passed American businessmen's interests in Cuba grew. While they feared the periodic disorder, their concerns were far from preeminent in the early Roosevelt years of the century. The President was primarily concerned with the role of Cuba in a hemisphere that he feared was vulnerable to the influence of the great European powers, especially Germany. The threat of civil war compelled Roosevelt to send in troops in 1906. He wanted to protect American lives and property, to be sure, but he also wanted to see the "experiment of democratic government" work.[23] Although Roosevelt removed the troops in 1909, interventions were to recur until Franklin Roosevelt's Good Neighbor Policy did away with the Platt Amendment in 1934.

Strategic concerns led Roosevelt to his decisions in assuring the construction of a canal through Panama. As in Cuba, Roosevelt inherited a series of McKinley's initiatives. The Spanish-American War and its aftermath had convinced McKinley of the military and strategic necessity of building an isthmian canal. Aside from reducing the time it would take to move the fleet from one ocean to another, the United States had new Pacific possessions to protect. Support of the canal was politically popular, especially among businessmen who sought expanded export markets in Latin America and Asia. McKinley's support of a canal—a clear goal of such groups as the NAM—won him more friends in that part of the business community interested in expanding foreign markets. McKinley sought to renegotiate the 1850 Clayton-Bulwer Treaty, which had provided that neither the United States nor Great Britain would seek unilateral control over an isthmian canal. The British found unacceptable a treaty signed by Hay in 1900, because amendments would have given the United States full control, and so McKinley sought a new treaty. He never saw it signed. Great Britain, however, was interested in American friendship and so made concessions to the United States in the November 1901 Hay-Pauncefote Treaty. This understanding set aside the Clayton-Bulwer agreement and approved American construction and operation of a canal. The United States was to keep the canal open equally to all nations. British acceptance of the terms of the treaty gained for her American friendship and cooperation, if not a direct alliance.

Roosevelt proceeded to secure for the United States a route across Panama. The unedifying story of America's heavy-handed role in gaining the Panama crossing need not be repeated here. Roosevelt secured his objective and considered the Panama Canal one of his greatest achievements. But America's role in encouraging and supporting a revolt in Colombia earned great ill will for the United States in Latin America. At home, Roosevelt gained general support, although influential voices protested the administration's bold interventionism. Business groups, especially those interested in increased trade with Latin America and Asia, generally applauded the President.[24]

The canal—opened finally in 1914—added greater force to America's concern with the Caribbean. It was a concrete strategic objective to be protected, a waterway essential to America's defense of her coasts and possessions in the Pacific. Thus, in the years that followed, concern for the canal's safety made policy makers more sensitive to threats of instability in Caribbean nations, lest a financial crisis somewhere in the area invite European intervention. And so the Roosevelt, Taft, and Wilson administrations intervened in a number of countries. To be sure, private economic interests pressured the government to protect their trade and investment in Caribbean nations. And, more generally, businessmen provided a locus of support when the government intervened in the Caribbean. Some public support was welcome in the face of criticism by anti-imperialists.

Roosevelt's policy in the Caribbean set patterns of tactics as well as of overall strategy. He acted boldly when America's predominance seemed threatened by unrest in Venezuela, the Dominican Republic, and Haiti. Troubles in Venezuela and the Dominican Republic led the United States to a more active role in the area. Venezuela's refusal to pay debts to European bond holders in 1902–3 prompted Britain, Germany, and Italy to establish a blockade. The American public reacted sharply, however, when the Europeans seized Venezuelan naval vessels, bombarded forts, and eventually landed troops. Roosevelt called for negotiations, and, despite German violence in response to provocation, the issue was submitted to a tribunal made up of judges from the International Court of Arbitration at The Hague. In a decision of February 1904, the tribunal directed Venezuela to pay. The implications were that the United States had little choice but to accept a more active role in the area. The British government acquiesced in America's growing activities in this hemisphere and indeed approved America's predisposition to keep order. While the pretext for American intervention was clearly economic disorder, the major consideration remained strategic. The United

States desired to keep foreign powers—especially Germany—from taking territory or increasing their influence in the hemisphere.[25]

Indeed, Roosevelt announced in December 1904 his famous "corollary"—as it was called—to the Monroe Doctrine. The United States, he asserted, might have to intervene in the face of "wrongdoing" and to act as the "international police power." Roosevelt applied his views soon after by accepting a protocol with the Dominican Republic which allowed the United States to collect customs and deal with that government's creditors. When revolution broke out on another part of the island in Haiti, Roosevelt warned the European powers not to interfere. Roosevelt increased American influence in other parts of the Caribbean as well. The United States tried to purchase the Danish West Indies. When the Danes rejected a treaty in 1902, Roosevelt made clear that the United States would not accept sale to another country. Finally, in 1916 the United States purchased the islands. In other places—like the Galapagos Islands off the coast of Ecuador—the United States asserted that it would not allow sites suitable for naval installations to fall into foreign hands.[26]

Taft followed the outlines of Roosevelt's Caribbean policies, although with considerably less sense of balance. Like Roosevelt, Taft and his Secretary of State, Philander Knox, sought stable Caribbean states to prevent pretexts for foreign intervention. Economic investment, they thought, was one way to achieve stability. Taft and Knox induced American banks to refinance loans in Nicaragua, Honduras, Guatemala, and Haiti. The Department of State monitored these loans to insure that undue advantage was not taken of the borrowers. To encourage American bankers, manufacturers, and merchants to invest, Taft and Knox insured swift protection for Americans and their property. In 1912 Taft landed marines in Nicaragua to prevent a revolution and keep a pro-American government in power. The force—a "legation" guard—remained until 1933. Woodrow Wilson came to office vowing to end "dollar diplomacy." In one of his last campaign speeches he criticized Knox's "dollar diplomacy." It was, he said, a foreign policy based "upon mere commercial exploitation and the selfish interests of a narrow circle of financiers extending their enterprises to the ends of the earth. . . ." But Wilson, too, ended by intervening in the Caribbean.[27]

ECONOMICS, MORALITY, AND ASIA

In the Far East, as in the Caribbean, Theodore Roosevelt inherited policies already begun by the McKinley administration, albeit more tentatively formed than those for the Caribbean. Beset by the crises in relations with Spain over Cuba, McKinley and Secretary of State Hay did little more than assert that America would have an interest in Asia, especially China. Any plans for an active Far Eastern policy were subordinated to the war with Spain and then the insurrection in the Philippines. Missionaries, however, continued their interest in China, and potential markets there intrigued vocal and well-organized groups of smaller businessmen.

China as a potential market for American manufacturers played a part in the formulation of the McKinley administration's view of policy in the Far East. The President, as we have seen, supported market expansion. The McKinley administration looked on with alarm as the major imperialist powers scrambled for ports, spheres of influence, and commercial concessions in China. Hay's open-door notes were to keep China available for future American economic activity. In the well-known series of events, the United States informed the major European powers of its desire to keep Chinese trade open to equal access by all powers. With the exception of Italy, which accepted the principles for the most part, the other powers paid little attention. Hay took the cool indifference of the other powers as acceptance, and America tried to gain the most that she could with the smallest commitment of resources and power. After all, the United States had rejected British overtures in 1898 and 1899 to maintain an open door in China, at first because of American troubles with Spain, but the second time because McKinley had no desire to be drawn directly into complicated relations with the other major powers. The President's

reluctance reflected the refusal of the public and Congress to accept such an enlargement of policy commitments.

But the United States was drawn into cooperation with the
European imperialist powers with the June 1900 Boxer rebellion,
sending 2,500 troops to join the expeditionary force to free the
besieged legations at Peking. As a result, Hay issued further clarification of the open door in a circular in July 1900. Domestic politics had as much to do with this document as the future of American business in China. Indeed it was very much a Republican
campaign document; it appeared as the opposition Democratic
Party was to meet in convention. With an eye to anti-imperialist
sentiment, Hay announced that the United States sought no territory in order to preserve China's "territorial and administrative
entity" and to maintain China's trade equally in all parts of the
Chinese Empire.[28]

The United States, thus, tried to keep China open for future rather than present American influence. American policy was
to be limited indeed. The United States refused to act on the
open-door principles—at least in concert with other powers. Secretary of State John Hay rejected Japanese appeals to join her in
thwarting Russian expansion into Manchuria early in 1901. He
responded that the United States did not want to get involved in
enforcing the concept of the open door if it would lead to hostile
relations with other powers. Indeed, as a guide to policy, the open-
door concept was a failure, for it certainly had not reduced foreign
rivalries for concessions in China, and probably involved the
United States more than Hay had intended when McKinley acted
to protect American life and property in the Boxer rebellion.[29]

As President, Roosevelt followed the outlines of the Mc-
Kinley and Hay policies in the Far East, although with a greater
attention to the rationales of a balance of power. The Far East
remained subordinate to Roosevelt's concerns in the Caribbean and
the European balance of power. He looked to a distant future for
a greater American role in Asia, but refused substantial commitments. Theodore Roosevelt hoped to encourage a balance of power
among the great powers engaged there, in part to keep China open
to future American economic activity, but also to check Russia

and later Japan. America supported and at times cooperated with British and Japanese efforts to restrain Russian ambitions in the area. And Roosevelt looked on approvingly when in 1902 the two powers signed a defensive Anglo-Japanese Alliance.

The United States became more involved there when Japan asked Roosevelt to mediate the Russo-Japanese war. Japan had tried to reach a compromise with Russia over two pressing issues—Manchuria and Korea. Japan wanted both areas for the logical growth of her Empire, and tried to reach an accommodation with Russia which had expanded into the area. After lengthy negotiations, the Japanese gave in to frustration with and mistrust of the Russians and surprised the Czar's fleet at Port Arthur in an attack in February 1904. Japan achieved early and impressive victories, ultimately destroying the Czar's fleet and defeating the entire Russian army. But the costs were high for Japan. Because of the severe financial strain, the Japanese approached Roosevelt to sponsor peace negotiations. Japan believed that American interests complemented hers. The agreement ultimately reached between Japan and Russia had a profound impact on the United States, for it clarified America's relations with the two powerful naval powers joined in the Anglo-Japanese Alliance, without drawing the United States into the alliance. The Japanese assured the United States that they did not have aggressive designs on the Philippines. In return, the United States recognized Japan's protectorate over Korea and approved Japan's alliance with Britain. Great Britain revised the treaty with Japan in 1905, stating that Britain would never direct the alliance against the United States.

Despite American assistance in the peace negotiations, relations with Japan did not remain friendly. Most notable was Japanese resentment at the San Francisco school board's attempt to segregate Japanese students, although Roosevelt and Root fashioned a moderate solution. Relations improved, and the following year the Roosevelt administration signed an important agreement with Japan that set out the basic American understanding of its position in the Far East. The Root-Takahira Agreement (November 1908) protected the status quo in the Pacific. Each power was to leave undisturbed the other's possessions: America in the Philippines and Japan in Korea and Manchuria. In regard to China, both agreed to support Chinese independence while keeping China open to foreign commerce and investment. Significantly, both parties agreed to consult on possible joint responses if these principles were threatened.

Roosevelt thus left to his successor a realistic Far Eastern policy which balanced America's military capabilities against a careful calculation of her interests. This is seen clearly in Theodore Roosevelt's views on the open door. "The Open Door in China," Roosevelt wrote to President Taft, "was an excellent thing, and I hope it will be a good thing in the future, as far as it can be maintained by general diplomatic agreement . . . [but it] completely disappears as soon as a powerful nation determines to disregard it, and is willing to run the risk of war." In December 1910, he made a similar point, summing up for Taft his views on the open door: "If the Japanese choose to follow a course of conduct to which we are adverse, we cannot stop it unless we are prepared to go to war." Aside from questions about public support for such a war, Roosevelt thought that we would need a fleet equal to Britain's and an army on a par with Germany's to defeat Japan.[30]

Nevertheless, the Taft administration reversed Roosevelt's moderate policy of acquiescing in Japan's growing influence in Manchuria. Taft and Knox recognized that Latin America was more significant for America's current strategic and future economic interests, but Taft sought to increase America's role in the East, in large part as a result of his personal interest and long experience in that part of the world. Taft and Knox explicitly used economic tactics to gain American objectives: the open door, the territorial integrity of China, and the protection of the Philippines. Roosevelt had sought similar goals, but he more cautiously attempted to accommodate American interests to American capabilities. In contrast, Taft wanted to weaken Japan's hold in Manchuria. At the prodding of State Department officials Willard Straight and F. M. Huntington Wilson, both of whom had opposed Theodore Roosevelt's policy toward Japan, Taft tried to increase American investment in China and to limit Japan's activities in Manchuria. Taft and Knox accompanied these changes in tactics with a highly moralistic rhetoric about China that continued to influence American thinking about that country. It was also a rhetoric very much out of step with changes in China, as the disintegration of the Manchu dynasty was accompanied by a sharpening of anti-Western feeling.

Taft and Knox embarked on a policy to enlarge American influence by increased investment in China in the hope of warding off threats to China's integrity by other powers. Central to their efforts were two financial projects. The United States wanted to take part in a French, German, and British bankers' consortium to finance the building of a railroad in southern and central China. The United States joined in May 1910. With the addition of Russia and Japan the following year, the group became known as the Six Power Consortium. Little positive came of these efforts. American bankers were far from enthusiastic—better investment opportunities existed in Latin America and Europe. American interest flagged further as the negotiations became strained and difficult. Indeed, the consortium's pressure on a weak Chinese government to accept its terms helped start the Revolution that overthrew the Manchus and led to the proclamation of the Chinese Republic in February 1912.

The second plan was more ambitious. In November 1909 the Taft administration proposed that the major powers help China raise the money to buy the Russian interest in the Chinese Eastern railroad in Manchuria and Japan's interest in the South Manchurian railroad. Taft and Knox also held out the possibility of building competing lines with British and American capital. This latter plan had little chance of success. It ignored growing antiforeign feeling in China and the reluctance of American financiers to get involved. Of more consequence, Taft and Knox drove the Japanese and Russians closer together. A 1907 understanding to divide Manchuria into spheres of influence was followed in July 1910 by another secret agreement to adopt common strategies to protect their spheres of influence in Manchuria. Britain and France were of little assistance to the United States. Knox had requested British assistance in 1909 to persuade her Japanese ally to accept plans for the neutralization of the Manchurian railroad. Britain needed her ally in Asia as the world became more complicated and dangerous. She was not about to force Japan to do what was not in her interests. Similarly, France was of no assistance with her Russian ally.

Taft's diplomacy was a failure. The United States alienated the Japanese, brought them closer to the Russians, raised questions in Britain and France over American naiveté, and helped to weaken the Chinese whom Taft had hoped to protect. But Wilson did no better than Taft in Asia. Indeed, by 1921 he created an abiding animosity between the United States and Japan. Wilson was not by any means entirely at fault for the strained relations, since the Japanese had taken advantage of World War I to expand.

The first Democratic President in twenty years, Wilson was less interested in foreign policy than his Republican predecessors. He drew back almost immediately from some of Taft's Asian policies. He withdrew from the Six Power Consortium, in part because he and Secretary of State William Jennings Bryan thought bankers already too influential in government. He also refused to approve a loan to China that threatened, in Wilson's eyes, the administrative independence of that country. Increasing involvement in Mexico and then the monumental questions of neutrality in the European war further forced Wilson to limit American policy in Asia.

Japan nevertheless gave Wilson cause for concern during World War I. The Japanese government tried to increase its control in China, with little fear that the warring European powers would hinder her ambitions. Indeed, the British and French encouraged Japan to take German possessions as part of an effort to weaken their enemy. The Japanese seized a German base at Tsingtas, took her concessions in Shantung, and occupied Pacific islands held by the Germans—the Marianas, Carolinas, and Marshalls.

The United States did not encourage these moves in late 1914, but neither did Wilson object. While desiring to protect American interests—"rights" the Wilson administration called them—in Asia, especially China, the United States did nothing. Secret instructions to the American ministers in Peking stated that the government would take all practicable peaceful means to insure Chinese welfare, but nothing more. Although the Japanese did not know of these instructions, they obviously surmised the basic American attitude. Early in 1915, Japan issued China an ultimatum with twenty-one demands. The document asked nothing less than a sharp reduction in Chinese power and territory. Chinese requests for American assistance were not met. Bryan admitted to the Chinese that the Japanese demands violated the open door and China's territorial integrity, but he also recognized that Japan had interests in areas close to the Japanese islands. In effect, America looked the other way as Japan increased its power in China. A short time later, Bryan sent identical notes to the Chinese and Japanese governments. The United States, he said, would not recognize any agreements that limited the rights of the American government, its citizens, the territorial integrity of China, or the open door.[31]

The Japanese were not deterred, but they were confused. As a result, they sought clarification of the American position in June 1917. The Japanese wanted an understanding like the 1908 Root-Takahira Agreement. Primarily, the government in Tokyo wanted to clarify with Lansing and Wilson the meaning of Bryan's principle of nonrecognition, although they worried too about whether political purposes lurked behind American bankers' loans to China. In an exchange of notes both America and Japan acknowledged the importance of China's territorial integrity and the open door; Lansing recognized nevertheless that geographical propinquity created special interests for the Japanese. They took these notes as an American recognition of their special political and economic interests in China.

The notes of November 1917, however, were in effect only until the end of World War I. After that, the Wilson administration attempted to thwart Japanese ambitions. As with Taft's policies, Wilson's failed and ended by alienating the Japanese. The United States revived the notion of a consortium to lend money to China to repurchase public works lost to foreigners. The Japanese, as earlier, objected because of their interests in Manchuria and Mongolia. America participated in the international brigade sent to Vladivostok to free Czech soldiers held by the Russians. American efforts were clearly designed to keep Allied supplies stored there out of German hands once Russia left the war. But the United States also hoped to keep an eye on the Japanese—70,000 of whose troops were in the brigade—and prevent them from turning Siberia into another Japanese preserve, as they had done in Manchuria.[32]

The Japanese took advantage of the Russian Revolution. They did not leave Siberia until the fall of 1922, after gaining special rights in northern Manchuria and some parts of Siberia. They also continued to occupy the northern part of the Sakhalin islands. Wilson's attempts to deflect the Japanese from such expansion failed. The Japanese refused to sign statements eschewing acquisitions they clearly wanted to make and they refused to leave Germany's Pacific islands. In response to pressure from Wilson, the Japanese threatened to leave the Versailles Conference and not join the League of Nations. The end of the war, then, saw America and Japan more and more suspicious of each other. Indeed, by the time Wilson left office, both countries had concluded that the other was the most likely enemy in a future war in the Pacific.

Like his predecessors, however, Wilson treated East Asia as less important than Latin America and the Caribbean. Overall, Wilson wanted to protect the Philippines, prevent the partition of China, and keep China open to future American trade and investment. Roosevelt had followed a moderate course in trying to achieve these objectives—a course in line with his perception of American interests and public willingness to support foreign initiatives. Taft took a more activist role in East Asia, more frankly using economic tactics like the Six Power Consortium to achieve larger political and strategic goals. Wilson abandoned his predecessors' economic tactics, amplifying instead some of the moral arguments first propounded by Taft to protect China and restrain Japan. America increasingly defended its policies by reference to the morality of protecting Chinese integrity from expansionist

Russia and Japan, although the United States continued to have an interest in expanded trade and investment.

ECONOMIC INTERESTS, LATIN AMERICA, AND EUROPE

The focus of the early Wilson years was in the Caribbean and Mexico. Wilson's involvement in the well-known interventions there needs no detailed repetition here. The new administration came to power criticizing its predecessor's dollar diplomacy, seeking instead friendly relations with Caribbean and Latin American nations. Wilson's goal was to foster democratic institutions there. America's major and dangerous involvement in Mexico clearly illustrated Wilson's early views of American foreign policy. Seeking to encourage the election of good men, he interfered directly in Mexican affairs. To the extent that he thought Great Britain supported the Huerta government to protect British economic interests, Wilson pledged support for an open door in Mexico.

Economic interests, however, were not foremost in Wilson's thinking. Indeed, Wilson's response to revolution in Mexico revealed a naive concern for political morality and for pressing upon different and unwilling societies American views of proper political institutions. At first, he ignored the pleas of businessmen who wanted to help protect their investments by recognizing the revolutionary Huerta government in Mexico. Not only did Wilson refuse; he blamed foreign investors for many of Mexico's problems. The domination of Mexican affairs by foreign concessionaires, the President asserted, led to intolerable conditions in Mexico. As late as May 1916, Wilson still believed that Americans interested in Mexican oil and minerals were the source of America's problems with Mexico.[33]

Investors' interests were not uppermost in other officials' thinking either, even though 22 percent of all American direct investment was in Mexico in 1914. Secretary of State Bryan, like Wilson, was hostile to the "selfish" interests of bankers and oil companies. Secretary Lansing was more sympathetic to the plight of Americans who owned property in Mexico. But the fear of German influence there constrained Lansing from taking strong action against what American investors considered outrages. Indeed the Wilson administration in August 1917 recognized the Carranza government, whose proposed land reforms were anathema to American businessmen in Mexico. By the end of the war, the administration's attention turned to the European peace. By that time too Lansing's ability to influence Wilson had declined markedly in a souring of personal relations between the two men.

Yet, as unsympathetic as Wilson was toward American investors in Mexico, he and even Bryan supported in principle the right of protection of American property. The administration faced what in later years was to become a more recurrent problem, threats to American property by foreign revolution. Those with significant investments in Mexico lamented Wilson's seeming obsession with moral questions to the exclusion of concern for economic interests. Yet the President did consider the safety of the 60,000 Americans in Mexico and the rights Americans had to property that they had acquired there. Wilson continued to subordinate economic interests to moral concerns in Mexico, although he never denied that investors had some claim on the government to help to protect their property.[34]

Economic considerations played a more direct role in Nicaragua, as Wilson reluctantly ended by following policies initiated by Taft and Knox. The United States continued its financial regulations and military presence. As in Mexico, Wilson intervened directly to influence the choice of a president, although without provoking the bloody resistance encountered in Mexico. In Haiti, the United States combined military intervention and economic supervision to maintain order. A treaty of 1915 set up a protectorate that lasted almost twenty years (until 1934). The Dominicans proved less receptive to American interference in their affairs, and Wilson set up a military government there in November 1916 when no political leader could be found to accept American terms for "reform." Military rule lasted six years, although extensive control of Dominican (and Haitian) finances lasted until World War II.[35]

Involvement in Asia and Latin America was not matched by America's role in Europe. With a few important exceptions, the United States did not play a major part in European affairs before World War I. This was ironic, for America's historic, cultural, and economic ties were greatest there. Theodore Roosevelt was the most knowledgeable about the culture and politics of Europe, and it was his administration that saw the United States take the most active role in what happened there, especially at the Algeciras Conference and in the naval rivalry between Britain and Germany.

America's lack of attention to European affairs did not mean, however, that the United States did not have interests there. On the contrary, as in the nineteenth century, American interests were similar or at least complementary to those of Britain. The Roosevelt administration tried—quietly, in view of anti-British feeling in the United States—to settle outstanding differences between the two nations. The British were interested because they could no longer afford to isolate themselves in a world where Germany and Japan could threaten their far-flung empire. Roosevelt wanted very much to cement relations with Great Britain, upon whose power in Europe the United States depended. America needed Great Britain to maintain the historic balance of power in Europe. And although understandings were not readily reached on troublesome issues like a long-standing boundary dispute over Alaskan territory, the Hay-Pauncefote Treaty in 1901 contained important concessions to America on the building and fortifying of our isthmian canal. Britain deferred more and more to the United States in Latin America, although the British expected to be able to trade and invest there freely.

The new rapprochement between the United States and Great Britain was not without its strains. Roosevelt took a hard line on the Alaskan border dispute. The Taft administration disturbed Britain over an abortive Canadian reciprocity treaty, and Taft's "dollar diplomacy" adversely affected British investments and trade in the Caribbean. An ugly dispute arose over Panama

Canal tolls, which angered the British too. Taft deferred the issue for the Wilson administration, which resolved it in 1914 by treating other nations equally in tolls charged to use the canal.

The European war that broke out in 1914 would further strain American relations with Britain in the two and a half years before America entered the war. But fundamentally America perceived its interests to be with Britain and her allies, and America still found its interests served by British maintenance of a balance of power in Europe. Wilson's entry into war against Germany was based on principle and his hopes for a new world order. Loans and trade played a part in the coming of American involvement, but the issue of neutral rights was more important to Wilson.

WORLD WAR AND THE INTERNATIONAL SYSTEM

President Wilson and his closest advisers were deeply suspicious of German power and motives when World War I began. In this respect, Wilson was in the mainstream of contemporary strategic thinking. When he left office, Roosevelt suspected that the Germans were the only major power that would threaten American predominance in the Caribbean. Planners in the army and the navy had concluded that Germany was the most likely enemy in the event of war. These attitudes were reflected publicly in the writings of Alfred Thayer Mahan and, more contemporaneously to Wilson, Walter Lippmann. The public at large, however, was not deeply interested in the war, although as time went on the efforts of British propaganda were successful in cultivating American sympathy.

Within the inner circle of the administration, Wilson's close adviser Edward M. House and his second Secretary of State, Robert Lansing, reflected the views of most informed observers that German power was a threat to the United States. Lansing became Secretary of State after serving as counselor to the State

Department, a position to which he brought great experience as an international lawyer. His experience in arbitration had stimulated Lansing to think systematically about America's role in world affairs. He became an architect of Wilson's neutrality policy toward Britain, but he was an influential opponent of Germany in the American administration. Lansing hoped that the Allies would win a full victory over Germany. Otherwise, Germany would continue to rival United States power in Latin America. Lansing's real fear was that Germany, Japan, and Russia would form an expansionist alliance that would limit American naval power in the Atlantic and the Pacific. Lansing was concerned with more than geopolitical issues in opposing Germany. The Secretary had a decidedly ideological view of the war, opposing autocracy and militarism as a threat to democracy and a liberal capitalistic order. He feared that in the future the United States would have to become more militaristic to counter the Germans if they were not clearly defeated. He was willing ultimately to risk American entry into the war in order to insure a full defeat of German power. As the major formulator of policies proposed by Wilson, Lansing tended to look the other way at British violations of American neutral rights, while holding the Germans to strict account.[36]

Colonel House shared Lansing's sentiments, even though his views were less systematically formulated than the Secretary's. But House was of greater significance, since he was much closer personally to Wilson. House envisioned foreign policy as an effort to create a stable balance of power. He was clearly pro-British and increasingly fearful of German militarism; he wanted the Allies to know as early as 1915 that America would come to their defense if necessary. House, however, distrusted the Russians and their unrestrained expansionism, and he saw the need for German power to hold back the Russian tide. But House, like Lansing, feared that a German victory would require a constant military preparedness on the part of the United States, something he wanted to avoid.

Wilson shared his advisers' apprehensions about Germany, and his initial reaction to the war was one of sympathy for the Allies whom he thought were resisting aggression. But during 1915

Wilson developed a broader outlook on the causes of war, and his view of the belligerents became more balanced. Although he shared the fears of House and Lansing concerning the consequences of a German victory, he came to believe that neutrality was the proper course for the United States. Only then would the United States be in a position to play a leading role in bringing about a new world order, which would ensure economically an open world for trade and investment and a peaceful means of conducting international relations. Wilson knew that such a world would benefit the American economy. But Wilson's vision of a new international order was not prompted primarily by a concern for America's economic self-interest. Wilson had not been among that number of politicians, bureaucrats, and businessmen who saw the American economy dependent on growing exports. Roosevelt, Taft, and Wilson believed that trade would expand primarily through private efforts, although they supported the State Department's efforts to ensure that American businessmen were not discriminated against. All three took note of and recognized the vocal support for increased government assistance to businessmen interested in expanding trade and investment. Wilson, like Roosevelt, however, did not believe that government should in effect eliminate risk in foreign business activities. Both Presidents, for ideological reasons, disdained too great a commitment to material values.[37]

But Wilson's ideological predispositions confronted hard political decisions. His policy of neutrality was eventually shaped by economic considerations. The President, more than House and Lansing, endeavored to maintain a genuine neutrality. But the United States became important to the warring alliances because of increasing trade and loans. America's economic ties were stronger with the British and their allies. The Royal Navy hindered German trade with America, and much of the Triple Entente's loans were tied to the need to buy American goods. Thus, at critical junctures, Wilson had to consider the economic consequences of a sharp response toward violations of American neutral rights by the warring powers. American prosperity and the safety of American loans were not the only considerations in Wilson's mind when he made decisions about Allied violations of neutral rights. The President's admiration for British culture and institutions, the pro-Entente feeling of his two key foreign policy advisers, and his generally high regard for the British leadership predisposed him to deal more gently with Britain and her allies.

Yet as trade and loans grew between 1914 and 1917, American prosperity became closely tied to war-related purchases. Economic conditions at home concerned Wilson because the economy had been depressed in 1913 and 1914. The large orders from abroad dramatically turned the situation around after an initial chaotic readjustment following the outbreak of the war in Europe. Technically, the United States had to keep its trade open to all to remain a neutral. Americans shipped abroad vast supplies of food, manufactured goods, and munitions. Since the Allies effectively controlled the seas, these products moved mostly to the Allied countries. Commercial ties to the Allied powers were followed by growing financial connections. By 1915 the administration had abandoned Bryan's plan to deny American loans to the belligerents. Despite Bryan's views, Wilson concluded that the purchase of foreign bonds and outright loans were necessary if the Europeans were going to continue to buy in the United States. By the time the United States entered the war, American bankers and bond purchasers held over $2 billion in Allied debts; in contrast Germany and Austria had borrowed only about $27 million.

This is not to say that Wilson's primary concern was domestic prosperity and the satisfaction of the interests of manufacturers, farmers, and bankers in the war trade. Domestic economic interests were simply a part of the consideration that Wilson had to give to the thorny question of defending America's neutral rights. Indeed, he dealt sharply with the British on more than one occasion when they dealt heavy-handedly with America. The British for their part realized the importance of American economic assistance and so reacted calmly to strong American protests about violations of neutral rights. In contrast, the Germans were less sensitive to American interests. Of equal importance, the administration was less sympathetic to the Germans and inclined to be more legalistic with them than with the British.[38]

Wilson wanted to remain neutral in order to play a major

role in the making of the peace. But America did not have the cultural, political, intellectual, institutional, and linguistic ties to Germany that she had to Great Britain. Since the Roosevelt administration America had developed a close relationship with Great Britain which predisposed America toward her. The growing trade and loans simply served to soften the Wilson administration's attitude toward Great Britain.

Yet when the President took the United States to war it was to build a new international order and not simply to serve the interests of the Allies. Wilson wanted American democratic principles and institutions to spread worldwide when the older imperialist relationships were done away with. American trade and investment were to play a part in the new order too. Wilson realized an open world was in America's interest, as the previous two decades had shown the vitality and strength of American economic expansion in trade and investment. Wilson did not conceive of this expansion as needing special American governmental protection and assistance. The new world order Wilson sought would ensure peace and security, which would also bring about stable economic growth. Wilson thought that American economic activity was in the interest of mankind, and happily what was in everyone's general interest coincided with America's economic interests, a happy framework in which to work for a statesman.

The United States entered World War I as an "associated power." Wilson intended to preserve an independent role for the United States in the making of peace. He anticipated that by then the Allied powers would be economically and financially dependent on America, enabling the United States to determine the terms of a settlement. Wilson wanted no less than a new international order, based on democratic political institutions and liberal capitalistic free-trade arrangements. This new international order would further the interests of small, less-developed countries and replace secret alliances and elitist diplomacy with an international politics of law and justice. These noble goals, Wilson thought, were in reach, because they coincided nicely with America's economic interests, ideological predispositions, and political prejudices. The President's objectives required little for the United

States to give up, although the achievement of Wilson's vision would have required sacrifices not only from the defeated but also from the victors in Europe.

Wilson, as is well known, had difficulty in obtaining his goals. Not only did the European leaders, especially the French, oppose Wilson on many issues, but he increasingly lost support at home by his inept handling of his Republican opponents in the Senate. Further complicating the negotiations was the Bolshevik Revolution in Russia, which only redoubled Wilson's efforts to get the new world order that he sought. The undemocratic regime in Russia replaced German autocracy as a major threat in the minds of many, including the President. Lenin's coup d'état in Russia threatened Wilson's vision of a new world order more than the machinations of European leaders at Versailles and American Senators in Washington.

American opinion was at first confused by the Bolshevik Revolution. Private investors were the most directly threatened by the revolution, but it proved to be only one more irritant in a time of profound disorder. Americans with investments overseas had become accustomed to the disruption of war. Attitudes were only tentative in part because many did not expect the revolution to succeed. In any event, businessmen tended to support the government's policy of nonrecognition.[39]

In summary, then, economic interests had played a part in the way policy makers conceived American interests and how they went about attempting to achieve their goals. The objectives that Theodore Roosevelt set out were to have a great influence on American diplomacy, although World War I was to alter drastically America's importance in the world. Unquestioned dominance in the Caribbean became possible with the defeat of Germany; America's role in European affairs increased whether Congress and the public liked it or not; and in Asia the United States became more and more involved with China in attempting to thwart the expansionist ambitions of Japan. Expansion of trade and increased investment were not the primary goals of American policy, although the right of Americans to trade and invest where they wanted was a part of Wilson's vision of a liberal world order.

POSTWAR AMERICA
AND THE WORLD ECONOMY

World War I had a profound impact on America's importance to the international economy. The system of international economic transactions established in London in the six decades before the Great War was so eroded by hostilities that it never recovered its prewar dominance. The London institutions did not disappear nor were they totally supplanted, but Great Britain was unable to balance and influence international economic life to the degree she once had. As the major financial and productive power after the war, many American business and governmental leaders understood that the United States had to assume greater responsibility for the smooth functioning of the international economic system. To some of these men, America's new power presented a great opportunity to rearrange the system to make American trade and finance flow more easily. Events confounded both those who wanted America to live up to its new responsibilities, on the one hand, and to take advantage of its new opportunities, on the other.

Many of the most prudent and advantageous international policies challenged the interests of powerful groups in the Congress and business. As a major creditor nation, the United States should have imported large quantities of goods, something that offended strong protectionist sentiments. To help revive the European economies, the American government should have postponed, reduced, or foregone wartime debts. But the Congress and the public, as well as members of the Executive branch, viewed these debts as business obligations that simply had to be paid. In such an atmosphere proposals to provide direct government loans for European reconstruction met stiff opposition. Critics maintained that private rather than governmental efforts should reconstruct Europe and indeed regulate the international economy.

Even had there been a consensus to support internationally minded policies, the American government and business did not have the institutions to assume Britain's role. There was little effective centralization or coordination in the foreign economic pol-

icy of the United States, as power and responsibility was dis-
bursed among a number of departments, bureaus, agencies, and
boards. Attempts at coordination of American economic diplomacy were centered in an Economic Liaison Committee of the
State Department, made up of middle-level experts from a number of different departments. This group did little more than
monitor economic conditions abroad, having no policy-making
powers. A high-level Central Foreign Trade Committee met only
once. Fundamentally, the Congress did not provide the State Department with the resources to take on coordination of policy. Indeed, the department's appropriations were cut back from wartime strength, although it was given responsibility to oversee the
dismantling of ad hoc wartime agencies and programs. Secretary
of Commerce William C. Redfield, who had hoped to coordinate
foreign trade policy in his department, quit the government, frustrated by the failure of the President and Congress to give him
the authority and resources needed to centralize commercial policy.

Private American economic institutions were no more able
to meet America's new international responsibilities. America's acceptance and exchange markets were undeveloped compared to
those in Britain. Similarly, the American Federal Reserve system
did not have great experience in international transactions, nor did
private American banks, which preferred domestic to foreign
lending.

America's task was formidable. She had to assume responsibilities and create institutions to take on a role Britain grew into
over five decades. That system had been sustained by a high volume of British trade and far-flung capital investment. Britain in
many of the six decades before 1914 had a negative balance of
trade on merchandise account. That is, she imported more than
she exported. But "invisible" earnings from foreign investments
more than assured a surplus on the total balance of payments. The
vastness of British investment in 1914—some eight times American foreign investment—assured funds to finance both long-term
capital projects (through foreign government securities usually) and
short-term capital to finance the movement of goods in interna-

tional trade. Moreover, sterling had become an international currency: abundant and available because of worldwide British trade and investment and relatively stable in value because it was closely tied to an international gold standard. The system was far from flawless, but it worked because of cooperation from other European countries. Leading European bankers adopted monetary policies that tried to adjust domestic policy to the needs of keeping exchange rates stable. World War I disturbed the institutions—the commercial banks, insurance companies, bill brokers, and the like—in London that kept the international economy operating. The gold standard was abandoned and domestic economic crises made it difficult for central bankers to follow policies that contributed to international stability. The United States was thus not alone in placing domestic economic and political consideration above the requirements of international economic stability. America's failure to create internationally minded policies, however, had grave consequences because of the country's great economic power.[40]

President Wilson realized the economic implications of America's new role in the postwar world. But he devoted his energies to the peace settlement and the League of Nations. The Senate's rejection of the Versailles Treaty undercut American influence with the European powers and embittered relations between the Congress and the Executive. Hostility between the two branches of government, combined with the President's debilitating illness, paralyzed American policy-making. The war raised issues as to reparations, war debts, tariffs, exchange rates, and reconstruction loans that had to be settled. Most of these problems were left unsolved in the uncertainty during negotiations for a peace treaty. Matters worsened during the years from the Senate's defeat of the peace treaty to the inauguration of the Harding administration. American officials had little to do with negotiations over reparations, as the British and French did as they pleased in determining them. Wilson refused to allow American officials to participate in conferences on currency and exchange problems. The President hoped to bring home to his domestic political opponents the consequences of American nonparticipation in the postwar treaty and the League of Nations.

Nevertheless, even if Wilson had been more cooperative, there were more fundamental problems in the United States' assumption of its responsibilities as the major power in the international economy. On almost every issue related to America's important new creditor status conflict arose between powerful domestic interests and those who believed that the United States should play a leading role in the international economy. Leaders in government and business who realized the broader implications of changed international economic conditions failed at almost every turn to get policies consistent with America's new responsibilities and power. The men arguing for an activist policy for the United States were not inconsequential members of the bureaucracy. In the Executive branch itself, aside from the President and Secretaries of State Lansing and Colby, there was the Secretary of the Treasury Carter Glass and Secretary of Commerce Redfield. Assistant Secretaries of the Treasury Rathbone and Leffingwell also contributed, as did Norman Davis, an influential adviser to the President. Leading bankers like Thomas Lamont, Otto Kahn, and Paul Warburg advocated policies that took a long-term view of America's interests. Leaders of prominent business associations (the Chamber of Commerce, the National Association of Manufacturers, and the National Foreign Trade Council) similarly advocated policies that looked beyond short-term interests.[41]

But public attitudes, the interests of small businessmen and agriculturists, congressional politics, and the remnants of the bitter disputes between Congress and the Executive all worked against America's taking a broad outlook in policy. These constraints did not preclude, however, the use of American economic power at times. But generally American policy was ineffective because of the President's irresolution, congressional intransigence, and the tendency of the public, businessmen, and farmers to consider their own particular interests above a more general and ill-defined international interest.

The tariff was one of the most obvious sources of conflict

between domestic and international interests. Leading members of the administration and prominent businessmen and bankers realized that the United States had to import more if the European economies were to revive, exchange rates stabilize, and foreign debts be paid. Treasury Department officials advocated lower tariffs. The prestigious business organization, the National Foreign Trade Council, wanted changes in the tariff, as did prominent bankers like Thomas Lamont and Paul Warburg. But internationalist sentiments were not easily translated into policy in a Congress pressed by agricultural and small business constituencies. Farmers in the summer of 1920 had responded to a fall in domestic prices with a call for emergency legislation to protect their markets. Agriculturalists pressured the Congress for increased tariff duties on a variety of agricultural products. President Wilson in March 1921 vetoed the tariff bill and was sustained by the Congress, although in May 1921 President Harding signed emergency tariff legislation that raised agricultural duties. Harding gave in to farmers' fears of an influx of cheap foreign agricultural goods into an already depressed and glutted American market. The bill, however, pleased small manufacturers too, because it contained anti-dumping provisions and embargoes against the imports of certain dyes and chemicals. Depreciating foreign currencies made American goods difficult to export, while European goods became more saleable in the American economy. Small manufacturers feared a glut of foreign, especially German, goods once foreign economies revived, something dreaded since German industry had not been substantially damaged by the war.

Domestic concerns also conflicted with wider American international economic responsibilities over war debts. Foreign economies would have revived more quickly had the United States rescheduled or cancelled the debts entirely. But cancellation, reapportionment, or extended deferment of interest, the President and Treasury officials feared, would have had a negative impact on the domestic economy, especially on taxes. Although the Treasury opposed cancellation, it reluctantly supported in 1919 a three-year moratorium on the payment of interest. Continued high taxes in the United States would have slowed domestic expansion.

Failure to collect the debts would have further complicated attempts to balance the budget, a prime goal of the conventional wisdom of the day. Overall, the President's concern for orderly economic growth at home and Congress' fear of overburdening American taxpayers with high taxes undermined the arguments of those who wanted to reapportion or defer debts.

To the Europeans the question of war debts was critical to the resolution of the reparations question. Wilson and Treasury officials, as well as American finance experts at Versailles, wanted reparations to be paid over thirty years and to be set within Germany's capacity to pay. Wilson assumed that the United States would play an important role in the Reparations Commission established to set the final figures. The United States, however, sent only unofficial observers when the Senate refused to ratify the treaty. By the end of Wilson's term, he and Secretary of State Bainbridge Colby had withdrawn even those officials in disgust at the terms the British and French were devising for reparations. American inability to be as flexible on the war debts as the Allies wanted contributed to the harsh reparations imposed on Germany, although one cannot entirely or even primarily blame the United States. Wilson's intransigence on the issues of the reservations to the treaty and the bitterness of congressional criticism of the President all contributed to uncertainty in the United States on the issue of reparations.

Attempts to create a program to help in European reconstruction ran into similar problems of conflict between Congress and the Executive, along with fears of damaging the domestic economy. But the issue of European reconstruction also brought to the fore ideological considerations. Leading American government officials and businessmen feared the growing power of the state. They wanted to allow private initiative and private capital to reconstruct Europe. Treasury plans in 1919 and 1920 to make government loans to the French for reconstruction ran into sharp opposition in the Congress. Congressmen feared that government lending to Europe would fuel inflation in the United States. Important advisers to Wilson such as Norman Davis and banker Thomas Lamont did not want to involve government too heavily in postwar reconstruction. Herbert Hoover and other prominent figures feared "politicization" of economic policy if the government was too directly involved. And learning a lesson from the war, they thought that the conflict had been in part a result of too heavy involvement of government in economic affairs in the first place.[42]

The private arrangements arrived at, however, were far from what was necessary to rebuild the European economies. The major instrument to provide loans to European governments was the so-called Edge Banks. Federal charters were authorized for these corporations in a 1919 amendment to the Federal Reserve Act. These banks were to help finance American exports and meet Europe's demands for capital. The Edge corporations, however, did not satisfy Europe's capital requirements, since the banks preferred to make short-term commercial loans of between six and nine months. The Europeans needed large-scale capital loans to be repaid over a decade and a half at least. American bankers were reluctant to commit themselves, however, to such extended loans so long as the question of peace remained unsettled and so long as the European currencies were depreciating. European reconstruction proceeded fitfully.

The inability to provide long-term loans and uncertainty over war debts only exacerbated Europe's problems. The value of European currencies continued to fluctuate, especially after the spring of 1919 when they were no longer pegged to the dollar. Such conditions only made the Congress and businessmen more reluctant to consider lower tariffs or long-term loans. Overall, then, although many government officials, prominent manufacturers, and international bankers saw the need for broader policies, they awaited a new administration. Wilson did not act on the larger responsibilities implied in America's new role in the international economy.

Despite the inability to effect long-term policies, there were businessmen and bankers who sought and obtained advantages abroad in those confused times. Officials in the State and Commerce Departments assisted American businesses in securing foreign investments and new markets. The dislocation in England

and Germany presented Americans with tempting opportunities to gain new markets, especially in Latin America. And businesses involved in communications, petroleum, and mining worked more closely than ever with government officials. The war had convinced many government officials of the need to keep close wartime contacts and, of more significance, of the general importance of foreign trade and investment to America.

Even though ad hoc assistance was forthcoming, there were nevertheless some institutional problems with making aid to business consistent and regular. Congress cut back appropriations and staff for the Departments of State and Commerce once the war ended. These departments were the victims of the bitter disputes between Congress and the Executive of the postwar years, of the Congress' reassertion of its authority. Secretary of Commerce Redfield resigned in disappointment, after a bruising battle to restore some of his department's programs to expand commerce which had been deferred during the war. Within the State Department, furthermore, there had been ambivalence about furthering particular business interests. Indeed, in July 1918 the Solicitor issued a memorandum making clear that promotion of trade and investment was to be a low priority of the administration. Such conflicts of view created tensions in the department and contributed to low morale, to say nothing of confusion in the minds of businessmen.[43]

CONCLUSION

America was incontestably one of the great powers by 1920. She had come out of the war militarily and economically ahead of the former great states of Europe. Part of America's power was her vast economic strength: her productive capacity, gold reserves, and capital. Decisions made in Washington affected the workings of the international economy as decisions made in London had affected it for the fifty years before. But the Wilson administration had proved incapable of living up to the vast economic responsibilities that came with peace in 1918. The President spent his political and physical strength in an unsuccessful struggle for his vision of America's role in the peace; the Congress looked more to domestic issues; and both government and private institutions were not equal to the tasks thrust upon the United States. The bureaucracies in Washington were eager to give assistance to private manufacturing and banking interests seeking markets or investments abroad. But there was little consistency to these efforts, because the bureaucratic institutions to provide such services were periodically the victims of cuts in appropriations by the Congress.

All of the Presidents in the years from 1899 to 1920 were aware of the growing economic power and interests of the United States in the world. Each in his own way took these interests into consideration in making foreign policy. But international economic issues and interests were not of central concern. Theodore Roosevelt and Woodrow Wilson, the two dominant figures in American diplomacy in those years, subordinated economics to wider considerations. Roosevelt conceived America's role in the world in political and strategic terms, although economic strength was an important part of his concept of power. Wilson concerned himself with the political institutions that would lead to collective security and peace, institutions that would also assure stability for foreign trade and investment. McKinley and Taft, men more easily identified with the special interests of the business community, nevertheless conceived of economics in diplomacy as something to be used for the achievement of wider goals too: security in the Caribbean and Asia. Economic interests were thus part of a larger diplomatic context that concerned itself with such issues as strategic security in the Caribbean, the balances of power in Europe and Asia, and the creation of international institutions to achieve peace.

Notes

1. Richard Leopold, *Elihu Root and Conservative Tradition* (Boston: Little, Brown, 1954), pp. 38–46: Robert L. Beisner, *From the Old Diplomacy to the New* (New York: Harlan Davidson, 1975), pp. 5–17; J. A. S. Grenville and G. B. Young, *Politics, Strategy and Diplomacy: Studies in American Foreign Policy 1873–1917* (New Haven: Yale University Press, 1966), pp. 297–336.

2. W. Arthur Lewis, "International Economics: International Competition in Manufactures," *American Economic Review* (May 1957), 47:579.

3. Mary Locke Eysenbach, *American Manufactured Exports, 1879–1914: A Study of Growth and Comparative Advantage* (New York: Arno, 1976), pp. 40–42.

4. U.S. Department of Commerce, Bureau of the Census, *Statistical Abstract of the United States for 1925* (Washington, D.C., GPO, 1926), pp. 449, 460.

5. Harold G. Vatter, *The Drive to Industrial Maturity: The U.S. Economy, 1860–1914* (Westport, Conn.: Greenwood, 1975), pp. 66–69; *Statistical Abstract 1925*, p. 449.

6. Alfred D. Chandler, Jr., "The Structure of American Industry in the Twentieth Century: A Historical Overview," *Business History Review* (Autumn 1969), 43:291–93; A. D. H. Kaplan, *Big Enterprise in a Competitive System*, rev. ed. (Washington, D.C., 1964; reprint, Greenwood), pp. 140–42; Eysenbach, p. 40.

7. Mira Wilkins, *The Emergence of Multinational Enterprise: American Business Abroad from the Colonial Era to 1914* (Cambridge: Harvard University Press, 1970), pp. 120–125; Robert B. Davis, *Peacefully Working to Conquer the World: Singer Sewing Machine in Foreign Markets, 1854–1920* (New York: Arno, 1976), pp. 116–18.

8. Burton I. Kaufman, *Efficiency and Expansion: Foreign Trade Organization in the Wilson Administration, 1913–1921* (Westport, Conn.: Greenwood, 1974), pp. 82–85.

9. *Ibid.*, pp. 117–30, 213–16.

10. Theodore Roosevelt, "Message to Senate and House of Representatives," March 1, 1905, James D. Richardson, ed., *A Compilation of the Messages and Papers of the Presidents*, 20 vols. (New York, 1897–1920), 14:6,948; U.S. Department of State, *Papers Relating to the Foreign Relations of the United States 1903* (Washington, D.C.: GPO, 1904), pp. 17–19, 91–118, 622–25.

11. Burton I. Kaufman, "The Organizational Dimension of United States Foreign Economic Policy, 1900–1920," *Business History Review* (1972), 46:17–44; Richard Hume Werking, *The Master Architects: Building the United States Foreign Service, 1890–1913* (Lexington: University Press of Kentucky, 1977), pp. 171–200.

12. Diary of Wilbur J. Carr, January 29, 1913, Wilbur J. Carr Papers, Library of Congress; Werking, pp. 234–35.

13. Mira Wilkins, *The Maturing of Multinational Enterprise: American Business Abroad from 1914 to 1970* (Cambridge: Harvard University Press, 1974), p. 31; Werking, pp. 229–31; Joseph L. Brandes, *Herbert Hoover and Economic Diplomacy: Department of Commerce Policy, 1921–28* (Pittsburgh: University of Pittsburgh Press, 1962), pp. 163–69.

14. The evolution of the government's view can be traced in its response to the Mexican Revolution. See Benjamin Taylor Harrison, "Chandler Anderson and American Foreign Relations (1896–1928)" (Ph.D. dissertation, University of California, Los Angeles, 1969), pp. 60, 112; Robert Freeman Smith, *The United States and Revolutionary Nationalism in Mexico, 1916–1932* (Chicago: University of Chicago Press, 1972), pp. 34–189; N. Ste-

phan Kane, "American Businessmen and Foreign Policy: The Recognition of Mexico, 1920–23," *Political Science Quarterly* (Summer 1975), 90:293–313.

15. Harrison, pp. 53ff; Joseph S. Tulchin, *The Aftermath of War: World War I and U.S. Policy Toward Latin America* (New York: New York University Press, 1971), p. 92.

16. National Association of Manufacturers, *Proceedings of the First Annual Meeting of the National Association of Manufacturers, 1895* (Philadelphia, 1896), pp. 12–13.

17. Theodore Roosevelt to Nicholas Murray Butler, August 12, 1902, and August 29, 1904, in E. E. Morison, ed., *The Letters of Theodore Roosevelt*, 8 vols. (Cambridge: Harvard University Press, 1951–54), 3:312–13 and 4:912–13; Tom E. Terrill, *The Tariff, Politics and American Foreign Policy, 1874–1901* (Westport, Conn.: Greenwood, 1973), pp. 202–08; Lewis L. Gould, "Diplomats in the Lobby: Franco-American Relations and the Dingley Tariff of 1897," *The Historian* (August 1977), 39:659–80.

18. Richard E. Welch, Jr., *Response to Imperialism, The United States and the Philippine-American War, 1899–1902* (Chapel Hill: University of North Carolina Press, 1979), pp. 3–23, 58–84; David Healy, *U.S. Expansionism: The Imperialist Urge in the 1890s* (Madison: University of Wisconsin Press, 1970), pp. 54–67.

19. William McKinley, "Second Annual Message," December 5, 1898, in Richardson, *Messages and Papers*, 13:6,326–27; John M. Dobson, *America's Ascent: The United States Becomes a Great Power* (Dekalb: Northern Illinois University Press, 1978), pp. 150–53; Grenville and Young, pp. 297–336.

20. Theodore Roosevelt, "First Annual Message," December 3, 1901, in Richardson, 13:6,645–48; John Morton Blum, *The Republican Roosevelt* (Cambridge: Harvard University Press, 1965), pp. 116–17.

21. Theodore Roosevelt to Maria Longworth Storer, October 28, 1889, in Morison, 2:1,089; Grenville and Young, pp. 239–66.

22. See, for example, U.S. Department of State, *Papers Relating to Foreign Relations of the United States, 1907* 2 vols. (Washington, D.C., GPO, 1910), 1:77–79, 266–68, 402–41, 477–508, 577–79.

23. Theodore Roosevelt to George Otto Trevelyan, September 9, 1906; and to Senator Joseph B. Foraker, September 28, 1906, in Morison, 5:399–401, 429–32.

24. See, for example, National Association of Manufacturers, *Proceedings of the Ninth Annual Convention, 1904* (New York, 1905).

25. Theodore Roosevelt to Elihu Root, June 7, 1904, in Morison, 4:821–22; Dana G. Munro, *Intervention and Dollar Diplomacy in the Caribbean, 1900–1921* (Princeton: Princeton University Press, 1964), pp. 65–77.

26. Theodore Roosevelt to John Hay, April 22, 1903, in Morison, 3:465.

27. *New York Times*, November 3, 1912; Harley Notter, *The Origins of the Foreign Policy of Woodrow Wilson* (Baltimore: Johns Hopkins University Press, 1937), pp. 197, 217, 232–34, 305; Ray Stannard Baker and William E. Dodd, *The Public Papers of Woodrow Wilson*, 6 vols. (New York, 1925–27; reprint, Kraus), 3:140–45.

28. Akira Iriye, *Across the Pacific, An Inner History of American-East Asian Relations* (New York: Harcourt, 1967) pp. 80–81, 88; Kenton J. Clymer, *John Hay, The Gentleman as Diplomat* (Ann Arbor: University of Michigan Press, 1975), pp. 143–51.

29. Clymer, pp. 151–52; Michael H. Hunt, *Frontier Defense and the Open Door: Manchuria In Chinese American Relations, 1895–1911* (New Haven: Yale University Press, 1973), pp. 33–34.

30. Theodore Roosevelt to William Howard Taft, December 22, 1910, in Morison, 7:190.

31. Arthur S. Link, *Wilson: The Struggle for Neutrality* (Princeton: Princeton University Press, 1960), pp. 267–308; Iriye, pp. 127–37.

32. *Ibid.*, pp. 133, 136.

33. *New York Times*, July 5, 1915; Harrison, pp. 53–77; Link, pp. 489–92; Smith, pp. 34–42; Wilkins, *Maturing*, p. 31.

34. Harrison, pp. 75–84; Smith, pp. 34–189.

35. Munro, pp. 160–425.

36. Link, pp. 45–48; Daniel M. Smith, *Robert Lansing and American Neutrality 1914–1917* (Berkeley: University of California Press, 1958), pp. 166–71.

37. Notter, pp. 9–10, 34, 55, 156–60; Healy, pp. 115–16.

38. Daniel M. Smith, "National Interest and American Intervention, 1917: An Historiographical Appraisal," *Journal of American History* (1965), 52:5–24; Paul Birdsall, "Neutrality and Economic Pressures, 1914–1917," *Science and Society* (Spring 1939), 3:217–28.

39. Joan Hoff Wilson, *Ideology and Economics: United States Relations with Soviet Russia, 1918–1933* (Columbia: University of Missouri Press, 1974), pp. 3–27.

40. William Ashworth, *A Short History of the International Economy since 1850*, 3rd ed. (London: Longman, 1975), pp. 191–230.

41. Robert H. Van Meter, "The United States and European Recovery, 1918–1923: A Study of Public Policy and Private Finance" (Ph.D. dissertation, University of Wisconsin, 1971), pp. 1–46; Melvyn P. Leffler, *The Elusive Quest: America's Pursuit of European Stability and French Security, 1919–1933* (Chapel Hill: University of North Carolina Press, 1979), pp. 18–30.

42. Van Meter, pp. 168–218.

43. Michael J. Hogan, *Informal Entente: The Private Structure of Cooperation in Anglo-American Economic Diplomacy, 1918–1928* (Columbia: University of Missouri Press, 1977), pp. 13–37; for a fuller discussion of these points see William H. Becker, *The Dynamics of Business-Government Relations: Industry and Exports, 1893–1921* (Chicago: University of Chicago Press, 1982), pp. 157–77.

5

1921–1932
Expansionist Impulses
and Domestic Constraints

Melvyn P. Leffler

Vanderbilt University

AFTER WORLD WAR I, economic considerations assumed a position of primacy in the shaping of American foreign policy. Economic factors played a decisive role because they were closely linked to ideological values, moral constructs, and legal concepts. Indeed the full impact of economic considerations cannot be assessed in quantitative terms. Studies of exports, imports, loans, and investments, however revealing they may be, do not elucidate the complex web of legal, institutional, ideological, and economic interrelationships that came to fruition in the aftermath of the Great War. American officials could extol the virtues of peace, support arbitration treaties, defend the rights of property, champion the sanctity of contracts, cultivate multinational efforts of cooperation in the private sector, and oppose revolutionary movements abroad because they realized that efforts to avert war, disseminate American ideals, and encourage world economic progress were compatible with the interests of a net creditor, exporting nation, increasingly concerned with foreign supplies of raw materials.

The primacy of economic considerations resulted at least in part from the absence of strategic apprehensions. With Germany defeated and Britain weakened, the vital security interests of the United States appeared safe. Japan was a potential menace to American interests in the western Pacific and in East Asia. But the Japanese did not seem to jeopardize the nation's security. No great power threatened the continental coastlines, challenged the Monroe Doctrine, or endangered the Panama Canal. Not having to worry about the nation's safety, even military thinking became increasingly linked to the vortex of economic factors. In part, this reflected the navy's effort to capitalize upon the nation's overseas commercial and financial interests in order to enhance its own organizational goals; in part, it reflected the ascendancy of economic factors in the shaping of diplomatic and military thinking.

American foreign policy goals were aimed at creating a stable and peaceful international order conducive to the expansion of American exports, the protection of American overseas investments, the control of foreign supplies of raw materials, and the dissemination of American ideals and values. The policy known as the open door, first applied to the Far East and subsequently universalized by Woodrow Wilson, increasingly influenced the conceptualization of policy objectives. American officials sought the right to trade and invest on equal terms with any other nation. They also wanted American access to raw materials and championed the cause of national self-determination. Such goals were expected to enhance American material interests. But these goals were also tied to ideological and legal principles that were considered prerequisite to world order, international prosperity, and universal justice.

Within the United States controversy did not center on the fundamental open-door objectives of American foreign policy. Instead debate focused on the tactics to implement foreign policy goals. Partisan politics, ethno-cultural divisions, bureaucratic rivalries, and rifts within the business community very much influenced the debates over tactics. And these disputes were significant because they implicitly revealed the degree of importance attached to foreign policy goals by interest groups, legislative representatives, and executive officials. The rejection of the League of Nations, imposition of higher tariff duties, insistence on war debt repayments, and antipathy to military commitments in Europe and East Asia revealed that as important as was the search for an open-door, liberal capitalist order, it did not take precedence over domestic priorities, many of them economic, nor supersede traditional non-entanglement inclinations.

In short, the matrix of economic-ideological concerns encompassed in the open-door approach to a stable, liberal capitalist world order determined the conceptualization of foreign policy goals. Yet the pursuit of these goals was not seen as *vital* to the national security or the economic well-being of the United States. Hence, when the depression came, and when there was not yet a threat from a totalitarian power, almost everyone concurred on the primacy (although not exclusiveness) of domestic tactics to solve the depression and on the need to refrain from military embroilments and political alliances that might divert energy and dissipate resources from these domestic approaches.

THE ECONOMIC VORTEX OF REPUBLICAN FOREIGN POLICY

World War I significantly influenced the position of the United States in the world economy. The nation entered the war as a net debtor on private account and emerged as a net creditor with a balance of over $3.5 billion. In addition, foreign governments owed the American government over $10 billion as a result of Allied war debt obligations. Not so dramatic, but also important, was the tremendous expansion of American trade during the war and immediate postwar years. The proportion of total world exports belonging to the United States climbed from 12.4 percent in 1913 to 16.9 percent in 1922. The percentage of total world imports going to the United States rose from 8.3 percent to 12.9 percent during the same period. If the effect of the 1921–22 recession is disregarded for a moment, the impact of world conflict on American exports and imports is even more startling. Between 1913 and 1920, American merchandise exports increased from $2.5 billion to $8 billion while American imports grew from $1.75 billion to over $5 billion. One of the most impressive developments between 1914 and 1920 was the 500 percent increase in the overseas sales of finished manufactured goods. In 1919, 14 percent of all manufactured goods produced in the country were exported compared to less than 10 percent in 1914.[1]

American officials and businessmen focused considerable attention on these foreign commercial and financial developments. When the postwar slump set in during the latter part of 1920 and exports precipitously declined, there was repeated stress on the interrelationships between export expansion and domestic prosperity. In the autumn of 1921, President Warren G. Harding and Secretary of Commerce Herbert C. Hoover convened a conference on unemployment to assess the workings of the business cycle and to propose suggestions to abet recovery and maintain prosperity. Emphasizing that "a small surplus of production over demand . . . fixes the price of the entire amount produced," the conferees maintained that export markets had to be cultivated or business would suffer and unemployment increase. Farm groups and business organizations concurred. During 1921 and 1922, the American Cotton Association, the American Farm Bureau Federation, the Southern Commercial Congress, the National Foreign Trade Council (NFTC), and the Chamber of Commerce of the United States clamored for governmental action to revive foreign markets.[2]

Farm commodities and raw materials were especially dependent on foreign markets. Using 1920 figures, the President's Committee on Unemployment reported that 61.5 percent of the cotton produced in the country was exported, 51.5 percent of the copper, 53.2 percent of the rice, 46.5 percent of the rye, 44.5 percent of the tobacco, 23.5 percent of the wheat, 19 percent of the zinc, and 17.8 percent of the tin plate.[3] Statistics of this sort and pressures from farm groups and their congressional spokesmen impelled Republican officials to reactivate the War Finance

Corporation in 1921 as a temporary expedient to help relieve the agricultural overproduction problem. Subsequently, when agricultural distress persisted, the Treasury Department and the Federal Reserve Bank of New York (FRBNY) sought to expedite Europe's financial stabilization and to augment her purchasing power in order to boost domestic farm prices and relieve agrarian discontent.[4]

Hoover and his colleagues in the Commerce Department did not think that farm problems could be solved permanently through overseas sales, but they were equally concerned with the nation's foreign trade. They maintained that crop diversification, more efficient marketing procedures, and an increasing home market would gradually eliminate agricultural distress. Accordingly, they focused their primary attention on the expansion of industrial exports. Foreign sales of manufactured goods, Commerce officials claimed, made "it possible to use our resources and energy to greater advantage; by widening the range of markets it gives to industry greater stability in output and thereby makes employment more secure." By the middle 1920s, the Bureau of Foreign and Domestic Commerce (BFDC) was answering 9,000 business requests daily for trade information. Export associations claimed that because prices were set in international markets, "our interest in foreign trade is far greater than the mere proportion which it bears to our total commerce."[5]

In order to maintain and expand American exports, policymakers recognized that private American capital would have to assume a more important role in the international economy. As early as April 1919 State and Commerce Department officials concurred that foreign investment "on a substantial scale is almost essential to the maintenance and extension of foreign trade on a sound financial basis." With the support of the Treasury Department, Congress passed the Edge Act in 1919. This legislation permitted new forms of business to engage in foreign lending. During the following year, hundreds of the nation's most prominent bankers and businessmen met in Chicago to support the formation of a new corporation under the Edge Act. As economic conditions worsened during 1921, businessmen continually reminded one another that, as a creditor nation, the United States had an obligation to make foreign loans in order to support foreign currencies and promote American exports. When the Harding administration took office in 1921, Secretary of State Charles Evans Hughes, Secretary of the Treasury Andrew W. Mellon, and Hoover focused immediate attention on how to promote the outflow of American capital for the well-being of the international community and for the advancement of the American economy.[6]

The evidence is now overwhelming that at the end of the Great War, executive officials and business leaders were cognizant of the creditor status of the United States and of its significance for American foreign policy. In the autumn of 1919, the State Department Economic Liaison Committee, including representatives from every important executive agency, discussed the commercial ramifications of the nation's creditor status. A new subcommittee was established "to prepare an exposition of the problems arising from the permanently adverse balance of trade which the United States, as a creditor nation, seems destined to have in the future."[7] Although imports did increase faster than exports in the postwar decade, the unfavorable merchandise balance did not materialize. Throughout the 1920s, officials in the Commerce Department paid close attention to the relationship of imports to exports. They maintained that capital outflows, immigrant remittances, tourist expenditures, and other so-called "invisible" items enabled the United States to reconcile a favorable trade balance with its creditor status. Yet they sensed that this was a temporary phenomenon.[8]

Indeed, one of the most striking aspects of the official American attitude toward the international economy after World War I was the growing belief in the nation's dependence on foreign supplies of raw materials. Hoover and Julius Klein, chief of the BFDC, repeatedly emphasized that "our standard of living is absolutely dependent upon certain import commodities." As the United States became increasingly industrialized, it seemed destined to import larger amounts of raw materials. The Commerce Department's systematic effort to expand exports was geared to the assumption that exports would eventually prove essential to pay for indispensable imports. "Foreign trade," the Commerce Department declared, "is of greater importance to our manufacturing industry in furnishing its raw materials than in providing markets for its finished products." Imports of raw materials and semi-manufactured goods constituted a growing proportion of all such materials used by American industry. The Commerce Department emphasized American dependence on foreign supplies of rubber, silk, and wood pulp, while the Navy noted the importance of nitrates, tin, nickel, rubber, wool, and coffee imports. In the mid-1920s, awareness of the growing dependence of an industrial nation on raw material imports impelled Hoover to combat the efforts of foreign government-sponsored cartels to control the marketing of important products, like rubber.[9]

At the conclusion of the Great War nothing worried American civilian and military officials more than the prospect of America's dependence on foreign petroleum sources. Oil seemed absolutely vital to American industry and the United States Navy. The assumption that America was quickly exhausting its oil reserves caused widespread alarm. State, Commerce, and Navy Department officials prodded private corporations to accelerate their search for foreign oil supplies. In negotiations with foreign governments, American policymakers insisted upon equal opportunity for American corporations and threatened to retaliate if such rights were not recognized.[10] Even in 1926, when new domestic discoveries were alleviating the worst apprehensions, the State Department's Economic Advisor's office maintained that "our whole industrial being as well as our security as a nation depends in a great measure on an assured supply of petroleum and in order to assure ourselves of supplies from foreign fields we want the control of those supplies to be in the hands of American companies." By this time American oil corporations were working out cooperative arrangements with their British counterparts to control much of the world's known oil reserves.[11]

After World War I, the search for export markets, the dependence on foreign supplies of raw materials, and the recognition of America's role as a creditor nation convinced policymakers and businessmen of the essential unity of the international economy.

Technological advancement and industrial progress bred world-wide interdependence. If it were not for the exchange of commodities, Hoover acknowledged, "Not a single automobile would run; not a dynamo would turn; not a telephone, telegraph, or radio would operate . . . Therefore, let no one think that international trade is but the noisy dickering of merchants and bankers,—it is the lifeblood of modern civilization." [12] This viewpoint impelled American officials to try to create a stable world order along open-door liberal capitalist lines. Such an order, they believed, would redound to the benefit of the American economy, promote international economic progress, and contribute to world peace. Peace, stability, prosperity, and capitalism were interlocking phenomena, each dependent upon the other. Such an all-encompassing Weltanschauung enabled American policymakers to reconcile their ideals with their self-interest, to blend their search for peace with their quest for markets, to harmonize their ethnocentrism with their generosity.

During the 1920s, in speech after speech, Harding, Hoover, Hughes, Mellon, Kellogg, and other influential officials dedicated American foreign policy to the construction of a peaceful and stable world order. Peace and stability, they never tired of saying, were prerequisite to the growth of world trade and the free flow of private capital. In turn, commercial exchange and private investment contributed to economic growth, fostered social stability, and destroyed the causes of mass discontent. Backwardness and poverty were the sources of social upheaval and revolutionary disorder; private investment and economic growth their cure. For Americans, self-interest and selflessness went hand in hand. "Were it not for commerce," Harding declared, "there would be no civilization." With genuine sincerity, the National Foreign Trade Council also emphasized the mutuality of interests between American businessmen and the "other peoples of the world. We wish them all peace, stability, and prosperity, so will their trade grow and thrive. So will ours advance." And as economic growth took place, the seeds of conflict would be removed and the prospects for peace would be enhanced. [13]

This outlook meant that the defeat of the League of Nations did not terminate American efforts to create a stable, liberal capitalist order. In fact, the League of Nations was not an end in itself, but a means toward an end. The League Covenant had been designed by Wilson without sufficient awareness of prevailing trends of internationalist thought in the United States. Wilson's covenant subordinated concepts of law and order and highlighted the use of political machinery. Most prewar internationalists, many of whom were Republicans, had had strong misgivings about the efficacy of Wilson's League. When the League issue became immersed in a matrix of partisan considerations, personality clashes, ethno-cultural divisions, and institutional struggles, it was predictable that many internationalists would seek other means to achieve a stable world order. Hughes and Hoover had supported the Treaty of Versailles with reservations. After taking office they believed that reviving the issue would engender controversy out of all proportion to the benefits that might be derived from the international organization. Like most internationalist-oriented business groups and peace organizations, they thought that a stable world order could be constructed upon an interrelated set of sound judicial institutions, wise economic policies, and enlightened multinational cooperation in the private sector.[14]

When Harding, Hughes, and Hoover supported the creation of a Central American tribunal and advocated American membership in the Permanent Court for International Justice, they were resuming the prewar American internationalist tradition. This orientation linked international law to a peaceful world order conducive to the flow of private capital, the advance of backward economies, and the growth of world trade. Republican officials did not expect legal institutions to insure world peace. Indeed, they believed it was naive to expect any international organization, however much force it might theoretically have at its disposal, to eliminate conflict. Their aim was to proceed gradually to establish legal processes that constituted alternatives to military force. Hughes and Hoover spoke frequently of codifying international law and enlarging the area of administered justice. They had no illusions but that this would be a slow, painful process. Yet respect for legal processes was indispensable to national and international stability. According to Hoover, "the whole great fabric of international commerce upon which the world is today dependent for its very existence rests . . . upon the sanctity of contract honestly entered upon under the laws of each country. But for confidence in the courts of different nations, the whole of our international economic relations would become hazardous and weakened. And the just decisions of the courts remove the friction of our respective citizens out of the field of diplomatic relations into the field of abstract justice."[15]

Viable judicial institutions and respect for legal processes were considered necessary for the maintenance of international stability, the cultivation of world commerce, and the protection of contractual obligations. Bolshevism constituted a challenge to the economic and legal world order sought by American officials. Bolshevik confiscation of private property, abrogation of contracts, and fomenting of revolutionary activity posed a long-term threat to the interests of a capitalist, creditor nation intent on expanding world trade and promoting economic growth in a stable international environment. Consequently, from 1919 to 1933, American officials refused to recognize the Soviet regime. This posture was not an ideological stand divorced from economic self-interest. Although a nonrecognition policy prevented the extension of long-term credits that might have aided exports to the Soviet Union, the loss of some direct trade with Soviet Russia was not considered as harmful to American interests as would be the adoption of Soviet precedents in other parts of the world. In a speech President Harding intended to deliver just before his death, he emphasized that "international good faith forbids any sort of sanction of the Bolshevist policy. . . . If there are no property rights there is little, if any, foundation for national rights, which we are ever being called upon to safeguard. The whole fabric of international commerce and righteous international relationship will fail if any great nation like ours shall abandon the underlying principles relating to sanctity of contract and the honor involved in respected rights." Such rhetoric did not compartmentalize ideology and economics; it blended them.[16]

In the 1920s, neither civilian nor military officials viewed the Bolshevik threat in strategic terms. The Soviet Union was too weak to jeopardize the national security interests of the United States. Notwithstanding this fact, the ideological posture and internal policies of the Soviet government constituted a threat to the worldwide legal order sought by a pragmatic capitalist nation. This was especially true when revolutionary nationalist movements were beginning to emerge in the Middle East, Far East, and Latin America. In Mexico, for example, Article 27 of the Constitution of 1917 declared all subsoil resources the patrimony of the nation. This provision endangered the property rights of American corporations, especially petroleum companies. Although the Department of State disagreed with American oil executives on many particulars, Hughes considered the "safeguarding of property rights against confiscation" the most important objective of the American government. "A confiscatory policy," he insisted, "strikes not only at the interests of particular individuals but at the foundations of international intercourse." Property rights, honestly acquired, had to be kept sacrosanct if cooperation and commerce were to flourish.[17] This was the natural ideological posture and legal position of an advanced industrial nation with a growing network of foreign investments and commercial ties around the globe.

The defense of property rights and aversion to revolution were integral parts of the American effort to disseminate open-door, liberal capitalist principles in the 1920s. American military officials accepted this as the major goal of American foreign policy. No longer fearing any imminent threat to the nation's coastlines, the Panama Canal, or the Monroe Doctrine, the army and particularly the navy increasingly defined their roles and justified their existence in economic terms. Surveying the world situation just prior to the depression, army officers complacently assessed the world strategic situation. Recognizing, however, that industrial development put America in the forefront of world commercial affairs, the army warned President Hoover that "it is a historical fact that ascendancy in world trade . . . has always been a great potential cause of war." Hence the nation's economic position demanded a viable, it not large, military establishment even when the international environment was not threatening. The navy's General Board constantly alluded to this economic argument when justifying its requests for appropriations. "When foreign markets close to us," the General Board maintained as early as 1922, "American prosperity ends. An efficient navy . . . is a necessary national contribution to our own economic prosperity. Moreover, it is the outward and visible force to ensure to the United States its ability to preserve for itself and for the world a rule of law, of order, and of justice."[18]

Throughout the 1920s Japan and Britain were pinpointed as prospective enemies not because they threatened vital security interests but because they posed threats to the open-door principles and commercial ambitions of the United States. Studies by the navy's General Board and its War Plans Division repeatedly and correctly emphasized that Japan, under prevailing conditions, had no capacity to attack in the eastern Pacific. The war plans drawn up by the army and navy emphasized that the focal point of possible Japanese-American friction was in the western Pacific and East Asia where America's open-door principles collided with Japan's quest for a sphere of influence. The Philippines, of course, constituted America's vulnerable spot, but their retention was constantly justified in terms of enabling the United States to expand its commerce into East Asia. In 1924, the General Board opposed Philippine independence. "Our country," it declared, "will depend more and more in the future on its sea-borne commerce [in the Far East], and for us to sacrifice this vital outlying position of commercial importance would be a very grave step that would cost us dearly in the future." Seven years later, when the world economy was in a tailspin and sentiment for Philippine independence had grown appreciably, the General Board's position still had not changed. Emphasizing America's open-door, commercial ambitions in East Asia, Admiral William V. Pratt wrote the Secretary of the Navy that

the Philippines constitute a potential commercial center upon which depend, to a large extent, the development and success of future American trade relations with Far Eastern countries and Australasia. . . . With the development of modern civilization in China, the United States will evince an increasing interest in the trade possibilities of the region of the

Western Pacific. Far-seeing statesmen, economists and writers are agreed that there lie the future great markets of the world.[19]

Most studies of the American navy in the interwar era have focused on American-Japanese rivalries. In the late 1920s, however, naval officials became less concerned with Japan and focused growing attention on Anglo-American differences. Discord over the limitation of cruisers was the ostensible cause of this acrimony. But economic competition was viewed as the real source of the tension. In 1927, the navy's War Plans Division recommended that plans for a possible war with Britain should be devised. "History indicated," wrote Frank Schofield, director of the War Plans Division, "that the world's two greatest nations eventually fight to decide superiority and to relieve trade competition." Three years later, when plans for a Blue (United States)–Red (Great Britain) war were drawn up, the Joint Board of the Army and Navy elaborated upon the economic considerations that might precipitate an Anglo-American conflict:

The most probable cause of war between RED and BLUE is the constantly increasing BLUE economic penetration and commercial expansion into regions formerly dominated by RED trade, to such extent as eventually to menace RED standards of living and to threaten economic ruin. . . . The foreign policy of BLUE . . . is primarily concerned with the advancement of the foreign trade of BLUE and demands equality of treatment in all political dependencies and backward countries, and unrestricted access to sources of raw materials. In this particular it comes in conflict with the foreign policies of RED.[20]

Without question the military's emphasis on economic considerations was prompted, at least in part, by organizational and bureaucratic imperatives. Nevertheless, it is significant that military leaders assumed that the best means of pursuing organizational interests was by underscoring the imperatives of open-door expansion. Such arguments, the army and navy believed, were most likely to win favor with other executive officials and congressional leaders. Yet once they admitted that the international environment was quiescent and that no strategic threats were on the horizon, military spokesmen found themselves in a very difficult position.

The absence of a threat to vital national security interests encouraged civilian leaders, especially Hoover, to press forward with arms limitation proposals. These officials assumed that their quest for an open-door, liberal capitalist world order would have a better chance of survival if it were built upon solid economic foundations than if it were imposed through military force. Moreover, there was a widespread consensus among Republican officials in the early 1920s that expenditures on armaments were one of the major causes of financial chaos, fluctuating exchange rates, commercial stagnation, and economic dislocation. By limiting armaments, Harding, Hughes, and Hoover hoped to curtail government expenditures, balance budgets, stabilize currencies, and establish an environment conducive to world economic growth.

This was the great achievement of the Washington Naval Conference of 1921–22. The agreements limited armaments, reaffirmed the principles of equal opportunity and self-determination in China, and provided for consultation among the great powers in the Pacific. With Germany no longer a military threat and Japanese power limited to the western Pacific, civilian officials believed that the best chance of stabilizing the international arena was by demonstrating the economic benefits to be derived from arms limitation and cooperative competition according to the principles of the open door. That policymakers believed this orientation would redound to their domestic political advantage does not mean they were unconcerned with foreign policy considerations. Indeed, the political appeal of the Washington Conference illustrates the American people's readiness to accept a foreign policy based on the economic and ideological foundations of the open door and arms limitation.[21]

Throughout the 1920s, Republican officials promoted arms limitation as an integral part of their foreign economic policy. This was not an unrealistic pursuit when implemented cautiously in an unthreatening international environment. Their aim was to establish the economic basis of a permanent peace. They also sought to end the dissipation of capital resources on military weaponry, find peaceful ways of settling contentious issues, and outlaw war as an acceptable means of pursuing national objectives. No great miracles were expected from any one of these developments. After the signing of the Kellogg-Briand Pact in 1928, Myron Herrick, the American ambassador to France, sarcastically remarked that "treaties are somewhat like children's games. When some child does not want to play any longer, he breaks up the game and that's the end of it." Yet American officials hoped that the slow evolution of arms limitation treaties, judicial processes, arbitration agreements, and antiwar pacts would gradually turn men's energy and attention from military preparations to economic undertakings.[22]

Indeed, even while the Washington Conference was underway, American policymakers remained very conscious that arms limitation treaties and open-door declarations had to be supplemented by wise policies capable of sustaining peaceful worldwide economic growth. William S. Culbertson, a member of the Tariff Commission, coordinated many of the economic studies used by Secretary of State Hughes during the arms limitation conference. Like many other officials, Culbertson urged the convocation of another international meeting to deal with commercial and investment issues. Culbertson believed that the arms conference would have lasting significance only if it were accompanied by efforts to tackle other economic and financial problems.[23] For a moment in early 1922 it seemed that Harding, Hughes, and Hoover might attend the British-sponsored international economic conference at Genoa. After careful deliberation, however, they decided to turn down an invitation lest they fall into the position of implicitly recognizing the Soviet Union and becoming overly embroiled in European political questions.[24]

Yet in the early 1920s both Republican officials and American businessmen agreed that the most important task of American foreign policy was to help rehabilitate European economies and stabilize European finances. Prior to the war Europe had consumed over 60 percent of American exports, including 83 percent of all crude material exports, and 71 percent of all foodstuff exports. Because the agricultural and raw material sectors of the American economy were so badly hit by the economic slump of

1920–22, it was natural for policymakers and businessmen to dwell upon the significance of Europe's pacification and reconstruction.[25] Moreover, they felt certain that the recovery of the Old World was necessary for the growth of backward economies, including those of Latin American nations. Europe constituted a critical market for the tropical goods and natural resources of underdeveloped areas. In turn, the latter purchased the manufactured goods and finished products of western Europe. Furthermore, with American capital still expected to find many lucrative opportunities at home, European capital was assumed to have a vital role to play in generating future international economic growth.[26]

The perception of an interdependent world economy, with the Old World occupying a major place in it, impelled American officials to grapple with European economic and financial problems. Even before the Washington Conference had been concluded, officials in the State, Commerce, Treasury, and Agriculture Departments as well as those in the FRBNY had begun to prepare for the reassessment of Germany's reparations burden, the reduction of Allied war debt obligations, the mobilization of private American capital for European reconstruction, and the readjustment of American tariff duties. These tasks were not easily undertaken because they clashed with protectionist demands, fiscal priorities, inflationary fears, and isolationist sentiment. Yet Harding, Hughes, Hoover, Mellon, Culbertson, and Benjamin Strong, governor of the FRBNY, moved cautiously and steadily to establish the World War Foreign Debt Commission, to strengthen the Tariff Commission, to oversee the outflow of private capital, to prepare for cooperation between European central banks and the FRBNY, and to depoliticize, so far as was possible, the European reparations imbroglio.[27]

By the latter part of 1923, Republican officials were ready to play a significant role in the financial rehabilitation of Germany and the stabilization of European currencies. With the mark worthless, the Weimar Republic on the verge of collapse, and revolutionary ardor on the upswing, American policymakers repeatedly emphasized that an American contribution to European stabilization efforts was prerequisite to sustained prosperity at home and to the prevention of revolution abroad. In the middle 1920s, American financial leverage, through capital outflows and war debt reductions, was applied to help arrange the Dawes Plan, consummate the Locarno treaties, stabilize European currencies, and establish the gold exchange standard. As European tensions abated, Franco-German relations improved, and economic growth resumed, Republican officials took great pride in their contribution to the restoration of stability in the Old World. Maintaining that a prosperous Germany would be a peaceful Germany, they reaffirmed their view that nations acted out of economic self-interest. They assumed that while they were laying the basis for Europe's recuperation and America's prosperity, they were also establishing the framework for a stable and peaceful world order along liberal capitalist lines.[28]

A Bolshevik Russia was perceived as an obstacle to American reconstruction efforts in Europe. Prior to the war Czarist Russia had served as a market for western European manufactured goods and as a supplier of foodstuffs and raw materials. If Russia once again could be integrated into the European economy, her markets and raw materials might abet Europe's recovery as well as constitute an outlet for American exports and investments.[29] All through the 1920s, there was some incentive to promote direct commercial relations, extend American aid, and recognize the Soviet government. These actions might gain the friendship of the Russian people and set the framework for the extension of American influence into Russia once the Bolshevik regime collapsed. Yet these possible advantages had to be weighed against the liabilities and repercussions of aiding and recognizing a government that disregarded the sanctity of contracts, denied the rights of property, and repudiated the legal basis for private investment and open-door commerce in the international marketplace.

During the 1920s, American policy toward Soviet Russia was beset with contradictions because policymakers could find no easy way of reconciling these interrelated yet often conflicting materialist and ideological considerations. Trade was permitted; famine relief extended; direct investments allowed; sale of Soviet securities prohibited; and recognition denied. These policies were designed to capture whatever meager markets were possible in the Soviet Union and to ward off European control of Russian raw materials without recognizing the Soviet regime or condoning its principles. Unexpectedly, these policies had the effect of strengthening the Soviet economy with American investments, relief, and technology while American officials sacrificed some export opportunities for the sake of pursuing a nonrecognition policy.[30]

Yet Secretary of State Hughes and other American officials were not mistaken when they minimized the economic benefits that were likely to be derived from recognition. From the perspective of the overall foreign economic interests of the United States Republican officials had reason to place the sanctity of contractual obligations and the protection of private property ahead of the promotion of exports to the Soviet Union. Even in the prewar era Russian-American trade constituted less than 2 percent of total American commerce.[31] Moreover, the contemporary efforts of western European nations to capture Soviet markets through formal recognition did not prove successful. Hence, insofar as American policies were premised on the imminent collapse of Bolshevism, they were shortsighted and naive. But the real dilemma of American policy stemmed from official efforts to harmonize short-term market aspirations and investment opportunities with the long-term needs of a capitalist, creditor nation.

With regard to Latin America, the overall foreign policy objectives of the United States were much easier to reconcile. The Monroe Doctrine still served as the cornerstone of American policy, but it no longer constituted a viable guide to action because European colonialism in the western hemisphere was almost over and European encroachments on the independence of Latin American nations were unlikely. American officials repeatedly proclaimed their desire to respect the territorial integrity of their Latin American neighbors, to refrain from direct military interventions, and to withdraw American troops from occupied countries. Nevertheless, the quest for stability remained the fundamental objective of American policy. Hughes and Hoover insisted that political instability "was the greatest menace to progress and prosperity." Indeed, American officials often promoted free elections because they considered them prerequisite to a stable order; yet the curtailment of democratic liberties also could be condoned when such liberties threatened to engender chaos. Hughes and other policymakers believed that disorder and revolution disrupted the flow of private capital, retarded economic growth, and set back educational, agricultural, and industrial advancements upon which democracy depended. They assumed that if stability could be preserved, American economic opportunities would multiply, Latin American economies would grow, and democratic institutions would flourish. The search for stability, then, was not simply a product of dollar diplomacy or economic imperialism. Nor was it a policy designed to protect the interests of any single firm or interest group. Instead, it was a policy that accepted the economic interdependence of the modern world; contemplated the parallel advancement of developed and undeveloped economies; postulated the mutual benefits of open-door commerce and overseas investments; and linked democratic institutions to economic foundations.[32]

With the exception of America's military intervention in Nicaragua in 1926, Republican officials steadily reduced America's military presence in Caribbean and Central American countries. They also began to withdraw from formal control over many of those nations' customs houses. Even in Mexico where pressure to intervene in the mid-1920s was substantial, President Calvin Coolidge and Secretary of State Kellogg resorted to more sophisticated and conciliatory tactics. Outright military intervention no longer maximized the interests of the United States. In fact, strong-arm tactics appeared to alienate Latin American peoples, stiffen resistance to American economic penetration, establish precedents for military solutions to other inter-American disputes, and encourage the growth of statist policies and confiscatory measures.

Therefore, American policymakers increasingly sought alternative means to achieve stability. State Department officials declared their respect for the sovereignty of other nations in the hemisphere, sought to limit armament expenditures, devised arbitration procedures for the peaceful resolution of inter-American disputes, endeavored to sign commercial treaties incorporating the equality of treatment principle, and tried to protect property rights. They also encouraged private corporate efforts to work out international agreements for American control of critical radio and cable facilities as well as petroleum resources. At the same time, Commerce Department officials encouraged the flow of private capital into Latin America's natural resource industries, advocated the construction of an inter-American transportation network, especially the Pan-American highway, and supported the efforts of unofficial American advisory missions to stabilize Latin American currencies and improve the management of Latin American finance ministries and central banks.

In East Asia, as elsewhere, the quest for a stable, liberal capitalist order dominated American policymaking. But in this area of the world, American policy was beset by the complications emanating from the disorder in China, the proximity of Japanese power, the vulnerability of the Philippines, and the uncertainty of whether to take a unilateral or cooperative approach toward Far Eastern affairs. The Washington Conference treaties aimed at establishing a cooperative orientation based on the acceptance of open-door principles, a subordination of military imperatives, and a concern for orderly economic growth in China. A multinational banking consortium, including Japanese and American financiers, sought to enhance financial cooperation, eliminate spheres of influence, and create a framework for America's trade expansion. The Commerce Department worked actively to foster exports to China. Hoover prodded the United States Congress to pass a series of China Trade Acts offering tax incentives to American firms operating in China. By the mid-1920s, however, the consortium had become inactive, business interest in China had languished, and prospects for a cooperative open-door approach had foundered upon the bedrock of Chinese nationalism. From 1921 to 1929 American exports to China were only about $115 million annually.[33]

During the mid-1920s American officials despaired as they observed the internecine warfare in China and watched the maneuverings of other powers to protect their interests. Seeking to abort a rise in Bolshevik influence, protect American lives and property, and coopt and moderate Chinese nationalism, the Coolidge administration acted quickly in 1928 to grant tariff autonomy and to recognize the Kuomintang government. Once the Nationalists had demonstrated some prospect of maintaining themselves in power, had revealed their willingness to accommodate American corporate interests, and had accepted the equality-of-treatment principle, Kellogg was prepared to relinquish treaty rights that infringed upon China's sovereignty. Like the Secretary of State, many Navy and Commerce Department officials hoped that American recognition would bolster the strength of the more conservative nationalists, enhance their ability to preserve stability, and undermine Communist influence.[34]

Throughout the 1920s, American policymakers never ceased stating that stability in China was the essential precondition for the growth of American exports and the extension of American loans. Whether they were institutionalizing multinational cooperation along open-door lines, condemning the proliferation of internal strife in China, or acting unilaterally to recognize the Nationalists, American policymakers were seeking to establish a stable order conducive to the safety of American lives and property and hospitable to the expansion of American commerce, investments, and values. The fundamental problem in the middle and late 1920s, however, was that the United States was unable to establish a policy that reconciled its ambitions in China with its existing interests in Japan.

Throughout the postwar decade there remained much potential for friction with Japan, America's number one economic partner in East Asia. Influential State and Commerce Department officials like William R. Castle and Julius Klein were well aware of this. In fact, as late as 1929 and 1930, the persistence of chaos in China and the brief revival of Japanese civilian efforts to cooperate with the West encouraged American policymakers to reaffirm the importance of Japanese-American relations. At this time Japanese-American trade still was more than twice the value of Chinese-American commerce. At the London Naval Conference of 1930, Secretary of State Henry L. Stimson and the rest of the

American delegation worked hard to reconcile Japanese-American differences. Japan's concurrent return to the gold standard seemed to bode well for the future development of economic relations in East Asia. Still not foreseeing the long-term ramifications of the stock market crash and the economic downturn, the Hoover administration desired to underscore naval arms limitation as a key component of America's economic diplomacy in East Asia and the rest of the world.[35] Although plagued by the difficulty of coordinating their quest for stability in China with their cultivation of a harmonious partnership with Japan, economic considerations remained critical to the conduct of diplomacy in East Asia.

THE EFFICACY OF REPUBLICAN POLICIES, 1921–1929

Despite the problems encountered by policymakers in some regions of the world, American exports, imports, loans, and investments grew steadily in the 1920s. Once the war-inspired cycle of boom and bust was over, the value of merchandise exports grew from $3,832,000,000 in 1922 to over $5,100,000,000 in 1929.[36] Particularly significant was the growth of finished manufactured products, which by 1929 totaled almost 50 percent of all American exports.[37] Most striking of all was the enormous surge in automobile exports. By the end of the decade automobiles constituted almost 10 percent of all exports and the value of automobile exports had increased almost 2,000 percent since the prewar era. In 1929, approximately 10 percent of all motor vehicles produced in the United States were exported abroad compared to 5.5 percent in 1913. Indeed the growth of the automobile industry in the 1920s was very much related to the increase in overseas sales. And since the automobile industry consumed 14 percent of the steel, 82 percent of the rubber, 63 percent of the plate glass, 60 percent of the upholstery leather, and 26 percent of the aluminum produced in the United States, overseas car sales had a bearing on

the well-being of the entire economy.[38] But in addition to automobile exports, foreign sales of other mass-produced goods also
mounted. All through the 1920s overseas sales of cash registers,
typewriters, sewing machines, and agricultural machinery were
especially noteworthy, and in 1930 machinery replaced unmanufactured cotton as America's number one export item.[39]

At the same time that exports were increasing, imports also
were growing from $3,113,000,000 in 1922 to $4,399,000,000 in
1929. Prior to the war, the value of imports was approximately 78
percent of exports; during the latter 1920s imports amounted to
84.4 percent of exports. Compared to the prewar years, the growth
in the value of wood pulp, newsprint, silk, and petroleum imports
was especially impressive. The quantitative leap in rubber imports
was also dramatic (over 800 percent), but price declines minimized
its significance. Commerce Department officials were captivated
by the rapid industrialization of the nation and worried about
American dependence upon foreign supplies of raw materials.
"Upon these highly essential imports," Hoover wrote, "is dependent not only much of our comfort but even the very existence of
the major part of our industrial life."[40]

Preoccupied with maintaining access to raw materials,
American officials were pleased by the overseas investments of
American corporations in natural resource industries. During the
1920s, private long-term American investments abroad grew dramatically, amounting to a little over $15 billion at the end of the
decade. Approximately $7.5 billion were in direct investments. Of
this amount slightly over 50 percent was in supply-oriented fields,
including mining, smelting, and oil production. In Latin America,
Asia, and even Africa, Americans began challenging Europe's
control of raw materials and developing access to their own supplies. Investments in foreign nitrates, oil, tin, copper, and rubber
grew dramatically. At the same time, market-oriented investments
also increased, especially in Europe. New manufacturing investments in Europe in 1928 and 1929 equalled the entire number of
such investments up to World War I. Yet the fastest growth of
American overseas foreign investments was in public utilities. In
sum, between 1922 and 1930, direct investments increased by

nearly $2.5 billion; portfolio investments by almost $7 billion. The result of these increments was that by 1930, United States direct foreign investments alone exceeded the direct *and* portfolio investments of France, Holland, and Germany *combined*. At the time of the stock market crash, American investments in Latin America for the first time equalled those of Great Britain. Between 1912 and 1928, United States investments in Colombia had increased by 15,150 percent; in Venezuela, by 4,566 percent; in Chile, by 4,200 percent; in Argentina, by 1,412 percent.[41]

The increase in American manufacturing exports, growth of raw material imports, and outflow of private capital reinforced American convictions about the interdependent nature of the world economy. During the late 1920s, Europe purchased about 47 percent of American exports, provided about 30 percent of American imports, and received about 30 percent of American investments. Yet American sales to and purchases from Asia were growing rapidly and American investments in Latin America surpassed even those in Europe. By the end of the decade, with the exception of Africa and Oceania, the United States had substantial economic and financial interests around the globe.[42] Moreover, policymakers, international financiers, and big businessmen gave increasing attention to the ways in which the interests of the continents were locked together. Studying international balance sheets led Commerce Department officials to emphasize the triangular nature of international commerce. Recognizing that the United States had a merchandise deficit with many raw-materials-producing nations in Latin America and Asia, Hoover and his assistants assumed that the dollars earned by these nations would buy European manufactured goods, thereby enabling Old World nations to pay for their net imports from the United States.[43]

This vision of a unitary world economy generated much rhetoric about the importance of all nations working together for the prosperity of one another. "It is a misfortune," Hoover stated in 1925, "that the terminology of trade has been so infected by military terms. . . . In larger vision our export trade does not grow by supplanting the other fellow but from the increased consuming power of the world." Accordingly, in the late 1920s,

American officials welcomed the revival of the European economy. In 1929 Secretary of Commerce Robert P. Lamont explained that

the restored prosperity of Europe to produce and export has been a major factor in building up our exports both to Europe itself and to other parts of the world, which in turn have found their buying power increased by the ability to sell more foodstuffs and raw materials to European countries. It is to our interest that Europe should expand still further in its export of manufactured goods. The prosperity of our farmers is much affected by the prosperity of European factories.[44]

The expansion of American trade and investments, however, was more a function of postwar international economic and financial developments than of any official American policies or actions. The great growth in manufacturing exports came in those very industries that had introduced mass production techniques and that benefitted from economies of scale. Official Commerce Department reports emphasized the relationship between efficient American mass production techniques and the growth of overseas sales of automobiles, agricultural machinery, and cash registers. In fact, there does not seem to have been any cause-and-effect relationship between the promotion of the unconditional most-favored-nation clause and the growth of these exports.[45] Likewise, an incisive study of American business firms in China suggests that government advocacy of the open door had little to do with the success or failure of American corporate marketing practices in that nation.[46] As the increment in manufactured exports can be best explained in terms of technological and industrial developments, the relative decline in overseas agricultural sales was related to the drive of many nations for national self-sufficiency in foodstuffs after the Great War as well as to the growth of foreign competition.[47] Even the value of American imports may well have been affected more by the general level of prosperity in the United States and by fluctuations in prices set in international markets than by the setting of American customs duties. The value of imports increased markedly in the mid-1920s despite the rate hikes in the Fordney-McCumber tariff schedule. At the end of the decade the quantity of imports reached an all-time high; but the unit value of these imports already was declining because of market forces somewhat beyond American control. Seen in this perspective, even the Hawley-Smoot tariff may well have had a smaller impact on world trade and American imports than is usually attributed to it.[48]

As with trade, the policies of the American government were not the key influence affecting the magnitude of overseas investments. Market-oriented direct investments in branch factories, for example, were most frequently the consequence of corporate attempts to leap over foreign tariff walls. Indeed Republican officials tended to be very circumspect about investments in branch factories because there was considerable apprehension that branch factories sacrificed American jobs.[49] On the other hand, American policymakers certainly supported overseas investments in raw materials like oil, rubber, and nitrates. Repeatedly, they called upon foreign governments to adhere to the open door for investment and to allow equal American access to undeveloped raw materials. Yet even in respect to these supply-oriented investments, official policy had only a marginal influence. Private American corporations, influenced by the dynamics of the marketplace, benefitting from superior technology and plentiful capital, and often encouraged by the governments of undeveloped nations, acted in accord with their own self-interest. As a result, the United States government often acquiesced in private corporate practices. In the cable, radio, and petroleum industries, for example, the open-door policy was compromised as Republican officials accepted private efforts to limit competition and establish multinational cooperation.[50]

In a similar manner, official efforts to encourage foreign loans and guide their use had little influence on events. The corporations established under the Edge legislation did not significantly augment the outflow of long-term capital. In the early 1920s, domestic economic recession and European financial and political instability undermined the efficacy of the Edge Act. As soon as recovery began at home and stability returned to Europe, there was an unprecedented outflow of American capital. As is well-known, State, Commerce, and Treasury officials tried informally to channel this capital into so-called productive pursuits. Yet their efforts were unsuccessful. Bankers ignored implicit warnings about the dangers of loans to German municipalities and found ingenious ways to circumvent an explicit ban on loans to France. New York did become the world's financial center, but this had more to do with the impact of the war on London than with any concrete measures taken by Washington. With the important exceptions of the State Department's informal support of the Dawes and Young Plans and the Treasury Department's strong encouragement of cooperation between the FRBNY and European central banks, financial developments were more closely related to the impact of the war, the evolution of political developments abroad, and the workings of the marketplace than to any official acts in Washington.[51]

This is not to say that Washington did not *try* to influence postwar economic, commercial, and financial developments. As outlined earlier in this essay, American officials very much sought to create a stable and prosperous world order conducive to the spread of liberal capitalist values and open-door principles. Yet there often was a gap between official aspirations and subsequent developments. Part of this related to the deep divisions within the business community and among economic interest groups. Disparate business organizations could agree on the need for a stable world order hospitable to the expansion of American trade, investments, and values. Recent studies demonstrate, however, that there was no consensus on tactics. Tariff debates pitted small manufacturers against international bankers, export-import interests against the Home Market Club, refiners against planters, meatpackers against ranchers, etc. Similarly, oil producers and international bankers disagreed on how the government should react to Mexican legislation implementing Article 27 of the 1917 constitution. J. P. Morgan and Company and Standard Oil could concur on the merits of a stable, liberal capitalist order, but their interests clashed when tax revenues on oil property might be used to liquidate outstanding debts. In China, members of the banking consortium and American exporters agreed on the wisdom of the open-door policy. Yet this did not stop businessmen from complaining bitterly about the reluctance of the consortium to finance major development projects.[52]

Rifts within the business community over tactics resulted not only from clashing interests but from honest differences of opinion over the importance to be attributed to foreign policy goals. Everyone, for example, wanted to restore financial stability in Europe. But one's willingness to reduce or cancel the Allied war debts and thereby accept a heavier tax burden depended on just how much importance one attached to the goal of European reconstruction. And this assessment would depend on whether one was an international banker in New York holding European securities, a cotton farmer in Mississippi seeking to recover European markets, an auto manufacturer in Detroit aspiring to expand overseas sales, or a haberdasher in Shenandoah, Iowa, hoping to increase business as a result of higher hog prices and enlarged farm income. Of course, the position one took was not exclusively based on a rational assessment of economic self-interest. The cotton farmer in Mississippi might be a Klansman who hated Catholics and therefore opposed any reduction of the Italian war debt. The essential point is that individuals and interest groups who shared a common goal might disagree sharply on tactics. And these tactical differences were significant because they reflected contrasting assessments of just how important foreign policy goals were vis-à-vis domestic priorities, like reducing taxes, protecting the local market, winning elections, or preventing speculation and inflation.[53]

American policymakers had to pursue foreign policy goals and reconcile clashing business interests without resorting to tactics that jeopardized domestic priorities or that engendered international complications out of proportion to the value attributed to the diplomatic objectives themselves. This was no easy task because competing interest groups often raised legitimate, albeit self-interested, concerns about difficult matters that were easy prey for politicians looking for demagogic issues. That complicated foreign policy questions might become the subject of political controversy always worried Hughes and Hoover. They were sensitive to ethnocultural divisions among the American people as well as to interest group pressures. Hence they sought to remove foreign policy issues from the political arena. They endeavored to establish general principles of policy that were designed to subordinate the narrow interests of particular firms, balance conflicting domestic pressures, and reconcile divergent national ambitions.

With regard to trade and investment American officials championed the unconditional most-favored-nation clause and the open-door policy. If all foreigners were treated equally in each nation's market, Hughes, Culbertson, and Hoover believed that world commerce would grow, international stability would be enhanced, and American exports would multiply. Accordingly, they were willing to sacrifice preferential treatment in the Brazilian market in order to disseminate the equality-of-treatment principle around the globe. At the same time, Republican officials were able to persuade Congress to strengthen the Tariff Commission, adopt a flexible tariff policy, and grant the President authority to adjust duties according to the difference in the costs-of-production at home and abroad. Hoover and Culbertson hoped that "scientific" protectionism would end congressional logrolling over customs duties and would permit experts on the Tariff Commission to adjust rates according to the needs of the national and international economy. Likewise, an open door for investments was advocated because this was considered the best means of promoting the unrestricted flow of private capital into productive pursuits. State and Commerce Department officials also believed that the open door would promote fair competition, stabilize international relations, and obviate the need to support any particular American firm. When necessary, however, Republican policymakers accepted business arrangements that established multinational monopolies so long as these could be justified in terms of maximizing efficiency, cultivating international cooperation, and enhancing overall American economic and strategic interests.[54]

In other ways as well Republican officials sought to depoliticize foreign policy issues, reconcile domestic pressures bearing on these issues, and harmonize competing national interests. The World War Foreign Debt Commission was established in 1922. Dominated by Mellon and Hoover, the commission negotiated war debt agreements with the Allied debtors in a way that balanced a desire to lower taxes with an eagerness to expand commerce and promote European financial stability. During the mid-1920s, the Treasury Department also encouraged the FRBNY to support European efforts to stabilize their currencies. The FRBNY extended credits, adjusted discount rates, and conducted operations in the open market in an effort to restore the gold standard and promote American exports without encouraging speculation, generating inflation, or injuring domestic business.[55]

Perhaps most importantly Republican officials made a calculated decision to rely upon the private sector and unofficial experts to implement foreign policy goals. The bankers consortium in China was intended to preserve the open door, enhance Japanese-American amity, and foster Chinese economic growth. Private financiers and businessmen, like Owen D. Young, J. P. Morgan, Thomas W. Lamont, Charles G. Dawes, and S. Parker Gilbert, were selected as unofficial experts to help settle the European reparations enigma and to arrange the financing of German indemnity payments. Hughes and Hoover looked to the major petroleum, electrical, mining, and rubber corporations to gain American control of critical overseas natural resources and communication facilities. The State Department relied upon private banking firms and professional economists, like Edwin Kemmerer, to mobilize capital and improve financial conditions in Central America, the Caribbean, and South America.[56]

Republican officials' reliance on the private sector reflected their views of how to structure and govern an industrial society in an interdependent world economy of competitive nation-states. The private sector was presumed to have the expertise to handle these complex matters. Moreover, by assigning responsibility to the private sector, government officials were trying both to minimize overt state intervention in the marketplace and reduce the chances that controversial foreign policy questions would become embroiled in partisan politics at home. They were also hoping to depoliticize the international economic environment. If economic and financial rivalries could be removed from the realm of government action, the prospects for peace would be greatly enhanced. Hoover, for example, deplored government-subsidized foreign cartels not only because they raised the price of critical raw materials but also because they further injected political considerations into international economic affairs and thereby increased the likelihood that economic competition could lead to war.

The dependence upon private businessmen, professional experts, and supposedly apolitical agencies eventually contributed to serious problems. Businessmen could not be counted upon to pursue the interests of the national polity when their self-interest was at stake. Relying upon the bankers consortium in China proved an ineffective way to implement the open door. Financiers would not make loans when persistent instability meant probable default.[57] Nor would private bankers forego the lure of high profits on German loans despite official warnings of their dangers.[58] Hoover and Mellon still depended upon central bankers and private experts to maintain European currency stability and to lighten Germany's reparations burden. Yet these methods were unlikely to succeed so long as American officials sought to avoid a clash with Congress over additional war debt reductions and so long as the Tariff Commission refused to use the flexible provisions of the Fordney-McCumber Act to reduce duties.[59] Even while the balance of payments problems of many nations mounted, Hoover and other officials continued to place great faith in the salutary effect of direct private foreign investments in backward economies. They disregarded or underestimated the significance of many things, including the decline in raw material and agricultural prices, the growth in the absolute value of America's export surplus, the weaknesses inherent in the gold exchange standard, and the discrepancy between supply and demand as well as between worldwide productive capacity and international purchasing power.[60]

In short, in the late 1920s American diplomacy became complacent and overly decentralized. Too much faith was placed in the efficacy of private market forces and too much responsibility was assigned to the private sector. Disconcerting developments were downplayed and tough decisions were postponed. The prevailing prosperity created great self-satisfaction and engendered a feeling that there was plenty of time to grapple with potential problems. Inertia set in. Policymaking mechanisms became routinized; old formulas institutionalized. The risks of changing policies seemed greater than the hazards of perpetuating them. Moreover, in the late 1920s, there was no widespread pressure for tariff or debt reductions or for recognition of Russia. Kellogg's recognition of the Chinese nationalists, Hoover's goodwill tour to Latin America, the State Department's rejection of military interventionism, and the FRBNY's experiments in central bank cooperation were about as innovative and progressive as anyone was proposing at the time. Hence no major initiatives were launched in the late 1920s to reduce tariffs, scale down the war debts, tackle European payments problems, bolster sagging raw material prices, stabilize conditions in China, or reintegrate Russia into the world economy. The stultification of the policymaking process was not so much a byproduct of bureaucratic imperatives as a reflection of officials' belief that they had already developed the best means of reconciling conflicting business pressures, of balancing internal and external economic imperatives, of harmonizing immediate market and investment demands with long-term ideological and economic aspirations.

ECONOMIC FOREIGN POLICY AND NATIONAL PRIORITIES, 1930–1933

During 1930 and 1931, of course, worldwide economic, financial, and political developments transformed the policymaking environment. The stock market crash in the autumn of 1929, the gradual erosion of values and growing political ferment in 1930, the dramatic financial crisis in the spring and summer of 1931, the eruption of warfare in Manchuria in September 1931, the precipitous decline in international trade, and the proliferation of revolutions throughout Latin America presented the Hoover administration with unprecedented foreign policy problems. Indeed, the very growth of American exports, imports, loans, and investments all through the 1920s had underscored the interdependence of the American and international economies and now highlighted the significance of unfolding events.

Under the circumstances, Hoover, Stimson, Mellon, and Treasury Undersecretary Ogden Mills reaffirmed the viability of the open-door economic orientation of the 1920s and tried to resuscitate outworn economic, commercial, and financial policies. Hoover emphasized the importance of arms limitation as a method of reducing expenditures, balancing budgets, stabilizing currencies, and revitalizing commerce. He sought to strengthen the flexible provisions of the tariff act, but still committed his administration to a policy of protectionism—scientifically applied. Stimson supported the open-door policy, chastised Japanese violations of the Washington treaties and Kellogg-Briand Pact, and proved unable to reconcile American rhetoric in China with American interests in Japan. Neither the lure of Russian markets nor the fear of Japanese ambitions persuaded Hoover or Stimson of the wisdom of recognizing the Soviet government. The potential for revolutionary ferment around the globe made Bolshevik precedents all the more threatening to the creditor and commercial interests of the United States. In Europe, Hoover proposed a one-year moratorium on debt payments. Yet he still depended on private financiers to maintain their credits in Germany, hoped that central bankers could preserve the gold standard, and proposed the recreation of the debt commission as a means of resolving the long-term problem of Allied war debt payments.[61]

Throughout the crisis of 1931–32, Hoover and Stimson refused to cancel the war debts, scale down tariffs, extend government loans to financially pressed nations in Latin America, assume strategic commitments in Europe, or intervene militarily in East Asia. Such actions might have contributed to the stable, open-door, liberal capitalist order that policymakers sought to establish. But these efforts also would have diverted attention from and interfered with domestic priorities that were considered of even greater importance. Likewise, such efforts would have conflicted with prevailing Republican views on the proper role of the government in economic affairs and on the appropriate responsibilities of the United States in the international arena. In other words, open-door, economic expansion remained critical to the conceptualization and implementation of American foreign policy during this era, but foreign policy goals remained of distinctly secondary importance to domestic concerns and to prevailing practices of privatism and independent internationalism.[62] This had been true all through the 1920s. During the first postwar decade, however, prosperity had eased the difficulty of making tactical choices. Once the depression set in, the subordination of "internationalist" options illustrated not the irrelevance of economic concerns to foreign policy goals but the subordination of foreign policy to domestic pursuits.

To understand this development, it is necessary to emphasize that during the 1920s foreign economic interests did not become proportionately more important to the functioning of the American economy. Notwithstanding the impressive gains in exports, imports, and investments, their relationship to domestic economic developments, albeit important, was not critical. Looking at broad trends, the proportion of exports to the total production of movable goods actually declined from 12.8 percent in 1899 to 9.8 percent in 1929.[63] The percentage of farm income derived from overseas sales diminished from 16.5 percent in 1914 to 15.0 percent in 1929.[64] Likewise, the book value of United States foreign direct investments as a percentage of gross national product did not change between 1914 and 1929.[65] Manufactured exports, to be sure, constituted a larger percentage of overseas sales. But the proportion of manufactured goods exported in relation to their total production decreased from a little less than 10 percent in 1914 to a little under 8 percent in 1929.[66] The importance of exports to the automobile industry, the fastest growing industry of the 1920s, cannot be denied. But petroleum refining was the fastest growing component of the nation's second most rapidly growing industrial grouping and the proportion of exports to total production dropped from 61 percent in 1899 to 36 percent in 1914 to 22 percent in 1927.[67] Chemicals constituted the third fastest growing industry and the proportion of exports to production remained less than 5 percent.[68] The textile industry was the largest manufacturing industry in the 1920s and exports constituted less than 4 percent of production.[69] Machinery was the second largest industry and machinery exports became the nation's number one export item in 1930. Yet the proportion of machinery exports to total machinery production decreased from 10.6 percent in 1914 to 8.6 percent in 1929.[70] Radios constituted one of the fastest growing sectors of the machinery industry. But once again exports remained a fairly constant 5 percent of production.[71] Cast iron pipe was the fastest growing component of the iron and steel industry, the nation's third largest. Exports in 1927, however, constituted only 3.6 percent of production.[72] Notwithstanding the growing interest in export markets, Commerce Department officials estimated in 1927 that only 4–5 percent of all manufacturers in the United States were engaged in foreign trade.[73]

During the 1920s, American officials never ceased talking about the interrelationships between peace and stability abroad and prosperity at home. Rhetoric and promotional activities aside, they were careful not to overestimate America's dependency on foreign markets. Year after year, the Commerce Department acknowledged that the "United States is self-contained to an exceptional degree." Exports had grown rapidly, Commerce officials reported, "but the data emphatically reveal that we are not becoming dependent to any greater degree on foreign commerce. . . . The significant fact is not that our foreign markets are unimportant, but rather that the domestic market predominates." Throughout the 1920s, when exporters and foreigners complained about the reluctance of bankers to pour even greater amounts of capital into East Asia and Latin America, American officials noted the existence of lucrative opportunities at home that circumscribed interest abroad.[74]

This orientation helps to explain why the Hoover administration focused its primary, although not exclusive, attention on domestic palliatives once the depression worsened. After several of the President's financial and disarmament initiatives encountered considerable foreign opposition, Hoover began an agonizing reappraisal of many previous assumptions. He even questioned whether industrialization bred worldwide economic interdependence. Faced with congressional demands for budgetary retrenchment, he rejected pleas from the BFDC that its budget not be cut.[75] BFDC officials already were reassessing their priorities in light of the declining interest in foreign trade and were placing an increasing emphasis on domestic commercial activities. Frederick M. Feiker, the new chief of the bureau, praised the recent completion of the first Census of Distribution. The statistical data in this study revealed the "vast array of opportunities" inside the United States. Domestic marketing, Feiker predicted, "will occupy the attention of men in business during the next five years." If the per capita domestic purchasing power throughout the country could be raised to the existing level in Michigan and California, Feiker believed there would be no overplant capacity. "We would have so much business we wouldn't know what to do with it."[76]

A major reason why foreign policy initiatives were circumscribed during the years 1930 to 1932 was because State and Commerce Department officials realized there was little support for such actions in the business community. During 1932, managers in the district offices of the BFDC repeatedly emphasized the absence of any great interest in foreign markets.[77] They were correctly assessing the situation. Faced with a deteriorating situation at home and abroad, business leaders placed primary, albeit not exclusive, emphasis on stabilizing the domestic market, linking domestic production and consumption, suspending the antitrust laws, and balancing the budget. At the annual meeting of stockholders of the United States Steel Corporation in 1931, James Farrell (also the president of the NFTC) was cheered when he claimed that "we can stimulate business in this country without waiting for the recovery of Europe." Later that year Charles M. Schwab, president of Bethlehem Steel, told the Iron and Steel Institute that it was not necessary to produce at full capacity to make a profit. An "80 percent operation," he claimed, "is an index of considerable prosperity." In the petroleum, electrical, and textile industries, corporate spokesmen emphasized the importance of curtailing production, ending price-cutting, and augmenting domestic purchasing power. The National Electrical Manufacturers Association stopped focusing on exports and contemplated an enlargement of the domestic market as more homes became electrified. Oil executives concurred that overproduction was their basic problem. The solution they recommended was to cut supply; there was little stress on enlarging demand through export expansion. By 1932, even General Motors abandoned hopes that there would be a rapid recovery in export markets. Likewise, in its annual reports, E. I. du Pont de Nemours and Company, the largest stockholder in General Motors, stressed the importance of reducing government expenditures. DuPont officials conspicuously ignored any mention of international economic developments. Chrysler executives, meanwhile, hustled to eke out a larger percentage of existing sales, especially within the domestic market. They no longer stressed the unlimited possibilities of overseas market expansion as they had in the late 1920s.[78]

This is not to suggest that the business community or Republican policymakers were repudiating the economic basis of American foreign policy. Support for the limitation of armaments, the stabilization of currencies, the maintenance of the open door, the sanctity of contracts, and the peaceful resolution of disputes remained the focal points of American diplomacy. But tactical attempts to implement such policies were too costly when they interfered with or diverted energy from domestic priorities as well as too dangerous when they demanded an enhanced role for government. In January 1931, the Department of Commerce rejected proposals to make a long-term silver loan to China. "The burden would largely fall on the American people" and this could not be accepted.[79] Similar fears about the budgetary and fiscal consequence of war debt readjustments prompted Congress to reject Hoover's proposal to recreate the debt commission. The President himself would not contemplate tariff reductions for fear that foreign goods might saturate the home market. Nor would he consider strong measures to enforce the open door in China. Most State, Commerce, and Naval officials concurred that Japanese actions in Manchuria did not threaten important American economic interests. Hence they rejected measures that might risk war and distract attention from domestic reconstruction efforts.[80] Foreign economic concerns, although critical to the conceptualization of diplomatic policy, remained subordinate to domestic economic approaches to American prosperity. "While reestablishment of stability abroad is helpful to us and to the world," Hoover insisted, "we can make a very large measure of recovery irrespective of foreign influence."[81]

The subordination of foreign to domestic policy was sustained, at least in part, by the belief that international developments, ominous as they were, did not jeopardize the nation's security. During 1932 military officials sneered at Stimson's efforts to bluff the Japanese into respect for the Kellogg-Briand Pact and the Nine-Power Treaty. Although naval officers worried about the growing strength of the Japanese navy relative to the American navy, they did not think Japanese actions in Manchuria threatened vital American interests. Admirals Bristol and Taylor, president of the General Board and commander of the Asiatic fleet respectively, believed that the Japanese and Chinese should be left to settle their differences by themselves. Writing in March 1932, even after Japanese military actions in Shanghai, Bristol emphasized that "the United States should put its own house in order without worrying about other nations unless we can help ourselves by helping others. . . . For my part I don't believe the financial or economic conditions of other nations have as much to do with our economic depression as do our home circumstances."[82]

In theory, Bristol agreed with Stimson that the United States had a definite responsibility to preserve the peace.[83] Yet policymakers had to assess carefully when preserving the peace was vital to the nation's security or economic well-being. Even Stimson concurred that the Manchurian "Incident" did not constitute such a situation. But he was so preoccupied with preserving the integrity of treaties as prerequisite to world peace, stability, and commercial growth that he was willing to resort to bluff. Hoover disparaged such an approach. Respect for treaties and maintenance of a stable order were long-term American diplomatic goals and linked to America's foreign economic aspirations. Hence their importance had to be reaffirmed. Yet Hoover distinguished between foreign policy goals, vital economic interests, and national security imperatives. Like most military officials, he did not think that Japanese aggression in 1931–32 threatened either of the two latter categories. Fearful that Stimson might overstate American interests and overcommit American prestige, Hoover tried to moderate the Secretary of State's more bellicose rhetoric.[84]

The President's refusal to incur strategic obligations in Europe, even if necessary to win approval of his arms limitation plans, was also a consequence of his belief that the nation's vital economic and strategic interests were not at stake. Like other influential policymakers in the postwar era, Hoover continually acknowledged that European controversies affected American foreign policy goals. But he refused to accept political commitments in the Old World. Such obligations, he feared, might entangle the United States in disputes it could not solve and might embroil the nation in conflicts that were unrelated to its vital interests. This orientation did not mean that the Hoover administration was unconcerned with or unaware of the incendiary state of Franco-German relations. During 1931 Hoover and Stimson constantly emphasized that the political disputes between France and Germany had to be resolved. At the same time American military officials carefully observed European developments and acknowledged the possibility of a European war. But in the context of 1931–32, they understandably could not see how these developments impinged upon the immediate security interests of the United States. France still maintained military predominance and Germany was wracked by civil strife. Even if Germany should achieve obvious foreign policy objectives, like the revision of the Polish Corridor, the right to rearm, and economic predominance in central Europe, the implications of these developments for American security were uncertain in the early 1930s. If they took place under Nazi tutelage they might mean one thing; if they occurred under other political auspices, they might mean quite another.[85]

In this uncertain environment, American civilian and military officials pondered what should be done. Stimson and Bristol, for example, both sympathized with French strategic anxieties. Army intelligence also stressed the mutuality of Franco-American economic interests. The two nations represented "the essence of capitalism and have the great common interest of saving this system from anarchy. . . . But today, in Europe at least, it is impossible to divorce economics from politics." But still no one advocated acceptance of French security demands. Guarantees of French security, the General Board of the Navy feared, might perpetuate "French hegemony over the Continent." This was unacceptable when everyone in American policymaking circles agreed that France had to make concessions to Germany in order to bolster the Weimar Republic, undermine support for Hitler, and enable Germany to take her rightful place as a great power. The prevailing fear, however, was that American commitments might embroil the United States without engendering a real change in French policy. The French, of course, were rightfully apprehensive that concessions on their part might not really alter the trend of developments in Germany and that additional foreign guarantees, even if secured, might not prove reliable. Hence there was a total impasse.[86]

Without a clear-cut threat to the nation's security, and there was none in 1931–32, foreign economic interests did not impel the Hoover administration to incur overseas strategic commitments. This did not mean that the United States was indifferent to European developments. Indeed Hoover was making real attempts at this time to alleviate financial distress in the Old World in order to promote prosperity at home. But foreign economic objectives, while continuing to demand certain types of economic and financial initiatives, did not lead to strategic obligations so long as policymakers did not think that national security interests were jeopardized.

CONCLUSIONS AND REFLECTIONS

Throughout the years 1921 to 1933, economic considerations were critical to the conceptualization of diplomatic goals, but foreign policy remained subordinate to domestic concerns and priorities. In the absence of any imminent threats to the nation's security, economic factors assumed a position of primacy because they were inextricably linked to a legalist-moralist framework that postulated the superiority of American values and institutions. But "realist" historians and political scientists are misleading students when they highlight the legal and moral aspects of American foreign policy in this era and treat them in isolation from the economic interests of a capitalist creditor nation. American officials sought to join the World Court, sign arbitration treaties, outlaw war, and protect property because they wanted to construct a stable world order conducive to the expansion of American interests and values. They did not expect these efforts to bring about any great and immediate changes in the nature of international relations. They did not assume any natural harmony among democratic nations. Modern industrialism and technology, they perceived, bred interdependence. But it did not eliminate the potentiality of conflict. Republican policymakers recognized the need for continuous efforts to cultivate worldwide stability and international economic growth. That they failed to achieve their task was not because they were naive but because they grew complacent in the late 1920s, bowed to domestic political expedients, mismanaged domestic economic affairs, exaggerated the benefits of the private marketplace, and shared in the pervasive economic ignorance of the time.

As important as the open door was to the molding of foreign policy, it was not considered *vital* to the nation's economic well-being or its national security. Revisionists err when they intimate that American officials during the Republican ascendancy believed that survival of the capitalist system at home depended upon the expansion of the open door abroad. This mistake is unfortunate because the Wisconsin School of diplomatic historians and their adherents have performed an important service in underscoring the domestic roots of foreign policy. Yet if further progress is to be made in our understanding, we must grapple not only with domestic expansionist imperatives but also with domestic economic constraints. Foreign policy, at least in this era, grew out of *and was limited by* internal economic imperatives and by prevailing ideas about the legitimate role of government in international economic affairs. Contemporaries viewed open door expansion as only one of several ways of coping with cyclical fluctuations, overproduction, and unemployment. Open-door expansion did not take precedence over domestic tactics; indeed it was subordinate to them. Encouraging foreign trade, as Hoover emphasized, was very valuable but not nearly so important as cultivating and protecting the domestic market. Business periodicals, trade association literature, and annual corporate reports indicate that once the depression intensified, efforts to balance production to meet consumption and proposals to cut government expenditures assumed greater importance than export expansion.

By the late 1920s, moreover, the perceived dependence on foreign raw materials may not have seemed as ominous as it had in the immediate postwar years. The discovery of new domestic sources of petroleum diminished the pervasive fears of oil shortages that had characterized the early 1920s. In fact, in its annual assessments of the international situation in the early 1930s, the navy stopped voicing concern over the inadequacy of petroleum supplies. In the plans drawn up in 1928 and 1930 for possible wars with Japan and Great Britain, the Joint Board of the Army and Navy noted that in an emergency the nation could fulfill most of its requirements for raw materials within the western hemisphere.[87] This may help to explain why in the early 1930s there was so much reluctance to intervene militarily in East Asia or to assume commitments in Europe. If most essential raw materials could be found in Latin America and Canada, and if European and Chinese markets were not vital to the nation's economic well-being, there were fewer reasons to take risks that were disproportionate to the nation's interests.

Prior to 1933, it was not unreasonable or unrealistic for American officials to pursue foreign policy objectives without incurring strategic obligations. It was a time when the Nazis still had not achieved power in Germany and when the Japanese still had limited ambitions. Moreover, since economic dislocation contributed to both German and Japanese bellicosity, and since American security interests were not immediately endangered, it was natural for the United States to play down geopolitical considerations and to concentrate on economic problems. Herein rested an area where the United States potentially could make a contribution to international stability. But Republican officials failed to devise a comprehensive approach that reconciled internal and external economic priorities. Ensnared by conflicting pressures and entrapped by an overzealous faith in the wisdom of the private sector and the beneficence of the open marketplace, policymakers failed to develop tactical approaches not only capable of achieving, but also commensurate with, their economic goals.

A study of the role of economic considerations in the shaping of American foreign policy in the post-Versailles era raises some interesting long-term issues that historians, political scientists, and economists need to reflect upon. Scholars need to do a much better job examining the complex interrelationships among economic aspirations, legal concepts, ideological tenets, and national security imperatives. They also must spend more time pinpointing key policymaking bodies, analyzing the interaction between these bureaucracies and influential interest groups, and tracing both bureaucratic and interest group linkages with relevant congressional committees. We need discrete analyses of interest group politics and organizational decision-making, but their utility will be limited if they are not synthesized into more comprehensive studies. We also need to have a much better understanding of those macro-economic developments that seem beyond the ability of policymakers to control and those micro-economic decisions that may moderate or accentuate these larger trends.

Practitioners of diplomacy might look at post-World War I American foreign policy and see that their forbears, in the context of their times, were neither so inept nor so naive as is commonly thought. A study of interwar diplomacy underscores the difficulties and complexities of reconciling foreign and domestic economic imperatives in a multipolar world. It also highlights the dilemmas of establishing tactics that are commensurate with the values accorded to diplomatic goals. Practitioners could learn some valuable lessons about the importance of setting priorities among goals and of distinguishing between economic interests and national security imperatives. Finally, practitioners and scholars alike might study the diplomacy of the 1920s and early 1930s and ponder the problems of reconciling American foreign policy goals with the objectives and needs of other powers. Republican officials in the 1920s never solved these issues. Let us hope we will do better in the future.

Notes

1. For statistics on the international payments and investment position of the United States as well as on American exports and imports, see U.S. Department of Commerce, Bureau of the Census, *Historical Statistics of the United States: Colonial Times to 1957* (Washington, D.C., GPO, 1960), pp. 564–65, 537, 539 (hereafter cited as *Historical Statistics*); for the proportion of world trade belonging to the United States, see U.S. Department of Commerce, Bureau of Foreign and Domestic Commerce (BFDC), *Commerce Yearbook*, 1929, 2 vols. (Washington, D.C.: GPO, 1929), 1:91 (hereafter cited as *Commerce Yearbook*, giving year, volume, and page); for the figures on manufactured goods, see *ibid.*, 1922, p. 476; *ibid.*, 1932, 1:94.

2. Conference on Unemployment, *Report of the President's Committee on Unemployment* (Washington, D.C.: GPO, 1921), p. 148; for the pressures of business and agricultural interest groups, see Joan Hoff Wilson, *American Business and Foreign Policy, 1920–1933* (Lexington: University of Kentucky Press, 1971); Melvyn P. Leffler, *The Elusive Quest: America's Pursuit of European Stability and French Security, 1919–1933* (Chapel Hill: University of North Carolina Press, 1979), pp. 40–44 ff.

3. Conference on Unemployment, *Report*, pp. 147–48.

4. Leffler, *Elusive Quest*, pp. 44, 54–58, 146–49.

5. For the quotation, see U.S. Department of Commerce, *Annual Report of the Secretary of Commerce, 1927* (Washington, D.C.: GPO, 1927), p. xxi; for the statistics, see Julius Klein to David Lawrence, December 29, 1927, Records of the BFDC, File No. 400, Record Group (RG) 151 (National Archives); for the view of exporters, see National Foreign Trade Council (NFTC), *Official Report of the Ninth National Foreign Trade Convention* (New York, 1922), p. vii.

6. For the quotation, see Minutes of Conference at the Office of Mr. Lay, April 22, 1919, Records of the BFDC, File No. 620, RG 151; also see, for example, Leffler, *Elusive Quest*, pp. 25–29, 58–59 ff.; Michael J. Hogan, *Informal Entente: The Private Structure of Cooperation in Anglo-American Economic Diplomacy, 1918–1928* (Columbia: University of

Missouri Press, 1977), pp. 78–79 ff.; Joan Hoff Wilson, *American Business and Foreign Policy*, pp. 101 ff.; Carl P. Parrini, *Heir to Empire: United States Economic Diplomacy, 1916–1923* (Pittsburgh: University of Pittsburgh Press, 1969).

7. Minutes of the 34th meeting of the State Department Economic Liaison Committee, November 19, 1919, Records of the BFDC, File No. 151.2, RG 151.

8. See especially Department of Commerce, BFDC, *The Balance of International Payments of the United States*, Trade Information Bulletin (TIB) nos. 144, 215, 340, 399, 503, 552, 625, 698, 761, 803, 814, 819 (Washington, D.C.: GPO, 1922–33).

9. For the quotations, see Department of Commerce, *Annual Report*, 1927, p. 27; *Commerce Yearbook*, 1926, 1:96–97; for the Navy's view of the raw material situation, see W. L. Rodgers to Secretary of Navy, September 27, 1921, General Board File No. 438 (Serial No. 1088), Records of the General Board (Washington Navy Yard); for Hoover's efforts against foreign cartels, see, for example, Joseph Brandes, *Herbert Hoover and Economic Diplomacy: Department of Commerce Policy, 1921–1928* (Pittsburgh: University of Pittsburgh Press, 1962), pp. 63–147.

10. See, for example, "Informal and Provisional Memorandum on the General Petroleum Situation, Outstanding Petroleum Questions, and the Position Taken by the Department Relative Thereto," by Arthur Millspaugh, General Records of the Department of State, File No. 800.6363/325, RG 59 (National Archives); Bainbridge Colby to Lord Curzon, November 20, 1920, File No. 800.6363/325, *ibid.*; Memo, April 16, 1919, Records of the BFDC, File No. 151.2 Economic Liaison Committee, RG 151; Joseph Tulchin, *The Aftermath of War: World War I and U.S. Policy Toward Latin America* (New York: New York University Press, 1971), pp. 118–54; John A. DeNovo, "The Movement for an Aggressive American Oil Policy Abroad, 1918–1920," *American Historical Review* (July 1956) 61:854–76.

11. For the quotation, see Memorandum, "The Petroleum Situation," Office of the Economic Advisor, March 31, 1926, File No. 800.6363/362½, RG 59; Hogan, *Informal Entente*, pp. 159–85.

12. Herbert C. Hoover, *Addresses Delivered During the Visit of Herbert Hoover, President-Elect of the United States, to Central and South America, November-December 1928* (Washington, D.C.: Pan American Union, 1929), p. 58.

13. For the quotation by Harding, see "What European Conditions Mean to American Business," *Nation's Business* (June 5, 1922) 10:9; for the view of the NFTC, see "Final Declaration," in NFTC, *Official Report*, 1928, p. x; also see, for example, Charles Evans Hughes, *The Pathway of Peace* (New York; Harper and Brothers, 1925), pp. 134–41; Hoover, *Addresses*.

14. See Warren F. Kuehl, *Seeking World Order: The United States and International Organization to 1920* (Nashville: Vanderbilt University Press, 1969), especially pp. 339–45; Charles DeBenedetti, *Origins of the Modern American Peace Movement, 1915–1929* (Millwood, N.Y.: Kraus, 1978); Charles Chatfield, *For Peace and Justice: Pacifism in America* (Knoxville: University of Tennessee Press, 1970), pp. 168–69; Hogan, *Informal Entente*.

15. Hoover, *Addresses*, p. 51; also see Hoover, "America's Next Step," World Peace Foundation *Pamphlets* (1923), 6:62–68; Hughes, *Pathway*, pp. 3–19, 65–88; Robert Freeman Smith, "Republican Policy and the Pax Americana, 1921–1932," in William A. Williams, ed., *From Colony to Empire: Essays in the History of American Foreign Relations* (New York: John Wiley and Sons, 1972), especially pp. 254–65.

16. For the view of Harding, see excerpt from *Address*, July 31, 1923, File No. 861.01/1765, RG 59; also see Hughes, *Pathway*, pp. 59–65; Department of State, *Papers*

Relating to the Foreign Relations of the United States, 1923, 2 vols. (Washington, D.C.: GPO, 1938), 2:755–64 (hereafter cited as *FR*, with year, volume, and page).

17. Hughes, *Pathway*, p. 158; *FR*, 1921, 2:406; also see Franklin K. Lane to Secretary of State, April 15, 1921, File No. 800.6363/257, RG 59.

18. For the quotations, see War Department General Staff, "Survey of the Military Establishment," War Plans Division (WPD) File No. 3345, RG 165 (National Archives); W. L. Rodgers to Secretary of the Navy, May 31, 1922, General Board Papers, File No. 420–2 (Serial No. 1130); also see, for example, Director, WPD, to Chief of Naval Operations (CNO), April 10, 1929, "Budget 1930: Estimate of the Situation and Base Development Program," File No. L1-1, Confidential Correspondence of the Secretary of the Navy, RG 80 (National Archives).

19. For the quotations referring to the Philippines, see Hilary Jones to Secretary of the Navy, March 12, 1924, General Board Papers, File No. 405 (Serial No. 1205); William V. Pratt to Secretary of the Navy, October 23, 1931, Joint Board Papers, File No. 305 (Serial 499), RG 225 (National Archives); also see the annual "Estimate of the Situation and Base Development Program," written by the director of the Navy's WPD, L1-1, Confidential Correspondence of the Secretary of the Navy, RG 80; "Estimate of the Situation: Blue-Orange," June 14, 1928, Joint Board Papers, File No. 325 (Serial 280), RG 225.

20. For the quotations, see Schofield to CNO, April 19, 1927, "Budget 1929: Estimate of the Situation and Base Development Program," File No. L1-1, Confidential Records of the Secretary of the Navy, RG 80; "Joint Estimate of the Situation, Blue-Red," May 8, 1930, Joint Board Papers, File No. 325 (Serial 435), RG 225.

21. For the interrelationship of arms limitation and economic stability, see Robert H. Van Meter, Jr., "The Washington Conference of 1921–1922: A New Look," *Pacific Historical Review* (November 1977), 46:603–24; Melvyn P. Leffler, "Political Isolationism, Economic Expansionism, or Diplomatic Realism: American Policy Toward Western Europe, 1921–1933," in Donald Fleming and Bernard Bailyn, eds., *Perspectives in American History* (Cambridge: Harvard University Press, 1974), 8:433–36; for the domestic and international political context see Roger Dingman, *Power in the Pacific: The Origin of Naval Arms Limitation, 1914–1922* (Chicago: University of Chicago Press, 1976).

22. For Herrick's remark, see Herrick to Robert W. Bliss, July 3, 1928, box 4, Myron T. Herrick Papers (Western Reserve Historical Society); also see, for example, Calvin C. Coolidge, "Promoting Peace Through Renunciation of War," *Ladies' Home Journal* (June 1929), 48:6, 160–61; William R. Castle to Nicholas Roosevelt, August 24, 1928, box 3, William R. Castle Papers (Herbert Hoover Presidential Library).

23. Culbertson to Hughes, January 21, 1922, box 47, William S. Culbertson Papers (Library of Congress).

24. Leffler, *Elusive Quest*, pp. 71–72.

25. *Commerce Yearbook*, 1932, 1:114; Leffler, *Elusive Quest*, pp. 40–42.

26. For the relationship of European recovery to the economic viability of other areas of the world, see Robert Neal Seidel, *Progressive Pan Americanism: Development and United States Policy Toward South America, 1906–1931*, Latin American Studies Program, Cornell University Dissertation Series No. 45 (Ithaca, N.Y., 1973), pp. 213–16.

27. Leffler, *Elusive Quest*, pp. 40–81.

28. *Ibid.*, pp. 82–157.

29. See, for example, Wesley Frost to Robert Lansing, February 3, 1920, General Records of the Department of State, File No. 661.1115/340, RG 59; Parrini, *Heir to Empire*, pp. 152–54 ff.

30. This paragraph and the preceeding one are based on Joan Hoff Wilson, *Ideology and Economics: U.S. Relations with the Soviet Union, 1918–1933* (Columbia: University of Missouri Press, 1974); Edward M. Bennett, *Recognition of Russia: An American Foreign Policy Dilemma* (Waltham, Mass.: Blaisdell, 1970); Peter G. Filene, *Americans and the Soviet Experiment, 1917–1933: American Attitudes Toward Russia from the February Revolution Until Diplomatic Recognition* (Cambridge; Harvard University Press, 1967); Benjamin M. Weissman, *Herbert Hoover and Famine Relief to Soviet Russia: 1921–1923* (Stanford: Stanford University Press, 1974); John Lewis Gaddis, *Russia, The Soviet Union, and the United States: An Interpretive History* (New York: Wiley, 1978), pp. 87–119; Robert Paul Browder, *The Origins of Soviet-American Diplomacy* (Princeton: Princeton University Press, 1953).

31. Hughes to Gompers, April 5, 1921, General Records of the Department of State, File No. 661.1115/266, RG 59.

32. For the quotation, see Hughes, *Pathway*, p. 167, also pp. 119 ff., 135–36. The sections in this paper on Latin America rely heavily upon the following: Dana G. Munro, *The United States and the Caribbean Republics, 1921–1933* (Princeton: Princeton University Press, 1974); Seidel, *Progressive Pan Americanism*; Paul W. Drake, "The Origins of United States Economic Supremacy in South America: Colombia's Dance of the Millions, 1923–33," paper delivered at the Woodrow Wilson International Center, 1979; Hogan, *Informal Entente;* Tulchin, *Aftermath of War;* Robert F. Smith, *The United States and Revolutionary Nationalism in Mexico, 1916–1932* (Chicago: University of Chicago Press, 1972); Samuel Flagg Bemis, *The Latin American Policy of the United States* (New York; W. W. Norton, 1943), pp. 202–76.

33. The sections in this essay discussing East Asia have been influenced by the following: Akira Iriye, *After Imperialism: The Search for a New Order in the Far East, 1921–31* (Cambridge: Harvard University Press, 1965); Dorothy Borg, *American Policy and the Chinese Revolution, 1925–28* (New York: Octagon, 1947); Warren I. Cohen, *America's Response to China: An Interpretative History of Sino-American Relations* (New York: Wiley, 1971), pp. 100–53; R. A. Dayer, *Bankers and Diplomats in China, 1917–1925* (London: Frank Cass, 1981); Brian T. George, "The State Department and Sun Yat-sen: American Policy and the Revolutionary Disintegration of China, 1920–24," *Pacific Historical Review* (August 1977); 46: 387–408; David A. Wilson, "Principles and Profits: Standard Oil Responds to Chinese Nationalism, 1925–27," *ibid.* (November 1977), 46: 625–47; Wilson, *American Business and Foreign Policy*, pp. 201–18; *Historical Statistics*, p. 550.

34. In addition to the citations above, the analysis of Commerce and Navy Department policy is informed by the following: Records of the BFDC, File 640: Foreign Loans-China Consortium; File 640: China Loans; File 492: China-General; File 036.1: China Trade Act, all in RG 151; manuscript collections of Mark Bristol, Charles McVay, and Montgomery Meigs Taylor, Library of Congress; Gerald Wheeler, *Prelude to Pearl Harbor: The United States Navy and the Far East, 1921–1931* (Columbia: University of Missouri Press, 1963).

35. For Japanese-American relations, see Wilson, *Business and Foreign Policy*, pp. 219–22; Iriye, *After Imperialism*, pp. 254–77; for the London Naval Conference, see Raymond G. O'Connor, *Perilous Equilibrium: The United States and the London Naval Conference of 1930* (Lawrence; University of Kansas Press, 1962); Leffler, *Elusive Quest*, pp. 219–28; for export and import figures, see *Historical Statistics*, pp. 550, 552.

36. *Historical Statistics*, p. 537.

37. *Commerce Yearbook*, 1932, 1:100.

38. For statistics on overseas automobile sales, see *ibid.*, 1929, 1:116, and 1932,

1:367; for information on the place of the automobile industry in the United States economy, see National Automobile Chamber of Commerce, *Facts and Figures of the Automobile Industry* (New York, 1928), p. 83; D. M. Phelps, *Effect of the Foreign Market on the Growth and Stability of the American Automobile Industry*, Michigan Business Studies (Ann Arbor: University of Michigan Press, 1931), 3:553–715.

39. For pertinent statistics, see *Commerce Yearbook*, 1925, pp. 96–97; 1929, 1:423–24; 1932, 1:102–4, 343.

40. For statistics on United States imports, see *Historical Statistics*, p. 537; *Commerce Yearbook*, 1932, 1:84, 105–8, and 1929, 1:118; for the quotation, see letter from the Secretary of Commerce, March 1, 1927, General Records of the Department of State, File No. 600.1115/583, RG 59.

41. For statistical analyses of the growth of American foreign investments, see Department of Commerce, BFDC, *American Direct Investments in Foreign Countries*, TIB No. 731 (Washington, D.C.: GPO, 1930); Department of Commerce, BFDC, *A New Estimate of American Investments Abroad*, TIB No. 767, (Washington, D.C.: GPO, 1931); for additional assessments, see Mira Wilkins, *The Maturing of Multinational Enterprise: America Business Abroad from 1914 to 1970* (Cambridge: Harvard University Press, 1974), pp. 49–163; Cleona Lewis, *America's Stake in International Investments* (Washington, D.C.: Brookings Institution, 1938); also see the figures in Klein to Bristol [Spring 1930], box 104, Bristol Papers.

42. For the global commercial and investment stake, see, for example, *Commerce Yearbook*, 1932, 1:111; Department of Commerce, BFDC, *American Investments Abroad*, TIB No. 767, p. 8.

43. For the study of the nation's balance of payments, see the analyses by the Department of Commerce cited in note 8.

44. For the quotations, see Herbert Hoover, *The Future of Our Foreign Trade* (Washington, D.C., 1925), pp. 7–8; Robert P. Lamont, "Prospects of United States Foreign Trade," in NFTC, *Official Report*, 1929, p. 18.

45. These generalizations are based on an analysis of the commentary, charts, and figures in the yearly edition of *Commerce Yearbook* as well as in the *Annual Report of the Secretary of Commerce* (Washington, D.C.: GPO, 1922–30).

46. Michael H. Hunt, "Americans in the China Market: Economic Opportunities and Economic Nationalism," *Business History Review* (Autumn 1977), 51:277–307.

47. For a statistical assessment of the change in the character of exports and the relative decline in agricultural exports, see *Commerce Yearbook*, 1930, 1:94 ff.

48. For statistics on imports, see *ibid.*, 1:85; also see M. E. Falkus, "U.S. Economic Policy and the Dollar Gap of the 1920's," *Economic History Review* (November 1971), 24:599–623.

49. See, for example, Klein to Alejandro E. Bunge, May 11, 1926, Records of the BFDC, File No. 620 Investments—Argentina, RG 151; Klein, "American Branch Factories Abroad—Arguments Pro and Con," *Textile World* (October 26, 1929), 76:55–56; Wilkins, *Multinational Enterprise*, pp. 60–61, 72–73, 75, 76, 85, 90; Department of Commerce, *Annual Report*, 1931, p. xxiii.

50. Hogan, *Informal Entente*, pp. 105–85; Wilkins, *Multinational Enterprise*, pp. 92–128; Seidel, *Progressive Pan Americanism*, pp. 317–417; Stephen J. Randall, *The Diplomacy of Modernization: Colombian-American Relations, 1920–1940* (Toronto: University of Toronto Press, 1977).

51. For American foreign loan and financial policy, see especially Stephen V. O. Clarke, *Central Bank Cooperation, 1924–1931* (New York: Federal Reserve Bank of New

York, 1967); Richard Meyer, *Bankers' Diplomacy: Monetary Stabilization in the Twenties* (New York: Columbia University Press, 1970); Lester V. Chandler, *Benjamin Strong: Central Banker* (Washington, D.C.: Brookings Institution, 1958); Frank Costigliola, "The Politics of Financial Stabilization: American Reconstruction Policy in Europe, 1924–1930" (Ph.D. dissertation, Cornell University, 1972); Leffler, *Elusive Quest*.

52. See, for example, Wilson, *American Business and Foreign Policy*, pp. 65–100, 201–7; N. Stephen Kane, "Corporate Power and Foreign Policy: Efforts of American Oil Companies to Influence United States Relations with Mexico, 1921–1928," *Diplomatic History* (Spring 1977): 1:170–98.

53. These themes are developed more expansively in Leffler, *Elusive Quest*.

54. *Ibid.*, especially pp. 43–53, 165–73, 195–202; Hogan, *Informal Entente;* Wilson, *American Business and Foreign Policy*, pp. 65–100, 157–219.

55. Leffler, *Elusive Quest*, pp. 64–70, 121–57, 187–91; Clarke, *Central Bank Cooperation;* Elmus Wicker, *Federal Reserve Monetary Policy, 1921–1932* (New York: Random House, 1966).

56. This paragraph and the succeeding one are based on Hogan, *Informal Entente;* Drake, "The Origins of United States Economic Supremacy in South America"; Costigliola, "The Politics of Financial Stabilization"; Leffler, *Elusive Quest;* Tulchin, *Aftermath of War;* Ellis Hawley's untitled essay in J. Joseph Huthmacher and Warren I. Susman, eds., *Herbert Hoover and the Crisis of American Capitalism* (Cambridge: Harvard University Press, 1973).

57. See, for example, Frederick E. Lee to Louis Domeratzky, November 14, 1923, Records of the BFDC, File No. 640 Loans-China, RG 151; Wilson, *American Business and Foreign Policy*, pp. 202–6; Frederick V. Field, *American Participation in the China Consortiums* (Chicago: University of Chicago Press, 1931); Dayer, *Bankers and Diplomats*, pp. 123–54.

58. For loans to Germany, see especially the materials in Records of the BDC, File 640 Foreign Loans—Germany, RG 151; Records of the Bureau of Accounts, box 85, RG 39, National Archives; boxes 376 and 377, OF, Herbert Hoover Commerce Department Papers, Herbert Hoover Presidential Library; also see Brandes, *Hoover and Economic Diplomacy*, pp. 180–91; Wilson, *American Business and Foreign Policy*, pp. 101–22.

59. Leffler, *Elusive Quest*, pp. 165–93.

60. For Hoover's faith in the salutary impact of direct foreign investments, see, for example, Hoover, *Addresses;* for problems in the international economy, see Charles P. Kindleberger, *The World in Depression, 1929–1939* (Berkeley: University of California Press, 1973), especially pp. 19–127.

61. For foreign policy developments outlined in this paragraph and the following one, see especially, Christopher Thorne, *The Limits of Foreign Policy: The West, the League, and the Far Eastern Crisis, 1931–33* (New York: G. P. Putnam's Sons, 1972); Wilson, *Ideology and Economics;* Leffler, *Elusive Quest;* Robert H. Ferrell, *American Diplomacy in the Great Depression: Hoover-Stimson Foreign Policy, 1929–1933* (New Haven: Yale University Press, 1957).

62. For fuller elaboration of the concepts of privatism and independent internationalism, see Hogan, *Informal Entente*, and Wilson, *American Business and Foreign Policy*.

63. *Commerce Yearbook*, 1932, 1:92.

64. *Historical Statistics*, p. 542.

65. Wilkins, *Multinational Enterprise*, p. 163.

66. Department of Commerce, Bureau of the Census, *Statistical Abstract of the United States, 1934* (Washington, D.C.: GPO, 1935), p. 403.

67. For industrial groupings and changes in physical output, see Solomon Fabri-

cant, *The Output of Manufacturing Industries* (New York: National Bureau of Economic Research, 1940), pp. 60–61. The percentages are computed from the tables (value of products and exports of value of refined oils) in *Commerce Yearbook*, 1929, 1:317, 323.

68. For the growth of the chemical industry, see Fabricant, *Manufacturing Industries*, pp. 60–61, 219 ff. The percentages are computed from the statistics pertaining to value of production and exports in *Statistical Abstract*, 1934, pp. 478, 710.

69. For the size of the textile industry, see Fabricant, *Manufacturing Industries*, pp. 57–59 ff., 84, 167 ff. The proportion of production exported is calculated from figures in *Statistical Abstract*, 1934, pp. 451, 704. (The figure for unmanufactured cotton has been subtracted from the total quantity of textile exports on p. 451 to make it comparable to the figures on p. 704 for the textile manufactures).

70. Percentages are computed from production and export figures in *Commerce Yearbook*, 1932, 1:342–44, and 1929, 1:423–24.

71. Percentages are computed from production and export figures in *ibid.*, 1932, 1:354, 356; also see Fabricant, *Manufacturing Industries*, p. 291.

72. Fabricant, *Manufacturing Industries*, pp. 58–59, 261–73; *Commerce Yearbook*, 1929, 1:387, 397.

73. A. S. Hillyer to Gardner Harding, January 7, 1927, Records of the BFDC, File 400, RG 151.

74. For the quotations, see *Commerce Yearbook*, 1930, 1:88, and 1932, 1:92–93; also see 1929, 1:102; Klein to Bunge, May 11, 1926, Records of the BFDC, File No. 620 Investments—Argentina, RG 151.

75. See, for example, Hoover to Lamont, July 20, 1932, Records of the BFDC, File No. 400 Trade Promotion—U.S., RG 151; Hoover to J. Clawson Roop, October 12, 1931, box 76, Fredrick M. Feiker Papers, RG 151.

76. For the quotations, see Feiker, "The Next Five Years in Business," July 1931, box 82, Feiker Papers; Feiker, "Doing Business on Facts Instead of Hunches," November 23, 1931; also see, for example, Feiker to Leslie C. Smith, September 18, 1931, box 81.

77. See, for example, J. S. Goff to Feiker, August 8, 1932, Records of the BFDC, File No. 400 Trade Promotion—U.S., RG 151; Memorandum, by John H. Farrell, "Selling Abroad," August 9, 1932, *ibid.*

78. For Farrell's statement, see United States Steel Corporation, *Minutes of the Annual Meeting of Stockholders*, April 20, 1931, p. 25; for Schwab's statement, see *Year Book of the American Iron and Steel Institute*, May meeting, (New York, 1931), p. 28, and October meeting, pp. 338–43; also see Standard Oil Company of Indiana, *Annual Report for the Year 1931*, pp. 3–6; "Institute Has Helped Minimize Distress," *Textile World* (October 24, 1931), 80:21–22; American Petroleum Institute, *Proceedings of the Twelfth Annual Meeting* (New York, 1931), pp. 4–8; *Report of Standard Oil Co. [New Jersey] for the Year Ended 31 December 1931*, pp. 4–10; "Stop Profitless Merchandising," in National Electrical Manufacturers Association, *Survey* (June 1931), 1:1; General Motors, *Twenty-Fourth Annual Report of GM Corporation, Year Ended 31 December 1932*, p. 17; E. I. du Pont de Nemours and Company, *Annual Reports* (for the years 1931–33); Chrysler Corporation, *Annual Reports* (for the years 1929–32).

79. William L. Cooper to Julean Arnold, January 2, 1931, Records of the BFDC, File No. 640 China—Loans, RG 151.

80. For war debt and tariff matters, see, for example, Leffler, *Elusive Quest*, pp. 267–70, 297–98, 303–4; for perceptions of Japanese actions in Manchuria, see, for example, Bristol to R. E. Bergeron, March 2, 1932, box 90, Bristol Papers; C. E. Moser to Henry

Sorenson, March 9, 1932, Records of the BFDC, File No. 492.1, RG 151; Thorne, *Limits of Foreign Policy*, pp. 152–67, 192–201, 225–72, 288–303, 345–53, 411–21.

81. William Starr Myers, ed., *The State Papers and Other Public Writings of Herbert Hoover*, 2 vols. (Garden City, N.Y.: Doubleday, Doran, 1934), 2:83.

82. Bristol to Bergeron, March 2, 1932, box 90, Bristol Papers; numerous letters from Montgomery M. Taylor to Pratt and to John Taylor, 1932, box 2, Taylor Papers; Director, WPD to CNO, "Annual Estimate of the Situation," March 31, 1933, File No. L1-1, Confidential Correspondence of the Secretary of the Navy, RG 80; for an excellent summation of the literature on American security policies, see John Braeman, "Power and Diplomacy: The 1920's Reappraised," *The Review of Politics* (July 1982), 44:342–69.

83. Bristol to James G. MacDonald, June 19, 1931, box 104, Bristol Papers.

84. Leffler, "Political Isolationism, Economic Expansionism, or Diplomatic Realism," pp. 459–61; Wilson, *American Business and Foreign Policy*, pp. 219–41; Thorne, *Limits of Foreign Policy*, especially pp. 161–62, 197–99; Gary B. Ostrower, *Collective Insecurity: The United States and the League of Nations During the Early Thirties* (Lewisburg: Bucknell University Press, 1979), pp. 132–34.

85. For European developments, see Leffler, *Elusive Quest*, pp. 231–315.

86. For the view of army intelligence, see Military Intelligence Division (MID), "Intelligence Summary," October 10–23, 1931, Records of the MID, RG 165; for the position of the General Board, see, for example, J. V. Chase to Secretary of the Navy, January 18, 1933, General Board Papers, File No. 438-2 (Serial 1521AA); Bristol to Secretary of the Navy, April 6, 1932, *ibid.*, File No. 438-2 (Serial 1521-0); Leffler, *Elusive Quest*, pp. 260–72, 277–88, 301–3, 314–15.

87. For the petroleum situation, see Director, WPD, to CNO, April 15, 1930, ND [April 1931], File No. L1-1, Confidential Records of the Secretary of the Navy, RG 80; for other raw materials, see "Estimate of the Situation: Blue-Orange," June 14, 1928, Records of the Joint-Army Navy Board, 1919–38, File No. 325 (Serial 280), RG 225; "Joint Estimate of the Situation: Blue-Red," May 8, 1930, *ibid.*, File No. 325 (Serial 435).

6

1933–1945
Economic Diplomacy
in a Time of Crisis

Robert M. Hathaway

Washington, D. C.

AMERICAN FOREIGN POLICY between 1933 and 1945 was, perforce, a diplomacy of crisis, for emergency and abnormality dominated the entire twelve-year period. First depression, then world war posed challenges as threatening as any the nation had faced since the Civil War. Particularly in the early 1930s, numerous observers openly worried whether American democracy and its attendant liberal capitalist order would prove sufficiently resilient to withstand the pressures directed against them by economic malady. This was the stage upon which Franklin Delano Roosevelt played out his assigned role in history, and in so doing led the United States from the edge of despair to a universally acknowledged position as the world's mightiest nation-state, an economic and military behemoth which overshadowed its rivals in a manner totally unimaginable a dozen years earlier.

  Nineteen thirty-three: unembellished statistics convey only inadequately the human suffering in that fourth winter of depression. The nation's GNP had plummeted from $98.4 billion in 1929 to barely half that three years later. The value of manufactured goods in 1933 was less than one-quarter what it had been in 1929. Nearly fifteen million workers had lost their jobs and were without any means of support. At least a million people roamed the countryside lacking homes of any sort, while millions more made do in flimsy shantytowns. Bank failures and mortgage foreclosures were legion. The number of marriages declined, while that of divorces and abandoned families increased, threatening the very social fabric of the nation. Husbands were unable to support wives, fathers to feed their children. Everywhere Americans had lost strength, confidence, hope.

The international position of the United States looked equally bleak. A series of revolutions and border clashes in Latin America menaced Washington's interests in that strategic region; the Japanese were on the move in Asia; America's traditional friends in Europe were reeling from the same hammer blows of deprivation as was the United States. All the world's major powers suffered from the disruption of normal patterns of trade, investment, and exchange relations. Measured in gold dollars, international commerce in 1932 had fallen nearly 60 percent from its 1929 levels. During this same period the value of American exports had decreased from $5.24 billion to $1.61 billion, a drop of 69 percent. Particularly worrisome was the fact that United States exports had declined more sharply than those of the other leading commercial nations. In 1929, America's share of the world's foreign trade had been 13.8 percent; by 1933, this figure had fallen to below 10 percent. Almost everywhere quota limitations, exchange controls, import licensing, and governmental monopolies betokened increased regimentation of international commerce and the division of the world into restrictive trade systems and regional blocs. Nor did the prospects for a reversal of these trends appear encouraging.

Into this maelstrom strode Roosevelt—Hudson River patrician, New York governor, and recently elected President of the United States. Confident, harboring an obvious zest for life, promising a "new deal" for Americans, Roosevelt assumed office in March of 1933 with a mandate for one critical task: to return prosperity and material well-being to Americans, many of whom in the 1920s had come to believe that these conditions were inseparable from United States citizenship.

Foreign affairs of necessity assumed a place of secondary importance among the priorities of the new administration. During the recently concluded presidential campaign, the Democratic nominee had spoken little of events beyond the nation's borders; Hoover's handling of the economic crisis had provided FDR with all the issues he needed. Roosevelt's inaugural address displayed this same indifference toward international relations. Clearly the administration's first priority was to fight the depression; active participation in European political developments, for instance, was to be forsaken. With very few exceptions, the new leadership viewed foreign affairs largely in the context of the grave domestic economic situation.

Of course a skillfully executed foreign policy might aid the domestic recovery. Farmers, for instance, would benefit if they could increase their sales abroad. Merchants and manufacturers of all types would profit by greater stability in foreign money markets. New outlets for United States goods had to be obtained "if American producers are to rebuild a full and enduring domestic prosperity for our people," the President told the nation. "There is no other way if we would avoid painful economic dislocations, social readjustments, and unemployment."[1] Ideas of this nature were accepted as truisms by most officials in the Roosevelt administration. But the unanswered question concerned the manner in which American foreign policy might be put to work to combat the depression, and particularly the methods by which American products might be marketed abroad.

Over the following years, certain broad principles which shaped this relationship between foreign affairs and America's economic well-being gradually won widespread acceptance within Washington officialdom. In the first place, economic considerations could only rarely be separated from, and were almost never ascendant over, strategic, political, and ideological objectives in the formulation of American foreign policy. Second, the great economic strength of the United States offered Washington officials a singular opportunity to employ economic means in pursuit of noneconomic ends. Third, the needs of private business groups would at times diverge from those of the administration and in such instances should be subordinated to a wider conception of the national interest. And last, as one component of this broader national interest, United States policymakers should seek to establish an international climate generally favorable to America's liberal capitalist economic system.

American businessmen not infrequently found the administration, in distinguishing between the interests of private persons and those of the nation as a whole, less responsive to pressure from individual groups than the NAM or the Chamber of Commerce would have liked. Not that Roosevelt or his top officials were hostile to either the American system of free enterprise or to businessmen. FDR himself, after all, counted among his friends such solid capitalists as Bernard Baruch, Jesse Straus, William Woodin, Vincent Astor, Averell Harriman, and Joseph Kennedy, and called upon these figures and others of their ilk to fill key administration posts. But occasional efforts to enlist private interests for specific purposes, such as Roosevelt's attempts to involve U.S. Steel in developing Brazil's steel industry, usually came to nought. Rather quickly, Washington decision makers concluded that, because different sets of American interests frequently conflicted, any direct effort to aid one (bondholders, for instance) might injure another (exporters or direct investors in overseas businesses, for example). Nonetheless, although the Roosevelt administration often found it difficult or undesirable to work in tandem with private interests, it was no less active in defending and extending the nation's capitalist system than any of its predecessors had been. Differences which did arise between officials and businessmen concerned means, not ends.

THE DIPLOMACY OF DOMESTIC RECOVERY

Roosevelt's Secretary of State, courtly Cordell Hull, had devoted the better part of his adult life to fostering increased commercial contacts among nations. As far back as 1908, in his maiden speech in the House of Representatives, he had boldly struck out against trade barriers, rather grandly labeling the protective tariff the "king of evils." In the succeeding years, he had built a national reputation as the country's foremost proponent of liberalized trade. Only through an international division of labor, he reasoned, could mankind in general and Americans in particular profit from technological advances and increased productivity. And only in a world of freely flowing trade unhampered by artificial barriers or superfluous governmental restrictions could the blessings of prosperity be extended to all peoples. Trade restrictions meant deprivation and want; liberalized trade inexorably led to prosperity, particularly for a country such as the United States which had so much to export. Over the years Hull's conviction of the absolute necessity of facilitating the exchange of goods and services among the various nations of the world had come to represent for him a goal second to none, an objective he pursued, one of his assistant secretaries has remembered, with "almost fanatical single-mindedness."[2]

But Cordell Hull saw something besides material well-being as the end result of freer trade. Lasting world peace, indeed human progress itself, was dependent upon liberalized commercial relations among nations. Economic rivalries promote political tensions, the Secretary argued; and political tensions lead to war. The improved standard of living which resulted from extensive trade contacts, on the other hand, made people less disposed to upset the world order or to listen to the wild rantings of demagogues and despots. "The truth is universally recognized," Hull confidently proclaimed in 1934, "that trade between nations is the greatest peacemaker and civilizer within human experience." Economics, he would later write, should be "the spear point of the approach to peace."[3]

For Hull yet another reason necessitated the liberation of trade from excessive governmental restrictions: the alternative—organization, regimentation, and control—would not only clog channels of trade, but would threaten the very foundations of American individual liberties and American democracy. Political freedom could not long endure without economic freedom. Quotas, exchange controls, subsidies all intruded into the domain of private initiative. Once individual freedom was lost in the economic sphere, its continued existence in other areas of life would be seriously jeopardized. For the defense of everything the United States cherished, then, freedom of economic activity and private enterprise must be maintained and expanded.

Weaving these various considerations of prosperity, peace, and the defense of American freedom together, and building upon the classic concepts of Adam Smith, Hull quickly established his position in the new administration as the leading advocate of an international approach to combating the depression. More so than any other Secretary of State in the nation's history, he set out to build a distinctive international economic order.

Roosevelt, on the other hand, shied away from such a precisely formulated approach to international affairs. A completely undogmatic thinker, the new President scorned abstract thought, broad principles, or finely woven theories. Practical results primarily concerned him, and he did not much care by what methods they were achieved. Improvisation, experimentation, flexibility—these were the hallmarks of the Roosevelt style. One can make too much of this mistrust of dogma, of course. Walter Lippmann's oft-repeated observation that Roosevelt was "a highly impressionable person . . . without very strong convictions" is not really correct, at least in the literal sense. Convictions FDR did have— beliefs about the desirability and propriety of capitalism, about the moral as well as economic benefits flowing from the American system of private enterprise, about the universal applicability of American methods and values and institutions. But these ideas, firmly if usually unconsciously held, set few practical limitations on the President's freedom of action. Certainly Roosevelt gave little evidence of unalterable allegiance to any single set of principles or theories such as those held by his Secretary of State. As a consequence, he lacked Hull's determination to create a multilateral world of freely flowing trade and was prepared to experiment with other methods for selling America's products overseas. Even after the major outlines of the Secretary's program had been officially adopted as administration policy with the signing of the Reciprocal Trade Agreements Act, Roosevelt failed to accept fully Hull's grand vision.

Indeed, a unilateral approach to the nation's economic worries, featuring preferential tariffs, bilateral barter agreements, and export subsidies, possessed certain attractions. Politically it was safer to follow the course least likely to arouse those Democrats most fearful of entangling commitments with other nations rather than risk splitting the party at its moment of victory into isolationist and internationalist wings. In addition, Roosevelt's domestic programs required the support of many of the Senate progressives—LaFollette, Norris, Wheeler, Borah, Johnson—who most feared anything smacking of collective security or international obligations. Furthermore, national action was more responsive to the President's manipulations than were programs that depended upon the cooperation of other countries. Finally, unilateral action was more direct; it gave an impression of decisiveness, of action. For reasons of politics and morale, Roosevelt did not have the luxury of waiting for slow recovery through international action; he had to give the appearance of doing something immediately.

Even before his inauguration FDR found himself called upon to choose between these two conflicting approaches of unilateralism and international cooperation. On November 12, 1932, Hoover informed the newly elected Roosevelt that the British had asked for an extension of the moratorium on intergovernmental war debts, payment of which was scheduled for resumption the following month. Counseled by his advisers that the debts could be paid, Roosevelt declined to work with Hoover to fashion a suitable American response. Having ridiculed Hoover's contentions throughout the campaign that the depression resulted from forces beyond the country's borders, FDR saw little reason to accept the Republican's assessment that international action was now necessary. Besides, postponing these debts would create unnecessary domestic opposition. His decision shortly after assuming office to take the country off the international gold standard demonstrated a similar inclination toward the unilateral solution. Roosevelt hoped that freeing the dollar from gold would boost domestic prices. At the same time, however, devaluation undercut efforts to achieve international monetary stability and greatly angered European statesmen.

But the new administration issued its strongest statement in behalf of economic nationalism during the World Monetary and Economic Conference, which convened in London in June 1933. Even before the delegates assembled, Roosevelt had antagonized the European participants by reversing Hoover's promise to discuss intergovernmental war debts. And as the conference progressed, Roosevelt, influenced no doubt by the conviction that the primary causes of the nation's sad economic plight were internal, grew increasingly leery of the meeting's other objectives as well. Hull, for instance, despite vague presidential orders to the contrary, seemed bound on using the gathering as a forum for propagating his own particular vision of a multilateral world, grandiloquently lecturing the assembled delegates in his opening address that "all past experience teaches that the power and influence of a nation are judged more by the extent and character of its commerce than by any other standard." By this time Roosevelt had become convinced that Hull's prescription of reduced trade restrictions would spell defeat for his efforts to raise American prices unless all other nations took similar steps to raise their own price levels, an unlikely occurrence. Whispered warnings that the Europeans sought to use the conference to commit the United States to an inflexible program of currency stabilization further alarmed the President, who dispatched Raymond Moley to London to steer the delegates away from such dangerous areas. Moley ultimately negotiated what he believed was a harmless stabilization agreement which committed the President to nothing. Given the expectations aroused by the conference, and the widespread publicity surrounding it, anything less would have been interpreted as unmitigated disaster. But at this juncture, Roosevelt publicly repudiated the handiwork of his agent, casually ridiculing "[o]ld fetishes of so-called international bankers" and declaring that a "sound internal economic system" in each nation would contribute far more to world recovery. Not surprisingly, most observers took this to signify that henceforth, the United States would pursue domestic recovery by means of a policy of unilateralism and economic nationalism.[4]

This conclusion was logical, but incorrect. In fact, Roosevelt had decided upon no one course of action. "In pure theory," he assured Hull, "you and I think alike, but every once in a while we have to modify a principle to meet a hard and disagreeable fact."[5] Among those "hard and disagreeable" facts which led the President to modify more than one of Hull's principles in these early months were the preoccupation with domestic recovery, a perception of political necessity, a desire for the appearance of immediate action and results, a national habit of policy formulation that gave little sustained thought to the impact American programs might have on other nations, Roosevelt's operating style of experimentation and groping, and not least in importance, a fundamental uncertainty about the effects various policies would have on the domestic and international scenes. The White House's acceptance of the 1934 Johnson Act, which prohibited the floating of loans in this country by any foreign government which had defaulted on its war debts, illustrates the way in which several of these considerations converged. Economically, the legislation did not make much sense, particularly for a nation that desired to increase its export trade, and the State and Treasury Departments raised objections to the bill on these grounds. But foreign debt default had by this time become as much a moral as a strictly economic question to millions of Americans; Coolidge's curt "they hired the money, didn't they?" struck a responsive chord in Americans hard pressed to pay their own debts (although FDR privately scoffed at the ex-President's remark). To administration strategists it seemed the better course of wisdom to ignore the international repercussions of the act rather than run the risk of alienating potential allies in the Congress.

Still, the utility of expanded foreign markets for reviving the economy could not be denied even by the stoutest of economic nationalists. No one in the administration proposed a policy of autarky; the debate concerned the most appropriate means for securing new markets without undercutting domestic programs of recovery. And gradually, hesitantly, Roosevelt turned to the ideas so repeatedly enunciated by his Secretary of State as one means of revitalizing the domestic economy. The Reconstruction Finance Corporation received a new charter expanding its activities into foreign fields. Early in 1934, the administration steered through Congress a bill creating the Export-Import Bank. Both the reconstituted RFC and the Eximbank were authorized to extend credits and loans to foreign purchasers of American exports, up to this time the job of private lending. An important new area of governmental operation had been opened in the pursuit of foreign markets. Even more tellingly, however, in March 1934, the President reversed his earlier decision and agreed to allow Hull to ask Congress for legislation authorizing the negotiation of trade agreements with foreign governments. Responding to this request, Congress passed the Reciprocal Trade Agreements Act in June 1934.

The preamble of the Reciprocal Trade Agreements Act explicitly acknowledged the link between the economic crisis of the 1930s and the bill. The act's purpose, it explained, was that "of expanding foreign markets" for American products "as a means of assisting in the present emergency" to restore the nation's standard of living, to overcome domestic unemployment "and the present economic depression," and to increase the purchasing power of the American public. The act authorized the President for a period of three years to enter into executive agreements with individual foreign countries that would lead to mutual reduction (or increase) in tariff duties of up to 50 percent. These agreements were to incorporate the principle so cherished by Hull of unconditional most-favored-nation (mfn) treatment. The act forbade any transfer of goods between the dutiable and free lists, stipulated that the public be given ample opportunity to express its views before any agreement was consummated, and expressly denied the President the power to reduce or cancel any debts owed the United States by foreign nations. And in a provision that violated its own stipulation of mfn treatment, the bill permitted a continuation of the exclusive preferential relationship that had tied Cuba to the United States since the beginning of the century. Opposition in both houses was spirited, although the margin of final passage in each was comfortable.

Despite cries of "unilateral economic disarmament," the Reciprocal Trade Agreements Act neither introduced free trade nor repudiated the nationalistic idea that concessions on America's part should be met with comparable concessions on the part of others. In fact, what stands out in assessing the manner in which Hull and his colleagues used this instrument over the succeeding years is not their eagerness in creating an entirely different global economic order from that of their Republican predecessors, but their apparent reluctance to depart in significant measure from previous policies. In the five years separating the passage of the act from the outbreak of war in Europe, Hull's State Department negotiated agreements with only twenty countries, most of which, like Haiti, El Salvador, Finland, and Switzerland, were too small or economically weak to promise American exporters significant new markets. Nor was Washington always eager to negotiate agreements, even when other nations took the initiative. Immediately after passage of the Reciprocal Trade Agreements Act, for instance, Australian officials suggested entering into negotiations. For months the State Department ignored their request, finally responding only in the following year, and then in the negative. The reason behind Washington's refusal was actually quite simple: the major Australian exports, wheat, butter, milk, and other agricultural products, were too highly competitive with American goods. And yet, when Canberra subsequently adopted an elaborate licensing system and prohibitive duties in an effort to divert trade toward those countries which bought heavily in Australia, Hull directed United States officials to lodge a protest against these restrictions. To Australians, however, American priorities were clear: despite his fine words, Hull's first concern was not with the establishment of a multilateral world embracing all nations, but with America's own well-being. The Secretary of State would have denied this, arguing that without continued congressional approval, which only a vigilant regard for American interests assured, there would be no possibility of the type of liberalized trade system he desired for either the United States or the world as a whole. To the Australians, this line of reasoning undoubtedly appeared as so much sophistry.

Latin American nations also found the State Department as interested in concrete material benefits as in the establishment of a cooperative international order. Argentina, for instance, desired an agreement with the United States but proved unable to surmount State Department fears of antagonizing domestic agricultural interests. "The negotiation of this treaty presents a fundamental problem of policy . . . ," Assistant Secretary of State Francis Sayre wrote Roosevelt, "i.e. whether our attempt shall be to negotiate a series of real exchanges embodying concessions of substantial value or a series of shadow treaties without real substance." Washington's ultimate choice was to do neither, but to avoid agreement altogether. "In all cases the concessions proposed seem advisable economically," Sayre explained. "The real question is as to political expediency."[6] Would reduced duties on Argentine agricultural products endanger the entire reciprocal trade agreements program? Political expediency won out.

The State Department, on the other hand, tried hard to sell American products to the Latin Americans, even when these nations did not want or could not afford them. Administration officials promoted American automobiles, for example, in spite of Latin American protests that they did not possess sufficient foreign reserves for such luxuries. Another tactic was to insist that the Latin American countries agree as a precondition to negotiations to eliminate all discriminatory preferences and adopt a mfn policy. In effect, Washington demanded that these countries sacrifice the immediate benefits of bilateral agreements with third parties in exchange for the hope of a trade treaty with the United States which often promised relatively little in return for these major concessions. At one point, the American ambassador in Santiago felt compelled to protest that Washington's terms were so one-sided that they threatened to undercut the entire Good Neighbor policy in Chile. Given such instances, the distinction between this administration and those of its allegedly business-dominated Republican predecessors is not immediately apparent.

The Eximbank also proved useful in developing new markets for American producers. Loans were generally accompanied by the requirement that the funds be used to purchase goods from the United States—perhaps not an onerous stipulation, but it did represent a break with Republican policies of the previous decade. And although American export interests usually initiated requests for Bank funds, they seldom played the decisive role in determining which applications would be approved. In this fashion administration officials acknowledged a distinction between private interest and a larger national interest. American exporters thought primarily in terms of short-term or immediate profits, while Washington officials were more likely to consider the long-term economic and political implications of the loans. Nonetheless, by using governmental funds to promote the sale of United States products, the administration provided a significant new service to American exporters, making the Bank, as Lloyd Gardner has noted, "no less a public works project than any PWA undertaking, no less a subsidy than AAA supports."[7] Here was certainly one embodiment of the idea that economic diplomacy could be employed to lift the nation out of depression.

Inevitably administration officials came to see that the Eximbank might serve other purposes in addition to its primary objective of promoting American exports. The Latin American development projects initiated by the Bank in 1938 unavoidably entangled the United States in the political and economic lives of those nations and were perceived by officials in Washington as important contributors to the creation of an inter-American security system. Occasionally the Bank postponed approval of loans until debtors had settled their earlier accounts with private American lenders. At other times the Bank evaded or pared down loan requests from countries considered unfriendly to United States purposes, most notably Germany, Italy, and Japan. Rather than using the Bank simply as a means of promoting American products, angry Republican congressmen charged, the administration was subverting the original intentions of the agency in a campaign to extend the nation's influence abroad. Privately, at any rate, the State Department and the Bank's directors would not have disagreed.

Still, despite the substantial assistance given American entrepreneurs by the administration, the feeling persisted, indeed
grew in many business circles, that the Roosevelt administration
was basically unfriendly to private enterprise. The President's domestic programs, of course, provoked much of this dissatisfaction,
but the government's dealings in international economic and financial transactions also drew critical comment. Whole volumes can
be filled with the complaints of disgruntled businessmen voiced
before congressional committees considering the renewal of the
reciprocal trade agreements program. The government's antimo-
nopoly policies of the later 1930s troubled businessmen interested
in foreign operations, as did occasional vague rumblings in the
Justice Department about the iniquities of "cartelization." Others
felt the government failed to exercise sufficient vigor in protecting
direct American investments abroad. When the rubber magnate
Harvey Firestone demanded a United States warship to coerce
Liberia into honoring its obligations to the industrialist, Roosevelt's answer was that "at all times we should remember that Firestone went into Liberia at his own financial risk and it is not the
business of the State Department to pull his financial chestnuts
out of the fire."[8] Perhaps it was the obvious lack of sympathy
implicit in this response rather than an actual neglect of American
business interests which so disturbed many American capitalists.

In extending diplomatic recognition to the Soviet Union,
however, Roosevelt took a step applauded by influential business
groups in the United States. Hull opposed recognition on much
the same grounds as had Hoover's Secretary of State: the communist regime in Moscow had, in repudiating the czarist debts,
failed to act in accordance with decent standards of international
behavior, and in addition represented an ideology and an economic system very much at odds with America's liberal capitalist
order. By 1933, on the other hand, many American business leaders looked longingly at the vast population and undeveloped markets in Russia and had come to the conclusion that Moscow's alleged immorality in international affairs was less important than
the impetus recognition might give the sale of American goods. In
moving toward recognition, Roosevelt overruled his Secretary of

State and seemed to be supporting those businessmen who hoped political ties would foster economic links. Actually, however, all available evidence indicates that FDR viewed resumption of relations not from a commercial standpoint but as a means of encouraging restraint among Japanese planners who might be contemplating aggressive moves in the Far East. Had recognition proceeded primarily from a desire for new markets, it would have been logical to couple this with the granting of credits to Moscow, but administration officials shied away from such action because of the uncertain state of Soviet-American relations. And the anticipated markets never did materialize. In fact, for a number of years after formal recognition was granted, American exports to the Soviet Union actually declined.

Closer to home, the administration found that economic tools could often be of use in achieving certain of its ends. The case of Cuba provides a good example. Soon after assuming office, Roosevelt dispatched his trusted confidant Sumner Welles to Havana to investigate the unrest threatening the island's political and economic stability. Welles initially held out the possibility of a new commercial treaty in an effort to force President Machado to grant political reforms. Failing in this, the American diplomat then worked behind the scenes for the Cuban leader's ouster. Eventually Machado did step down and after further jockeying was replaced by the reformist Ramón Grau San Martín. Fearing that Grau's allegedly radical ideas might challenge American economic hegemony in the island, and motivated in part by a personal antipathy toward the Cuban leader, Welles next maneuvered to replace Grau with a president more amenable to United States interests. By refusing to extend diplomatic recognition to Grau's government, Washington insured that the regime would be unable to secure the foreign loans essential to the survival of any Cuban government. After only four months, these intrigues bore fruit in the form of another coup, which established Fulgencio Batista as the country's new strongman. Almost immediately thereafter, the administration proffered diplomatic recognition, a trade agreement, and direct loans. Although the 1934 trade treaty, signed under Hull's recently secured Reciprocal Trade Agreements Act, helped stimulate the island's depressed economy, it also had the effect, recognized in Washington at the time, of undercutting Cuban hopes for economic diversification and locked the small country ever more tightly into the American economic sphere.

With the rise of Batista, Cuban political life assumed some semblance of stability, always one of the primary American desires for the island nation. And perhaps nowhere else was the usefulness of America's economic might more apparent than in maintaining this stability. In addition to a sugar quota granted Cuba by the Jones-Costigan Act, the Eximbank made silver loans to Havana, replacing private financing with official governmental aid here as elsewhere. Other credits followed throughout the remainder of the decade, always after Cuban concessions: a settlement for American bondholders, reforms in Cuba's monetary and fiscal systems, legislation to protect United States sugar companies. By the time of Roosevelt's death, the United States exercised far greater control over the Cuban economy than it had prior to 1933. And although Washington had pledged to refrain from intervention in the political affairs of its small neighbors to the south, its overwhelming economic power made inevitable active participation in and supervision of Cuban political matters. Economic diplomacy proved just as effective and a good deal less objectionable than had the old-fashioned military and political intervention.

Elsewhere in Latin America, as in Cuba, the Good Neighbor policy worked out to be something less than the total repudiation of traditional American assumptions and methods that administration spokesmen claimed for it, although the degree to which Washington was able to accomplish its objectives varied from country to country. Broadly speaking, the administration's principal goal was not the creation of new markets for American goods, nor the establishment of American client states for their own sake, but the fostering of a generally favorable atmosphere in which American interests—economic, political, military—would receive fair treatment and a sympathetic hearing. And judged by the compliant attitude adopted by nearly all the Latin American nations during the Second World War (Argentina being the obvious exception), the administration's primary objective seems to have been fulfilled, at least up to 1945, to an unusual degree.

Still, many government officials and private business interests hoped that neighborliness would also entail more extensive commercial and financial contacts. The early years of the depression had seen Britain, France, and Germany make significant inroads into American trade with Latin America, primarily through various forms of barter arrangements. Whereas, for instance, goods from the United States had accounted in 1926 for 24.7 percent of Argentina's imports, by 1933 that figure had been halved. Such a trend, if allowed to continue, might eventually challenge fundamental American security interests in the hemisphere, and not the least of Roosevelt's successes was in reversing this pattern of commercial dealings. Trade between the United States and its neighbors to the south more than doubled in the first four years following Roosevelt's announcement of the Good Neighbor policy, although it failed to regain its pre-1929 levels until the following decade. In some instances, however, good neighborliness proved insufficient, and Washington found itself resorting to the tactics employed so successfully in Cuba. "We do not intend to let [the Latin Americans] trade upon the sense that our need for their friendship is so great that we must overlook all impairment of our interests," warned the State Department's adviser on international economic affairs in 1939, at the time the department was rejecting a Peruvian request for an Eximbank credit on the grounds that the Lima government had failed to honor its financial commitments to American bondholders. "The decision not to use gunboats to collect private debts did not mean an end to all attempts to collect them or—more importantly—an end to using dollar diplomacy to further American interests," one scholar has rightly pointed out.[9]

Nevertheless, American businessmen not infrequently complained that the State Department neglected to exercise the proper vigilance in defending their private interests in Latin America. Beginning in 1934, the reformist Mexican government of Lázaro Cárdenas embarked on a vast program of land redistribution, a policy that saw numerous seizures of property owned by United States citizens. Three years later, Bolivia's military junta nationalized the Jersey Standard concession. In both instances, the administration's response was one of restraint. Although Hull in particular was appalled by the idea of expropriation of private property, the principle guiding Washington throughout these episodes was that there existed other American concerns—the need for generally friendly relations with Latin America, hemispheric collaboration for security purposes, a more benevolent image among the peoples of the south—that were more important than private American business interests.

A similar conclusion directed the administration's response to Cárdenas' 1938 nationalization of foreign oil holdings in Mexico. Again, Hull was particularly upset, complaining that without minimum standards of conduct, international relations would be impossible. "In eight cases out of ten," he fumed, a country that seized the property of others soon became "a decadent nation," steadily slipping "backward and downward" in "its most vital processes of progress and civilization."[10] Nine days after the expropriations were announced, Hull persuaded a reluctant Henry Morgenthau, Secretary of the Treasury, to suspend the agreement by which the United States supplied the Mexican government with valuable foreign exchange through regular purchases of silver. But second thoughts by Morgenthau led him to undercut the effect of this action by continuing to buy silver on the open market. Several months later, worried that further pressure on the Mexicans would drive them toward Germany and Japan, Morgenthau turned down Hull's request to drop the price of silver. Administration insiders did not miss the irony involved in the Treasury Secretary refusing, for political reasons, to accede to a request by the Secretary of State for the employment of economic pressure.

Hull continued to fret about the iniquity of the Mexican action for the next three years, but could not induce Morgenthau, Roosevelt, or even his ambassador in Mexico City to accept his alarmist views, despite repeated protests that inaction in this instance threatened all other oil concessions in Latin America. The President, for his part, believed the exorbitant demands of the oil companies voided any obligation the administration might otherwise have had to push their case with much vigor. Furthermore, he was skeptical of the effectiveness of any pressure the United States could employ against Cárdenas and found persuasive Ambassador Daniels' warnings of the danger of driving Mexico toward unfriendly powers.

Ultimately Hull, faced with a deteriorating international situation and an intransigent attitude on the part of the oil companies, agreed to permit talks looking toward a negotiated settlement. The subsequent discussions produced a package arrangement whereby Washington, in exchange for satisfaction of all American claims, pledged to resume its silver purchase program, to spend up to $40 million to stabilize the Mexican peso, and to grant Mexico a $30 million loan for completion of the Pan American Highway. The United States had not forsaken the principle of property rights, Hull assured American oilmen, but the general world situation and the ineffectualness of previous American actions had made compromise necessary. Put a slightly different way, the administration had determined that the protection of the property of American nationals no longer deserved the priority it had once enjoyed. The United States had certain interests different from and superior to the private interests of American business. This perception of the national interest meant that the occasional loss of property might be the unavoidable price to be paid in the pursuit of a more broadly defined national interest—in this instance, a Mexican government and people prepared to support Washington in its confrontation with Germany and Japan.

Roosevelt's Good Neighbor policy, then, incorporated a blend of continuity and innovation. In opposing high or discriminatory tariffs for the undeveloped Latin American countries, Washington made it much more difficult for them to industrialize, thereby perpetuating the favorable economic relationship enjoyed by the United States. Financial hegemony, moreover, made easier a continuation of the political sway traditionally maintained by American diplomats. On the other hand, the administration's readiness to sacrifice private property in pursuit of other objectives seemed to many businessmen an unfortunate departure from past practices. Somewhat more to their liking was the greater willingness in Washington to use the economic might of the American government itself—credits, development loans, trade agreements—to achieve and maintain a climate favorable to United States interests in their totality—political, economic, strategic, and ideological.

But if one judges the ultimate success of the administration's policies by the standard Roosevelt himself established—easing the depression—then the results are at best mixed, for economic stagnation still plagued the United States as late as 1939. Domestic recovery took much longer to achieve in the United States than in most of the other major industrialized nations of the world; war, not the New Deal, was the ultimate antidote. In this sense, it is difficult to escape the conclusion that New Deal diplomacy, including economic diplomacy, failed in a fundamental respect. Despite more legislation designed to open up channels of trade than in any previous period of American history, the value of United States exports rose between 1932 and 1939 only from $1.61 billion to $3.18 billion, a level far below 1929's figure of $5.24 billion. Similarly, imports in 1939 amounted only to $2.32 billion, a rise of one billion dollars since 1932 but still two billion dollars short of the 1929 levels. Moreover, even these minimal increases cannot be attributed solely to American policies, for improvements in the national economies of other countries also contributed to greater trade. Nor was the sale of goods abroad as important to the economy by the end of the 1930s as it had been a decade earlier. In 1929, exports represented 5 percent of the nation's GNP; in 1939, the comparable figure was only 3.5 percent. In like fashion, direct American investment in foreign enterprises remained lower at the end of the decade than it had been at the beginning. The 1935 claim of one of Hull's top assistants that "we are to a greater degree than ever before meshing our domestic economy into the world economy" represented aspiration more than reality.[11]

Administration officials had particularly desired to export agricultural surpluses in an effort to aid the hard-hit farmer, and nowhere is the failure of their policies more evident than in this area. Whereas exports had amounted to 15.0 percent of farm income in 1929 and 14.0 percent as late as 1932, the corresponding figure by 1939 had fallen to a woeful 8.4 percent. Only in 1942 did the quantity of agricultural exports begin to rise. In 1929 American producers sold 90 million bushels of wheat overseas, but barely two-thirds this number ten years later. Cotton exports, so vital to the American South, fell from 3.98 billion pounds in 1929 to 2.56 billion at the end of the following decade. By 1940, the total value of farm exports was at its lowest level since 1888. Foreign nations, frightened by the spectre of dependence upon a distant and unpredictable United States, had embarked upon a program of self-sufficiency that included bounties and subsidies for farmers and the creation of a synthetic-fiber industry designed to replace American cotton.

Angry congressmen from agricultural districts grumbled that the treaties Hull negotiated under the provisions of the Reciprocal Trade Agreements Act "sold out" the farmer in favor of the manufacturer, pointing to the fact that most of the agreements negotiated during the 1930s were with underdeveloped countries, which had agricultural goods and raw materials to sell the United States in return for finished products from American factories. Actually, however, Hull's cherished treaties produced only modest results in promoting the export of American goods of any nature. Sales to nations which had concluded trade agreements with the United States did mount faster than exports to other states. But only eight of the countries with which treaties had been negotiated by the outbreak of war took as much as $50 million of American goods in 1938. Argentina, on the other hand, in 1937 and again the following year took more products from the United States than did any other nation in Latin America, without the benefit of a trade treaty.

Nor did the Reciprocal Trade Agreements Act lead to the dismantling of barriers to the exchange of goods to the extent Hull had hoped. Some of the largest countries in Latin America, Chile, Brazil, and Argentina among them, persisted throughout the mid-1930s in entering into bilateral agreements that discriminated against goods from the United States. The 1938 trade agreement with the United Kingdom, the most comprehensive by far of all the prewar treaties, did not reverse London's protectionist trade policy nor prevent the British from negotiating subsequent bilateral arrangements antagonistic to American businesses. Even American duties, although they declined from 59.1 percent in 1932 to 39.3 percent in 1939, remained substantial. In its annual report for 1939, the Bureau of Foreign and Domestic Commerce was led to conclude: "Obstacles to foreign intercourse . . . became perhaps even more numerous and more complex during the past year than in preceding years."[12]

Hull, however, attributed another benefit to his precious trade agreements. Some years later he would write: "The political line-up followed the economic line-up," meaning that once war broke out in 1939, none of the nations with which trade treaties had been negotiated bore arms against the United States.[13] But one suspects the causal relationship between trade agreements and political orientation was somewhat more involved than the Secretary's comment would indicate. Rather than economic collaboration leading to political partnership, as Hull subsequently contended, it appears only that the United States concluded trade agreements with a somewhat selective group of nations. The majority of the treaties negotiated by the end of 1939 were with countries in Latin America, an area in which Washington's influence was already extensive and one in which openly siding with the enemies of the United States during the war would have been foolhardy. Others which signed trade agreements included Belgium, the Netherlands, Czechoslovakia, and France, all subsequently invaded by the Germans; Switzerland and Sweden, whose neutrality during at least the early years of the war was heavily tilted in favor of the Axis; and Finland, which ultimately became one of Germany's satellites. Russia and China, on the other hand, were two of Washington's closest allies during the war, despite the fact that neither had signed into Hull's program. So one can hardly escape the conclusion that the Secretary's claims are misleading, if not largely fatuous.

Of one thing there can be little doubt: the word "isolation" has no meaning in describing the economic diplomacy of the Roosevelt administration in the 1930s, and it is well past time historians buried that term once and for all. "Economic self-sufficiency is a policy of retrogression and runs counter to the entire course of civilization's advance," Sayre wrote in 1939, accurately reflecting official thinking.[14] At the same time, it is equally incorrect to portray American policy in these years as driven by any one mainspring or motive, such as a belief that the American economic system had to expand in order to survive. There was simply not that sort of consistency in the policies pursued by Roosevelt and his subordinates. Even Hull, who possessed a more clearly defined picture of what American policies should be than anyone else in the government, often backtracked or vacillated, unable to decide whether immediate gains or long-term results, domestic or international considerations, political or economic factors should prevail. And Roosevelt, who harbored none of his Secretary of State's certainty about the most desirable directions for American policy, was still more inconsistent in his ideas and programs. Moreover, his subordination of foreign affairs to the more pressing task of economic recovery further undermined any coherence his programs might otherwise have possessed. Perhaps a steadier vision of the future would have induced an economic diplomacy capable of achieving greater success in easing the Depression. Given the times, the uncertainties, and most importantly, Roosevelt himself, such a vision was neither likely nor forthcoming.

ECONOMICS AND THE SLIDE TOWARD WAR

As the somber clouds of approaching war darkened the world's skies after 1935 or '36, the nature of the foreign affairs issues engaging the Roosevelt administration began to shift. During their first several years in office, FDR, Hull, and their associates, surrounded by deprivation and misery, had focused most heavily on policies that promised to mitigate the nation's economic distress. As the decade progressed, however, and the forces of change increasingly undermined the stability of both Europe and the Far

East, considerations of a political or strategic nature came to over-shadow economic worries in the minds of American diplomats. As the President told Congress early in 1936, the point had been reached "where the people of the Americas must take cognizance of growing ill-will, of marked trends toward aggression, of increasing armaments, of shortening tempers—a situation which has in it many of the elements that lead to the tragedy of general war."[15]

Of course, the nation's leaders did not simply shove aside economic considerations as they became more and more preoccupied with the ominous behavior of Germany, Italy, and Japan. In fact, the three Axis nations troubled Washington officials in part because they posed threats to various American economic interests of both a short- and a long-term nature. Writing to Henry Stimson in 1939, Herbert Feis observed: "Mr. Hitler has become so decisive a factor in determining what lies ahead of every producer in this country that the economist simply cannot think in terms of steady, ordinary development." German efforts to create a closed European economic order administered from Berlin struck directly at American hopes for greater trade and the return of domestic prosperity. A German-controlled Europe, warned one Assistant Secretary of State, would result in "falling prices and declining profits" in the United States "and a lowering of our standard of living with the consequent social and political disturbances." Hitler need not conquer even all of Europe, FDR told Harold Ickes at one point, "to make it difficult for us economically."[16]

The use of quotas, bilateral agreements, and state monopolies to divert Europe's trade from the United States disturbed American officials, but Germany's transgressions went further. Berlin imposed severe restrictions on the transfer of funds from the Reich, and American companies in Germany found themselves with no alternative to plowing their profits back into the local economy, thereby stimulating German recovery at the expense of Hull's theories concerning the unhampered flow of goods and capital. Even more galling to the American Secretary of State, United States firms did not hesitate to negotiate restrictive and discriminatory agreements with their German counterparts, a practice that undercut his efforts to guide the rest of the world into the paths of multilateralism. Even traditional American markets were no longer safe from Berlin's grasping reach. Beginning in 1935, Germany launched an aggressive drive for expanded commercial ties with Latin America, employing barter transactions, state subsidies, and blocked credits. Such arrangements held a special appeal for nations suffering from shortages of foreign exchange, and Berlin's share of the Latin American market began to rise perceptibly. In 1935 alone, German trade with Latin America increased by almost 50 percent. Between 1934 and 1937, Germany's share of Brazilian imports climbed from 14 to 25 percent; of Mexico's imports, from 9 to almost 20 percent; of Chile's, from 10 to 25 percent. By 1936, Germany had surpassed the United States as Chile's chief supplier of foreign goods. Worried by these developments, Roosevelt publicly warned against the danger of Latin America falling under Axis sway without the introduction of a single enemy soldier. Hitler's Germany, then, threatened both individual private American interests and Hull's hopes for a multilateral world economy.

United States economic concerns found themselves similarly challenged on the opposite side of the globe. Japan's attempt to establish a position of hegemony in East Asia ran directly counter to longstanding American involvement in China and other areas of the region. Placed into jeopardy were both immediate commercial dealings with the peoples of the Orient and dreams of developing the fabled China market. Of the two, the latter was probably the more important to Washington officials. American investment on the Asian mainland was never large, and trade contacts with the Chinese and neighboring regions represented only a small proportion of total United States overseas sales. Still, the vision of providing for the daily needs of millions of Chinese peasants proved as enticing to this generation of Americans as it had to their forebears. "Across that sea lies the underdeveloped Orient, and in it lie comparatively unexhausted riches," Rexford Tugwell told Roosevelt at one point. In China were located "the great potential markets of the future," Hull added.[17] But in 1938, for the first time, Japan surpassed the United States as China's leading supplier. Those Americans interested in Far Eastern affairs stirred uneasily. "Since the Open Door policy of John Hay, the United States has looked to China as a valuable market, and has done much to cultivate it," the president of the Eximbank gloomily noted; "I do not believe that we should abandon it to the Japanese or anyone else."[18]

But if Japanese policy bode ill for future commercial dealings with the Chinese, its more immediate effects appeared hardly less distasteful. Should the Japanese succeed in overrunning China, Roosevelt's Commerce Secretary warned in 1937, they would be able to substitute cotton grown on the mainland for that produced in the American South, endangering in the process nearly $100 million of annual sales to Japan. The export of iron, steel, copper, paper products, industrial machinery, and numerous other goods would also be threatened as Japan achieved self-sufficiency and advanced toward Indochina, India, and the South Seas. Tokyo's consolidation of its position on the Asian mainland even generated concern among United States businessmen about Japanese competition in third markets as far away as Latin America.

Finally, the Japanese forward movement into Asia jeopardized America's supplies of key raw materials needed for both industrial and strategic purposes. In the 1930s, the United States imported from the Philippines, Malaya, and the Netherlands East Indies 100 percent of its manila fiber, 95 percent of its quinine, 90 percent of its natural rubber, and 85 percent of its tin. Japan itself supplied all of America's loffa sponges and 75 percent of its pyrethrum, used for insecticides and to combat certain skin disorders. Such essential commodities as nickel, jute, copra, tung oil, antimony, beryllium, manganese, mica, and tungsten were either not produced at all in the United States or were obtainable only in insufficient quantities; every one of these vital materials came from the Far East. Here were economic interests the uncompensated loss of which could have grave repercussions on America's well-being. Quite obviously, American diplomats could not afford to ignore these multifaceted economic considerations in analyzing the steady deterioration of relations between their country and the Axis powers.

Economic competition by itself, however, simply does not explain either Washington's initial opposition to these nations, or the reasons why the United States ultimately found itself at war with Germany, Japan, and Italy. Real worries about an autarkic German economy notwithstanding, the absolute dollar value of trade between the United States and Germany held steady in the five years following Hitler's assumption of power. Moreover, the balance of trade was substantially in Washington's favor. Direct American investments also rose, although this may have been largely due to German restrictions on the export of capital. A similar picture held true in Asia. Despite the long-term impact of being squeezed out of the China market, short-term considerations argued for friendly relations with Tokyo. In 1938, the United States supplied nearly 44 percent of Japan's imports, at a value of almost $240 million. This figure was far higher than anything American exporters could realistically hope to obtain from the Chinese market anytime in the foreseeable future. In fact, in the mid-1930s, the United States sold more goods to Japan than to all the rest of Asia combined. The bulk of American Far Eastern investments, too, lay in Japanese, not Chinese enterprises. United States interests in the rest of Asia, Ambassador Grew cabled from Tokyo, were simply not sufficient to warrant the risk of war with Japan. It was common thinking, Norman Graebner has written, that American trade with China amounted to less than the cost of one week's war against Japan.[19] Given these stakes, there was every reason for promoting stronger ties with Berlin and Tokyo.

Nor did the business community demand a more aggressive stand against either Germany or Japan. Like their countrymen generally, American businessmen held no one attitude toward Nazism, neutrality legislation, internationalism, or multilateralism in the years preceding the war. Many corporate executives personally deplored the lawlessness and brutality that characterized the policies of the Axis nations, but just as many found it profitable to turn a blind eye toward these excesses and engaged in extensive dealings with German and Japanese firms. It was not uncommon, particularly in Hitler's early years, to hear the Nazis praised in American business circles for providing stability and economic rationality in central Europe. Some businessmen even professed to find Germany's restrictions on private enterprise no more onerous than those of the New Deal. Mira Wilkins' investigation of business attitudes toward Japan seems to support this contention that few called for firmer American action to protect threatened Far Eastern opportunities. Businessmen shared only one common sentiment, she writes: they did not want the United States to become involved in an Asian war.[20] Had American capitalists been inclined to engage in crusades against closed economies, their target would not have been the Axis nations, but the Soviet Union. And virtually no one in the 1930s demanded war with Russia in defense of free enterprise. Britain, too, pursued commercial and financial policies that placed American businessmen at a serious disadvantage, but again no one advocated war. In short, there existed simply no major constituency for a rift with either Germany or Japan on economic grounds.

In fact, when given the opportunity to obtain immediate economic benefits at the expense of other objectives, American policymakers usually chose to sacrifice the economic gains. As early as the spring of 1934, the State Department advised against making economic concessions to Berlin, even if American trade had to be sacrificed. Part of the department's opposition arose from Hull's disinclination to deal with Germany on a barter basis, but Sayre's warning that credits to Berlin would aid Germany in rearming was also a factor in the rejection of the German overtures. Moreover, the American consul general in Berlin advised against an agreement of any sort in the hope that an economic crisis in Germany might topple Hitler. Later in the year, Roosevelt's ambassador in Berlin informed the Foreign Ministry that Washington's refusal to renew the German-American commercial treaty was "more attributable to *political* than to economic reasons."[21] In the administration's scale of priorities, temporary relief for American producers was of lesser importance than refusing to support a German government pursuing policies contrary to United States interests. Four years later, a similar situation involving the Japanese arose. Faced with a request from Tokyo for credit to purchase 500,000 bales of American cotton, Warren Pierson, the president of the Eximbank, frankly replied that Japan's activities in China made consideration of the application out of the question.

Pierson's response is illuminating, for it clearly demonstrates that to Washington officials, the economic challenge posed by the Axis nations comprised only part of a more extensive threat. Roosevelt himself had by 1937 drawn some rather stark conclusions concerning the actual nature of that menace. His famous "quarantine speech" in Chicago in October of that year can be viewed as an early effort on his part to alert the American people to the dangers confronting them. The President spoke of "the present reign of terror and international lawlessness" threatening "the very foundations of civilization." He mentioned "violations of treaties" and the "ignorings of humane instincts" and warned that no nation could isolate itself from these pestilences. Ninety percent of the world's people were being threatened by this "breakdown of all international order and law," he declared, and not even the United States could have complete protection in a world of disorder. In private he used the term "armed banditry" to characterize the policies of Berlin, Rome, and Tokyo.[22] Quite obviously, Roosevelt had decided by 1937 that more than simple economic interests were involved. Peace, progress, security, civilization itself were at stake.

Other Washington officials described the German threat in more concrete terms. American military leaders voiced anxiety about the continued security of the Panama Canal and increasingly expressed concern about an eventual strategic challenge to the United States should Hitler continue to get his way in Europe. Berlin's economic penetration of South America raised the disturbing possibility of these Latin American nations becoming susceptible to German political pressures. The State Department worried that the countries to the south might become ideological as well as economic bases for Nazism. At the very least, important sources of strategic raw materials, essential should the country ever find itself at war, would be placed in jeopardy. More generally, the substitution of German for American economic predominance in Latin America would undermine Washington's position of hegemony.

Well before the commencement of hostilities, Roosevelt spoke fatalistically of the forces driving Germany inexorably toward war, and by the spring of 1941, he was publicly warning that if Britain fell, Germany would close in relentlessly on the western hemisphere. At this same time, the President wrote a friend: "Even if our continental limits remained intact I, personally, should hate to live the rest of my days in a world dominated by the Hitler philosophy." The conflict in Europe, he added, was ultimately between "right and wrong," a view reinforced in the minds of many by the brutal treatment accorded German Jews and other domestic groups.[23] In sum, American diplomats found themselves repelled by the militarism, racism, and expansionism of the German regime as well as by its flagrant disregard for the basic rights of other peoples. The American national interest was seen to have strategic, political, economic, ideological, and even moral components, all of which Germany threatened and not any one of which could be entirely divorced from the others.

A similar assessment of United States interests governed the Roosevelt administration's perception of relations with Japan, but events in Europe as well influenced American thinking about Far Eastern matters. As early as October 1937, FDR was telling friends that Japanese actions in China imperiled American "security and stability."[24] Only an independent and vigorous China, capable of maintaining the Asian balance of power, could safeguard American interests from the maraudings of predatory powers. Stable relations with Tokyo were also desirable, but Japanese actions in East Asia, coupled with the large reservoir of sympathy for China in the United States and naive but widespread American notions about helping the Chinese, continually undercut the prospects for enduring Japanese-American bonds. And as the European situation deteriorated, increasing numbers of Americans came to view Asian affairs through a European lens. "The problem of peace and national relations in the Far East is today directly connected with the same problems in Europe," Henry Stimson warned Roosevelt near the end of 1937. The "world crisis of freedom" was "trembling in the balance on the fields of China," for the Chinese were fighting "our battle for freedom and peace."[25] With the conclusion of the Tripartite Pact in September 1940, few questioned the essential unity of German and Japanese purposes. "The fundamental proposition," FDR wrote Grew early the following year, "is that we must recognize that the hostilities in Europe, in Africa, and in Asia are all parts of a single world conflict. . . . We are engaged in the task of defending our way of life and our vital national interests." Consequently, if Britain deserved Washington's support in Europe, she equally deserved it in Asia. If Japan drove the British from the Far East, the State Department informed Roosevelt in December 1940, "our general diplomatic and strategic position would be considerably weakened."[26] It was this linkage of European and Asian affairs, of Berlin and Tokyo, of American and British interests in the Pacific that ultimately led to Pearl Harbor. Economic rivalries and Japan's efforts to close the open door in China caused relations between Washington and Tokyo to cool, but by themselves were not sufficient cause for war.

Economic factors might not have been the primary forces behind the ultimate American involvement in the global conflict, but both Congress and the Roosevelt administration did assign economic considerations a place of prominence in the conduct of affairs with the Axis powers. Nowhere was this more evident—or less successful—than in the neutrality laws, a misguided attempt to avoid European entanglements by sacrificing ill-gotten economic profits. Reflecting the popular consensus that American participation in the First World War had been terribly mistaken, and determined to prevent a few selfish economic interests from getting the nation embroiled in future hostilities, Congress in 1935 established a mandatory arms embargo in case of war. Six months later the legislators added a prohibition on loans to any belligerent power.

This, however, turned out to be the extent to which the lawmakers were willing to go, despite their obvious failure to pre-

vent American supplies from fueling overseas aggression. By the
end of 1939, Congress had repealed even the ban on arms exports,
and the cash-and-carry provisions of the legislation enacted that
November appeared designed as much to aid one side in the European conflict while maintaining the profits of neutral trade as to
isolate the United States from the contagion of war. In four brief
years American policy had largely reversed itself, from foregoing
war-induced gains to promoting them in a fashion that minimized
the risks for United States businessmen. Instead of protecting vital American interests, the laws demonstrated that private businessmen were unsatisfactory agents of national policy if being so
demanded pecuniary loss, and that congressmen forced to seek
periodic reaffirmation from the voters had little will to impose
heavy sacrifices upon their constituents. More importantly, the
aggressor states had been encouraged to believe they could with
impunity employ naked force to redraw the world map.

The economic sanctions implied in Roosevelt's quarantine
address offered a more promising approach to the problem of relations with those nations which would upset the world order, but
his subsequent retreat from any commitments undercut whatever
utility such an idea might have possessed and demonstrated the
President was not yet willing to risk domestic opposition for the
sake of international issues. The same pattern can be detected time
and again. He refrained from aiding the Spanish loyalists, despite
private hopes for their victory and even though simple inaction
would have rendered them assistance, for fear of embroiling himself in domestic controversy which might alienate supporters in
Congress or unfavorably influence the impending election. Following the Italian invasion of Ethiopia, Roosevelt denounced prof-
iteering in the form of increased sales to Italy and was eager to
apply an arms embargo, believing these actions would assist the
Ethiopians. But the inescapable fact is that Washington's measures
were totally inadequate. Exports to Italy, especially the critical
sale of petroleum, rose dramatically. Ethiopia as well as Italy was
denied arms and other much-needed supplies, and eventually the
helpless African nation succumbed to Mussolini's tanks and war-
planes. American oil companies, one industry journal commented,
took the attitude that no reason existed for curtailing the sale of

petroleum to "a country that is formally on good terms with the United States."[27]

Other attempts at employing economic diplomacy to express American dissatisfaction with the Axis states proved no more successful. Hull, for instance, had viewed the 1938 trade agreement with Great Britain as an important means of convincing Hitler of American solidarity with the western European democracies, but the German chancellor hesitated not a whit in his campaign of expansion. Countervailing duties placed upon United States purchases of German goods a short time later were no more effective. Earlier in the decade, the American Treasury had initiated a policy of purchasing Chinese silver in an effort to shore up the government of Chiang Kai-shek. This step and other monetary arrangements instituted over the following two years may have helped China avoid severe monetary fluctuation, but did not noticeably augment Chiang's military efforts against the Japanese. In 1938, Roosevelt overrode State Department objections and approved a $25 million credit to Chiang's government after receiving assurances that Chinese military resistance against the Japanese would continue. That summer Hull announced a moral embargo against the sale of aircraft and related parts to Japan, while the Commerce Department began to discourage exporters from extending private credits to Japanese firms. On October 6, 1938, the State Department lodged a formal complaint with Tokyo for violating the principles of the open door in China. Finally, in mid-1939, Hull gave notice that the 1911 commercial treaty with Japan would be allowed to lapse. But in neither Asia nor Europe did these steps result in a reversal of the undesired behavior that had prompted them. In none of these instances were American actions sufficiently strong to deter Berlin or Tokyo. Hull, for instance, was careful to explain to the Japanese that the decision not to renew the trade agreement did not presage any immediate changes in commercial relations between the two countries. Every one of these steps, in short, served to antagonize Germany or Japan without providing meaningful aid to the opponents of these nations. FDR's economic diplomacy created enemies without winning friends or supporting prospective allies.

Only in Latin America did United States officials experi-

ence any degree of success employing economic tools. Beginning
in 1938, Washington adopted a much more vigorous response to
German penetration of the western hemisphere. The Eximbank in
particular took an aggressive attitude toward extending credits to
the nations to the south. Bank officials arranged to finance a loan
to Haiti for a program of public works, despite the fact that this
involved the American government to a greater extent than any-
time since the inauguration of the Good Neighbor policy in the
internal affairs of a small Caribbean country, and despite the assessment of the bank's vice-president that the financial risks were
greater than prudent banking would dictate. The economic hazards, he explained, were "dwarfed into insignificance" by the political considerations of keeping Germany out of the country.[28]
The following year a loan to Nicaragua from the Public Roads
Administration helped to stabilize the political situation in that
country. Private American companies, such as Pan Am and IT&T,
received government funds to expand their operations in Latin
America and thereby oust German and Italian firms. These same
corporations, on the other hand, were also required by Washington to purge their affiliates of any Axis connections and to refrain
from doing business with German, Italian, or Japanese companies
located in South America. As tensions continued to heighten in
Europe, the American government created subsidiaries to stock-
pile strategic materials and to deny these items to unfriendly nations. Bolivia, for instance, contracted to sell its entire supply of
tungsten ore concentrate to the United States. By means such as
these, the threat of German penetration in Latin America had
considerably lessened well before Pearl Harbor.

In the twenty-seven months between the outbreak of war
in Poland and America's formal entry into the fray, Washington
continued to rely on economic means for the accomplishment of
two objectives. In Europe United States officials attempted to use
their economic resources to bolster Germany's enemies. Toward
that end, they employed export controls, blacklists, restrictions on
the transfer of foreign funds, further preclusive buying, and of
course, lend-lease. Roosevelt's actions in negotiating the de-
stroyer-bases exchange are instructive. Churchill desperately sought

to avoid tying the two parts of the deal together, for he wished to shun the appearance of a business arrangement. This, however, is exactly what appealed to FDR. By making it appear as a shrewd, hard-headed bargain, he could defuse domestic criticism about the neutrality of his action. He sought, in essence, to use the language of economic gain to defend a step taken for entirely different, noneconomic reasons. Constrained by a continuing public demand that the nation keep out of war, the administration turned to economic measures as one of the few ways available to express its growing conviction that the allied cause was America's as well.

In the Far East, Washington hoped that gradual economic coercion would persuade the Japanese of the foolhardy nature of provoking the United States into war. American economic policy, counseled Ambassador Grew from Tokyo, could be used as "a sword of Damocles" dangling over Japan's head. Through a graduated series of pressures, Roosevelt hoped to guide the Japanese back into more peaceful and acceptable policies. The President did not wish to strangle Tokyo, Harold Ickes decided, but sought only to "slip the noose around Japan's neck," and to "give it a jerk now and then."[29] The trick, Hull and his State Department colleagues repeatedly cautioned, was to avoid jerking the Japanese so frequently or so vigorously as to drive them into Indochina or toward the Dutch East Indies. Ultimately, of course, even Hull's geographical vistas proved too limited.

The years preceding Pearl Harbor, then, had demonstrated that the concept of national security clearly had an economic side. To be secure, the United States had to be reasonably prosperous, and most Americans in policymaking positions in the 1930s believed that prosperity required a healthy international trade. To the extent that liberal commercial rules contributed to an increase in America's share of that trade, therefore, national security demanded some sort of multilateral global system. This comes very close to saying that the perception of the national interest held by most officials in the Roosevelt administration required the existence of an international system in which private American capitalism could operate with a minimum of restrictions. But having said this does not mean that the United States went to war with

Germany and Japan primarily for economic reasons. While economic competition did play a role in the growing rift between Washington and its eventual enemies, these considerations were only part of a larger complex of political, military, ideological, and moral factors. And not all economic interests pointed toward antagonism; powerful forces argued for a continuation of normal commercial and financial transactions.

Where economic considerations may have contributed most heavily to the ultimate recourse to arms was in the administration's attempt to employ economic pressure against Japan. The ever-cautious Hull may have been correct after all, for economic coercion, rather than blocking the Japanese, only pushed them into an early attack on the Dutch East Indies in order to replace the American oil they had lost. Washington's sanctions represented token actions, gestures of pique, not concerted policy, and to oppose Japan in this fashion served no useful purpose and further embittered key policymakers in Tokyo. Largely as a consequence, Japan moved before the American military was prepared to respond. Economic diplomacy, it seems, had been doubly unfortunate, provoking the Japanese to attack, and leading them to do so before American defenses were in place.

But in the long run, Hull showed himself no better able than anyone else in Washington to devise a set of policies that would adequately protect American interests and at the same time keep the country out of war. His solution, as he told Neville Chamberlain just as the Japanese were preparing to expand the war in China in 1937, was to develop healthy trade relations, which would then create a state of mind conducive to international collaboration. As late as November 26, 1941, when he handed the Japanese ambassador Washington's final proposals for averting war, the Secretary persisted in this idea that economic cooperation could ease the crisis. Of the nine general principles contained in the Secretary's plan, six concerned steps designed to create a greater flow of commerce. Such single-minded devotion to inappropriate policies increasingly exasperated Roosevelt. "Henry," he at last exploded, speaking with Morgenthau of Hull's reciprocal trade agreements, "these trade treaties are just too goddamned slow. The world is marching too fast."[30] Probably he was right, although we will never know for sure. For by the latter part of the decade, time had run out.

THE ECONOMICS OF WARFARE

After Pearl Harbor, American diplomats directed their efforts primarily toward two objectives: total victory over the Axis powers, and the creation of a postwar world in which American interests would be adequately safeguarded. Economic tools played a leading role in pursuit of both these goals. In fact, in the final three and one-half years of Roosevelt's presidency, the United States government found itself involved in international economic and financial dealings to a totally unprecedented degree. The growth of the State Department reflects the vast expansion of its duties which occurred during the war years. From an organization of 974 employees in 1939, it had mushroomed by the spring of 1945 into an operation nearly four times that size. At the same time, the department's traditional responsibilities had been scattered among literally scores of competing agencies and bureaus, so that Hull and his associates often exercised less day-to-day supervision of the nation's foreign policies than ever before. This proliferation of bureaucracies made possible a much more comprehensive utilization of economic diplomacy, but it also created major problems of coordination and implementation.

The most pressing question facing Washington officials was, of course, the war, and World War II saw the employment of economic warfare on a scale never before attained. Initially, a hodgepodge of bureaus, departments, and committees emerged, each concerned with one particular facet of the economic war effort. It became apparent very quickly, however, that these agencies were devoting as much time to fighting off one another's encroachments as to combating the enemy, and in September 1943, Roosevelt consolidated the foreign economic functions and staffs of fourteen of these bureaucracies in an effort to eliminate this costly competition. Thereafter, the Foreign Economic Administration, headed by Leo Crowley, supervised the major overseas economic operations of the United States. Its activities included administration of the lend-lease program; procurement of strategic materials for war production and domestic consumption; preclusive buying to deny valuable materials to the enemy; oversight of export controls; direction of relief operations in liberated countries; and collection and analysis of information about the economies of the Axis nations for use by the armed forces.

As might be expected, this massive program achieved only mixed results. Efforts to obtain vital materials needed to fulfill America's role as the supply master of the allied coalition met with a good deal of success, but Washington's ability to keep similar goods from the enemy turned out to be severely limited. Until the tide of military battle had clearly shifted in favor of the allies, the neutral states—primarily Switzerland, Sweden, Spain, and Portugal—had no real incentive to cooperate with Washington's efforts to blockade the Axis powers. Even as late as 1944, Germany was still deriving nearly one-quarter of its iron ore—an essential ingredient in the production of steel—from Sweden, a percentage only marginally smaller than in 1941. Similarly, although Britain and the United States made a great effort to cut off Spanish and Portugese wolfram exports to Germany, supplies from the two Iberian countries accounted for 63 percent of Germany's consumption between 1941 and 1944, and by the latter date Germany had stockpiles adequate for two more years. Economic diplomacy, one must conclude, had a definite usefulness as a means of warfare, but equally prominent limitations.

Lend-lease, the most expensive of the programs of economic warfare, also proved the most successful, and must be viewed as a significant exception to this generally cautious assessment. Between March 11, 1941, and June 30, 1945, the United States extended $42 billion in goods and services to its military allies. Before Pearl Harbor, this aid stimulated the domestic conversion to war production, provided crucial jobs to American workers still seeking recovery from the depression, and helped to maintain Great Britain's military resistance, thereby buying more time for America's own preparations. Following formal United States entry into the war, lend-lease assistance supplied vital materials to both the military forces and the civilian populations of America's allies, increasing the pressure being brought to bear on the enemy and unquestionably shortening the war and saving thousands of American lives. Moreover, by writing into the original legislation repayment clauses that were deliberately vague, Roosevelt guaranteed that the country would be spared the disastrous political and economic consequences that had followed in the wake of the loans made during the First World War. By all accounts, the lend-lease program was an inspired utilization of America's great economic might.

Of course, economic assistance of this magnitude might also be employed for other purposes not directly connected with the waging of war, a fact immediately appreciated by virtually everyone connected with lend-lease. It is difficult to escape the conclusion, for instance, that the aid granted Bolivia or Ecuador had more to do with Washington's desire to increase its influence in the hemisphere than with promoting military victory. In like fashion, the extension of lend-lease assistance to Saudi Arabia produced little additional oil for the allied war machine, but it did hold forth the promise of countering British influence in the Middle East and of creating an atmosphere of good will which might prove highly advantageous after the war. But it was America's closest ally, the United Kingdom, which experienced most acutely this determination to obtain non-military benefits from lend-lease. Hull saw the aid program as an excellent means to break down the British system of imperial preference, thus opening the Empire to American goods and promoting a multilateral global economy. Although Roosevelt assured Churchill that the United States had no intentions of using the promise of lend-lease assistance as a club against the British, the long months of negotiations which preceded the signing of the Anglo-American lend-lease agreement attest to the persistence with which Washington officials held to the idea that wartime aid might be exchanged for British concessions regarding postwar commercial dealings. At times the diplomats in Whitehall had occasion to wonder whether it was actually the Germans who posed the greater long-term threat to Britain's well-being. "It would indeed be ironical," worried one London newspaper, "if the lifeline thrown to us in 1941 served only to strangle us in 1944 and 1945."[31]

Still, this aspect of lend-lease can be overemphasized. Despite the lever that London's desperate need provided them, Washington officials ultimately accepted a vague formula that committed Great Britain to little more than further consultations on postwar economic policy. And notwithstanding the bitterness that often characterized these discussions, the fact remains that Washington and London forged a wartime coalition more extensive, more intimate, and ultimately more effective than any which had ever linked two major states together. In the case of Great Britain, the nonmilitary objectives which a judicious use of lend-lease might promote were clearly inferior to its primary function of assisting in the defeat of the enemy.

This policy of granting priority to military over political or economic goals in the employment of lend-lease appears to have been repeated elsewhere as well. While lend-lease clearly played a political role in Latin America, total aid to the republics south of the Rio Grande amounted to only one percent of all lend-lease expenditures, indicating the relatively minor importance given these purposes. China also received only a tiny proportion of the total lend-lease budget, a figure far too small to have prompted hopes for significant postwar benefits. The manner in which aid was extended to the Soviet Union, however, provides the best indication of this subordination of nonmilitary to military goals, for Roosevelt, over the objections of his State Department, steadfastly refused to attach any political conditions whatsoever to Russian lend-lease. His reasons for doing so derived from his perception of military necessity. In the absence of a second front, American lend-lease aid played a vital role in holding the anti-Axis alliance together, and this, rather than attempting to advance democracy, promote capitalism, or lower trade barriers, was the President's fundamental purpose. (Ultimately, of course, defeating the Axis would promote these other goals as well. Here is an excellent illustration of the hazards involved in attempting to segregate diplomatic intentions into neat, distinct categories.)

In Latin America, military and nonmilitary objectives mingled together until it proved impossible to determine where one left off and the next began. Washington officials were deeply concerned about Nazi influences in the western hemisphere and adopted a far-reaching program utilizing numerous economic projects to combat this threat. An elaborate regulatory system was devised to supervise all commercial and financial exchanges with enemy states. RFC subsidiaries signed preclusive purchasing contracts with Brazil, Bolivia, Peru, Mexico, Chile, Colombia, and several other Latin American republics, guaranteeing the United States a stable source of raw materials and the producing nations an assured market and a steady flow of income. Because of the importance of coffee to the economies of many of the countries of South and Central America, an arrangement to divide the United States into separate sales regions was drawn up to insure each producer an equitable share of the market. Even before Pearl Harbor, the administration secured congressional authorization to raise the Eximbank's loan ceiling from $200 million to $700 million, the additional funds being earmarked to assist the development, stabilization, and marketing of the economies of the western hemisphere. By easing economic distress in Latin America, administration spokesmen argued, the Bank could curb the growth of fascist influence and maintain hemispheric solidarity. The creation of the office of the Coordinator of Inter-American Affairs gave this heightened level of economic assistance a bureaucratic mooring and signified a new interest among Washington officialdom which would in later years develop into the more highly publicized Point Four program.

It could be argued that all these actions advanced the goal of military victory, but it would be just as accurate to maintain that each served other American interests as well. As Axis commercial concerns were driven out of Latin America, United States firms as often as not took their places. Many of the preclusive buying agreements meant added profits for American investors, who owned the companies producing the goods sought by the

United States government. Credits and grants contributed not only to wartime collaboration but also to the internal stability desired by American economic interests. When the State Department's petroleum advisor played a central role in writing a new petroleum law for Venezuela, he both insured that the oil needed for the prosecution of the war would continue flowing and secured legislation that conferred substantial benefits on Jersey Standard. In short, wartime exigencies provided the opportunity for further economic penetration of Latin America and significantly reinforced the dependency relationship already linking the economies of these nations with that of the United States.

The Middle East also saw an enlarged American presence during the war years, a heightened level of activity pushed by both private economic interests and certain elements within the United States government. American oil companies sought to have Washington employ its power to ease the way for private enterprise to exploit the petroleum reserves of the region. The motives of administration officials were somewhat more complex. Ickes and the navy were chiefly concerned with insuring sufficient supplies for the prosecution of the war while at the same time conserving domestic and hemispheric oil, a preoccupation spurred by surveys purporting to demonstrate United States reserves were being exhausted. The Middle East's strategic location athwart the world's routes of communication attracted other proponents of a more conspicuous American presence in the region. Competition with Great Britain for postwar trade, commercial air transportation, and communications systems prompted a desire to counteract British influence in that part of the world. A feeling that if the United States expected to contribute to international security and stability, it must participate in the life of the Middle East influenced still others. Thus, while both private economic groups and government representatives worked for a more active American interest in the Middle East, their reasons for doing so were not identical.

And despite sharing similar objectives, Washington officials and oil company executives clashed sufficiently often to belie the notion of any tight partnership between the two groups. At the very time when the industry was pushing for lend-lease aid for Saudi Arabia, Commerce Secretary Jesse Jones was persuading Roosevelt that to bow to these demands would create unacceptable domestic opposition. Jones, acting upon instructions from the President, then proceeded to inform the British that Washington continued to consider Saudi Arabia within London's sphere of interest. Two more years passed before the White House acknowledged the desirability of providing Jidda with lend-lease.

Other administration programs demonstrated this same dissimilarity in outlook between business and government. In mid-1943, Ickes moved to acquire shares of private American firms for joint private-government oil production, a project the companies bitterly opposed as an unwarranted intrusion into their exclusive domain. A year later, the Petroleum Reserves Corporation sponsored construction of a government-owned pipeline from Saudi Arabia to the Mediterranean, again prompting massive opposition from private interests. A proposed treaty with Great Britain designed to promote the orderly development of Middle Eastern oil represented still another government move denounced by important segments of the industry. Ultimately all three of these projects were abandoned, in large measure because of vociferous opposition from the private companies. But the bitter public struggle in each instance indicates the absence of any real harmony of purpose between industry officials and the administration. Despite the apparent similarity of objectives between the government and the oil companies, despite even the massive influx of industry executives into the government's policymaking process during the wartime emergency, to say that the administration's Middle Eastern policy merely served the needs of private enterprise would be a gross distortion. Where a parallelism of interests existed, each found the other's assistance useful; but when their interests diverged, a perception of the national interest different from the claims of the oil companies prevailed.

In other areas as well, American policymakers demonstrated a willingness to stake out positions independent of business desires, even at the sacrifice of immediate economic profits. In a revealing memorandum circulated throughout the State Department in the summer of 1944, one official pointedly observed that the serious economic problems besetting Great Britain presented the United States with "a choice with far reaching consequences." "We can take advantage of the difficulties to extend our foreign trade and push into markets formerly British," he noted. Alternatively, Washington could "overlook possible immediate gains to the United States and make every effort to re-establish the United Kingdom in the belief that American interests over the long run are best served economically and politically by a strong United Kingdom." An accurate reading of American needs, this analysis concluded, dictated selection of the latter approach.[32] Those higher up in the administration generally concurred in this assessment. In an August 1944 meeting of the Executive Committee on Economic Foreign Policy, William Clayton, Surplus War Property Administrator and soon to be nominated as Assistant Secretary of State for Economic Affairs, argued that the United States should facilitate the establishment of foreign industries even when these competed directly with American firms. In the long run, he reasoned, this would raise living standards abroad and contribute to an expansion of United States trade. The President himself acknowledged this distinction between the interests of American business and of the country as a whole, warning his subordinates at one point against appearing "as though we were trying to steal the economic position away from other nations."[33]

But at the same time that they were prepared to forego short-term gains, Washington policymakers seldom lost sight of their long-term objective: the creation of a multilateral global economy which would bring economic harmony and political stability to the postwar world—and financial benefits to American workers and businessmen. Genuine concern for the well-being of other peoples, and hard-headed awareness of America's own self-interest—these twin themes underlay virtually all administration thinking about the postwar period.

The international financial institutions established at Bretton Woods under American leadership nicely illustrate these dual concerns. The International Bank for Reconstruction and Development was designed to make funds available for large reconstruction projects, while the International Monetary Fund was to assist in maintaining stable currencies and restoring currency convertability. Only through massive development programs and economic stability, Washington officials argued, could the world repair the ravages of war and gradually achieve economic justice for all peoples. In selling these agencies to Congress and the public, however, administration spokesmen emphasized not the benefits which would accrue to Italians or Egyptians, but the increased volume of American goods which a prosperous world would purchase. The Bretton Woods agreements, Clayton assured congressional doubters, contained "not one single element of Santa Claus philosophy."[34]

The Assistant Secretary of State was unquestionably correct in this remark, and yet, the Bretton Woods programs cannot be seen merely as an instrument of American economic imperialism forced upon a fearful world by threats and coercion. John Maynard Keynes, Britain's representative to the conference and widely regarded as the century's most innovative economist, played a leading role in creating these institutions. If his ideas were not always accepted by the American delegation, differences between the United States and Great Britain concerned means, not fundamental objectives. More generally, Keynes was a devout disciple of a multilateral economy similar in many respects to Hull's. Any other approach, he believed, would threaten the sterling area and jeopardize London's position as a leading global financial center. Nor were Britain and America alone in pushing for a postwar order linked by interdependent economies. Technical experts in Canada, Latin America, and other smaller nations that counted upon increased exports also viewed multilateralism as in their nations' interests.

The opponents that Bretton Woods attracted also say something about its nature and purposes. Morgenthau, the moving force behind the creation of the institutions, harbored a deep distrust of international bankers, whom he felt had badly mishandled reconstruction after the First World War. He was determined they would not be given a second chance, and his barely masked dislike prompted a reciprocal antagonism from the nation's financial community, a hostility that focused upon the IMF. The president of the American Bankers Association urged Congress to reject the IMF, solemnly warning that it contained "very grave dangers." Other New York bankers feared that the fund would permit an influx of foreign goods that would fuel domestic inflation. A "special country club of business and the Federal Reserve" comprised the IMF's chief opposition, Morgenthau acidly replied.[35] Again, one is left to marvel at the complexity and diversity of American economic interests—public and private—a patchwork that makes sweeping generalizations a risky enterprise.

Because of Britain's particular vulnerability, the United States enjoyed great leeway in using its economic might to achieve certain diplomatic ends vis-à-vis its principal ally, and a closer look at Anglo-American ties during these years reveals a number of important points about Washington's conduct of its foreign affairs. In the first place, American businessmen, as should already be obvious, found that governmental actions provided them numerous opportunities to expand the geographical range of their activities, often at Britain's expense. In Latin America, in the Middle East, in the southwest Pacific, long-term British interests complained of being squeezed out by aggressive American firms enjoying indirect official sanction. Washington's stipulation that Britain not export anything constructed with lend-lease materials resulted from the administration's desire not to undermine congressional support for its program of aid, but this provision further hampered the British in their efforts to continue supplying their traditional customers. Other American actions were more deliberate, as when FDR bluntly wired Churchill that if he wished generous lend-lease assistance in the future, he had better accept the administration's views concerning postwar commercial aviation.

Washington's position in this controversy over the future of international aviation illustrates the comprehensive scope of the American concept of multilateralism. Essentially, the British sought a formal agreement guaranteeing all interested parties a share of peacetime international air traffic, while the Americans preferred to permit individual carriers to settle these issues on a competitive basis. "In its own way," explained Assistant Secretary of State Adolf Berle, this dispute was "the counterpart of the same fight which Mr. Hull has been making for years against closed trade areas." All the United States desired, added Herbert Feis, was that the "prevailing principle should be 'equality of opportunity.'" Once again, however, Washington officials seemed unable or unwilling to recognize that given America's prewar leadership in the field, coupled with the huge productive facilities and experienced carriers it had developed during the war, "equality of opportunity" would in fact drive all competitors from the skies. Berle's endeavor "to write the charter of the open sky," then, was simply the latest development in a continuing performance.[36] The proceedings had begun with Hull's efforts to secure London's agreement to forsake discriminatory trade barriers, had reappeared during the Argentia conference with Churchill's resistance to American attempts to commit him to a statement assuring equal access for all nations to the trade and raw materials of the world, and had repeatedly resurfaced in the years since in the protracted negotiations concerning the obligations Britain had assumed under Article VII of the lend-lease agreement. As Warren Kimball has written, American officials, fearful that London would continue the policies that had initially led to depression and war, were determined to save Great Britain from herself.[37]

But here again, this aggressive element in American diplomacy must be balanced by another less assertive side. "The United Kingdom is the best friend of the United States and no one in his right mind can visualize our two countries lining up on opposite sides in armed conflict," one of the State Department's senior Europeanists wrote in 1944.[38] Roosevelt evidently agreed. Pressed by his Secretary of State that autumn to extract concessions from the British in return for a promise of financial aid following the German surrender, the President chose instead to attach no conditions to American assistance, prompting the British War Cabinet to congratulate Churchill for an agreement "which is more favourable than we could ever have expected." Hull, on the other hand, was incensed at losing his principal lever for prying open British preferential restrictions, later recalling that this episode "angered me as much as anything that had happened during my career as Secretary of State."[39] The incident also demonstrates that in Roosevelt's scale of priorities, the achievement of a multilateral order had at times to be subordinated to other concerns. Returning to London near the end of 1944 after a difficult set of negotiations in Washington, Keynes wrote of "the ever increasing and ever deepening conviction in the minds of all responsible Americans that a strong Britain after the war is a vital, indeed an indispensable, requirement of American policy."[40] This being the case, administration officials felt able to push the British only so far.

        This perception of the need to balance economic considerations with other factors colored American policy across a whole range of issues. Planning for the future of a defeated Germany is a case in point. While obviously the Morgenthau Plan contained weighty economic ramifications, the American Treasury Secretary promoted this program primarily as a means of insuring that German militarism would not drive the world into a third global war. Subsequently, adverse public opinion as much as a careful study of the implications of the program caused the President to back away from the plan. Roosevelt's oft-expressed anticolonial views also opened the possibility of American economic advantage, but the most recent scholarship attributes his distaste for imperialism primarily to political and moral rather than economic considerations. In the Middle East, the majority of Washington officials had come to the conclusion by 1944 that the strategic interests of the United States demanded a continuation of the traditional British presence, even though this might interfere with the American search for profits. And though unilateral Soviet actions threatened the open door in Eastern Europe, growing doubts within the administration about Russian activity in that region arose more from anxieties about the effect this behavior might have on a stable peace and continuing Big Power cooperation than from any desire for penetration of an area in which American economic interests were at best marginal. Washington officials were hardly happy with Moscow's apparent determination to seal off Eastern Europe from contact with American capitalists, but this displeasure was not sufficient cause to jeopardize good relations with the Russians.

Of all the world's powers, in fact, the Soviet Union proved the least susceptible to economic blandishments proffered by American diplomats. Despite huge shipments of lend-lease supplies, Stalin and his lieutenants remained secretive, suspicious, and stubbornly disinclined to meet United States desires with regard to Poland, postwar boundaries, or many of the other issues that made the Grand Alliance a troubled one throughout the war years. Having failed with military aid, Washington policymakers next turned to the possibility of a large postwar loan. Indications of the administration's good will in this manner, Morgenthau believed, would provide "a sound basis for continued collaboration" in the political sphere. Opponents of this measure readily acknowledged that American dollars were "one of the most effective weapons at our disposal to influence European political events," but wanted a firm understanding that "our willingness to cooperate wholeheartedly with them in their vast reconstruction problems will depend upon their behavior in international matters."[41] Not all American thinking about the Soviets was this hard-headed. Morgenthau, for one, remained wildly overconfident that socialist Russia would become a willing member of the capitalist global order created at Bretton Woods. Ultimately, of course, such naiveté was disappointed; all semblance of Big Power harmony collapsed, Russia's need for American reconstruction aid notwithstanding. Economic diplomacy, it appeared, had reached the limits of its effectiveness.

ECONOMIC DIPLOMACY
AND THE ROOSEVELT LEGACY

The spring of 1945 saw the passing of two giants. One, the Führer of the Thousand-Year Reich, ended his days in a concrete bunker, his world toppling down around his head. The other, the New York patrician, died in the knowledge that his world was secure.

Indeed, the transformation in American life between 1933 and 1945 was little short of remarkable. Domestic crisis had been banished; internationally the United States towered over the remainder of the world. Franklin Roosevelt stood vindicated.

Also rescued was America's system of private enterprise. Neither depression nor war had been able to shatter the conviction cherished by most Americans that their liberal capitalist order held forth the promise of peace, freedom, and plenty. Quite the reverse, in fact—American capitalism was more firmly entrenched than ever. And having established a new deal at home, Americans now prepared to seek wider spheres of endeavor. Even while memories of global warfare remained fresh, Washington geared up for another confrontation, this time against the alien social and economic doctrine of Soviet communism.

In this new conflict the United States drew strength from a number of the policies laid down during the twelve years in which Franklin Roosevelt occupied the White House. The movement toward economic as well as political cooperation with other nations, exemplified by the Good Neighbor policy and the Reciprocal Trade Agreements Act, smoothed over old antagonisms and established friendships that would prove useful throughout the period of the cold war. The heightened awareness that the United States possessed vast resources to influence events abroad—captured in Roosevelt's advice to Congress that "there are many methods short of war, but stronger and more effective than mere words, of bringing home to aggressor governments the aggregate sentiments of our own people"—gave Washington policymakers additional tools with which to fight the communists.[42] Moreover, the more encompassing definition of what were properly official concerns broadened opportunities for the utilization of these immense riches.

American actions in these years also reinforced a principle earlier administrations had advanced. By 1945 it no longer even provoked controversy to suggest that the national interest could be distinct from the interests of specific American economic concerns. Firestone, Jersey Standard, Pan Am, National City Bank, Ford, General Electric—each discovered at a critical juncture in its operations that the Roosevelt administration was not particularly receptive to its pleadings. Speaking of American interests in the Far East early in 1938, Hull explained the administration's perspective. "Orderly processes in international relations must be maintained," he declared. "This interest far transcends in importance the value of American trade with China or American interests in China, it transcends even the question of safeguarding the immediate welfare of American citizens in China."[43] This assessment would have been equally true in describing United States policy in Europe or the western hemisphere. Economic considerations were important, at times they were paramount; but overall they comprised only a portion of a larger complex of political, strategic, ideological, moral, and domestic factors which went into the making of American foreign policy. In this respect, the comments of an observer somewhat removed from the immediate stresses of Washington politics might be pertinent. Writing in March 1945 of the American policymaking process, John C. Donnelly of the British Foreign Office found "a sort of cauldron in which all the special interests, the various schools of political and moral thought, the extremely powerful and completely individualistic organs of information and publicity and the governmental structure are all cooking together, all more or less as ingredients of equal value and importance." American policy, he continued, "is rarely deliberately formulated by the Administration, it is rather the vapour which derives from this cauldron in which the Administration itself is only one ingredient."[44] Given the fact that the United States was a democratic as well a capitalistic country, it is hardly surprising that the product of this process should have followed a course generally favorable to American business interests. This is altogether different, however, from concluding that Washington's foreign policy existed largely to serve the needs of American capitalism.

Nor should Hull's ambiguous position within the administration be forgotten in considering these matters. Popularly acclaimed and publicly courted, the Secretary of State was throughout his nearly twelve years in office privately ridiculed and systematically excluded from important areas in the conduct of the nation's foreign affairs. In those fields in which he had a special interest, Roosevelt exercised daily supervision, ignoring, even circumventing, the unfortunate Hull. The matters he left to the Secretary's direction were those in which he was not particularly interested, and hence, those of lesser importance to the nation's position in world affairs. To ignore this relationship, for instance to credit Hull's schemes for a multilateral world as the central driving force behind American policy, is to misread the distribution of power within the administration. As the years passed, the President allowed Hull wide latitude in matters relating to international commerce largely because in Roosevelt's scheme of things, these issues were of lesser importance.

How successful was the Roosevelt administration in using economic diplomacy to safeguard the national interest? The ultimate assessment must be a mixed one. The same foreign policies which failed to lift the depression laid the groundwork for an extraordinary postwar boom which encompassed both the United States and most of America's major trading partners. The failure of the Reciprocal Trade Agreements Act to promote substantially greater commercial exchange or to pave the way for political stability and international peace, as Hull had anticipated, must be balanced by the Eximbank's success in entwining the economic futures of many of the Latin American nations more tightly with that of the United States. But even this statement must be qualified. In the short run, Washington's dominance over its neighbors to the south served a useful purpose in promoting hemispheric solidarity, protecting American economic and financial interests, and maintaining the nation's security. This same hegemony, however, had long-run consequences of a less favorable nature, as events in Cuba since 1959, to cite only the most obvious example, have demonstrated.

And so it is with virtually all of America's overseas economic activities. The short-term does not necessarily complement the long-term. Private interests do not always parallel the public interest. Nor is it easy to determine the public interest; Morgenthau many times defined the term in a fashion quite unlike that of Hull and the State Department, and the FEA, the Commerce and

Agriculture Departments, the military, and not least in importance, the White House often saw the matter in still different ways. Means become confused with objectives, rationalizations with innermost motivations. Bureaucratic concerns intrude, to jostle with personal ambitions, private interest groups, and various and conflicting ideals about America and its role in the world. Within this welter of competing claims, economic considerations assumed an important role in the thinking of those officials charged with directing America's foreign policy. Just as certainly, however, they rarely stood out from the political, strategic, ideological, or domestic factors also present. Tempered in the crucible of Great Power responsibilities, these various elements ran together into one indissoluble blend, called for lack of a better name, the national interest.

Notes

1. Samuel I. Rosenman, ed., *The Public Papers and Addresses of Franklin D. Roosevelt,* 13 vols. (New York: Harper, 1938–50), 4:463.

2. Cordell Hull, *Memoirs,* 2 vols. (New York: Macmillan, 1948), 1:52; Dean Acheson, *Present at the Creation: My Years in the State Department* (New York: Norton, 1969), p. 9.

3. Arthur W. Schatz, "The Anglo-American Trade Agreement and Cordell Hull's Search for Peace, 1936–1938," *Journal of American History* (June 1970), 57:86; Hull, *Memoirs,* 1:525.

4. Hull quoted in Lloyd C. Gardner, *Economic Aspects of New Deal Diplomacy* (Madison: University of Wisconsin Press, 1964), p. 29; Roosevelt in Robert Dallek, *Franklin D. Roosevelt and American Foreign Policy, 1932–1945* (New York: Oxford University Press, 1979), p. 54.

5. James MacGregor Burns, *Roosevelt: The Lion and the Fox* (New York: Harcourt, 1956), p. 252.

6. Edgar B. Nixon, ed., *Franklin D. Roosevelt and Foreign Affairs,* 3 vols. (Cambridge: Harvard University Press, 1969), 1:556–57.

7. Gardner, *Economic Aspects of New Deal Diplomacy,* p. 59.

8. Mira Wilkins, *The Maturing of Multinational Enterprise: American Business Abroad from 1914 to 1970* (Cambridge: Harvard University Press, 1974), p. 180.

9. Herbert Feis to Laurence Steinhardt, Feb. 10, 1939, box 26, Herbert Feis Papers, Library of Congress; Gardner, *Economic Aspects of New Deal Diplomacy*, p. 61.

10. Clayton R. Koppes, "The Good Neighbor Policy and the Nationalization of Mexican Oil: A Reinterpretation," *Journal of American History* (June 1982), 69:69.

11. Quoted in Gardner, *Economic Aspects of New Deal Diplomacy*, p. 93.

12. Paul A. Varg, "The Economic Side of the Good Neighbor Policy: The Reciprocal Trade Program and South America," *Pacific Historical Review* (Feb. 1976), 45:71.

13. Hull, *Memoirs*, 1:365.

14. Francis Bowes Sayre, *The Way Forward: The American Trade Agreements Program* (New York: Macmillan, 1939), p. ix.

15. Rosenman, *Public Papers and Addresses of Franklin D. Roosevelt*, 5:9.

16. Feis to Stimson, Oct. 16, 1939, box 26, Feis Papers; Fred L. Israel, ed., *The War Diary of Breckinridge Long* (Lincoln: University of Nebraska Press, 1966), p. 98; Roosevelt quoted in James V. Compton, *The Swastika and the Eagle: Hitler, the United States, and the Origins of World War II* (Boston: Houghton Mifflin, 1967), p. 258.

17. Tugwell quoted in Gardner, *Economic Aspects of New Deal Diplomacy*, p. 15; Hull quoted in Arthur F. Sewall, "Key Pittman and the Quest for the China Market, 1933–1940," *Pacific Historical Review* (Aug. 1975), 44:352.

18. Frederick C. Adams, *Economic Diplomacy: The Export-Import Bank and American Foreign Policy, 1934–1939* (Columbia: University of Missouri Press, 1976), p. 178.

19. Norman Graebner, "Hoover, Roosevelt, and the Japanese," in Dorothy Borg and Shumpei Okamoto, eds., *Pearl Harbor as History* (New York: Columbia University Press, 1973), p. 41.

20. Mira Wilkins, "The Role of U.S. Business," in Borg and Okamoto, *Pearl Harbor as History*, p. 370.

21. Arnold A. Offner, "Appeasement Revisited: The United States, Great Britain, and Germany, 1933–1940," *Journal of American History* (Sept. 1977), 64:375.

22. Burns, *The Lion and the Fox*, p. 352.

23. Willard Range, *Franklin D. Roosevelt's World Order* (Athens: University of Georgia Press, 1959), p. 79.

24. Gardner, *Economic Aspects of New Deal Diplomacy*, p. 81.

25. Stimson to Roosevelt, Nov. 15, 1937, copy in box 26, Feis Papers.

26. Roosevelt's letter is in Arnold A. Offner, *The Origins of the Second World War: American Foreign Policy and World Politics, 1917–1941* (New York: Praeger, 1975), p. 193; State Department memorandum cited in Gardner, *Economic Aspects of New Deal Diplomacy*, p. 145.

27. Quoted in Roland N. Stromberg, "American Business and the Approach of War, 1935–1941," *Journal of Economic History*, (Winter 1953), 13:65.

28. Adams, *Economic Diplomacy*, p. 201; Gerald K. Haines, "American Myopia and the Japanese Monroe Doctrine, 1931–41," *Prologue* (Summer 1981), 13:108.

29. Grew quoted in Irvine H. Anderson, Jr., *The Standard-Vacuum Oil Company and United States East Asian Policy, 1933–1941* (Princeton: Princeton University Press, 1975), p. ii; Harold Ickes, *The Secret Diary of Harold Ickes*, 3 vols. (New York: Da Capo, 1953–54), 3:588.

30. John Morton Blum, ed., *From the Morgenthau Diaries: Years of Crisis, 1928–1938* (Boston: Houghton Mifflin, 1959), p. 524.

31. W. J. Gallman to Secretary of State, Nov. 15, 1944, 841.9111/11-1544, Department of State Decimal File, RG 59, National Archives.

32. John E. Orchard memorandum, "Thoughts on Phase Two," Aug. 15, 1944, box 7, Clayton-Thorp Files, Harry S. Truman Library.

33. Gardner, *Economic Aspects of New Deal Diplomacy*, p. 221.

34. *New York Times*, March 21, 1945, p. 12.

35. *Ibid.*, March 22, 1945, p. 16; Morgenthau quoted in Alfred E. Eckes, Jr., "Open Door Expansionism Reconsidered: The World War II Experience," *Journal of American History* (March 1973), 59:920.

36. Berle memorandum, Dec. 2, 1944, box 216, Adolf A. Berle Papers, Franklin D. Roosevelt Library; Herbert Feis, "On Our Economic Relations With Britain," *Foreign Affairs* (April 1943), 21:469; Beatrice Bishop Berle and Travis Beal Jacobs, eds., *Navigating the Rapids, 1918–1971: From the Papers of Adolf A. Berle* (New York: Harcourt Brace 1973), p. 502.

37. Warren F. Kimball, "Lend-Lease and the Open Door: The Temptation of British Opulence, 1937–1942," *Political Science Quarterly* (June 1971), 86:259.

38. U.S. Department of State, *Foreign Relations of the United States, 1944* (Washington, D.C.: GPO, 1965), 3:70.

39. Deputy Prime Minister to Prime Minister, Sept. 18, 1944, F.O. 800/412, Foreign Office Records, Public Record Office, London; Hull, *Memoirs*, 2:1614.

40. "The Washington Negotiations for Lend-Lease in Stage II," Dec. 12, 1944, PREM 4, 18/6, Prime Minister's Office Records, Public Record Office.

41. Morgenthau quoted in Eckes, "Open Door Expansionism Reconsidered," p. 921; *Foreign Relations of the United States, 1944*, 4:951; Gardner, *Economic Aspects of New Deal Diplomacy*, p. 316.

42. Rosenman, *Public Papers and Addresses of Franklin D. Roosevelt*, 8:3.

43. Wilkins, "The Role of U.S. Business," p. 352.

44. Minute by J. C. Donnelly, March 23, 1945, AN 929/22/45, F.O. 371.

7

1945–1960
The Era of American
Economic Hegemony

Robert A. Pollard
and Samuel F. Wells, Jr.

Woodrow Wilson International
Center for Scholars

AMERICA EMERGED FROM the Second World War as the preeminent economic power in the world. Unlike virtually every other industrialized country, the United States escaped the conflict with its productive capacity unscathed. Indeed, the war fueled an unprecedented boom in American industrial production while the economies of all other powers lay shattered or damaged. The U.S. gross national product (GNP) expanded from $91 billion in 1939 to $220 billion in 1945. Steel production grew by more than one-half. By 1947, the American share of world trade had climbed to one-third, compared to one-seventh in 1938, and by 1948, the United States produced 41 percent of the world's goods and services. Since it controlled so much of the world's industrial and financial assets, any action or inaction by the United States in the economic sphere had a profound impact on the postwar world order. And conversely, any major economic development abroad necessarily influenced America's economy and security interests.[1]

Two other general conditions encouraged an activist economic diplomacy on the part of the United States. In the first place, America's traditional economic competitors lay prostrate. With Japan, Germany, and Italy vanquished, and France and Britian (let alone China and Russia) exhausted by war, the United States had an unprecedented opportunity to shape the future conduct of international commerce and finance. The absence of any immediate military threat to its security, moreover, both permitted and encouraged the United States to rely upon economic power as the main instrument of diplomacy.

Second, American leaders in 1945 were not reluctant to assume leadership in the reform of international economic institutions. Unlike American officials after the First World War, who had relied mostly on private and informal means to achieve similar policy objectives, the post–World War II generation of leadership more readily endorsed governmental action and multilateral institutions as instruments of foreign economic policy. Policymakers in Washington keenly appreciated the opportunity that this country's vast military and economic power afforded them.

PRINCIPLES WITHOUT POLICY

A common set of beliefs, attitudes, and experiences informed the American prescriptions for world peace and prosperity. Almost every official concerned with economic diplomacy believed that the high tariffs, currency instability, and autarky which so many nations had practiced during the 1930s had set the stage for global depression and war. In certain societies, the poverty, despair, and uncertainty of these years had bred totalitarianism and militarism. American officials believed that the erection of closed economic blocs by fascist Germany in Eastern Europe, Japan in the Far East, and Britain in the Commonwealth countries had exacerbated economic rivalries and set the great powers on the road to world war. The prewar decade had demonstrated the dangers of depression, economic isolationism, and bilateralism to peaceful and democratic societies. For leaders in Washington, recent history showed that American prosperity and security depended upon an economically stable and open world order.

American leaders purposefully attempted to build a distinctly different world economic order after the war. In addition to promoting traditional objectives such as freedom of the seas, national self-determination, and democratic government, American officials sought to build an open-door world in which nations enjoyed equal opportunities for trade and investment. At Bretton Woods, for instance, the United States sponsored institutions designed to ease the convertibility of currencies (the International Monetary Fund) and to prime the pump of world production and trade through reconstruction and development loans (the International Bank for Reconstruction and Development or World Bank). The presumption was that a free-trading, nondiscriminatory environment would offer the benefits of peaceful economic competition, equal access to raw materials, and maximum efficiency through the principle of comparative advantage. An open, multilateral economic system would also tend to support the interdependent economic and political structure that American officials felt was conducive to peace, prosperity, and democracy.

Generally, American planners favored private enterprise over state ownership of the means of production. Similarly, they believed that commerce through private channels would most likely ensure fair trading practices; state trading, on the other hand, smacked of the exploitative and autarkic practices utilized by the fascist regimes in the 1930s to dominate satellite countries. For most Americans, the New Deal and the war had taught that steady economic growth under a modified capitalist system, rather than radical redistributive reforms under a socialist system, constituted the best way to remedy social ills. In practice, this meant that the United States would put primary emphasis upon increased production and efficiency in its foreign aid programs. But the New Deal and the war had also greatly expanded the role of the federal government, and after 1945 executive agencies and the Congress became increasingly important in the protection and promotion of free enterprise abroad.

To a remarkable extent, this consensus guided American foreign economic policies throughout the Truman and Eisenhower administrations. Economic diplomacy was the main instrument of U.S. foreign policy before the Korean War. While policymakers generally subordinated economic interests to strategic objectives, they relied so heavily upon economic diplomacy as a tool of security policy during the years 1945 to 1950 that the two were sometimes indistinguishable. American leaders, moreover, had both the resources and the will to reshape international economic relations.

INITIAL AID PROGRAMS

American foreign economic interests in 1945 were massive and far-flung. Foreign (and domestic) demand for American goods in the aftermath of war was almost insatiable. Merchandise exports (excluding military sales) rose to $9.8 billion in 1945, more than triple the average annual level from 1936 to 1938 and almost double that in the boom years 1927–29. (Unlike the American experience after World War I, moreover, exports rose steadily until 1950.) Beyond immense domestic consumer demand, the only restraints on the American export trade were limits on the productive capacity of America's farms and factories and on the capacity of foreign customers to pay for American goods. Imports doubled over the same period to $5.2 billion in 1945. American private investment abroad grew more slowly since the war had destroyed both overseas physical properties and investors' confidence in such ventures. Nonetheless, investment income was already $570 million in 1945, roughly the same as the 1936–38 average, and promised to expand rapidly once financial conditions stabilized.[2]

Yet the war had disrupted the traditional pattern of world

trade. The United States had maintained sizable, but not excessive, export surpluses in trade with Europe ($530 million) and the British Commonwealth of nations ($350 million), and small import surpluses in trade with the Far East ($200 million) and Latin America ($60 million) during the years 1936 to 1938. But after the war, the United States enjoyed huge trade surpluses in every region of the world: in 1946, for instance, a $3.3 billion surplus in trade with Europe, $1.1 billion with the British Commonwealth, $450 million with the Far East, and $320 million with Latin America. Meanwhile, the European countries lacked the productive capacity to earn the hard currency necessary to pay for imports of manufactured and agricultural goods from the dollar area. Lagging productivity also meant that Europe lost some of its traditional markets in Latin America and other raw material-producing areas to the United States.[3]

Budgetary constraints, high domestic inflation, and fiscal conservatism discouraged bold initiatives by the Truman administration in the foreign economic field until 1947. When the war ended, the United States was already committed to a variety of relief programs which would cost several billion dollars over the next two years, with most aid going to Europe. The conservative, and after 1946, Republican-controlled Congress sharply curtailed relief programs such as the United Nations Relief and Rehabilitation Administration (UNRRA). And while the lending authority of the Export-Import Bank (Eximbank) was extended from $700 million to $3.5 billion in July 1945, the intent of Congress was clear: the bank should only extend loans which directly stimulated U.S. exports and for which repayment was assured.[4] Furthermore, as a condition for renewing lend-lease into the early postwar years, the nation's lawmakers had expressly prohibited the direct use of such funds for reconstruction purposes, although the Roosevelt and Truman administrations later exploited loopholes in the law to divert some lend-lease to European reconstruction. Yet Congress was not wholly to blame for the timidity of early postwar economic diplomacy.

Key members of the administration, including President Harry S. Truman, firmly believed that an unbalanced budget in peacetime threatened the health of the national economy. A failure to put a ceiling on foreign aid, moreover, would inhibit self-help on the part of recipient countries. American planners felt that small and temporary doses of direct aid to major European countries would suffice to start the world economy on the road to recovery. Thereafter, they hoped, American private investment and multilateral mechanisms such as the Bretton Woods institutions would generate the liquidity and stability necessary to restore equilibrium. The net effect of these constraints and attitudes was the adoption of piecemeal, limited relief programs.

With relatively small resources for foreign aid purposes and heavy foreign demands for aid, the Truman administration needed to be selective in distributing assistance. In order to encourage other countries to adopt free-trading, multilateral practices, the United States sometimes used foreign aid as a political weapon. In response to the autarkic and politically repressive system which the Soviet Union imposed upon Eastern Europe, the United States sharply restricted loans to the Soviet bloc beginning in the fall of 1946 while concentrating most of its aid in more cooperative West European countries. U.S. governmental grants and credits to Western Europe grew from approximately $600 million in 1945 to $4.3 billion in 1947, but those to Eastern Europe fell from $390 million to $210 million in the same years.[5]

The most important American effort to promote multilateralism in this period was the set of Anglo-American agreements signed in December 1945 and approved by Congress in July 1946. In exchange for a low-interest, desperately needed $3.75 billion credit, the British promised to reduce discrimination against dollar imports and to dismantle the restrictive trading bloc they had created in conjunction with the Commonwealth countries before the war. While the Anglo-American agreements offered aid on more favorable terms than those of the Eximbank, the loan proved insufficient to sustain the British through the transitional period.[6] Basically, the administration's piecemeal approach to Europe's economic problems addressed immediate relief needs, rather than the real obstacles to long-term reconstruction.

ORIGINS OF CONTAINMENT

During the first two years of peace, events in Eastern Europe precipitated a marked deterioration in Soviet-American relations. Having fought in two world wars to defend democratic government, national self-determination, free enterprise, and an open international economic environment, the United States abhorred the politically repressive and economically exploitative system that the Soviet Union imposed upon some, if not all, East European countries immediately after the war. In addition to levying heavy reparation settlements upon the former Axis states, the Soviet Union concluded barter trade agreements which tied up a large portion of potential East European exports (Polish coal, for example) and effectively foreclosed unfettered commercial relations with the West. Although the Soviets did not create an autarkic trading bloc in Eastern Europe until after the Marshall Plan, aspects of the discriminatory system in the initial postwar years unpleasantly reminded American officials of prewar German practices.

Soviet political practices proved even more disturbing. The erection of a Communist-dominated government in Poland immediately after the war, without the elections promised at Yalta, particularly incensed President Truman and other American officials. Washington expressed its displeasure with Moscow by stern complaints, by withholding reconstruction credits, estimates of which had ranged from $1 to $6 billion in wartime discussions, and by cutting back loans to other Soviet bloc countries.

But aside from the tensions over Eastern Europe, numerous obstacles stood in the way of harmonious and expanded economic relations between the two powers. The Soviet refusal to ratify the Bretton Woods accords by the end of 1945 called into question the Kremlin's willingness to cooperate on international economic problems. The Soviets' reluctance to repay even a small amount of their lend-lease debt, as had many other countries, also did not inspire confidence within American financial and governmental circles.

The Truman administration, on the other hand, did not improve the prospects for great power cooperation by adopting a quid pro quo policy toward the Soviet Union on various political and economic issues. In sharply rebuking Soviet Foreign Minister V. M. Molotov in April 1945 for Soviet transgressions in Eastern Europe, President Truman inadvertently gave the impression that he did not intend to honor Roosevelt's commitments at Yalta. The speed with which American negotiators concluded the loan agreements with Great Britain also contrasted vividly with their treatment of the prospective Russian loan. And in steadfastly resisting the allocation of a fixed amount of German reparations to the Soviet Union during the Potsdam conference (July–August 1945), American officials appeared in Soviet eyes to favor German over Russian reconstruction.

Yet even if these difficulties had been surmounted, the Soviets had little to offer in the way of trade, and without trade, they could not very well repay an American loan. U.S. trade with the Soviet Union before the war had been minimal, reaching a peak of 2.3 percent of American exports ($70 million) and 1.2 percent of American imports ($24 million) in 1938. The vast flow of goods through the lend-lease pipeline, comprising one-fourth of American exports in 1944, encouraged false hopes among American businessmen of a huge postwar market in Russia. But even before the intensification of the Cold War in 1947–48 brought about an outcry for tougher export controls, American exports plummeted from $1.8 billion in 1945 (mostly lend-lease and relief programs) to $360 million in 1946, and $150 million in 1947, or 1 percent of total U.S. exports.[7]

The Soviets, moreover, bluntly refused to make any political concessions to gain American credits and trade. Moscow did not strongly press the Americans for a loan, apparently in the belief that the Soviet Union could gain more from a harsh German (and East European) reparations settlement than from loans from the West. With no political or economic basis for a Russian loan, American officials effectively withdrew Eximbank funds earmarked for that purpose in the spring of 1946.

Stalin's election speech of February 1946, which seemed to

signify renewed Soviet hostility toward the capitalist West, alarmed Washington. Asked to analyze the Kremlin's seeming about-face, George F. Kennan, the American chargé d'affaires in Moscow, responded with a long telegram which contended that Soviet history, ideology, and internal political and economic factors militated against a modus vivendi with the West. American lend-lease, the prospect of a large postwar loan, or other positive incentives, Kennan argued, would in no way soften Soviet policies within their sphere. Kennan emphasized the political and economic, as opposed to military, threat posed by the Soviet Union to American interests. In particular, he feared that Soviet-controlled Communist parties would take over unstable West European countries. In this cable and subsequent writings, Kennan prescribed an effort to contain Soviet expansionism in Europe and Asia through a coordinated policy of economic aid and political support to friendly and strategically important countries, such as Britain, France, Germany, Italy, and Japan.

The Truman administration enthusiastically embraced Kennan's recommendations. Countering what appeared to Washington as Soviet aggression, the United States acted forcefully in 1946 to rebuff Soviet pressure on Iran and Turkey. The goal of containment would hereafter lend a strongly political coloring to American foreign economic policies as well. Beginning in the fall of 1946, Washington denied reconstruction loans to certain East European countries presumably under Soviet domination, such as Poland and Czechoslovakia. Prewar American investment and trade with Eastern Europe (excluding the Soviet Union) had been minimal—4 percent of American foreign investment, and 2.1 percent of American exports between 1936 and 1938—and future prospects were not much better. Soviet political and economic domination of Eastern Europe, to the potential exclusion of West European interests, disturbed American officials for political reasons far more than did the loss of those markets to American businessmen. Unfortunately, the withdrawal of American (and other Western) aid, trade, and technology may have actually accelerated the subordination of those countries to Soviet rule. The Kremlin, in fact, responded to American pressure by gradually extending its bilateral commercial agreements and mutual defense treaties with the subject countries, thereby further limiting Western access to that region.[8]

THE TRUMAN DOCTRINE

In a speech of March 12, 1947, the President established containment as American policy in enunciating the Truman Doctrine. While he focused upon the security threat to Greece and Turkey, Truman basically sought to build a broad public and congressional mandate for a bold new policy of American intervention abroad, wherever Soviet aggression or internal Communist subversion threatened "free" governments. Although military expenditures did not expand significantly after this speech, the United States did establish a permanent naval presence in the Eastern Mediterranean to counter an apparent Soviet bid to expand into that region.

The Truman Doctrine also became an instrument of economic diplomacy, although not in the conventional sense. The President's speech emphasized economic over military aid, yet just under one-half of the $400 million requested in the Greek-Turkish bill was designated for economic assistance. And while American economic interests in the Near East would grow enormously in the postwar years, they were not extensive at the time of the Truman Doctrine. Some American officials believed that the support of friendly governments in Greece and Turkey was necessary to maintain important trading routes between the Middle East and Europe, especially to secure the flow of newly developed Middle Eastern oil to European industry. But this was a secondary consideration compared with the immediate security needs of Greece and Turkey and of the European economy in general.

The Truman Doctrine set a precedent and provided the justification for the Marshall Plan, and in this context it should be viewed as an instrument of economic containment. Administra-

tion officials, such as Dean Acheson, had found to their dismay
during the debate on the British loan during early 1946 that anticommunism and the specter of the Soviet threat in Europe won
congressional support far more effectively than the rather prosaic
and abstract multilateral principles—free trade, the open door,
peace and prosperity—which economic planners voiced. The Re-
publican-dominated Eightieth Congress, moreover, showed signs
of extreme reluctance to support foreign aid legislation in the winter of 1947. Until Republican Senator Arthur H. Vandenberg of
Michigan intervened on behalf of the White House, members of
his party had attempted to dismantle the Reciprocal Trade Agreements program, to raise protectionist tariffs, and to slash post-
UNRRA relief during the weeks preceding the Truman Doctrine.
The Congress and the public refused to recognize the severity of
European problems and their political and economic importance
to the United States.

Administration leaders recognized that the situation in
Greece and Turkey represented only a minor part of the larger
problem of European distress. But the dramatic events which precipitated the Truman Doctrine—the accelerating guerrilla warfare
in Greece, against a backdrop of Soviet-American confrontation
over Eastern Europe, Iran, and the Turkish Straits—provided just
the occasion the administration needed to alert the public and the
Congress to the European crisis.

The Truman Doctrine was a landmark in U.S. foreign economic policy. The Truman Doctrine marked the virtual end of
efforts to cooperate with the Soviet bloc in the economic field.
The administration thereafter usually harnessed economic aid in
the service of political and strategic ends. In practice, then, the
distinction between military and economic aid (and military and
economic containment) that Kennan had sought to maintain became blurred. After the Truman Doctrine, moreover, the United
States seldom engaged in aid programs run by international agencies like UNRRA. Instead, the administration favored bilateral
programs which it could control. As Under Secretary of State
William L. Clayton stated in May 1947 in planning for a European recovery program, *The United States must run this show.* The

United States still backed the faltering Bretton Woods institutions and was the major force behind efforts to lower trade barriers on a multilateral basis through the General Agreement on Tariffs and Trade (GATT) negotiations. But these activities, while highly important in the long run, now assumed a secondary status in American foreign economic policy.[9]

THE MARSHALL PLAN

The Truman administration soon applied the containment doctrine to Western Europe. For instance, the National Advisory Council (NAC), an interdepartmental executive group charged with overseeing U.S. policies in the Eximbank, IBRD, IMF, and other institutions, approved a $650 million loan to France in the spring of 1946, in part to bolster moderate democratic forces at a time of Communist electoral gains. On purely economic grounds, the NAC would have rejected, or reduced the size of, this and other political loans.

Yet American policymakers had greatly overestimated the strength of the West European economies. The initial postwar resilience of the European economies (except for Germany and Italy) had raised hopes for a swift recovery, but the economic crisis during the winter of 1946–47 exposed the hollowness of American optimism. European countries, notably France and Great Britain, built up huge balance-of-payments deficits with non-European trading partners, in particular the United States. A severe blizzard paralyzed much of Northern European industry, while lagging coal production, a key resource for Continental industry, forced the importation of eleven millions tons of high-priced American coal in 1946, and even more in 1947. German coal production in 1947 reached only two-thirds the prewar average, and steel production only one-fourth. Stocks of raw materials began to run out, and successive droughts caused acute food shortages. Restrictive bilateral commercial agreements (about 200 by late 1946) and currency regulations choked off the free flow of goods among European countries. Faced with a rapid increase in the cost of imports and a sharp decline in export income, the British government was forced to exhaust all but a small part of its loan from the United States. The perilous state of British reserves, moreover, compelled the British to renege on their commitments to liberalize their foreign commercial policies and to restore sterling convertibility in the summer of 1947. American investors, meanwhile, were understandably wary about risking their capital in rubble-strewn Europe. And the Bretton Woods institutions remained largely inactive.[10]

From the perspective of Washington, the economic dislocation in Europe threatened to undermine both American prosperity and the economic foundations of the peace. In 1947, exports were responsible for 6.5 percent of U.S. GNP and directly or indirectly accounted for the jobs of an estimated 2.4 million American workers. Key industries, such as steel and automobiles, registered more than 10 percent of their sales overseas in 1947, while 13 percent of farm income was derived from exports. Administration spokesmen stressed these figures in statements designed to win public support, but privately, they were more alarmed by the specter of Communist takeovers in such key European countries as France and Italy. Given the subservience of West European Communist parties to the Kremlin at that time, Communist electoral victories or takeovers in France and Italy would have completely upset the European balance of power and overturned democratic institutions in the very countries American troops had liberated.[11]

The mere fact that American leaders recognized the gravity of the West European political and economic crisis in early 1947 did not mean that they welcomed the costs and responsibilities of European reconstruction. A new recovery program required a major campaign on Capitol Hill and a diversion of scarce resources from domestic programs at a time when inflation and pressures on the budget were very high and the President's popularity and political clout were both quite low.

But once having made the commitment to aid Europe, the

Truman administration, partly reflecting the desires of the Eightieth Congress, insisted upon fundamental changes in European institutions. In the first place, German reconstruction became a precondition of further American aid. The Marshall Plan in this sense represented the price the United States was willing to pay for French acquiesence in the rebuilding of Germany.

Second, the Economic Cooperation Administration (ECA), the American agency in charge of implementing the Marshall Plan, generally acted to slow the pace of social reforms in Europe, particularly those which seemed to drain energy and attention from the more immediate task of raising industrial and agricultural production. The emphasis of the Marshall Plan, in short, was on productivity rather than redistribution of income as a means to resolve social ills. In Britain, this meant a curtailment of public housing and other popular social welfare programs in order to conserve scarce capital for industrial expansion. Yet the American program did not require the imposition of alien practices upon Western Europe. The American stress on productivity only reinforced parallel developments in postwar Europe, where labor unions and leftist parties, unlike those immediately after the First World War, were adopting a relatively docile and cooperative attitude toward capital and management.

Third, the United States used the considerable leverage afforded by its aid to promote economic, if not political, integration in Europe. In addition to efforts toward freer trade, currency convertibility, and equal access to markets and raw materials through European participation in the GATT, the IMF, and the IBRD, the United States heartily endorsed the European Coal Organization, the Schuman Plan, and the Organization for European Economic Cooperation (OEEC), which together helped to create a common market in Western Europe and set the stage for later industrial and technological cooperation. American intervention in this regard was doubly useful in that it both reversed the postwar economic nationalist trend of certain West European governments (notably the French) and relieved West European governments of the responsibility for politically unpopular and economically painful reforms. French officials, for example, recognized that they

needed to hold down wages and to improve tax collection in order
to combat inflation and to balance their government's budget, but
the fragility of French coalition governments in the late 1940s discouraged bold action on these issues. These same officials, however, could more easily weather the storm of public protest arising
from unpopular reforms if the ECA appeared to initiate them.

And last, the United States used the Marshall Plan as a
tool to seal off the Soviet bloc from Western trade, credits, investment, and technology. The political object of the recovery
program was to create a Europe sufficiently coherent and cohesive
to resist Soviet pressure and influence. Despite Polish, Yugoslav,
and Czechoslovak interest in the plan, the Soviets refused to allow
East European participation on the grounds that the satellites might
fall under American domination. Trade with Eastern Europe had
never been substantial, and after the war American exports to this
region consisted largely of relief shipments. With the introduction
of controls, American exports dropped from $103 million in 1948
to $72 million in 1949; by 1952, the United States had negligible
trade with that region. Commerce between Eastern and Western
Europe continued at a substantial, albeit lower, level ($1.3 billion
annually, 1947–49) until the United States pressed the Europeans into adopting a systematic program of export controls immediately following the outbreak of the Korean War, after which this
trade declined sharply.[12]

Total Marshall Plan aid—$13 billion from 1948 to 1952—
was not in itself sufficient to revive European production and trade.
Progress was slow. Since the balance-of-payments problems of
European countries forced them to maintain some restrictive trade
and currency practices, especially against the dollar area, the liberalizing measures undertaken by GATT did not spur a large expansion in trade between Western Europe and the United States
until the mid-1950s.

But the Marshall Plan provided the margin of capital
equipment, machine tools, raw materials, and foodstuffs necessary
to buoy confidence on both sides of the Atlantic. By 1952, industrial production in ERP countries exceeded the prewar figure by
35 percent and agricultural production by 10 percent. Investors

could look forward to relative political stability and security of ownership in the years to come. European governments could plan economic and defense agendas with some certainty of a sustained American presence on the continent. And the United States, having practically broken the European deadlock on Germany, could depend upon a sizable export market in Europe. Moreover, the United States could now build mutual defense institutions upon the base of European economic and political cooperation.[13]

AID AND RECONSTRUCTION IN ASIA

National security objectives increasingly dominated U.S. foreign economic policy toward other parts of the world in the late 1940s. In Asia, American political and strategic interests vastly outweighed real or potential economic involvement. The United States restored Japanese industry for roughly the same reasons it restored German manufacturing capacity. American officials saw Japan as the key to general Asian reconstruction. American planners had originally hoped to disperse Japanese industry or trade throughout other Asian and Pacific countries (especially China, the Philippines, and Australia), partly through Japanese reparations and American aid. But by 1947 they realized that these largely underdeveloped countries could not fill the economic void left by the Japanese collapse. Japanese reconstruction was necessary, American officials reasoned, to help exclude Soviet influence from the region, to revive Far Eastern trade, to preserve a major U.S. trading partner, and—not the least of their considerations—to cut U.S. occupation costs. What is more, American leaders, including General Douglas MacArthur, firmly believed that a democratic and peaceful Japan would flourish only if its people prospered under the occupation. An open, nondiscriminatory economic order would also breed interdependence in the Far East and reduce the economic rivalries that had helped cause World War II.

The United States concentrated most of its funds for Asian aid in Japanese reconstruction because American economic stakes in that country, actual and potential, far exceeded those of any other country in the Far East. American exports to strife-torn mainland China during the 1930s never exceeded $100 million annually (and averaged about $60 million), while those to Japan never fell short of $200 million from 1934 to 1940. At first, American trade with Japan recovered slowly after the war, but by 1948 and 1949, exports to the island nation ($325 million and $468 million, respectively) rapidly overtook those to mainland China ($273 million and $83 million, respectively), then wracked by civil war.[14]

China, for all its historical allure for American businessmen, actually offered few investment returns. The prolonged Japanese occupation of China and the subsequent civil war ravaged American properties and trade in that country. After 1945 U.S. economic policy was limited to stopgap financial measures to help prop up the inept and corrupt Nationalist regime. American officials disagreed over the strategic importance of China and over whether or not Communist advances signified the expansion of Soviet power into Asia, but they largely agreed that the United States could not decisively influence the outcome of the civil war. In any case, American economic interests in China were far too small to justify a large foreign aid investment in what most knowledgeable Americans considered a losing cause. During the Korean War, however, Cold War political pressures forced an increase in American aid to the Nationalists exiled on Taiwan from $18 million in 1950 to $80 million in 1952.[15]

Political and strategic imperatives also dictated the course of American economic policy in Southeast Asia. U.S. economic interests in Southeast Asia were minimal, although the region was an important, but by no means the sole, source of commodities such as tin and rubber for Western industrialized countries. Furthermore, the anticolonial tradition of U.S. foreign policy militated against direct involvement in the war between French imperial forces and Indochinese nationalists.[16]

But during late 1949 and much of 1950, several developments forced a reappraisal of American policy in Southeast Asia.

The Communist victory in China in the fall of 1949, the rise of domestic anticommunism in the United States, and the outbreak of the Korean War in June 1950 made the defense of Indochina against a Communist takeover politically necessary. Consequently, the United States vastly accelerated military and economic aid to the French and to indigenous allied forces in Indochina. From 1950 to 1954, the United States provided the French and their Asian allies with $1.2 billion in aid. Aside from the political necessity of containing Asian Communism, the Truman and Eisenhower administrations aided the French in order to win their participation in, and adherence to, a NATO that included a rearmed Germany. Furthermore, once the United States had decided to rebuild the Japanese economy, Southeast Asia assumed much greater importance both as a market and as a source of raw materials for Japan and other allied nations in the Far East. Thus, the origins of U.S. involvement in the Indochinese quagmire lay less in direct American economic interests in the region than in political obligations to allied countries.[17]

APPROACHES TO
THE UNDERDEVELOPED WORLD

American enthusiasm for national independence movements in less developed countries (LDCs) waned as the Cold War intensified. Unstable and underdeveloped, newly independent countries appeared especially susceptible to Communist influence and takeover. The breakup of European empires now seemed a mixed blessing. American officials tended to subordinate the needs of the LDCs to European reconstruction and to the struggle against Soviet Communism, and they sometimes regarded the LDCs as mere appendages to the metropolitan (European) economies. Hence, ECA officials used a substantial portion ($240 million) of Marshall Plan aid to France to develop raw material production in overseas territories, especially French Africa.[18]

Despite growing American dependence upon imports of certain raw materials and semi-finished goods from the LDCs, the Truman administration gave infrequent attention to these countries. The United States was far more self-sufficient in natural resources than other major industrialized countries, with the exception of the Soviet Union. In many cases, the United States imported foreign materials not because domestic supplies were unavailable, but because it proved marginally cheaper to extract them overseas. In many cases, the United States enjoyed numerous foreign (as well as domestic) sources of certain materials so that their continued flow was never endangered.

Some American officials realized the security implications of the nation's growing dependence upon imported strategic minerals and raw materials. In 1947, the United States became a net importer of petroleum for the first time, and by the end of the Truman presidency oil imports had grown to one million barrels per day, or 13 percent of total U.S. oil consumption. As the President's Materials Policy Commission (Paley Commission) forcefully argued in mid-1952, long-term American security and prosperity depended upon access to foreign sources of raw materials.

Recognition of this problem caused the Truman administration to take several important, but halting, steps toward correcting the situation. The government accelerated its stockpiling program in order to prevent shortages of strategic materials in wartime. It also began to plan for a national energy program after temporary, worldwide oil shortages in the early postwar years pointed up the growing dependence of the United States and other developed countries upon foreign oil. Without an assured supply of oil, neither American and European factories, then in the process of shifting from coal to oil, nor the American and NATO war machines could function efficiently. But the early effort to promote energy independence foundered after a glut of Middle Eastern (and new domestic) oil ended the shortages and after the Korean War shifted governmental attention and resources to defense activities.

The steps taken were inadequate, and the administration underestimated future U.S. dependence upon such commodities as oil. Fears of resource scarcity did not significantly influence the making of American foreign economic policy in this period, but the government did initiate action to expand overseas commodity production in order to ensure supplies for Western Europe and for NATO in time of war.

The Truman administration strongly supported, in word if not always in deed, the development of overseas industrial and raw material production through direct investment by American corporations. The commitment to open, nondiscriminatory trade dictated the reduction of wartime subsidies to domestic mining and other extractive industries. The State and Treasury Departments, the Reconstruction Finance Corporation, the Eximbank, and other agencies of the U.S. government, as well as the U.S.-controlled World Bank and IMF, also began securing agreements with foreign governments that facilitated the entry of U.S. business abroad. American business was at first wary of investing heavily abroad, even in such traditional and relatively safe markets as Western Europe. But during the 1950s, American foreign investment picked up sharply. Total U.S. private investment abroad, which had grown slowly from 1945 ($14.7 billion) to 1950 ($19 billion), soared to $29.1 billion in 1955 and $49.3 billion in 1960. Direct U.S. foreign investment grew from $8.4 billion in 1945 to $31.9 billion in 1960.[19]

In the expansion of American multinational corporations, the strategic, political, and economic threads of national policy formed a tight, coherent fabric. The case of Iran illustrates the nexus of U.S. security and economic concerns. Through fair means and foul, American oil companies, with the help of the State Department, secured access to a large portion of the oil reserves of the Persian Gulf, in the process totally excluding the Russians and partially displacing the British. By 1950, the U.S. government had succeeded in denying political influence and oil (and arguably, territory) in Iran to the Soviets, helped establish a friendly government under the Shah in Iran, secured a large and reliable source of oil for the West, and opened the way for highly profitable participation in Iranian oil development by American companies.

Americans assumed that this development process would

create stable, free societies with ties to the West. In the case of Iran, the people would benefit through a trickling down of wealth through all layers of society. As Iran and other LDCs progressed through the various stages of capitalist growth, this reasoning went, a large and educated middle class would provide the foundations for democratic government.

The flow of American investment capital to LDCs after World War II produced mixed results for its recipients. The problem with the "modernization thesis," as this line of thinking came to be called, was that foreign corporations often dominated local economies, distorted development, and exported profits. LDCs became locked into a pattern of specialized raw material production; the infrastructure, light industry, and agricultural development necessary for sustained economic growth did not materalize. In political terms as well, capitalist modernization often failed to produce the promised benefits. Authoritarian regimes raised the specter of Communism to help maximize U.S. foreign aid and to justify delays in internal reforms. Locked into a symbiotic relationship with local elites, the United States in some instances— Taiwan, Nicaragua, South Korea, Cuba—became committed to the preservation of regimes with dubious claims to legitimacy, however fervent their professions of democracy and anticommunism.

U.S. technical aid achieved no greater degree of success. Funding for Point Four, the Truman administration's only major foreign economic initiative during its second term, was pathetically small. Technical aid to all of Latin America for 1949–50, excluding that under military aid appropriations, totalled only $54 million. Congressional enthusiasm for purely economic aid programs wavered after the North Korean invasion. The Truman administration did very little to promote Point Four, and the reasons are not hard to find. The conventional wisdom of the day held that the developing countries, like the early American republic, should rely upon self-help, free enterprise, and foreign private investment, rather than foreign aid, as the means to economic growth. While the President had proclaimed that the main purpose of Point Four was to assist in the economic development of the LDCs, he bluntly told an aide in 1952 that the program was also meant to create conditions conducive to American overseas investment. Point Four would help build the infrastructure in LDCs which American multinationals needed to develop markets, and in the process such assistance would supposedly silence foreign criticisms of American indifference toward the developing world.[20]

American investment in the extractive industries and manufacturing plants of the LDCs grew dramatically during the Truman and Eisenhower years. U.S. investment in Latin American oil, for instance, more than doubled between 1940 ($570 million) and 1950 ($1.2 billion), and once again more than doubled by 1960 ($2.7 billion). Total U.S. investment in Latin America grew from $2.8 billion in 1940 to $7.5 billion in 1960. In addition to direct investment income, the United States gained both secure access to relatively inexpensive raw materials and new markets for its exports. The inclusion of the LDCs in the multilateral world order provided some of the same benefits to America's allies in Europe. And although the exact causes remain the subject of debate, many LDCs in the Middle East, Latin America, and Southeast Asia experienced explosive, if highly uneven, growth during this period.[21]

By 1960, the American economy had become far more integrated into the world economy than wartime planners had ever anticipated. Officials in Washington believed that interdependence indirectly served American security by reducing the economic rivalries which allegedly had helped precipitate the last war. But interdependence also carried a price. As its economic interests expanded, the United States also increased its political and military responsibilities overseas at a time when the effort to contain the Soviet Union and Communist revolution had already stretched national resources to the limit.

EAST-WEST TRADE AND MILITARY CONTAINMENT

The autarkic practices of the Soviet bloc violated basic American economic principles. American officials felt multilateral agreements with these countries were impossible as long as governmental authorities engaged in state trading, sharply restricted foreign trade, manipulated currency valuations, expropriated foreign investment, stole Western patents, and refused to cooperate in the Bretton Woods institutions. In response to the Marshall Plan, the Soviet Union imposed a highly exploitative series of bilateral commercial treaties upon its satellites, thereby further heightening American suspicions. Once again, a foreign power was creating an economic bloc in Eastern Europe in order to achieve political domination of the region.

The United States responded to this Soviet economic policy by creating a neomercantilist system of export controls. The motivation for these controls was more political and strategic than economic. This is not to say that export controls did not serve an economic purpose. During the early stages of the Marshall Plan, the ECA discouraged exports of certain scarce materials needed for West European reconstruction. But the emphasis soon shifted to one of denying strategic goods and materials to the Soviet bloc. At first, only items with obvious military uses, such as airplanes and uranium, were restricted. But soon the Commerce Department's Office of International Trade, which held primary responsibility for the controls, extended the program to include even civilian-use items, on the grounds that such trade would allow the Soviets to divert resources normally used in civilian-goods production to the manufacture of military items. Technology transfers came to be equally controlled. With the outbreak of the Korean War, the Truman administration began pressing the West Europeans to adopt increasingly stringent export controls against the Soviet bloc, now expanded to include the People's Republic of China and North Korea. By the early 1950s, American trade with the East was negligible, while trade between Eastern and Western Europe continued but at much reduced levels.[22]

The virtual cessation of East-West trade worked, on balance, against the interests of the United States and its allies. The West had good reason to curtail Soviet access to military hardware and technology, as well as certain items with limited military utility, such as trucks, optical equipment, and machine tools. But by extending the controlled list to include many consumer goods as well, the Truman administration inadvertently eliminated the one remaining means of contact and influence with the captive peoples of Eastern Europe. Export controls, in addition, reduced the economic dependence of the Soviet bloc upon the West since controls forced the bloc countries to develop substitute industries. Finally, and most importantly, the decline of East-West trade may have retarded West European recovery almost as much as that of Eastern Europe. The higher prices which West European countries had to pay for raw materials from alternate sources—such as coal, timber, potash, and grain, all traditionally imported from Eastern Europe—and the loss of East European export markets may partly explain the stalled recovery of the Marshall Plan countries during the eary 1950s.

The Korean War significantly reduced the importance of economic instruments in American diplomacy. Beginning in 1950, military containment supplanted economic containment essentially because the latter strategy proved inadequate to satisfy U.S. security needs in Western Europe (NATO) and the Far East. American policymakers, notably Secretary of State Dean Acheson (1949–53) and Secretary of Defense Robert Lovett (1951–53), felt that the use of economic assistance and sanctions would not suffice to hold together America's allies against the political and military danger posed by the Soviet Union, Communist China, and revolutionary parties directed by the Cominform. Military aid and rearmament increasingly replaced economic assistance and reconstruction as the West's main weapons against Soviet aggression and Communist revolution. By 1952, 80 percent of American aid to Western Europe consisted of security assistance.[23]

The rearmament precipitated by the Korean War caused a

scramble for raw materials, which sharply forced up the prices of basic commodities in world markets. Although the West European countries fell far short of the rearmament goals set forth by NATO at Lisbon in 1952, the substantial increases in military spending actually achieved did divert scarce resources and capital from economic reconstruction. Some conflict arose between the United States and its allies over the issue of military procurement. Congress attached various "Buy American" provisions to appropriations bills that established the amount of U.S. defense dollars available for the purchase of military materiel outside of the United States.

During the course of the Korean War, the Truman administration increasingly supported the allied countries through direct spending at foreign military bases and security assistance, rather than through economic aid. Indeed, the Marshall Plan ended for all practical purposes by mid-1951 and officially terminated in 1952. U.S. private trade with, and investment in, Europe and the Far East tended to follow the flag and to some extent helped fill those areas' persistent dollar gaps. Meanwhile, the outstanding if unspectacular accomplishments of the GATT negotiations steadily reduced trade and investment barriers among participating countries.

The Truman administration achieved most of its objectives in foreign economic policy. It helped create an interdependent world order which bound together most of the major industrial economies, sustained American prosperity, and nurtured the growth of free enterprise and democracy based on the American model. In doing so, it also laid the economic foundations for American security.

THE EISENHOWER ADMINISTRATION: NEW LOOK, OLD POLICY

Newly inaugurated Presidents often enter the White House with great confidence in their ability to effect far-reaching change and reform in national policies, only to find after a short period in office that the weight of precedent and limitations upon presidential power overwhelm their firmest resolve. Dwight D. Eisenhower was no exception. As the Republican candidate for President in 1952, he had pledged to cut foreign (especially economic) aid and to rely more heavily upon private, as opposed to governmental, instruments of American economic power. Yet within two years of entering office, Eisenhower emerged as the foremost champion within his administration of the multilateralist institutions initiated by his predecessor.

Eisenhower's foreign economic policies diverged far less from those of the Truman years than Republican rhetoric had suggested. Like Truman, Eisenhower believed that American national security depended upon a healthy domestic economy and that high defense spending hurt the economy by generating less real growth than an equivalent amount of private sector expenditure would create. Both Presidents also feared the consequences of sustained deficit spending, but believed that unbalanced budgets could be justified by national emergencies or recessions.

Yet they differed over whether the country faced a serious emergency in the early 1950s. Forecasting that 1954 would be the year of greatest peril to the United States, the Truman administration had launched a massive rearmament and foreign aid program entailing huge spending increases and budget deficits in the early 1950s. As part of its New Look at defense policies, the Eisenhower administration argued that the United States could stretch out its rearmament efforts over several years' time. To Eisenhower, fiscal irresponsibility might pose as great a danger to the Free World as Communist aggression. Indeed, the President and other top officials in his administration, notably Treasury Secretary George Humphrey, suspected that the Soviets were deliberately escalating the arms race in order to bankrupt the United States.

The administration's emphasis upon a balanced budget created pressure for spending cutbacks in all fields, including defense. Yet the New Look did not herald a significant decline in foreign aid. Total foreign aid expenditures did plummet from $6.35

billion in 1953 (a transitional year at the end of the war in Korea when defense expenditures in the Truman-Eisenhower era peaked at $43.6 billion) to an annual average of $4.8 billion during the 1954–60 period. But the latter figure was almost identical to the annual average foreign aid ($4.85 billion) during the Truman years (1945–52).[24]

The New Look also sustained the military emphasis of foreign aid programs during the last two years of the Truman presidency. In ruling out the use of conventional forces in wars like Korea, the Eisenhower strategy placed a premium upon military aid to equip American allies for "local" conflicts. Thus, security assistance comprised roughly two-thirds of total U.S. foreign aid during 1953–54 and one-half of total aid during the balance of the 1950s.[25]

An important reason for the continuity of foreign economic policies under Truman and Eisenhower was the widespread agreement among Republicans and Democrats, big businessmen and financiers, farm and labor groups that an open and nondiscriminatory international economic environment—frequently subsumed under the slogan "free trade"—benefitted the American economy as a whole. Even the competition of imported manufactured goods acted to hold down domestic prices and to spur American industry to greater efficiency. Freer trade worked to the great advantage of the United States given the high productivity of American industry and agriculture. As a result, top corporate leaders and governmental officials, who during Eisenhower's presidency were largely interchangeable, recognized the need for American leadership in the international economic sphere. The President himself was an ardent free-trade advocate who frequently acted to moderate protectionist forces in his own party. Indeed, to the extent that Eisenhower and his colleagues hoped that private trade and investment would replace governmental aid as an instrument of U.S. foreign policy, the multilateralist economic system was an increasingly important ingredient in the administration's prescription for a stable and peaceful world.

The main innovation of the Eisenhower White House in economic diplomacy lay in the shift of its assistance programs from

Europe to underdeveloped countries. Economic development in the Third World received greater attention because West European countries, following the economic recovery sparked by the Korean War, needed less aid, and because planners and businessmen recognized the importance of securing the energy and raw material resources of the newly emerging nation-states for the industrialized world.

The administration's concern for political developments in the Third World also encouraged an activist foreign economic policy. Through technical, economic, and military aid programs, the Eisenhower administration sought to minimize Communist influence in the former colonial areas, as well as to create new trade and investment opportunities and to open up additional sources of strategic raw materials. In doing so, Eisenhower extended the containment policy from Western Europe and Japan to developing regions of the world.

TRADE AND AID POLICY

Although Eisenhower readily accepted the main thrust of Truman's foreign economic policies, he initially adopted different tactics to achieve the same ends. In particular, the new administration hoped to use trade as a partial substitute for foreign aid. A favorite target of foreign aid opponents was economic assistance to Europe. The Marshall Plan, the critics argued, had not closed the dollar gap, spurred productivity, or dampened inflation as successfully as the plan's proponents had promised. Long-term aid commitments had also removed national economic incentives which might have forced European recipients to restore production, stabilize currencies, and balance trading accounts. With its growing military aid burden in Europe, moreover, the United States could afford only limited economic aid.[26]

In May 1953, Eisenhower appointed a Commission for Foreign Economic Policy headed by industrialist and free trader

Clarence Randall to investigate how the administration might reform assistance and other overseas economic programs. The CFEP recommended in early 1954 that in order to reduce economic aid, the United States government should reduce tariffs to spur imports from Europe (and other areas), encourage increased investment overseas (to relieve the European balance-of-payments problem in particular), and seek the early restoration of currency convertibility in Europe. The developing countries, the CFEP reasoned, would also profit from increased export opportunities and the influx of American investment. As in Europe, needy countries presumably would require less American assistance than before. In essence, the early Eisenhower White House embraced a variety of Dollar Diplomacy designed to complement a slimmed-down foreign aid program.

Preoccupied with a domestic recession and other issues and deterred by a Republican split on tariff legislation, Eisenhower did not press for a major reform of foreign economic policy in the spring of 1954. In blocking the Randall Commission's recommendations for liberalized trade, Republican Congressmen undermined the "trade not aid" strategy. The Congress, in fact, had earlier inserted an escape clause and a "peril point" provision in trade legislation to help protect American industries supposedly threatened by the foreign competition unleashed by the GATT accords. In later extensions of the Reciprocal Trade Agreements (in 1955 for three years and 1958 for four years), the Congress strengthened the escape clause and added a similarly protectionist National Defense Amendment. Together with the already extant Buy American amendment which favored government procurement from U.S. companies, those measures indicated that the Congress viewed reciprocal trade and other commercial agreements primarily as means to expanded U.S. exports, rather than as means to increase industrial efficiency, foster international specialization, or reduce costs to domestic consumers.[27]

The White House achieved only moderate success in liberalizing trade during Eisenhower's first administration. In particular, its lackluster performance in promoting multilateral cooperation in the reduction of trade barriers drew fire from free traders.

Having already succumbed to congressional pressure on the Recip-rocal Trade Agreements, the President was not immune to protec-tionist and budget-cutting sentiments within his own party, espe-cially when they emanated from members of his cabinet. Eisenhower acceded to the desires of his conservative Treasury Secretary, George Humphrey, and curtailed the independence of the Eximbank. Humphrey wished to confine the bank to the ac-tivities mandated in its charter, namely the promotion of Ameri-can exports, and to curtail the bank's extension of loans for polit-ical purposes. While the Eximbank's lending power was raised $500 million in 1954 to $5 billion, Humphrey, as the Chairman of the National Advisory Council, strictly held down its developmental assistance during Eisenhower's first term.

The most important new program in foreign economic pol-icy during Eisenhower's initial term conflicted directly with the free-market gospel espoused by Republican officials. The passage in July 1954 of Public Law 480, a federal program to dispose of farm surpluses overseas, directly involved the government in the regulation and marketing of agricultural products. P.L. 480 sup-plemented surplus sales by the Commodity Credit Corporation, which sold surplus goods at a discount for dollars, by offering surplus goods for foreign currencies, again below cost. Aside from its benefits to domestic agriculture, P.L. 480 was useful as a weapon to award or to punish other countries. Yet critics charged that the farm program, by dumping American surpluses abroad, undermined relations with nations which exported agricultural goods and retarded agricultural development in some Third World recipient countries.

The government also launched a campaign to promote ex-ports through Eximbank loans and American foreign investment. The United States supported the creation in late 1955 of the In-ternational Finance Corporation (IFC), an affiliate of the World Bank designed to encourage private investment in the Third World with soft loans. But lagging development and the Communist ad-vance in the Third World forced the Eisenhower administration to rethink its foreign economic policy beginning in early 1955.

Postwar U.S. foreign aid programs had evolved in three

stages by 1955. From 1945 through 1949, most American assistance was economic in nature and destined for Europe. With the formation of NATO and the outbreak of the Korean War, the emphasis during the years 1950 to 1953 shifted to military aid to Europe. Beginning in 1953, an increasing proportion of aid consisted of security assistance to client states in Asia (especially South Vietnam, South Korea, and Taiwan). Purely economic aid, aside from some development projects, was almost nonexistent by 1955–56, for much of the "economic" assistance was military-related and was concentrated in states closely allied with the United States. The administration, moreover, had turned increasingly toward soft loans (those allowing repayment in local currencies, rather than "hard" dollars), both in order to cut grant aid and to win congressional backing.[28]

SOVIET OFFENSIVE IN THE DEVELOPING WORLD

Communist advances in the Third World, most dramatically illustrated by the Viet Minh victory over the French at Dienbienphu in May 1954, forced a rethinking of foreign aid policy. Eisenhower and CFEP Chairman Joseph Dodge, among others, became convinced that private channels of trade and investment could not provide a sufficient stimulus to spark economic growth in developing countries. Without additional U.S. and West European aid, they reasoned, the Third World countries would slip into economic and social chaos and perhaps fall prey to Communist subversion and Soviet influence.

Soviet economic efforts in the Third World lent a sense of urgency to economic aid. Soviet trade with developing countries grew 70 percent from 1954 ($850 million) to 1956 ($1.44 billion), while Soviet credits and technical assistance increased even more rapidly. Soviet trade and aid appealed to developing nations because they found the USSR's growth record impressive and because Moscow offered trade on a barter basis and credits with few strings attached.

Eisenhower feared that Soviet influence might displace the American (and West European) economic presence in the Third World, threaten sources of strategic materials, and undermine American security. As a first step, the President asked Congress in April 1955 for $200 million under the Mutual Security Program (MSP) toward establishment of a Fund for Asian Economic Development. Still skeptical of economic aid programs—it appropriated only four-fifths of the President's MSP requests for fiscal years 1955 and 1956—the Congress sliced the Asian fund in half to $100 million. The Congress also refused Eisenhower's request in March 1956 for an additional $100 million per year to meet the Soviet challenge in the LDCs.

In subsequent years, the administration's campaign for developmental assistance enjoyed greater success. While the Congress slashed the White House's military aid portion of MSP by almost $1 billion in fiscal 1957, nonmilitary aid suffered only a $73 million cut. And while Congress had been openly hostile toward economic assistance (much of which still went to Europe) in the early 1950s, the trend was reversed in the late 1950s, when most economic aid went to developing countries. A rising chorus of criticism questioned the efficacy of military aid in fighting the spread of Communism. Although in retrospect both the administration and its critics clearly exaggerated the ability of the Soviets to lure developing nations into the Communist or neutralist camp with economic incentives, Cold War competition over the Third World did have the beneficial effect of sensitizing Americans to the problems of economic development and of setting in motion a reevaluation of the Mutual Security Program.

OIL AND NATIONAL SECURITY

No single commodity better symbolized the nexus of economic diplomacy and national security policy than oil. National security objectives and economic interests on oil policy often coincided, but when they conflicted, strategic aims usually took precedence over economic concerns. Following Truman's precedent, Eisenhower early in his first administration permitted the major American oil companies to participate in a consortium in order to help solve the political and economic crisis in Iran. By doing so, the President undercut the Justice Department's long-standing antitrust suit against the major oil companies. During the Suez crisis of 1956–57, Eisenhower similarly relied upon the oil corporations to execute national policy. To alleviate a petroleum shortage in Europe, the administration encouraged organization of an emergency supply system in which the majors functioned like a cartel.

National security considerations again overruled antitrust and free trade objectives in the President's restriction of oil imports to the United States. Under pressure from oil- and coal-producing states such as Texas and West Virginia, the White House established voluntary import quotas in 1955. These worked fairly well until the Suez crisis forced the temporary suspension of the controls program. By 1956, 10 percent of national oil supplies came from abroad.

When imports rose to 11 percent of total supplies, Eisenhower invoked the national security amendment to the Reciprocal Trade Agreement extension act and created, at the cabinet level, the President's Special Committee to Investigate Crude Oil Imports. The committee reported to the President in July 1957 that the rising tide of cheap imported oil, estimated to reach almost 18 percent of total supplies by the second half of 1957, discouraged domestic drilling, thereby undermining this country's defense mobilization base in oil. The committee dismissed the concept of a strategic oil reserve on the grounds of expense and impracticality and rejected both subsidies to domestic drilling and governmental participation in oil exploration and development as "contrary to the principles of free enterprise." The President's advisers also contended that to allow increased oil imports in order to preserve domestic reserves would leave the United States vulnerable to the interruption of foreign supplies in times of crisis. The committee recommended that the President instead establish voluntary import quotas for use by private companies.[29]

The Eisenhower administration's rationale for import quotas conveniently ignored the fact that even with growing import levels U.S. oil exploration and reserves were at an all-time high in 1957. The President's committee also never clarified what level of imports threatened national security, other than to state that the current level was undesirable. Since the late 1950s were a time of a vast oil glut with oil distributors doing almost everything to boost consumption, any level of imports, according to this logic, would have threatened both the domestic oil industry and the national security.

The committee's report left unanswered a number of other disturbing questions. In light of the fact that new drilling did not match the increase in demand, the critics asked, would not the imposition of import quotas exhaust domestic reserves more rapidly? And did not import quotas violate the free enterprise principles which the administration professed to uphold? In actuality, the answers to both questions were affirmative. By controlling imports, the administration also undercut the Justice Department's antitrust suit against the majors (in part instigated because of their alleged collusion in limiting imports) and contributed indirectly to the formation of the Organization of Petroleum Exporting Countries (OPEC) in 1960. Despite the highly contentious nature of the debate, it is hard to escape the conclusion that the oil industry's political power at least partly explains the administration's sensitivity toward the supposed "national security" implications of domestic oil development.

While the voluntary quotas proved temporarily effective, natural market forces, especially the low cost of Middle Eastern and other foreign oil, encouraged the oil companies to circumvent the quotas. Imports soon inched upward. In 1959, the White House felt compelled to impose mandatory controls on oil imports. The quota system temporarily succeeded in protecting the domestic oil industry, but at the price of postponing a national energy policy.

EUROPE, THE ALLIANCE, AND SUEZ

Despite the increasing attention which the United States devoted to the developing countries, Western Europe remained America's main trading partner and ally during the Eisenhower period. American exports to Europe grew from $3.3 billion in 1950 to $7.4 billion in 1958, remaining at about one-third of total U.S. exports during those years.[30] The European economies recovered smartly in the years following the Korean War, thereby largely obviating the need for further U.S. assistance. While the United States continued to register a sizable trade surplus with Western Europe, several factors, including burgeoning American military expenditures, military aid, and private investment in Europe, contributed to American balance-of-payments problems by the end of the decade. Interestingly, however, American investors remained less enthusiastic about prospects in Europe than in other areas. While total U.S. direct investment rose from approximately $12 billion in 1950 to $27 billion in 1958, Canada ($5.9 billion), for instance, gained far more of the $15 billion increase than did all of Western Europe ($2.9 billion).[31]

American endorsement of the European Common Market, with its unitary external tariff and continuing discrimination against American goods, ran against the free-trade universalism which the United States had promoted during the initial postwar period. During the 1950s, however, American officials could easily argue that the political gains of a European union outweighed the economic costs. A strong Western Europe could help contain the Soviet Union, integrate West Germany into the Alliance, and provide a growing market for American exports and investment. During the late 1950s, the return of European currency convertibility, the GATT's success in promoting broad tariff cuts, and the boom in transatlantic trade and investment heralded growing economic interdependence between Europe and America. European economic regionalism marked at least a partial fulfillment of American multilaterialism.[32]

Yet European and American interests sometimes clashed,

as the Suez crisis of 1956 demonstrated. During the Truman period, the United States had provided military aid to Israel and sought to safeguard British and French economic interests in the Middle East, while showing less regard for the Arab states. In contrast, the Eisenhower administration, especially after its intervention in Iran during the summer of 1953, sought to build closer ties with the Arab states by dissociating the United States from British and French colonialism and by putting a greater distance between the United States and Israel. By building a new balance of power between Israel and the Arab states and among the Arabs themselves, Eisenhower and Dulles hoped to minimize Soviet influence in the Middle East.[33] In March 1956, Eisenhower confided in his diary that "our efforts should be directed toward separating the Saudi Arabians from the Egyptians and concentrating, for the moment at least, in making the former see that their best interests lie with us, not with the Egyptians and with the Russians."[34]

In order to minimize Soviet influence in the region, the United States supported, but did not join, the Baghdad Pact, a military treaty which included Britain, Turkey, Iran, Iraq, and Pakistan as of October 1955. In an unsuccessful effort to win Egyptian adherence to the pact, the United States had also pressured the British to withdraw from their huge military base at Suez during the fall of 1954 and offered Egypt extensive economic aid to help build the Aswan Dam. But Egypt's arms purchases from, and growing political and economic intimacy with, the Soviet Union and its allies caused Eisenhower to withdraw the Aswan offer in July 1956. Egyptian President Gamal Abdel Nasser responded by seizing the Suez Canal, whose revenues he claimed would help finance Aswan. Eisenhower and Dulles despised Nasser and feared the Egyptian operation of the canal would endanger the flow of oil and raw materials to Europe, but they did not wish to appear to align the United States with European colonialism in North Africa. The United States could not act against Nasser, Eisenhower told Dulles in late July, because "now we are in the position of just protecting someone's private property."[35]

Meanwhile, the Americans did little to assuage British and French fears of economic strangulation at the hands of the Egyptians. For both countries, the Suez Canal was a lifeline to Mideastern oil and strategic outposts throughout their crumbling empires. About two-thirds of Western Europe's oil passed through the canal, while another one-third flowed through Mideastern pipelines. Although they appreciated the importance of the region's oil for the European economies, Eisenhower and Dulles did not seem to appreciate the blow to Anglo-French prestige which the seizure of the canal represented, nor the urgency which those countries felt about retaliating against Nasser's Egypt.[36]

For several weeks before the invasion, the President staked his personal prestige on diplomatic efforts to find a solution to the canal crisis. Given the apparent willingness of the Egyptians to compromise on the canal issue, Eisenhower stated in a private meeting just before fighting began that "the French and the British do not have an adequate cause for war."[37] Yet the Europeans were less concerned about resolving the canal issue itself than they were about restoring European prestige in the Middle East, if necessary by overthrowing Nasser. Without consulting the United States, the British and French attacked the Port Said area of Egypt in late October 1956 following an Israeli invasion of the Sinai.

The Anglo-French assault upon Port Said infuriated Eisenhower. For one thing, the timing of the Suez invasion could not have been worse. The Anglo-French armada approached the Egyptian coast at the very moment that the Red Army was crushing the Hungarian rebellion. The United States found itself in the uncomfortable position of joining hands with the Soviets in the United Nations in an attack upon France and Britain while the Soviets were slaughtering Hungarians with impunity. The Eisenhower administration also temporarily withheld oil shipments to Europe and refused to help stem heavy speculation against sterling during the crisis.[38]

The Suez crisis shook the Atlantic Alliance. For that the British and the French deserve most of the blame, but one can also fault Eisenhower and Dulles for pursuing a policy that alienated America's main allies without appeasing Arab nationalists. In any case, the main result of this Alliance crisis was the rapid displacement of Anglo-French influence in the Middle East by the

United States. Since 1945 the United States had aggressively promoted the expansion of American oil companies in major oil-producing states—Saudi Arabia, Iran, Iraq, Kuwait—at the expense of the British and French in particular. At the same time, the United States sought to replace Great Britain as the dominant political and military power in the area. But in doing so, the United States undermined Anglo-French interests in the region and thereby called upon itself a much larger part of the defense burden in the Middle East.

The Soviet Union took advantage of the crisis by improving its ties with Egypt and Syria, but the United States retained predominant influence with the oil-producing states of Iraq and Saudi Arabia. While the United States refused to become a formal member of the Baghdad Pact, Eisenhower did ask the Congress on January 5, 1957, for a joint resolution authorizing the President to expend up to $200 million in military and economic aid in the Middle East and to use American armed forces in defense of any Middle Eastern country facing "overt armed aggression from any country controlled by international communism." The Eisenhower Doctrine was flawed in that administration leaders identified the Soviet Union and international Communism as the major sources of instability in the Arab world, when in fact economic underdevelopment, enmity toward Israel, and intense nationalism were the main factors. Nonetheless, both houses of Congress approved the new doctrine by overwhelming margins in March 1957.[39]

Economic interests clearly influenced the American response to Nasser and the Suez episode, and security concerns dictated action along similar lines. The Egyptian nationalization of the canal threatened the flow of oil and other materials essential to European prosperity and security. On the other hand, the Eisenhower administration opposed military intervention against Egypt precisely because it feared that such action would stimulate a rash of nationalizations and other retaliatory measures against American oil companies. But in the final analysis, American policy in the Suez crisis, as in most of the its dealings with the underdeveloped world, was governed as much by the determination to prevent a further intrusion of Soviet influence in the region as by the need to protect Western economic interests.[40]

THE UNITED STATES AND THE DEVELOPING COUNTRIES

Two themes dominated U.S. policies in the Third World during the Eisenhower administration: the Cold War and private investment. Competition with the Soviet Union (and, to a lesser extent, Red China) in the Third World spurred larger U.S. aid programs in developing countries. The main American instrument against the spread of Communist influence in those countries, however, remained U.S. trade and investment. The expansion of American-based multinational corporations was to provide technology, jobs, capital, and consumer goods, and a model of economic growth for emerging nations. While economists, businessmen, Congressmen, and administration officials differed over the ideal mixture of trade, investment, and aid, they agreed that economic growth on the capitalist model, sustained by an influx of American dollars, was necessary to foster stable and democratic societies which would share the foreign policy interests of the United States. Most Americans, in short, assumed that it was possible to graft the American model of economic growth and Anglo-American political institutions onto developing countries.

The underdeveloped nations led the fight for additional aid. They sought the creation of a Special United Nations Fund for Economic Development (SUNFED). The United States opposed SUNFED because it hoped to keep aid costs down, preferred private investment over governmental aid, and wished to control the use of American aid through unilateral programs. To preempt SUNFED, the White House in the spring of 1957 announced its support for a revolving, multiyear Development Loan Fund for the newly independent countries, consisting of $500 million in fiscal 1958 (trimmed to $300 million by Congress) and greater sums in later years.[41]

Beginning in the mid-1950s, the Eisenhower administration increasingly advocated soft loans to meet the developmental needs of the LDCs. In part, the various American soft loan proposals were devices to head off criticism from developing countries. But the United States also favored soft loans, which recipients could repay in local, inconvertible currencies, because private trade and investment had failed to meet LDC needs, and many of those countries faced bankruptcy as a result. In addition, the Congress had failed to lower tariff barriers sufficiently to boost the LDCs' export earnings, which, consisting as they did largely of commodities, already fluctuated widely. The mood in Congress was also highly critical of foreign aid, especially grants. Thus, soft loans both provided the LDCs with needed American goods and services and circumvented congressional obstacles to conventional foreign aid.

Numerous other programs during the late 1950s demonstrated the Eisenhower administration's commitment to economic development. The P.L. 480 program provided billions of dollars' worth of agricultural products in exchange for local currencies, which the United States then recycled back to recipient governments through economic development and defense grants, loans to local private enterprise, and direct U.S. expenditure in the developing country for such purposes as cultural exchange. The Congress raised the Eximbank's lending authority from $5 to $7 billion in 1958, and increasing proportions of aid went toward economic development following the resignation of Treasury Secretary Humphrey in 1957. In 1959, the United States and other members doubled their subscriptions to the World Bank while increasing their IMF subscriptions by one-half, thereby raising the amount of funds available for economic development and currency stabilization. The United States also supported creation in 1960 of the International Development Association, a soft-loan affiliate of the World Bank, of whose initial $1 billion capitalization the United States supplied $320 million. Finally, the administration persuaded the Congress in 1959 to appropriate $280 million as the initial U.S. subscription to the Inter-American Development Bank to provide aid to Latin America.[42]

Altogether American economic and technical assistance (grants and credits, including surplus farm products) to developing countries rose from an average of about $1 billion annually during the 1950–54 period to $2.5 billion during 1958–60. By way of comparison, U.S. assistance to industrialized countries—the Marshall Plan nations in particular—shrank during the same period. As initial recipients began to repay loans, the balance in the aid budget for industrialized countries shifted from an annual average net payment of $1.5 billion in 1950–54 to a net receipt of $200 million in 1958–60.[43]

Yet even this level of aid could not satisfy more than a fraction of the developing countries' needs. Indeed, the administration's continuing opposition to SUNFED alienated many Third World countries, and certain U.S. aid programs had dubious results. For instance, the flood of U.S. surplus commodities released under the P.L. 480 program, in conjunction with restrictions on agricultural imports, overwhelmed less efficient producers in certain recipient (such as India) and farm surplus (such as Denmark) nations. While the White House publicly endorsed the program as a temporary expedient, the Agriculture Department, despite repeated protests by the State Department, privately sought to expand P.L. 480 as a central and permanent part of its efforts to relieve the mounting farm surplus. In this case domestic economic and political imperatives took precedence over foreign policy considerations.[44]

Reductions in U.S. tariffs through the GATT negotiations were also designed to benefit the LDCs, but in general, the administration's aid and trade policies did little to help commodity-producing nations, which suffered from instability in the prices of primary products. The Eisenhower administration did create incentives for private development in the LDCs. Through the creation of Foreign Business Corporations, which were entitled to tax deferrals on non-repatriated, reinvested earnings in LDCs, American business could benefit from investment in LDCs and encourage economic development at the same time.

LATIN AMERICAN CHALLENGES

Perhaps the greatest problems facing the United States in the developing world lay in Latin America, a region traditionally of great importance but one which American policymakers had largely neglected during the 1940s. Washington continued to show little concern over Latin America during the early 1950s because American interests in the region seemed secure and because officials complacently believed that the growth of U.S. investment and Eximbank and World Bank credits would satisfy developmental needs. Hence, most assistance under the Mutual Security Program to Latin America consisted of military rather than economic aid.

The Eisenhower administration remained firmly committed to the proposition that private enterprise offered the best prospects for the economic development of Latin America. Consequently, Washington officials believed that one of the main functions of the United States government in the region was to help provide a conducive environment for private investment. For the most part, the administration sought to achieve these objectives through conventional diplomacy, such as the partially successful effort to negotiate treaties of friendship, commerce, and navigation with the Latin American republics.

Yet as the CIA-sponsored overthrow of the Guatemalan government in June 1954 demonstrated, the Eisenhower administration could use forceful intervention to protect U.S. business in Latin America, especially when international Communism appeared to be a factor in local unrest. The Guatemalan revolution had begun in December 1944 with the overthrow of a brutal dictatorship and the election of a government which quickly instituted land reforms and raised living standards for the masses of Indian laborers who worked in the country's huge banana, coffee, and cotton plantations. In March 1951, Jacobo Arbenz Guzmán, one of the original revolutionary officers and a former minister of defense, became President of Guatemala. The Guatemalan congress in 1952 passed a law providing for the expropriation of all idle lands. On the basis of that legislation, the Arbenz government in March 1953 seized several hundred thousand acres belonging to the United Fruit Company.

As one of the main owners of plantations, railroads, and other assets in Guatemala, United Fruit did not look with favor upon the new reforms. Not insignificantly, the company had close ties to the Eisenhower administration: John Foster Dulles' law firm had acted as counsel for United Fruit in its land acquisitions in Guatemala during the 1930s, and his brother Allen Dulles, Director of the CIA, had once served as the company's president. When the Arbenz government offered compensation for the land based upon the value the company itself had set the year before for tax purposes ($600,000), United Fruit, with the support of the State Department, demanded $16 million.

Even before passage of the nationalization law, American corporations had cut back operations in Guatemala, and the World Bank and the Mutual Security Administration had withheld aid. In 1953, the presence of Communists in the Arbenz government prompted the Eisenhower administration to begin organizing a counterrevolution directed and supplied by the CIA. Secretary of State Dulles in March 1954 secured lukewarm agreement from the Tenth Inter-American Conference in Caracas to a resolution calling for "appropriate action" against intervention by international Communism in the western hemisphere. The Guatemalan government's purchase of Czechoslovakian arms in the spring of 1954, following fruitless efforts to buy them in the West, provided the Eisenhower administration with the pretext it needed for intervention. The U.S. Navy instituted a partial blockade against Guatemala in late May. Then, on June 18, 1954, fighter-bombers piloted by American mercenaries began bombing Guatemalan towns in support of a rightist army of liberation trained by the CIA. Within a week, Arbenz had resigned, leading Dulles to claim later that the "evil purpose of the Kremlin" in infiltrating Latin America had been thwarted. A wave of repression followed in Guatemala, with land reform repealed and United Fruit's property restored.[45]

Such blatant intervention was atypical of U.S. policy in

Latin America under Eisenhower. The administration normally used more subtle methods—diplomacy, loans, military aid and training, and the threat of force—to pursue its objectives, which included the elimination of Soviet and Communist influence and economic development along capitalist, multilateralist lines. Yet ironically, the shortcomings of the American model of development opened the way for precisely those influences that the United States most strongly opposed.

While U.S. investment in, and trade with, the region grew substantially during the 1950s, the Latin American countries did not achieve the sustained economic growth which the crude economic data might suggest. U.S. direct investment in the region grew from $5.6 billion in 1953 to $8.3 billion in 1961. These figures, however, represented a drop from 34 percent to 24 percent in the proportion of total U.S. direct investment abroad. Moreover, fully 70 percent of new U.S. investment in Latin America during the Eisenhower years took place in extractive industries. By the late 1950s, one-half of all direct U.S. investment in Latin America was concentrated in mining, smelting, and petroleum. These industries, critics noted, tended to be isolated outposts within the larger economies of the developing nations. Their presence did not generate comprehensive investment and growth in all sectors of the economy, nor did wealth and jobs trickle down to the general population. The American-based multinationals also expatriated much of the profits from their foreign holdings. Partly as a consequence of uneven development and of the extreme volatility (mostly downward) of commodity prices during the 1950s, the economic situation of most Latin American countries actually deteriorated during the Eisenhower years. Feeling deprived of adequate foreign assistance, oppressed by defense and political commitments which infringed upon national sovereignty, and harnessed to a commercial and financial system which largely benefitted foreign enterprise and a tiny minority of their countrymen, Latin Americans increasingly blamed the United States for their economic problems. At times, this resentment erupted into violence, as in the mob attack upon Vice President Richard M. Nixon during his visit to Caracas, Venezuela, in May 1958.[46]

To his credit, President Eisenhower recognized during his second term that the source of most development in Latin America, as well as in other LDCs, would have to come from public sources. The Congress helped initiate a shift in policy by allocating Development Loan Fund credits to Latin America in 1957. Formation of the Inter-American Development Bank in 1959 also guaranteed a new source of aid. Compared with only $40 million in 1954, U.S. aid to Latin America soared in the late 1950s ($570 million in 1958, $340 million in 1959, and $190 million in 1960). Yet Cold War considerations—primarily, the fear that the Soviets and their clients might make political inroads into underdeveloped and unstable countries—rather than a profound sympathy for, or understanding of, the social and economic problems of development, prompted the Eisenhower administration to revise its policies toward Latin America in the mid-1950s.

The Castro revolution in Cuba in 1959 exposed the superficiality of U.S. understanding of regional problems and the inadequacy of the North American model of economic growth for Latin American countries. The Cuban economy during the 1950s had become unhealthily dependent upon the U.S. market. With a large proportion of its economy committed to the production of a few crops, Cuba suffered from abrupt swings in the prices of primary products (especially sugar, which provided most export earnings). U.S. capital, moreover, controlled much of the large-scale agriculture and manufacturing in Cuba, including virtually all oil production. Most profits from foreign investment were exported from the country. Well before Castro, Cuban nationalists began to challenge U.S. dominance of the island's economy, despite the special preferences which Cuban sugar had won in the U.S. market.[47]

Most U.S. officials, particularly Secretary of State Christian A. Herter, hoped that Castro's ambitions to pursue autonomous development of his country would not preclude cooperation with American investors and the U.S. government. The critical question from Washington's perspective was Castro's relationship with the Cuban Communist Party and the Soviet Union, rather than Havana's actions regarding U.S. property on the island. It is still impossible to know today, as it was then, whether Fidel Castro was a confirmed Communist when he took power. But it is clear that Washington's tough economic sanctions in response to Castro's decrees nationalizing U.S. property and harsh treatment of political dissidents in 1960 set off a chain reaction of unforeseen events, perhaps forcing, and certainly encouraging, the Cuban leader to seek Soviet support. Once Cuba accepted Soviet aid and advisers, relations between Cuba and the United States quickly deteriorated. Under White House orders, the CIA organized and supported an invasion of Cuba by anti-Castro exiles that resulted in the debacle at the Bay of Pigs in April 1961. Meanwhile, administration officials took steps to prevent Castro's revolution from spreading. Following a visit in 1960 to several Latin American countries, Eisenhower persuaded Congress to authorize $500 million for a social development fund for the region, plus $100 million for Chilean reconstruction following a devastating earthquake. Congress appropriated these funds in 1961.

Deeply rooted ideological antipathy toward Communism led Eisenhower to underestimate the indigenous sources of revolutionary nationalism in LDCs and to overestimate the role of the Soviet Union in initiating and supporting foreign revolutionary movements. Cold War objectives, especially the desire to contain Communist revolution and aggression, meant that most aid was concentrated in newly independent countries on the periphery of the USSR and Red China (e.g., Pakistan, Turkey, Iran, South Vietnam, Taiwan, and South Korea), and that most such aid consisted of military material and related equipment. Internal reforms in recipient countries usually fell far short of American goals. Once a recipient country won American aid, it had little incentive to meet U.S. criteria for reform.

Yet the Eisenhower administration was still the first to reorient U.S. foreign aid toward the developing countries. The Eisenhower White House also shared credit with the Congress for partially shifting the focus of the Mutual Security Program from military to economic aid. And in supporting new multilateral forms of economic assistance, such as the International Development Association, Eisenhower helped provide the LDCs with more aid with fewer strings attached. In just a decade, the Third World had moved from the bottom to the top of the agenda in U.S. foreign aid programs.[48]

THE GOLD DRAIN

Balance-of-payments problems had developed almost unnoticed in the early Eisenhower years, but a sudden hemorrhage of dollars in 1958 drew national attention to the problem. For every year beginning in 1948, the United States had suffered a payments deficit, growing from $200 million in 1948 to $3.8 billion in 1958. Since the United States enjoyed a healthy trade surplus ($3.3 billion in 1958), as well as a sizable dollar inflow from investment income ($2.9 billion in 1958) throughout these years, American deficits were due to the burgeoning foreign aid program ($2.6 billion in lending and economic aid, 1958), overseas military expenditures ($3.4 billion, 1958), and private investment abroad ($2.8 billion, 1958). Until the late 1950s, however, the deficits were not a cause for alarm, since most countries enjoying a positive payments balance with the United States preferred to increase their reserve holdings of dollars rather than demand payment in U.S. gold.[49]

In 1958, the gold drain grew to $2.3 billion. Since it facilitated the return of West European convertibility, a U.S. goal since the end of the war, this development was not entirely adverse to American interests. In the short term, in fact, the payments deficit, or to put it another way, the dollar glut—was not a major problem. U.S. gold reserves ($19 billion in 1959) still exceeded foreign liabilities. The American deficits also increased world liquidity. Furthermore, the dollar glut signaled the restoration of European economic health and a rough equilibrium in world trade. As one scholar of Eisenhower's economic diplomacy has written, "it was the relative strengthening of the European economy and the rough balancing of world trade rather than any fundamental economic weakness on the part of the United States that accounted for the imbalance of payments."[50]

Still, the Eisenhower administration correctly discerned that the deficits of the late 1950s, if unchecked, could force painful adjustments in America's international economic relations. The economic leverage of the United States relative to Europe, Japan, and even some LDCs, would decline, for the payments deficits would constrain the amount of foreign aid, overseas military expenditures, and political influence that the United States could afford. Thus, it was only appropriate that the Eisenhower administration, in addition to tying aid to trade, sought to shift more of the defense burden to the European allies. To cooperate on economic issues such as the balance of payments and to encourage multilateral foreign aid programs for the LDCs, the White House also supported the creation in October 1960 of the Organization for Economic Cooperation and Development (OECD), which included the West European countries, Canada, and the United States. But when economic partnership failed to alleviate U.S. payments difficulties, Eisenhower resolved in the fall of 1960 to cut overseas military expenditures by ordering home military dependents and by further tying economic aid and defense support to procurement in the United States.[51]

In comparison with the problems of later years, Eisenhower faced few economic constraints on foreign policy. Even in the summer of 1959, the President did not seriously consider devaluing the dollar, raising interest rates, or restricting imports to offset the payments deficit. Yet the persistence of this problem in succeeding years would pose painful limitations upon U.S. foreign policy. The United States could not expand its commitments—foreign aid, military expenditures, and politico-military alliances—without eroding its economic position in the world.

Probably the greatest achievement of the Eisenhower administration was its skill in balancing foreign commitments with U.S. resources. Although the administration greatly expanded American obligations in the Third World, it simultaneously cut aid to the developed world. When payments problems arose in the late 1950s, Eisenhower curtailed foreign spending, supported stronger multilateral aid institutions (to replace some unilateral American assistance), and encouraged the West European countries and Japan to pick up a larger share of the cost of their own defense and of Western aid to the LDCs.

Furthermore, the Eisenhower administration firmly committed the Republican Party to an open and nondiscriminatory trade program (notably the reciprocal trade program) and laid the basis for future reductions in trade barriers. All too often the administration cloaked liberalizing commercial measures in anticommunist garb, with the consequence that pro-American but authoritarian regimes received the lion's share of American aid. By emphasizing Cold War rhetoric, the President's strategy was to overcome congressional protectionism and to harness foreign economic programs to political ends such as the containment of Communism. But in the process, Eisenhower consolidated the main features of the Bretton Woods system, fostered integration of the world economy, and ushered in unprecedented affluence at home.

CONCLUSION

During the administrations of Harry S. Truman and Dwight D. Eisenhower, the United States and the rest of the industrialized world enjoyed the greatest sustained economic boom of the twentieth century. There is no dispute about the striking growth in production, trade, and investment of all the developed nations. Yet, in acknowledging significant American contributions, it is impossible to state with any precision the degree to which postwar prosperity resulted from U.S. policies and actions. American leaders, whether in the government or the private sector, recognized the very limited extent to which they could control major developments in the world economy. Still, there is no question that the leadership of the United States in Bretton Woods and later multilateral enterprises, such as the Marshall Plan and GATT, did help to dismantle trade and investment barriers and to stabilize the world's currencies. These steps, in turn, facilitated world trade and recovery. The fact that the United States was acting in its own interest in doing so should surprise or dismay no one. We have only to remember the post–World War I experience to appreciate why leaders of the industrialized democracies welcomed U.S. leadership in the management of the post–World War II world economy.

Not all countries benefitted equally in the postwar boom. The industrialized countries prospered more than developing countries, and as the industrialized nation least scarred by war, the United States was in a position to gain most from an open economic order. The degree to which developing countries benefitted under this system varied widely, and in almost every case, the economic growth of the developing states was less even and more painful.

Yet it is a distortion to lay all the blame for the maladjustment and suffering of the developing countries upon the multilateral system that the United States sponsored. In the first place, the United States was not responsible for every factor in the world economy that worked to the disadvantage of the developing countries. For instance, the invention of alternative materials, such as synthetic rubber and certain alloys, reduced the income of some developing countries whose national economies depended heavily upon primary production. The relative decline in the prices of primary, as compared to semi-finished and finished, products was a long-term development which would have taken place with or without Bretton Woods and subsequent American policies. Governments could, and often did, cushion the blow to primary producers suffering from international competition through subsidies and other methods. In practice, American policymakers often tolerated, albeit grudgingly, the restrictive economic practices, such as tariffs, import quotas, and currency regulations, that developing countries like Argentina designed to protect infant industries. The problem with such "temporary" measures was that they tended to become permanent. In the long run, the alternative for most countries to participation in an open market economy was stagnation, inefficiency, and higher prices.

Insofar as American officials could influence the economic policies of other countries, they tended to support local policies weighted in favor of increased productivity, rather than a redistribution of income. One of the lessons for domestic policy that American leaders had drawn from the New Deal and wartime experiences was that an increase in productivity, accompanied by a trickling down of wealth to every social class, would do more to distribute income and to ameliorate social ills than radical social reforms or open class conflict, which discouraged investment and disrupted normal economic activity. In American leaders' understanding of the national experience, free enterprise had proven the most productive and rational means to prosperity and social harmony. In the domestic arena, these attitudes translated into a governmental role in social and economic policies limited to maintaining equal opportunity and competition, compensating for the most severe social inequities, and stimulating the economy in times of recession. In the foreign economic arena, the role of the U.S. government was conceived in broader terms, for the interwar experience had taught American leaders the need for vigorous promotion of an open economic order through regulation of international currencies and large-scale aid for reconstruction and development.

In numerous cases, American policymakers opted for economic growth over socialistic reform. In the western zones of Germany immediately after the war, American officials openly opposed efforts by the Social Democratic Union (SPD) to socialize major extractive and manufacturing industries of the Ruhr. In this case, the reduction of American occupation costs, the restoration of German steel and coal production, and general European recovery took precedence over the restructuring of German society. In Latin America, although the Truman and Eisenhower administrations regularly pressed for land reform, they strongly opposed state trading, government enterprises, and curbs on private enterprise. Through the IMF, the United States also pressured Latin American (and other Third World) governments to stabilize currencies and to reduce foreign debt before undertaking extensive industrialization. The object in each of these cases was not so much to protect entrenched elites or to retard local development as to build an economic base upon which free enterpise and democratic reform could grow.

Economic considerations alone cannot explain American

economic diplomacy in this period. The exigencies of the Cold War forced major changes in American multilateral programs. Through the denial of credits and the use of export controls in the early postwar period, the United States sought to isolate the Soviet bloc economies. The Eximbank and other governmental agencies used "political" loans to prop up U.S. allies when, as in the cases of Italy, Greece, and Nationalist China, purely economic considerations would not have justified such loans. In the 1950s, Cold War politics again dictated disproportionately large loans to South Vietnam, South Korea, Taiwan, Turkey, and other countries. And generally, the foreign aid programs of the Truman and Eisenhower administrations included a large proportion of direct military and military-related aid designed to serve strategic, rather than economic, ends.

Domestic economic conditions also played an important part in American decisionmaking, although Truman and Eisenhower generally faced fewer constraints in economic diplomacy than their successors. Fears of a postwar depression initially encouraged officials in the Truman administration to promote exports. But after 1946, in the face of huge export surpluses and double-digit inflation, these fears subsided, and the administration sought to increase imports and to control domestic demand instead. Later, during the Eisenhower presidency, massive overproduction by American farmers encouraged efforts to promote agricultural exports through the Commodity Control Corporation and the P.L. 480 program. A more significant and lasting domestic constraint was the widespread belief that uncontrolled deficit spending in peacetime could drive the country to bankruptcy.

The Congress sometimes curtailed certain executive policies by slowing the liberalization of trade or trimming foreign aid programs, as in its stubborn refusal to approve the International Trade Organization during the late 1940s and its opposition to the continuation of economic aid to Europe after the Korean invasion. The powerful pro-Israeli lobby in the United States also compelled the Truman and Eisenhower administrations to adopt policies toward Israel which bore little relation to American economic interests, real or potential, in that country, and which proved positively harmful to American relations with the Arab states.[52]

But once again, it is difficult to measure precisely the impact of internal factors upon policymaking. An enduring foreign policy consensus emerged from the common experience of the Second World War and the early Cold War, and the Truman and Eisenhower administrations were remarkably adept at exploiting this consensus and winning over congressional leaders, influential journalists, prominent businessmen, and other opinion makers to the official view on foreign policy issues. Both administrations also had a clear sense of the limits of what the economy and the public would sustain in the way of foreign policy commitments. Perhaps the only time when American officials lost sight of these limits was during and immediately after the Korean War, when the United States launched a massive rearmament program and greatly expanded its military responsibilities abroad. Thus, executive political skill, rather than the absence of domestic constraints, may best explain the relative ease with which major foreign policy programs made their way through Congress during these years.

American corporate and financial interests rarely exerted a direct influence upon American policy. When larger political and strategic objectives came in conflict with the needs of specific business interests, American decisionmakers usually abandoned the latter to their own devices. In spite of determined opposition from some business and financial circles (such as the National Association of Manufacturers), the Truman administration pursued liberalizing commercial and financial policies in the British loan agreements of 1945, the Marshall Plan, and the GATT negotiations. The Truman administration also foreclosed American business opportunities in Eastern Europe when it imposed export controls for political and strategic reasons against the Soviet bloc countries. The Eisenhower administration similarly resisted protectionist forces and maintained foreign aid programs in the face of business criticism. Throughout the postwar period, moreover, the American commitment to Israel greatly complicated the operations of American oil (and other) companies in the Arab world, not to mention broader U.S. relations in the Middle East.

In an indirect way, the U.S. government was very sensitive to the general and long-term needs of American business abroad, in particular the need for an open economic environment if American exports and investment were to expand. American officials recognized the link between foreign trade and American prosperity, and that between access to foreign sources of raw materials and the continued well-being of American business. Finally, they appreciated the value of business as a spearhead for American political and cultural penetration of other countries. A clear case in point is the role which U.S. oil companies played in the Middle East. By providing the capital and technology to develop Mideastern petroleum reserves, the oil companies provided Western Europe with an essential resource, stabilized friendly local regimes, and set the stage for closer political and military ties with the United States, while earning themselves a handsome profit in the process. The multilateral system helped serve all of these purposes.

The key concept behind multilateralism was interdependence. By definition, multilateralism implied a mutuality of interests among participating countries and a rejection of economic nationalism. It implied, too, an American willingness to accept responsibility for world economic problems. American officials recognized that the worldwide dollar shortage of the late 1940s and early 1950s required a reduction of American import barriers, for ultimately the American export trade could grow only in tandem with imports. By the same token, the United States promoted the stabilization of currencies relative to the dollar, the revival and integration of the European and Far Eastern economies, and the reduction of trade barriers through GATT and other devices. In every case, the object was equilibrium in world trade. The fact that the Truman and Eisenhower administrations did not always live up to multilateralist ideals is less important than the fact that they accomplished as much as they did.

Interestingly, the expansion of U.S. management of the world economy did not occur when foreign trade played the greatest role in the American economy. As a percentage of the gross national product, U.S. exports during the Truman and Eisenhower years ranged from a high of 6.5 percent in 1947 to a low of 3.6 percent in 1950. The corresponding figures for the 1920s are higher, and yet U.S. governmental intervention in international

economic affairs was certainly less in the 1920s than in the 1945–
60 period. (The same generalization holds if one compares imports
as a percentage of GNP, or exports and imports as a percentage
of production of movable goods, for the 1920s and the 1945–60
period.) In fact, exports constituted a much more important part
of the national economy during the 1889–1917 period, when they
averaged more than 6.5 percent, than they did for the Truman-
Eisenhower era.[53]

The explanation for the postwar activism of the United
States in international economic affairs lies more in the realm of
perceptions than economic interests. The interwar period, in which
the United States had seemingly abjured its responsibilities as a
Great Power, had left a deep impression upon the generation of
Americans who became national policy makers after 1945. International economic conditions, they believed, had a direct bearing
upon national security and prosperity. Rather than rely primarily
upon private institutions, postwar American leaders were determined to make extensive use of governmental agencies and multilateral institutions to reshape the international commercial, monetary, and financial systems. The fact that the United States
enjoyed unrivaled economic power after the Second World War,
of course, made it easier for American officials to achieve these
objectives.

The global and comprehensive nature of American foreign
economic policies and ideas makes it difficult to distinguish among
the political, strategic, and economic sources of American conduct
in the postwar years. Indeed, one of the main lessons American
postwar leaders drew from the interwar years was the inseparabil-
ity of foreign economic conditions from the national security and
the domestic economy.

From the beginning, the U.S. multilateral plan was designed to serve strategic, as well as economic, ends. American
wartime planners believed that an economically interdependent
world would be a peaceful and prosperous one in which democratic societies could flourish. The division of Europe (and later,
Asia) into economic blocs came as a rude shock to American mul-
tilateralists. Soviet-American tensions arose from the competition

of the superpowers over the political future of Europe and objective security considerations more than economic conflict.

But with the advent of the Cold War, American officials found multilateral institutions to be useful in unifying the Western democracies and in containing Communist influence. Within the Free World, American leaders believed that economic recovery and development on the American model would foster stable and democratic societies with an interest in sustaining the peace.

Economic diplomacy was perceived as an integral part of national security policy. American economic policies promoted the strength and unity of the Western world. To a remarkable extent, Truman and Eisenhower succeeded in designing foreign economic policies that served domestic economic objectives as well. The unprecedented prosperity of the 1945–60 period helped foster an enduring consensus behind multilateral American policies, which in turn sustained the Western alliance and prevented a resurgence of autarky and economic rivalry.

Notes

1. Thomas G. Paterson, *Soviet-American Confrontation: Postwar Reconstruction and the Origins of the Cold War* (Baltimore: Johns Hopkins University Press, 1973), pp. 15, 84.

2. U.S. Bureau of the Census, *Historical Statistics of the United States: Colonial Times to 1970, Bicentennial Edition, Part 2* (Washington, D.C.: GPO, 1975), pp. 864, 903 (hereafter cited as *HSUS*).

3. U.S. Bureau of Foreign and Domestic Commerce, Office of International Trade, *Foreign Trade of the United States, 1936–69* (Washington, D.C.: GPO, 1951), p. 47 (hereafter cited as *Trade*).

4. Paterson, *Confrontation*, p. 42.

5. *HSUS*, p. 874. All figures rounded off to nearest $10 million.

6. After December 31, 1946, the British were obligated to end the sterling area dollar pool and quantitative import controls on American goods. In addition, Britain was required to restore sterling convertibility in mid-1947, that is, to allow countries enjoying

export surpluses with the U.K. to exchange sterling for scarce dollars. Finally, the agreement compelled the U.K. to scale down the vast sterling balances accumulated by other countries during the war, presumably to facilitate the transition to a multilateral regime. Yet owing to numerous loopholes, only the provisions concerning QRs and sterling convertibility would pose major problems for the British. See Richard N. Gardner, *Sterling-Dollar Diplomacy: The Origins and Prospects of Our International Economic Order* (New York: McGraw-Hill, 1969), pp. 213–21.

7. Paterson, *Confrontation*, pp. 60, 66, 71.

8. *Ibid.*, pp. 101–2.

9. William L. Clayton, memorandum of May 27, 1947, *Foreign Relations of the United States*, 1947 (Washington, D.C.: GPO, 1972), 3:232.

10. Richard Mayne, *The Recovery of Europe, 1945–1973* (Garden City, N.Y.: Anchor Press/Doubleday, 1973), p. 118.

11. *HSUS*, p. 887; Paterson, *Confrontation*, pp. 6, 6n.

12. Paterson, *Confrontation*, p. 102.

13. *Ibid.*, p. 232.

14. *HSUS*, p. 903.

15. *Ibid.*, p. 875.

16. *Trade*, p. 44.

17. Walter LaFeber, *America, Russia, and the Cold War, 1945–1975*, 3d ed. (New York: John Wiley, 1976), p. 161.

18. Paterson, *Confrontation*, p. 234.

19. *HSUS*, p. 869. U.S. private investment includes all long-term and short-term investment abroad, exclusive of U.S. governmental investment. Direct investment is long-term private investment by American companies with physical plant, sales, and services established in the foreign country; direct investment excludes private U.S. holdings of foreign stocks, bonds, and other notes.

20. Peter B. Kenen, *Giant among Nations: Problems in United States Foreign Economic Policy* (New York: Harcourt, Brace, 1960), p. 150; Ayers' Diary, April 14, 1952, Papers of Eben A. Ayers, File "Diary (Ayers) 1952," Harry S. Truman Library.

21. *HSUS*, pp. 870, 871.

22. Paterson, *Confrontation*, p. 72.

23. *Ibid.*, p. 232.

24. *HSUS*, pp. 872, 874; Congressional Quarterly Service, *Congress and the Nation, Volume I, 1945–1964* (Washington, D.C.: Congressional Quarterly, 1965), p. 391.

25. All figures exclude aid to five international agencies. *HSUS*, pp. 872, 874. The Eisenhower administration's tilt toward military aid is more readily apparent when one considers that military aid had totalled less than 2 percent of U.S. foreign aid in 1946 and 1947 and had risen to only 12 percent in 1950, the year of the Korean invasion.

26. Thomas V. Dibacco, "American Business and Foreign Aid: The Eisenhower Years," *Business History Review* (1967), 41:24–25.

27. Kenen, *Giant*, pp. 46–57, 77–78; Robert A. Pastor, *Congress and the Politics of U.S. Foreign Economic Policy, 1929–1976* (Berkeley: University of California Press, 1980), pp. 101–4.

28. Burton I. Kaufman, *Trade and Aid: Eisenhower's Foreign Economic Policy, 1953–1961* (Baltimore: Johns Hopkins University Press, 1982), p. 58. See David A. Baldwin, *Economic Development and American Foreign Policy, 1943–62* (Chicago: University of Chicago Press, 1966), ch. 4 passim.

29. See Kenen, *Giant*, pp. 76–77; Gerald D. Nash, *United States Oil Policy, 1890–1964: Business and Government in Twentieth Century America* (Pittsburgh: University of Pittsburgh Press, 1968), pp. 202–6; and Sinclair Weeks to Eisenhower, July 29, 1957, with attached report by Special Committee to Investigate Crude Oil Imports, "Petroleum Imports," n.d., Records of Council of Economic Advisers: 1953–61, File "Oil Imports (1957)," Dwight D. Eisenhower Library (hereafter cited as DDEL). Eisenhower approved the report in a memo to the Secretary of the Interior (Weeks) dated July 29, 1957.

30. *HSUS*, p. 903. U.S. imports from Europe rose from $1.4 billion to $3.3 billion over the same period. *HSUS*, p. 905.

31. *Ibid.*, p. 870.

32. David P. Calleo and Benjamin M. Rowland, *America and the World Political Economy: Atlantic Dreams and National Realities* (Bloomington: Indiana University Press, 1973), pp. 62–65.

33. Charles C. Alexander, *Holding the Line: The Eisenhower Era, 1952–1961* (Bloomington: Indiana University Press, 1975), pp. 172–73.

34. Eisenhower diary entry, March 8, 1956, DDE Diary Series, Eisenhower Papers (Ann Whitman File), DDEL. Also, see March 13, 1956 diary entry in same folder.

35. Telephone call from the President (to Dulles), July 30, 1956, Dulles telephone conversations, DDEL.

36. Alexander, *Holding*, pp. 173–76.

37. A. J. Goodpaster, "Memorandum of Conference with the President," October 30, 1956, DDE Diary Series, DDEL.

38. Alexander, *Holding*, pp. 176–78.

39. *Ibid.*, pp. 186–87.

40. *Ibid.*, pp. 173–76.

41. Kaufman, *Trade and Aid*, pp. 100–12 passim.

42. *Ibid.*, chs. 7, 8, 9 passim.

43. *HSUS*, pp. 873, 874.

44. Kaufman, *Trade and Aid*, pp. 147–51.

45. Peter Lyon, *Eisenhower: Portrait of the Hero* (Boston: Little, Brown, 1974), pp. 588–92, 596–98, 607–14; Stephen Schlesinger and Stephen Kinzer, *Bitter Fruit: The Untold Story of the American Coup in Guatemala* (Garden City, N.Y.: Doubleday, 1982), passim.

46. *HSUS*, p. 870.

47. Alexander, *Holding*, pp. 256–57.

48. Kaufman, *Trade and Aid*, p. 208.

49. Kenen, *Giant*, pp. 20–21.

50. Kaufman, *Trade and Aid*, p. 179.

51. *Ibid.*, pp. 182–88, 192–96.

52. See Pastor, *Congress and U.S. Foreign Economic Policy*, pp. 325–53, for a comprehensive analysis of the role of Congress in shaping U.S. policy on foreign trade, investment, and assistance.

53. *HSUS*, p. 887. For a contrary interpretation, see Harry Magdoff, *The Age of Imperialism* (New York: Monthly Review Press, 1969), pp. 173–201 passim.

8

Since 1961
American Power
in a New World Economy

David P. Calleo

Johns Hopkins University

THE AMERICAN WORLD SYSTEM
AND ITS CHALLENGERS

Historians may well come to see 1960 to 1980 as the golden age of the postwar *Pax Americana*. Thanks to the success of American leadership in the early years after the war, American policy had achieved a reasonable approximation of its declared goal—an open international system managed by multilateral global institutions. By 1960, the world was settling down to a tolerable approximation of the liberal visions of Cordell Hull and Woodrow Wilson. The Soviets had been contained and Europe's recovery accomplished. If the United Nations had not lived up to expectations, the other international institutions that had sprung from the American political imagination—the GATT, the IMF, the NATO—were beginning to function in a fashion reasonably similar to what had been intended.

The achievement of this open international "system," with its various multilateral structures, was inseparable from the dominant postwar position achieved by the United States itself, a "hegemony" of vision and initiative as well as power and wealth. American success was embodied in four great postwar accomplishments. These may seem obvious but are useful to recall, if only to lay bare the foundations of the system built upon them.

First was the American economy's successful transformation to peacetime. Contrary to what was widely expected, no depression followed the war. The transformation in economic structures and policy that emerged from the war seemed to have resolved the prewar malaise. A confident new affluence permitted, as well as reflected, the surge of American power and enterprise throughout the world.

Second was the "containing" of the Soviet Union without a major war. By 1960, the United States had successfully blunted the challenge of its principal international rival—the Soviet Union. America's world order encompassed the greater part, by far, of the globe's space and resources. Even the self-conscious "neutralism" of India, Egypt, Yugoslavia, and several other Third World countries was turning out to be less a hostile alienation from the American-sponsored world system than a tactic to increase their weight within it.

America's third great postwar success lay within the industrial capitalist world itself. The same remarkable prosperity that sustained postwar America had also spread to the other industrial capitalist nations. Thanks to the Russian threat, Japan and the states of Western Europe soon became American military protectorates. Their economies revived and their democratic traditions, native and imported, flourished as never before. The industrial West—with Japan added in due course—became an increasingly integrated economic bloc, linked not only by common democratic political institutions, but also by a certain common outlook toward economic management. An imposing battery of multilateral institutions grew up to manage common economic as well as military affairs. Thus, the great capitalist states were revived within a context that promised an end to those internecine quarrels that had brought them two world wars within three decades.

The fourth success lay in the transformation of the old colonial empires into independent states still closely integrated into a world economy. Within this Third World, rapid decolonization was to be accompanied by "development" that would reconcile domestic self-determination and progress with continuing international integration. The principal opponents were nationalist Communists, aided by Soviet or Chinese power. American economic and military aid stood in their path. While some new nation states were diffident about institutionalized military links, development, particularly as mediated through multilateral agencies like the World Bank, was almost universally welcomed.

Success with this "Far Empire" reinforced the Atlantic "Near Empire." American power underwrote not only direct security for Europe and Japan, but also that secure access to vital raw materials, markets, and investment opportunities, which was once the principal justification for their own imperial systems. Likewise, the variety of rich industrial nations participating, made the system less constricting and threatening to the new nations.

These four achievements—domestic prosperity, containment of Communism, the recovery and containment of other major capitalist powers, and the refashioning of the old colonial order—were all highly conscious and interdependent goals. In particular, a broad American consensus believed domestic prosperity depended upon maintaining the liberal international order. This consensus inevitably provided the context within which postwar American foreign economic policy was made. In other periods, when domestic prosperity was not believed to be so dependent upon a world system, American foreign economic policy often resembled merely an agglomeration of special interests. But in this postwar period, when national prosperity was seen to depend upon running a world-wide political economy, American policy was inevitably more "structural" than agglomerative. The overriding aim of foreign economic policy was to sustain the structure and functioning of the international system.

Naturally, the interests of particular economic actors and groups, or competing bureaucratic forces, were never absent in policymaking, and at times had to be appeased for the sake of a broad working consensus. But the wide belief that creating and preserving a certain kind of international order was an overriding national interest allowed successive administrations to confront particular interests with the discipline imposed by a larger definition of national welfare. Thus, for example, liberal trade legislation triumphed repeatedly over seemingly formidable coalitions of special interests.

By 1960, the heroic phase of American policy was over. The pan-Atlantic structure was in place and beginning to work as intended. NATO was well established. Europe, with American encouragement, had formed its own economic union and started relinquishing the protectionist concessions permitted to encourage its recovery. The GATT had begun to dismantle transatlantic trade barriers; monetary convertibility had finally been achieved and the Bretton Woods system had begun to function. American policy settled down to manage its achievements. The task proved far from easy.

American policy faced three sets of interrelated challenges. First was the growing restiveness of the European Near Empire, given its most articulate voice in the eloquent pronouncements and enterprising diplomacy of General de Gaulle. While this European challenge had important military and diplomatic dimensions, it was perhaps felt most strongly in the economic sphere. The new European Community successfully restricted American efforts to integrate transatlantic agricultural markets. Above all, Europeans grew increasingly critical of American monetary hegemony.

Restiveness in the Third World formed a second major challenge. Third World countries either wanted to withdraw from the international order, as with Vietnam or perhaps Chile, or wished a repartition of world economic wealth and function within the world system, as with OPEC or the Group of 77.

The third major challenge came from within: the growing disaffection inside the domestic American political economy over the economic and moral costs of trying to manage the world. The domestic revolt over Vietnam provides the obvious illustration. In the economic sphere, growing nationalism gradually transformed the quality of American world leadership. Attempts to juggle competing domestic and international claims fueled a mounting inflation that both weakened the American economy and fed dissension within the world system.

The historical outline that follows presents American foreign economic policy in the light of these three challenges. The analysis weaves together the evolution of American foreign and domestic policy and the changing character of the rest of the international system. The term foreign economic policy is meant to be taken broadly. All three challenges, as well as the policies designed in response, almost inevitably had political and economic dimensions mixed together. In many instances, a meaningful distinction between political and economic spheres cannot easily be drawn. And since a major threat to the international order came from a revolt within the domestic American political economy itself, the line between domestic and foreign policy is similarly elusive. The politics of domestic economic management often determined not only the balance of resources available for foreign policy, but also the domestic demands on the international system that foreign policy was forced to reflect. The channel of interdependence, of course, ran both ways. Thus the politics of domestic economic management also reflected the demands of other states in the system, to which American domestic demands had occasionally to defer.

American policy throughout the sixties and seventies can certainly be considered at least a limited success. By 1980, despite many particular trials and several disturbing trends, the system's capacity to withstand shocks and survive ailments was undeniable. This durability reflects not only the strength of the defense, but also the conservative nature of the challenges. Few, even among the challengers, wished to dismantle the international system, or even to withdraw from it. Rather they wished to reform apparent inequities. In the quarrels over monetary structure, for example, the French wanted less American hegemony, which they believed would also mean less inflation. Their initiatives were framed to save the integrated monetary system, not to destroy it. Similarly, the prominent OPEC countries had no desire to wreck the international economy. On the contrary, they showed great solicitude lest the industrial geese stop laying their golden eggs. To a large extent, the domestic American rebels were not neo-isolationists hoping to lay down the pains and pleasures of world management. Rather they wanted leadership that cost less morally and economically—hegemony "on the cheap." Even the "The New International Economic Order" demanded by the Group of 77 wanted a bigger share of the system's wealth, rather than a disintegration of the system itself.

In a sense, most rebels were seeking a more "plural" system, one that would be, among other things, less dependent upon American power, resources, and leadership. The historical question was whether the integrated postwar system, fashioned by the Americans, could evolve a sufficient consensus to sustain integration under more plural management. In other words, could a more plural international order remain liberal and integrated or would a decline of American hegemony, sapped from within and without, mean a return to the protectionist blocs of the interwar period, or perhaps the "New Imperialism" of the later nineteenth century? In the face of such momentous uncertainty, should American policy have resisted the trend to pluralism, or instead sought to promote an orderly transition to it?

Actual American policy went through two distinct periods. Two administrations—those of Kennedy and Nixon—created the broad policies for their respective decades. In a sense, each represented opposite reactions to the same broad challenges. Kennedy began at the high point of American imperial power and commitment. He nevertheless sensed the potential force of the challenges. His solution was a bolstering of American hegemony, both by a reassertion of power abroad and by a renewal of strength and commitment at home. A decade later, Nixon faced more urgent problems with fewer options. International and domestic disintegration had proceeded. Nixon's solution was a certain selective disengagement from hegemonic responsibilities, but not hegemonic power. In effect, Nixon's strategy was more "national" or "mercantilist," less "imperial" than Kennedy's.

Common to American policy in both the sixties and seventies was an inability to balance combined domestic aspirations and international commitments within the resources available. American inflation was a natural consequence. Its progressive worsening—and export throughout the system—was the persistent theme running through the twenty years. Since much of inflation's momentum is psychological, with labor and capital markets progressively losing their "money illusion" and thereby learning to discount for inflationary effects, inflationary growth had a certain progressive and cumulative rhythm. Raising the inflation rate from 1 percent to 2 percent took five years. Within the next five years, it had more than tripled. By the end of the next decade, the annual rate had doubled again.[1] The consequences grew more and more destructive at home and abroad, and more and more disabling for American foreign and domestic policy.

THE KENNEDY STRATEGY, 1960–1971

If 1960 now seems a high point of American postwar success, it did not seem so to the incoming Kennedy administration. On the contrary, Kennedy foresaw an urgent Russian strategic challenge, one that was not to become actual until the later seventies. Kennedy felt an equally urgent need for accelerated growth and social reform to forestall conflict at home. He was also worried that as Europe's rapid recovery lowered America's relative competitiveness and productivity, American world leadership would be more and more difficult to sustain. Quite rightly, he saw the dollar's troubles—minor compared to what was to follow—as a dangerous signal of coming weakness.

But if Kennedy may be praised for foreseeing difficulties that lay in the future, he may also be criticized for pursuing remedies that ultimately made the difficulties more severe. In general,

he reacted to anticipations of a decline of American power by vigorous reassertions of hegemony abroad and stimulation of growth
and reform at home. In their excess of zeal, these reactions worsened the conditions they were meant to forestall. Thus the Grand
Design for Europe exacerbated the transatlantic quarrel, while the
new emphasis on development and counterinsurgency in the Third
World pointed toward Vietnam. In the domestic economy, heavy
rearmament and an aggressive full-employment policy both contributed substantially to stoking inflation. Inflation, in due course,
combined with declining productivity to erode the trade balance, thus weakening America at home and abroad. While it may
certainly be argued that Kennedy cannot be held responsible for
those decisions of the Johnson administration that had such traumatic results, a distressing continuity nevertheless links Kennedy's aspirations for domestic growth and foreign predominance
early in the decade with Johnson's inflation and war at the decade's end.[2]

In many respects, history may prove kinder to Eisenhower
than to Kennedy. With his fear of inflation and overextension,
Eisenhower now seems possessed of a sounder and more prudent
vision of America's long-range interests.[3] By contrast, Kennedy
seems to represent a militant but untimely return of conventional
wisdom. Kennedy's programs were not radically new in substance, but rather an intelligent updating of those Rooseveltian
policies that had become the mainstream of American politics.
What was new was the eloquence, dedication, and impatience with
which traditional policies were pressed.

Five aspects of Kennedy's economic policy seem particularly significant for the international system: these were his fiscal,
trade, investment, development, and monetary policies. Each was
a significant aspect of an overall strategy for accelerated domestic
growth and heightened foreign predominance. Much of the history of the sixties, and in particular the contradictions that came
to disable American policy by the end of the decade, can be traced
in the original character and subsequent evolution of each of these
policies.

Kennedy's ambitions required a substantial increase in the

rate of economic growth. Rapid growth would make vastly easier the sharply increased military spending designed for renewed foreign leadership as well as the new jobs and social programs needed for domestic transformation. Fortunately, Kennedy inherited a domestic economy ripe for expansion. Eisenhower came into office determined to extinguish the "Korean" inflation and the controls that had suppressed it. While reconciled to large counter-cyclical deficits, he was skeptical of the efficacy of tax cuts and government projects as a cure for recession, and fearful of their inflationary consequences. The recessions of 1953 and 1957 were thus permitted to run their course without the more activist Keynesian policies urged by several of his advisers, including, interestingly enough, Vice-President Nixon and Arthur Burns, head of the Council of Economic Advisers until 1956. Eisenhower's insistence upon returning to a balanced budget in fiscal 1960 helped slow 1959's sharp recovery to a 2.2 precent growth rate by 1960, and thus prepared the way for Kennedy.[4]

Kennedy's fiscal policy was immediately expansive. Military spending jumped sharply in 1961, and again in 1962. Not only was an ambitious strategic missiles program put in place, to close what turned out to be an illusory gap, but reserves were called up to strengthen forces in Europe in response to Soviet maneuvers over Berlin.[5] Substantial increases in nondefense spending started in 1962, including the commitment to put a man on the moon. As rising spending was meant to increase demand, an investment tax credit was supposed to encourage investment to meet it.[6] GNP growth remained a slow 2.6 percent in 1961, jumped to 5.8 percent in 1962, but dropped down to 4.1 percent in 1963. Unemployment was high in 1961 (6.7 percent), fell in 1962 (5.5 percent), but rose slightly in 1963 (5.7 percent).

After 1960's small surplus, fiscal deficits resumed in 1961, and jumped rather sharply in fiscal 1962—from $3.4 to $7.1 billion—and fell back to $4.8 billion in 1963.[7] As deficits continued, Kennedy, who personally had trouble accepting the more advanced fiscal notions of his advisers, began thinking of a tax increase. His Keynesian counselors stressed still high unemployment and the possibility that the declining growth rate for 1963

signalled a new recession. Eventually the President, having under-
gone a crash course in fashionable economics, was talked into a
tax cut.[8] To sell it to Congress and the public, the neo-Keynesian
concept of a "full-employment budget" was embraced officially
and widely popularized.[9] Whereas the Truman and Eisenhower
version of postwar Keynesianism called for fiscal deficits in recession and surpluses in boom, the fiscal theories embodied in the
concept of the full-employment budget committed the government to maintaining the economy in a perpetual boom. Thereafter, the full-employment budget was to serve as a rationale for
deficits under almost every sort of economic condition. The tax
cut ran into considerable congressional opposition, but was finally
passed in the early days of the Johnson administration (January
1964). Eisenhower's balanced budget for fiscal 1960 turned out to
have marked the end of an era. For the next two decades, the
United States government ran fiscal deficits every year but one
(1969), a trend likely to continue at least well into the 1980s.[10]

Fiscal deficits in the Kennedy-Johnson era were generally
accompanied by an accommodating monetary policy. Discretionary monetary policy had fallen into relative disuse during the war,
when managing the ballooning national debt was the principal
concern. Since the traditional liberal view favored easy money in
every event, the Federal Reserve had considerable difficulty re-
gaining even some degree of autonomy under the Truman administration. Kennedy and his economists shared the general liberal
perspective on monetary policy. Their plans for economic growth
depended, they believed, upon the country's abundant capital being
cheap and available for business investment. The same view was
firmly entrenched in Congress—where a host of special interests
raised cries of alarm at the first sign of higher interest rates. Agricultural interests, for example, traditionally favored cheap money.
The huge building industry was also extremely sensitive to monetary stringency. With support neither from the administration,
nor from Congress, the Federal Reserve was in a weak position to
use restrictive monetary policy to balance an expansive fiscal policy. The same commitment to perpetual "full employment" that
animated fiscal policy denied legitimacy to restrictive monetary
policy.[11]

By comparison with its dramatic advances later in the decade, inflation was scarcely visible in the early sixties. The figures registering the inflation of domestic prices, however, are rather misleading. Price inflation tends to move according to a rhythm dictated by the program of psychological expectations. Inflation gathers force slowly and then accelerates as the policy begins to lose its "money illusion."[12] In addition, much of America's early inflation was "exported" through its regular balance-of-payments deficit, a topic dealt with in detail below.

Keynesian liberals, prominent throughout the Kennedy administration, were traditionally indulgent toward inflation. Their approach to economic management had been nurtured throughout a prolonged depression, whose principal problem was diagnosed as a too feeble demand. Postwar "neo-Keynesians" were impressed by a "Phillips Curve" that appeared to suggest a stable trade-off between regular small doses of inflation and full employment.[13] Inflation, moreover, was seen less as the consequence of overly expansionist monetary and fiscal policies than of the oligarchic market structures characteristic of modern capitalism. In an economy with markets controlled by giant corporations and giant labor unions, government controls seemed the appropriate check against inflation. The Kennedy administration thus set up and defended a system of wage-and-price guidelines. Such a system of controls, however, could not withstand the pressure of relentlessly expansive fiscal and monetary policy. Since fiscal policy remained ever more expansive, and monetary policy its captive, the wage-price guidelines were fated to collapse, as they did in 1966.[14]

By early 1965, inflation was growing harder to ignore. The effects of the steady expansionist policies, including the tax cut of 1964, had begun to have noticeable effects on domestic prices. By late 1965, military spending for Vietnam was also starting to have a major effect on government outlays. Unemployment, meanwhile, dropped from 4.5 percent in 1965 to 3.3 percent in 1966.[15] In practical terms, unemployment had vanished. Nineteen sixty-six saw full employment overachieved, war spending up sharply and growing, and an ambitious social program, "The Great Society," going forward apace. Johnson's economic counsellors finally advised a tax increase. Johnson refused, afraid that Congress would cut his domestic programs. Johnson's refusal was a great blow to the pretensions of economic technocracy. When the tax cut had been passed in 1964, a good deal had been heard about the new capacity of economic experts to "fine tune" the economy in order to abolish the business cycle. By 1966, however, fine tuning was lost in the static of budgetary politics. The American political system hardly seemed to favor sensitive discretionary adjustments of fiscal policy.

With fiscal policy paralyzed, the Federal Reserve stepped into the breach with tight monetary policy. The result was a "pause" in inflation in 1967. Accused by both the administration and Congress of policies threatening a recession, the Fed soon began to give way and the inflation rate rose to 4.2 percent in 1968. Johnson had meanwhile finally asked for a tax increase in January of that year, but it was not passed until June. As he had feared, Congress insisted upon substantial cuts in his Great Society programs. Meanwhile, the Federal Reserve, thoroughly alarmed at the inflation's momentum, had regained its resolve. Renewed monetary stringency accompanied the June 1968 tax increase. The Kennedy-Johnson era thus ended in a period of combined monetary and fiscal restraint, fated to last under Nixon until the congressional election year of 1970.[16]

Inflation, however, proved to have a momentum of its own that did not respond immediately to the abrupt change in government policy. The consequence was "stagflation," declining economic activity combined with still high inflation. Nineteen seventy witnessed the first recession since 1958, but with inflation rising to an annual rate of 5.9 percent. In response to the monetary and fiscal stringency that was already ending in 1970, inflation did recede somewhat in 1971 and 1972. It nevertheless remained at a higher level than before 1968. With policy switching to "reflation" in 1970, inflation gathered its strength for a bound that was to carry it to an annual rate of 11 percent by 1974.[17] In retrospect, Eisenhower's fears had proved all too correct: by 1970 inflation was well on its way to becoming the country's overriding economic malady.

The consequences of America's domestic inflation came to dictate much of America's foreign economic policy. But the causes of that inflation may themselves be linked to foreign policy.

The rise of serious inflation, it is often argued, came with the ill-starred war in Vietnam. And, to be sure, with Johnson unwilling either to raise taxes or cut his rapidly expanding domestic programs, sharply rising military expenditures did unquestionably pour fuel on the inflationary fire. But to see the Vietnam war as an exogenous catastrophe upsetting an otherwise noninflationary set of economic policies does not match the evidence. To begin with, as the French kept saying, America's persistent balance-of-payments deficit was, in itself, the sign of a domestic inflation whose consequences are being "exported" to the world at large.[18] If so, American inflation had started long before 1965. In any event, America's domestic price inflation was clearly visible in 1965, before Vietnam's military costs began affecting government spending.

The war itself can be counted a natural outcome of long-standing policies—the ambitious foreign goals and corresponding military buildup launched in 1961. Even before the war, American defense expenditures were extremely high by any standard but that of the Soviet Union. Rising government spending cannot be traced, moreover, to rising defense outlays. From 1960 to 1970, federal nondefense expenditures increased far more rapidly than defense expenditures, even with Vietnam added in.[19] In short, inflation was already entrenched in the American economy before the Vietnam War, and was being nourished by policies that reflect less an unexpected catastrophe than long-standing trends in domestic and foreign policy.

Conservative analysts, of course, tend to blame inflation on the welfare state. But even with the large increases for Johnson's Great Society, American civilian expenditures were not beyond standards set by other advanced industrial countries, nor was the American standard of full employment more ambitious, at least in crude statistical terms. On the contrary, U.S. unemployment rates were consistently higher than in most Western European countries.[20]

David P. Calleo

America's relatively high unemployment absorbed a good deal of expert attention in the sixties and provided, for one school of economists, a major clue to the causes of inflation. The Phillips Curve was found to be "shifting to the right," meaning that sustaining the same rate of unemployment was requiring increasing doses of inflationary stimulus. According to Milton Friedman's classic analysis, such a shift merely records the natural progress of any neo-Keynesian full-employment policy. Full-employment budgets produce inflation, which, in turn, produces employment through "money illusion."[21] Initially, wage demands do not adequately cover price inflation. The public's imagination cannot keep up with the government's printing press. So long as prices rise faster than wages, real wages fall and employment naturally increases. But as public expectations begin to adjust more accurately to inflation, more and more money, hence inflation, is required to provide the illusion needed to sustain the same level of employment.

While Friedman's analysis could explain inflation's inherent dynamism, the rightward shift of the Phillips Curve in America could also be attributed to various demographic factors, among them the exceptionally large number of teenagers and women seeking jobs.[22] Since both groups change jobs more frequently than the general norm, their relative increase in the work force raises the unemployment averages. Something of the rightward shift might also be attributed to the success of the Kennedy-Johnson domestic reforms. Civil rights and Great Society programs brought large numbers of formerly marginal workers into the labor market, a great social achievement, which nevertheless required an increasingly vigorous economic growth to absorb the new labor and meet its rising expectations. Stimulating that growth presumably required more and more inflationary policies.

It is interesting, in this regard, to compare America's unemployment rate with that of a country with regularly lower inflation, like the Federal Republic of Germany. Germany's low inflation could not be ascribed to its citizens' tolerance for unemployment. Germany's jobless rate was much lower than in the United States, and no higher than in other European countries with much higher rates of inflation. Unlike America, or European countries like Britain or Italy, Germany had a relatively homogeneous and well-educated work force, without great social, racial, or educational cleavages. Germany also had a large supply of foreign labor which it was able to send home whenever controlling inflation called for policies of restraint.[23]

Whatever the significance of such domestic differences for comparative inflation rates, America's combination of a welfare state at home and military hegemony abroad produced budgetary claims inherently more severe than in other major capitalist industrial states. Kennedy sought to augment both domestic welfare and foreign hegemony. Johnson followed with less restraint. Under the circumstances, even if structural conditions had been otherwise equal, more inflation in America than in the Federal Republic was only to be expected.

Strictly speaking, blaming inflation on budgetary deficits may be considered rather simplistic. In theory, if tight monetary policy forces a deficit to be financed from real savings in the capital market rather than from an expanded money supply, no inflationary pressure need result. Germany's Federal Republic, after all, has often run substantial fiscal deficits, but used tight monetary policy to contain inflation.[24] Whether tight money can be preserved in such circumstances depends upon political attitudes and institutional structures. Germany has a powerful central bank and deep public aversion to monetary instability. In the United States, by contrast, the Federal Reserve lacked the independence and support needed to impose a consistently tight monetary policy of this kind. Inflation might thus be blamed on the American political system, which not only produced a chaotic budgetary processs, but denied its central bank the independent power needed to compensate.

Whatever its causes, U.S. inflation came to shape not only the national but the world economy. American foreign economic policy was caught up in the consequences, as the examination of trade, investment, and international monetary policy makes clear. It was within the last of these, international monetary policy, that inflation finally precipitated a crisis that forced a major mutation in American strategy, a shift that ended the Age of Kennedy and began the Age of Nixon.

Following the best liberal traditions, the Kennedy and Johnson administrations pursued a major trade initiative. The Trade Adjustment Act of 1962 gave the President substantially greater power to bargain for reciprocal tariff cuts.[25] The ensuing "Kennedy Round" of GATT negotiations was a major element in Kennedy's plans for reasserting American leadership in the West. Trade and monetary barriers, once tolerated as necessary for European and Japanese postwar recovery, were to be dismantled, lest the recently formed European Economic Community grow into a protectionist bloc with imperial ambitions.

The assumptions were traditional. Trade integration was to promote transatlantic political interdependence and thus reinforce the already close military ties. As world markets opened up to major sectors of the American economy, the domestic consensus supporting America's world role would broaden. The opportunity was particularly great in agriculture, where the United States had a clear comparative advantage over Europe and was suffering from serious problems of overproduction. Lower tariffs were also expected to encourage U.S. firms to invest and produce more at home for export rather than to invest and produce abroad. Freer trade would thus reinforce domestic investment, growth, and employment, reduce capital outflow, and bolster the faltering balance of payments.

Unfortunately, few of the assumptions proved correct.[26] The actual negotiations proved unexpectedly arduous and dragged on until 1967. Rather than a reinforcement of pan-Atlantic political cohesion, they proved a major occasion of U.S.-European discord. The French obstinately set themselves against transatlantic agricultural integration. As the French understood the Common Market, their markets had been opened to German industrial competition only on condition that German agricultural markets were kept a privileged preserve for the French farmer. If this, the constituent deal of the EEC were not honored, France would withdraw. The United States tried to shift the Community's internal balance by encouraging the hitherto reluctant British to join. De

Gaulle flatly vetoed the whole initiative. Britain, he argued, had a political and economic orientation incompatible with the close economic integration of the continent France wished to see.[27]

Agriculture aside, the Europeans, including the French, were not at all opposed to freer trade. Hence negotiations to cut industrial tariffs were much more successful, but with consequences quite different from what American policy had expected. By the time lower industrial tariffs began to go into effect in the late sixties, inflation had greatly weakened America's competitive position. Deterioration was marked after 1964. By 1971, as Nixon's reflation took hold, American trade had deteriorated into its first deficit since 1883.[28] The growing foreign presence in the domestic American market provoked strong protectionist sentiment, particularly from domestic-based heavy industry.[29] Protectionist pressure was to rise sharply until assuaged by Nixon's New Economic Policy, in effect a policy of continuous devaluation.

At the same time as it was trying to liberalize transatlantic trade, the Kennedy administration also pointed the way toward liberalization of East-West trade. It soon experienced, however, the domestic resistance that was to hobble America's own participation. In the early glimmerings of détente that followed the Cuban missile crisis, and with Europeans demanding an easing of Alliance restrictions, the administration moved to unfreeze Soviet-American commerce. Kennedy thought trade might liberalize the Eastern European regimes and wean them from their Soviet dependence. Despite its war in Vietnam, the Johnson administration had similar views and disparaged the notion that trade would give strategic benefits to the Soviets. But even as East-West European trade grew swiftly, congressional opposition discouraged any sustained U.S.-Soviet opening.[30]

As the Kennedy Round was supposed to strengthen the *Pax Americana's* transatlantic center, so a broad new policy of economic development was designed to speed progress and integration in the Third World. American aid to developing countries increased by roughly one-half over the later fifties. The Kennedy and Johnson administrations lavished energy and idealism upon such enterprises as the Alliance for Progress and the Peace Corps.

Fashionable theories about "stages" of economic growth fostered expectations of rapid "modernization." Properly encouraged, economically backward countries were to "take off" into self-sustaining development.[31]

The notion of a take-off stage lent itself to a military corollary: once a country reached its moment of ascent, its prosperous future within the international liberal order would sustain a liberal-democratic domestic system as well. The danger of Communism, Fascism, and other forms of economic nationalism, if prevented until maturity, would pass. The administration's heavy emphasis on counterinsurgency tactics could thus be presented as a phase of preventive medicine during adolescence rather than a permanent system of repression between haves and have-nots. The Green Berets and the Peace Corps thus represented the two halves of the Kennedy administration's views on the Third World.

The link between these perspectives and the involvement in Vietnam is too obvious to belabor. Whether the balance would have been the same had Kennedy lived is, of course, impossible to determine. Many of Kennedy's Keynesians would have no doubt preferred a policy based more on Cobden and less on Hobbes. Had Kennedy lived, they might have been able to shift the balance. Nevertheless, the logical affinity between Kennedy's dreams and Johnson's nightmares is clear. American determination to impose its liberal vision over the Third World was bound, almost inevitably, to conflict violently with the untidy and angry realities of the non-Western world. A collision course was set, even if a more nimble pilot might have backed off from Vietnam.

Kennedy's liberal world vision had strong appeal in more imaginative sectors of the business community, particularly in its rapidly growing international sectors. American corporations had been investing heavily in Europe since the fifties and were also beginning to invest strongly in Third World countries. Foreign investment was hardly unknown in earlier periods, but the postwar investments were greater in scale and different in character. In brief, the balance began to change markedly toward industrial investment.[32] Along with spreading multinational enterprise also came a great expansion of the international capital markets and, in due course, an extraordinary internationalization of American banking, developments with great consequences for American international monetary policy, as will be discussed presently.

Growing enterprise was accompanied by a growing ideology. A plethora of academic studies weighed the great significance for the world political economy of the spreading American multinational corporation. A sort of business Hegelianism began to depict the multinational corporation as a world-historical actor transforming an international arena of mercantilist states into a fragmented pluralistic system of mutual restraint and interdependence. Culture, too, was thought to be growing less national; the new world economy was soon to be a global village. The view had great appeal, not only as a practical ideology for internationally rampant business interests, but also for academics and journalists steeped in free trade and world federalism, the latter updated into "functionalism" and "neo-functionalism" by political scientists drawn to the study of European integration[33]

On balance, however, neither the Kennedy nor the Johnson administrations had great enthusiasm for the multinational phenomenon. Their statist liberalism was philosophically ill at ease with the pretensions of big business to escape from political control. On a practical level, the ever-worsening balance-of-payments problem made them wish to discourage American corporations from foreign investment. In addition, foreign investment seemed to divert capital from the domestic industrial growth needed to pay for social and international goals and counted on to restore faltering American competitiveness. As inflation continued to worsen the balance of payments, the government's disincentives to capital exports multiplied until, by the end of Johnson era, large-scale outflows were prohibited altogether.[34] Needless to say, such a policy not only fitted badly with the international aspirations of American business but was in grave tension with the official vision of an ever-more-integrated liberal international system.

While Vietnam and de Gaulle's withdrawal from NATO were more dramatic challenges, the faltering dollar was no less a sign of America's mounting geopolitical difficulties. The international monetary issue reflected not only growing resistance to

American hegemony abroad, but also growing resistance to paying its costs at home. The Bretton Woods Agreements of 1944 codified the world monetary order desired by the United States. It not only established an international monetary system with fixed rates, but made the dollar the "key" currency against which other currencies were to be measured. The system's theoretical anchor lay in the dollar's link to gold, at a fixed price of $35 per ounce.[35] The dollar was also the system's principal "reserve currency." As the vast American outflow to finance postwar reconstruction and rearmament permitted European states to reconstitute their finances, most foreign central banks kept a large part of their reserves in dollars, which earned interest, rather than in gold, which did not. Along with its key and reserve roles, the dollar was also the world's principal "vehicle" currency, the universally acceptable medium of payment in multinational transactions. The demand for dollars grew together with the remarkable growth of international trade and enterprise. Since controls restrained foreign borrowers in the domestic American money market, a large dollar market developed in Europe. By the late sixties, this expatriate "Eurodollar" market had attracted funds that dwarfed the international monetary reserves not only of the United States, but of all the world's central banks combined.[36]

Despite the large international demand for dollars, the rate at which the United States was increasing the supply gradually began to seem excessive. With the end of heavy U.S. economic and military aid to Europe, the progressive liberalization of trade, and the restoration of convertibility in 1958, the American balance of payments was supposed to return to equilibrium, if not to surplus. On the contrary, the payments deficit continued from the fifties through the sixties. As early as 1958, American external short-term obligations exceeded American monetary reserves. Various crises of confidence followed in the sixties.[37] With the dollar in a periodic sinking spell, in 1965, General de Gaulle attacked America's "inflationary" monetary policy and demanded an end to its perpetual payments deficits.[38] Early 1968 saw another crisis that forced an end to the dollar's link to gold in private markets, and was contained only as American policy shifted to mon-

etary and fiscal stringency in Johnson's final year. Nixon's continuation of the stringency, plus Europe's chain of social dislocations,
provided a further respite in 1969. No sooner did Nixon reflate,
however, than a massive crisis of confidence developed once again.
By August of 1971, Nixon was unwilling and, indeed, unable to
defend the dollar's parity any longer.

Nixon's suspending of convertibility, after a long struggle
engaging a great deal of prestige, was America's monetary Vietnam. As in Southeast Asia, the strategy that eventually failed
stretched back to the Kennedy administration. Kennedy was troubled by the payments deficits of his time, but his administration
neither knew what they signified nor how to end them. Policy was
a series of short-term measures to finance, manipulate, or hide the
deficits—a policy aptly termed *ad hocery*. [39]

As the monetary situation grew increasingly precarious, the
Johnson administration used heavy diplomatic pressure to persuade the central banks of America's major creditors to go on ac-
cumulating dollars. [40] As foreign resistance mounted, the administration grew interested in academic arguments for structural
reform of the international monetary mechanism. It was America's critics who had initially pressed structural reform. According
to the thesis tirelessly elaborated since the 1920s by de Gaulle's
economic adviser, Jacques Rueff, any system with reserve currencies permitted favored countries the exorbitant privilege of running balance-of-payments deficits without restraint. Such deficits,
creating credit in the country that received them without reducing
credit in the country that issued them, were bound to flood the
world with excess money. [41] Hence the gold standard should be
restored and reserve currencies proscribed.

The Belgian-American economist, Robert Triffin, gave the
old argument a novel twist. Unlike Rueff, Triffin believed new
"liquidity" was, in fact, constantly needed to finance a swelling
postwar volume of international transactions. But Triffin argued
that adequate liquidity could never be created safely by a national
currency, even the dollar. A national currency's issue was controlled by the particular needs and conditions of its domestic, rather
than of the international, economy. To be a reserve currency meant

exporting money to the outside world; hence balance-of-payments deficits. But a national reserve currency also had to compete in currency markets with the money of surplus countries whose reserve positions would grow relatively stronger as their surpluses continued. Preserving the parity of a national reserve currency would thus grow more and more difficult. But if the reserve currency's outflow ceased, a burgeoning international economy would soon grow short of liquidity. Triffin's solution was to have a new international money created multilaterally by the IMF, in quantities dictated by the needs of stable monetary growth in the international economy as a whole.[42] After the mid-sixties, the idea began to find favor within the besieged Johnson administration. With *de facto* control over the IMF, the United States would control the process and receive the greater part of any new credits created. The administration accordingly launched a major campaign to permit the IMF to issue "Special Drawing Rights" to augment world "liquidity." A long struggle ensued, with most Europeans skeptical and the French opposed. The United States prevailed in 1968, but only after permitting the EEC a collective veto over SDR creation.[43] The first SDR issue finally appeared in 1970, after the dollar's position had deteriorated so drastically that the few billions of extra credit permitted could not arrest its decline.

While the debate absorbed a good deal of academic attention, and was an important diplomatic struggle, it was irrelevant to the real economic problem, which was a superfluity rather than a shortage of liquidity.[44] In theory, had the United States abruptly ended its balance-of-payments deficits, a real shortage of world money might have developed. But the United States was never ready to adopt the policies needed to end its regular deficits. To do so would have required curtailing its foreign or domestic goals. The deficits therefore continued and a collapse of the dollar's parity grew inevitable. As early as 1966, the dollar's depreciation began to be anticipated in the Treasury and among more perspicacious private economists. A sophisticated ideology began to appear, justifying the dollar's fall, and counseling "benign neglect" of its further defense.[45] By the time the dollar did fall in 1971, the superiority of a "floating -rate system" was becoming the new economic orthodoxy.

It is difficult to determine the extent to which America's failure to end its balance-of-payments deficit was the result of conscious decisions as opposed to incompetent analysis. In view of the intensity and duration of America's balance-of-payments difficulties, the technical analysis prevailing in the American government, and among American economists generally, was surprisingly undeveloped. Two broad approaches have dominated American policy toward the balance of payments: the item-by-item approach and the monetarist approach.

Balance-of-payments policy in both Kennedy and Johnson administrations based itself on an essentially item-by-item approach to the deficit.[46] Analysts noted that the United States regularly ran a considerable trade surplus (until 1971) and a large profit on "invisibles." The U.S. current account was thus always in surplus. But this surplus was regularly exceeded by the combined net outflows for overseas military costs, foreign aid, and private long-term capital investment abroad. The balance-of-payments deficit, looked at in this fashion, could easily be traced to the costs of the Vietnam War, although the government could claim that the actual exchange costs of the war were minimal.[47] No one, however, could deny the exchange costs of American troops in Europe. From this perspective, curing the payments deficit presumably depended upon either limiting the world role or extracting more "burden sharing" from the allies. This way of thinking reached its climax in the months before the Nixon administration suspended convertibility. The incumbent Secretary of the Treasury, John Connally, kept noting the remarkable congruence between the annual "basic" balance-of-payments deficit and the exchange costs of the American troops in Europe.[48] Needless to say, partisans of the *Pax Americana* found such analysis highly inconvenient.

It also seemed increasingly irrelevant. The flows involved in the basic balance had only to do with the "real" economy—the exchange of goods and services. But as a huge offshore dollar market developed, the net flows for real goods and services were easily dwarfed by giant flows of "hot money" seeking a safe refuge and higher short-term interest rates. With the shifting reserves of multinational corporations and banks regularly causing flows of ten and twenty billions of dollars in and out, withdrawing American troops from Europe to save two or three billions in foreign exchange annually seemed preposterous. Managing short-term capital flows, however, meant regulating domestic interest rates to affect international capital flows. Comprehending this connection between domestic monetary policy and the balance of payments required, moreover, shifting from an item-by-item to a monetarist approach to analyzing the balance-of-payments problem itself.

In the broad monetarist approach, a country runs a deficit when its rate of monetary creation is more inflationary than the norm for the international system as a whole.[49] Stopping America's payments deficit required reducing America's inflation to at least the norm for the system as a whole. For the monetarist, monetary policy was the most efficacious instrument.

Monetarism was coming into fashion by the later sixties. This reflected not only changing economic fashion, but also the gradual paralysis of fiscal policy. The war in Vietnam piled on the military expenditures and Johnson's Great Society added more and more civilian entitlements. Policymakers, hard-pressed by rising military and civilian demands, and unable to raise taxes adequately, were gradually losing control over fiscal policy. To stem the consequent inflation, governments were driven to using their monetarist levers. Policy increasingly oscillated between concern for inflation and concern over the effects of tight monetary policy.

Unlike the liberal Keynesians, most monetarists, were preoccupied with inflation. They might therefore have been expected to favor defending the balance of payments. In theory, bringing the balance of payments to equilibrium would have meant lowering American inflation at least to the general world level. But even conservative monetarists, like Haberler or Friedman, counseled abandoning the dollar's parity rather than giving up control over domestic monetary conditions.[50] Their prescription thus differed sharply from the French monetarists, like Jacques Rueff, who believed domestic inflation could be prevented only under an international system that automatically imposed monetary stringency whenever a currency's parity was threatened. In Rueff's view, the United States had developed domestic inflation because its reserve-currency role had permitted ignoring balance-of-payments constraints. From this Rueffian perspective, Friedman's enthusiasm for floating was perversely inappropriate.

Rueff's analysis, however, had its own deficiency. If the reserve-currency privilege could explain why American inflation ran unchecked, it did not locate its initial causes. To blame inflation on an excessive creation of money was to describe the efficient but not the underlying causes. To say that America's exorbitant privilege to run payments deficits allowed it to continue its inflation unchecked did not explain why, or for what, the privilege was used. Unless inflation was to be blamed merely on incompetence or weakness at the Federal Reserve, or Original Sin in general, something more concrete was needed to explain why the United States was exercising its exorbitant privilege to create excessive money.

From Friedman's purely domestic perspective, America's inflation might be blamed on full-employment policies relying on money illusion. But its balance-of-payments deficit indicated that the United States was more inflationary than the norm for the system as a whole. But why? America's neo-Keynesian counter-cyclical policies were hardly unique. The U.S. unemployment rate was, in fact, higher than in most other capitalist countries. Domestic spending was certainly no more generous than elsewhere, in many respects less so.[51]

One logical explanation lay in America's relatively intractable structural problems. Its multiracial work force and demographic trends generally could be seen to impose more formidable hindrances to full employment and hence require more inflationary stimulation than elsewhere.[52] A less speculative explanation lay in the obvious pressure on America's fiscal policy of its defense budget, large by comparison with the European states, and gigantic by comparison with Japan.[53] With the political system unwilling to raise taxes to cover the combined domestic and defense outlays, perennial fiscal deficits pressed insistently for monetary expansion. The links between inflation and a fiscal policy aiming simultaneously at world leadership and major advances in domestic welfare should have been obvious. A logical cure for inflation and the balance-of-payments deficit presumably lay in reducing America's combined domestic and foreign aspirations, or establishing a clearer priority between them.

American economists, however, showed a remarkable capacity to resist the obvious. Not surprisingly, Keynesians hoped to resolve inflation through growth. Enhanced demand, they hoped, would eventually stimulate adequate supply, a more and more implausible expectation as rampant inflation began to slow productivity, saving, and growth. Conservative monetarists concentrated on restoring the "market," attacking the welfare state, or lecturing the Federal Reserve on how to control the money supply. Seldom, however, did they suggest reducing the defense budget or defending the dollar.

Events followed a more or less inevitable course. By 1968, confidence in the dollar had so eroded that the juggling act was approaching its end. The United States lacked the reserves to defy speculation in the huge offshore market; foreign monetary authorities had neither the will nor indeed the ability to sustain the dollar in the face of American inflation.[54] In the end, the United States was itself trapped in the logic of that international interdependence it had been so eager to create. Liberal integration meant that policies in one country could not indefinitely exceed the norms set by the system as a whole. Staying within the Bretton Woods system would have meant facing squarely the causes of American inflation and drawing the consequences for foreign and domestic policy. No administration was willing to do so. Europe's problems in 1968 and 1969, plus the early Nixon administration's relatively restrained U.S. fiscal and monetary policy, did save the dollar's parity until 1971. But the domestic political economy found the restraint intolerable. Hence, Nixon's escape from Bretton Woods in August of 1971, a moment that in many ways was the real end of the Kennedy era. The consequences of this escape for Nixon and his successors form the drama of the seventies.

THE NIXON REVOLUTION

In recent years, an "iron law" of the presidency apparently leads every new President to enhance the reputation of his predecessor. At the time Eisenhower left office, Truman's reputation—at its nadir in 1952—was well on the way to restoration. Kennedy's tragically premature death shifted the process of Eisenhower's rehabilitation to the Johnson administration. Conditions by 1968 were more than ample to promote a renewed appreciation for Eisenhower. Along with Vietnam and the quarrel with France, the American economy was heading into serious trouble. With a recession more extreme than that of 1958 already underway, the underlying inflation rate was nevertheless nearly five times higher than in 1960. The inflationary spiral was undermining not only domestic prosperity but also free trade and open monetary convertibility, the twin pillars of America's new international order. The dollar's defenses were nearly exhausted and abandoning Bretton Woods was only a matter of time. Meanwhile, the competitive position of American industry had so deteriorated that the once mighty trade balance was heading into a deficit, while powerful forces were gathering to demand tariffs, as well as serious restraints on corporate investment overseas. Faced with such an inheritance in 1969, Nixon's administration, not surprisingly, looked to major shifts in foreign and domestic policy.

Nixon's new policies took two years to develop. In 1969 and into 1970, he continued the fiscal restraint of Johnson's final months, paralleled by continuing severe monetary restraint from the Federal Reserve.[55] The new policy had certain austere rewards. In 1969, a fiscal surplus was achieved for the first time since 1960, a feat never to be repeated in the 1970s. The 1969 basic balance of payments achieved its only surplus since World War II. The new virtue had high costs. The continuing restraint brought mounting unemployment and acute discomfort to over-extended debtors in the business community. The rewards seemed slim as inflation receded very slowly. With congressional elections coming in 1970, Nixon began pressing for reflation. A bad showing for the Republicans spurred him on. Monetary policy quickly accommodated.[56]

The predictable international consequences followed swiftly. By the spring of 1971, an immense wave of speculation against the dollar hit the currency markets. Under enormous pressure, the German mark floated in July. Flight from the dollar nevertheless continued and the dollar's parity grew indefensible.[57] On August 15, Nixon himself announced his revolutionary "New Economic Policy," the centerpiece of which was a temporary end to the dollar's convertibility and, as it happened, the final demise of the Bretton Woods system.

Nixon was determined that the new policy not seem an American defeat, an all too obvious parallel with Vietnam. His new policy was presented not as a retreat from an overextended position, but as a bold offensive to correct long-standing failings of the international monetary system. The United States, it was argued, had been the principal victim of those failings. A new American policy would combine international reform with national economic renewal.

Nixon's policy involved several measures besides suspension of convertibility.[58] A surcharge of 15 percent on all imports was meant to reverse the deteriorating trade balance and to force formal allied acquiescence in a substantial devaluation. Meanwhile, wage and price controls were imposed on the domestic economy, along with cuts in fiscal spending.

The rationale for Nixon's revolutionary policy combined four elements: structural criticism of the Bretton Woods system, liberal academic enthusiasm for floating exchange rates, a political attack on America's allies, and a mercantilist drive to restore American trade.

Criticism of the Bretton Woods structure emphasized that the dollar, as the key currency, was the only currency unable to devalue to correct a persistent payments deficit.[59] Since nothing pressured surplus countries to revalue, the system was inherently biased against the American economy. Initially, the dollar had been deliberately overvalued to aid European and Japanese recovery. No subsequent adjustments had been made. Subsequent devaluations had increased still further the original distortion of parities. Discriminatory trade practices, permitted during recovery, had been reinforced by discrimination, like the European Community's Common Agricultural Policy. The United States, moreover, had discriminated against itself by continuing with barriers to East-West trade in the interest of common security, while West Europeans took energetic steps to capture Comecon markets.[60] Discrimination against the United States in the economic sphere was paralleled by disproportionate burdens in the military. America's mercantilist allies refused to assist adequately in their own defense, let alone support the United States in maintaining security elsewhere, as in Vietnam. In short, Europeans and Japanese had become classic "free riders" of an imperial system.[61]

As a result of the system's unequal biases and burdens, it was argued, the dollar had grown more and more overvalued, a condition, in turn, that had slowly been undermining the domestic American economy. American products grew less competitive. Investment abroad grew more attractive. Stop/go policies to bolster the weak dollar were having the effects on American growth and employment long familiar in Britain, the textbook case of a country whose systemic responsibilities had sapped its national vitality. Unless the United States could break out of this same imperial trap, it would eventually suffer the same fate.

A more technical economic analysis explained why traditional policies of restraint short of devaluation were so ineffective.[62] In postwar democracies, thanks to labor unions and automatic subsidies to the unemployed, wages almost never fell. Deflationary policies, therefore, soon produced a politically unacceptable degree of unemployment. In addition, automatic unemployment benefits led to rises in fiscal spending that undermined the deflationary policy's effectiveness. Deflation, thus, aroused too much political opposition to be sustained and worked too slowly to be effective within the time politics permitted. "Stagflation" damaged the economy's general vitality. For all these reasons, devaluation was a remedy preferable to deflation. An international system that prevented the United States from devaluing thus condemned the American economy to prolonged maladjustment.

Since, for selfish mercantilistic reasons, surplus countries had resolutely refused to revalue adequately, and nothing in the system's structure compelled them to do so, the United States had to seize the initiative.[63] It was now up to the rich allies to accept the devaluation. With an appropriately reduced parity for the dollar, and with the understanding that the United States would no longer allow itself to be exploited, Bretton Woods might be reestablished. Otherwise, Nixon made clear, the dollar would remain inconvertible and American trade would be protected.

Nixon's New Economic Policy had immediate and wide appeal. For domestic producers and their workers, devaluation provided a much-needed competitive boost. After the customary lags, America's trade position did improve dramatically and gradually cut the ground out from beneath the partisans of more direct protectionism.[64] For multinational business, moreover, the inconvenience of a changing dollar parity seemed preferable to those tariffs and capital controls that a further defense of the dollar seemed to imply. The new policy particularly pleased the big American banks, for it was accompanied by the gradual end to all restraints on capital exports. The controls attempting to insulate the domestic from the world capital market, restrictions which had hitherto inhibited American banks in the offshore dollar market, were to be abandoned. Giving up the insulation also implied an end to limits on domestic interest rates, a development also deeply gratifying to the country's banks.[65]

Not only did the New Economic Policy please a wide range of domestic interests, it also appeared to work. Domestic growth resumed and unemployment diminished. By December of 1971, the affluent allies had acquiesced in a substantial formal devaluation. The Bretton Woods system seemed restored, although the United States pointedly refused to pledge support of the dollar should it once more come under severe pressure.

Europe and Japan, needless to say, were not so pleased, but faced a fundamental dilemma. They disliked a declining dollar because it hurt their trade and, in countries where trade involved a large part of the economy, had a depressing effect on investment and employment generally. But if they went on supporting the dollar in the face of market pressures, they would import inflation into their own economies, which also had deleterious effects on their international competitiveness and domestic growth. The only real resolution was some sort of monetary and trading bloc that would permit stabilizing their own currencies against each other while imposing collective capital controls and tariffs to compensate for the dollar's decline. Such a policy was hardly possible, given their own conflicting national interests and perspectives, as well as their heavy military dependence upon the United States. Under the circumstances, a declaration of economic independence would, at the very least, require a long preparation. It was easier to hope the Nixon Revolution would prove a once-for-all cure to which they could adjust. The departure, in May 1972, of Nixon's openly mercantilist Secretary of the Treasury, John Connally, and his replacement by a conventional liberal, George Shultz, seemed to presage a return to normal. Nixon, meanwhile, went on to an overwhelming electoral victory in November of 1972, providing an example, rare in America, of a successfully managed political business cycle.[66]

Politically, Nixon's Revolution was an adroit maneuver to extricate the United States from the wreckage of its previous grand strategy. As an economic policy, however, it suffered from a fatal defect. The dollar's problem stemmed not from the technical inadequacies of Bretton Woods but from an underlying American inflation. Devaluation could not, in itself, cure that inflation. At best, it could provide a respite from inflation's consequences—time for more fundamental policies to eliminate the need for further devaluations. At worst, it could lead to repeated currency depreciations that would accelerate the inflation. The latter, unfortunately, is what happened.

Once Nixon had disposed of Bretton Woods, U.S. inflationary pressure grew sharply. For a year and a half, wage and price controls masked the consequences. When controls were dropped after the 1972 presidential election, prices exploded. The Consumer Price Index nearly doubled in 1973 and redoubled in 1974.[67] By the first quarter of 1974, growth in the Consumer Price Index had reached the hitherto unimaginable rate of 12.3 percent.

By mid-1973, the Nixon boom was turning into a crash. Consumer spending was falling, squeezed by higher prices, sharply rising food prices in particular. With the Fed belatedly reacting to the inflation, interest rates shot up to record levels. As events seemed increasingly out of control, frightened businessmen and consumers curtailed spending further. OPEC's fourfold raising of world oil prices in December was another sharp blow to confidence and was, in due course, another major source of the inflationary squeeze on consumer spending.[68]

Nineteen seventy-four was the worst year for the American economy since World War II. With the administration entangled in Watergate, inflation remained at its record height, while numerous other signs indicated an oncoming depression. Real GNP declined 2 percent. Unemployment reached 7.2 percent, the highest rate in fourteen years. As government policy had aggravated the boom, so it aggravated the recession. The Fed continued to keep money tight and, as inflation raised tax rates, fiscal policy turned from a stimulus to a "drag."[69] The Great Inflation became the Great Recession.

Nixon was cast from power almost three years to the day from his August revolution of 1971. The economy was in even greater disarray than in Johnson's final year. Freeing the domestic economy from international restraint had proved a disaster. The evil consequences, moreover, were hardly limited to the United States.

As usual, a considerable part of American inflation was exported abroad, even more, perhaps, with Nixon's controls holding down domestic prices through 1972. The general inflation rate in capitalist industrial countries jumped sharply in 1972 and again in 1973. By 1974, the ten largest non-Communist industrial economies had reached an aggregate price inflation of 13 percent for the year. All along, of course, world inflation had paralleled American inflation. In the mid-sixties, the general rate among the ten largest industrial countries was only 2½ percent per annum. But in the eight years from the first quarter of 1968 through the fourth quarter of 1975, consumer prices rose 62 percent in the United States and Canada, 127 percent in Britain, 85 percent in

France, 92 percent in Italy, 106 percent in Japan, and 47 percent in Germany.[70] A general phenomenon suggested a general cause.

One view blamed world inflation on the broad sociological evolution of most capitalist countries. Self-indulgent publics of "post-industrial societies," it was said, were demanding benefits greater than the resources available. Governments, frightened by the explosions of discontent in the late sixties, were giving way. Easy monetary policy financed the consequent fiscal deficits.[71] As workers demanded more and more, cost-push inflation of wages and prices paralleled excessive public spending. In addition, fashionable environmentalism, another offshoot of the new culture, was starting to reduce growth, thus further stimulating inflation. In broad terms, prolonged capitalist prosperity had nourished a reborn socialism. As its ideology and values spread, capitalist societies were becoming "ungovernable."[72] Universal accelerating inflation was the consequence. The view had obvious elements of truth. It was also congenial to conservative American academics, like Secretary of State Henry Kissinger, and suited a certain *Schadenfreude* characteristic of the Nixon administration in general.

A more embarrassing view linked world inflation directly to America's own economic policy. Hardly anyone denied that all postwar capitalist societies had developed a chronic tendency toward inflation. But those tendencies might have been kept under control, had it not been for the particularly egregious collapse of fiscal and monetary discipline in America. Thanks to America's central role in the word economy, and the world's monetary system in particular, excessive U.S. liquidity was rapidly injected elsewhere, thus reinforcing the homegrown forces of inflation.[73] Under the prevailing monetary arrangements, not only was American inflation exported, but the system had lost its natural balance.[74] Thanks to the dollar's international role, money exported from America increased foreign money supplies, but without any corresponding decrease in the American money supply. Hence, with demand increased abroad but not cut in America, the system had lost its natural tendency to return to equilibrium.

After 1971, as the world's monetary system moved de facto to a regime of floating rates, it was supposedly easier for surplus countries to let their currencies appreciate, and thus to compensate somewhat for the inflationary effects of America's exported dollars. But countries deeply involved in international trade were reluctant to appreciate because of the danger to their export industries and to domestic growth and employment generally. And since the dollar's relative depreciation gave many trading advantages to American industry, the relative appreciation of other currencies removed any international incentive for the Americans to stop their inflation. Hence floating seemed to mean a progressively mounting American inflation, accompanied by a perpetual, if erratic, depreciation of the dollar.

Nixon's gradual ending of capital controls was also blamed for the spreading of American inflation throughout the world. Big American banks, entering wholeheartedly into the booming Eurodollar business, were behaving, it was said, like the Federal Reserve under the old system: they created money abroad without reducing it at home,[75] with the oil crisis creating an enormous demand for funds to finance balance-of-payments deficits. The Eurodollar market, which nearly tripled in size from 1971 to 1975, doubled again by 1979 to a net size estimated at $600 billion.[76] Under such conditions, any credit-worthy borrower could find financing. Several countries with large current account deficits actually increased their reserves by borrowing from the Eurodollar market.[77] In effect, other countries, developing countries in particular, imitated the United States and ignored their balance of payments altogether. As the seventies progressed toward the eighties, the swollen credit system began to come under increasing pressure. Obviously shaky borrowers from among Third World or East European countries found trouble arranging new credit, needed often not only for current deficits but also to service already excessive debts. Fears of some eventual world banking collapse grew increasingly vivid.[78] Whatever the ultimate fate of this banking structure, its inflationary propensities in the seventies were beyond question.

In this perspective on the international economy, the United States was itself playing the crucial role in fueling world inflation. The world was hooked on cheap credit from America, and America was still exercising monetary hegemony. But its leadership was that of an attractive bad companion, initiating the rest of the world into its own addictive vices. While domestic pressures for inflation may have existed in every advanced economy, they were powerfully reinforced in an international context that encouraged profligacy and made inflation difficult to avoid in any event.

The Nixon era saw not only a rampant American inflation reaching toward a new cyclical high, but a major explosion in the world prices of raw materials—food and oil most notably.[79] Sharp rises in commodity prices are not unusual at the peak of an inflated boom. But certain policies of the American government could also be blamed for worsening the shortages. The explosions of 1973, however, appear to reflect a more fundamental shift, even if exacerbated by mismanagement. A number of distinguished economic historians believe raw materials prices normally follow a long cycle of their own. This "Kondratieff cycle" postulates a complete revolution in primary prices roughly every forty years. Changes in the direction of prices within the cycle, although long in preparation, are often abrupt and severe. The 1973 explosion of oil and food prices appear to fit the Kondratieff pattern quite well. Prices of primary products had been falling relative to industrial goods since the peaks of the early 1950s. A sharp rise was therefore due around the early seventies.

Alternate phases within the Kondratieff cycle seem to correlate historically with the world booms and depressions.[80] Logically, a downswing in primary prices meant terms of trade shifting to favor industrial products; income thus fell in the primary producing countries. Since the primary producing countries were, before World War II, the principal markets for industrial products, a decisive improvement in the terms of trade for industrial countries also meant a decisive falling off in demand for industrial goods. Hence, a depression followed, presumably until a Kondratieff upswing restored the income of primary producers and hence the demand for industrial products.

The pattern did not repeat itself after World War II. An apparent Kondratieff downswing did occur around 1950, but without a fall in demand for industrial goods, and hence a depression in the industrial countries. A plausible explanation seems to lie in the changing nature of industrial products and their markets. After World War II, consumer goods replaced the railroads, ships, and other capital goods that formerly composed the leading sectors of industry. The markets for postwar consumer goods were not in the primary producing countries, but in the industrial nations themselves. Keynesian full-employment policies in the industrial countries could thus sustain demand for manufactures, despite the falling income of the Third World. Trade among industrial nations could grow by leaps and bounds, even while trade with producers of primary products languished. Once the Kondratieff cycle went into its upswing, however, and the prices of raw materials rose sharply, industrial countries would predictably face great difficulty. To adjust to the shift in world income, they would have to turn from producing mass consumer goods for the home market to producing the capital goods demanded by the newly affluent primary producers. Considerable dislocation was inevitable, particularly with the Western consumer habituated to the neo-Keynesian combination of high income and full employment. To avoid unemployment while industry shifted from domestic toward foreign production, Western governments would go on stimulating domestic demand. Widespread inflation was the probable consequence.

While a Kondratieff upswing may have been inevitable, in the cases of both food and petroleum long-standing domestic and international policies of the American government worked to exaggerate the effects. For years, the United States had been subsidizing roughly half its wheat exports. Developing countries had become more and more dependent upon this cheap American wheat. Investment to improve agriculture in other countries was thus discouraged and world production slowly fell farther and farther behind. Meanwhile, the United States was letting its buffer stocks run down. When sudden shortfalls occurred, U.S. reserves were inadequate and prices naturally shot up. Explanations at the time invariably blamed particular catastrophes—disappearing anchovies or failed Russian harvests. But harvests frequently fail and nature abounds with catastrophes. In short, the chronic shortages and exploding prices typical of food markets in the early seventies were the consequence not only of normal long-range trends, but also of U.S. government policies that heedlessly augmented world demand while reducing world supply.[81]

The explosion in petroleum prices demonstrates a similar pattern—an unfavorable long-range trend combined with a short-sighted government policy that made it worse. Throughout the fifties and sixties, oil prices fell absolutely in constant dollars, as well as in relation to overall industrial prices. During this period, domestic American suppliers effectively limited world petroleum prices.[82] American excise taxes on petroleum products were far lower than in most other industrial countries. Hence American retail prices were much lower than elsewhere, a condition that naturally encouraged higher American domestic consumption. Contrary to the general trend among advanced industrial states, American energy use per capita increased rather than decreased with the rise of GNP. The gap between American per capita consumption and the average among advanced countries kept growing.[83]

In due course, this package of policies and trends had a predictable result. American demand began to outstrip American supply. As the United States grew to depend more on imports, its capacity to block world price increases gradually disappeared.[84] OPEC, founded in 1960 but powerless for a decade, finally had a market in which an effective cartel became possible. Shorter trends and special events helped precipitate the turnaround. OPEC found the Yom Kippur War a useful trigger to cooperative action. The rapid inflation of industrial prices no doubt also bolstered solidarity among the oil producers. In the perspective of a Kondratieff cycle, however, some sharp rise in oil prices was inevitable. But the long-standing American oil policy worked to make the inevitable price shift more explosive and traumatic.

The Kondratieff upswing could hardly have come at a worse time. Rising food and petroleum prices, by sucking purchasing power from other products, exaggerated the cyclical collapse of demand that was, in any event, the natural consequence of the overheated inflationary boom that had just preceded it. The recession of 1974 and 1975 was far and away the most severe setback suffered by the American economy since the Second World War. Nixon's revolution in economic policy, like his presidency, appeared to end in unprecedented disaster. Nineteen seventy-four was worse even than 1968. The "Iron Law" of the presidency was triumphantly confirmed.

THE FORD-CARTER YEARS:
THE RECOVERY OF THE NIXON STRATEGY

Nixon's economic policy proved more durable than its author. Ironically, an international environment in which vital raw materials were subject to bounding prices and unpredictable supplies appreciated precisely those assets in which the United States was better endowed than its rival partners—self-sufficiency and military power. The United States was the world's major exporter of food and still a major world oil producer. Despite its voracious appetite for energy, it was far less dependent on external sources for oil than Japan or most states in Western Europe. And alone among the big capitalist states, the United States had the power to threaten to meet economic blackmail with military force. In effect, the United States enjoyed a comparative advantage in surviving the international shocks its policies did so much to engender. All rich industrial states were worse off, but America less than the others.

The United States proved not in the least bashful about its advantages. All through 1973, Secretary of State Kissinger had been trying unsuccessfully to strengthen American diplomatic hegemony over Western Europe. The oil crisis provided a new chance. The United States made a direct bid to manage a common Western response to OPEC's challenge.[85] The usual Franco-American quarrel resulted, as the French tried to lead Europe toward more accommodation of the Middle East and more independence from the Americans. The results were equally familiar. Europeans were too divided among themselves for a concerted policy toward either the United States or the Middle East. France excepted, the others acquiesced formally in various American schemes for collective action, but only after depriving them of any serious content. A new multilateral International Energy Agency was hatched and provided useful statistics and studies. But the pretense of a common approach under American leadership was a polite fiction. Instead, Europeans pursued their own separate national interests directly with the Middle Eastern oil producers. A certain common European policy appeared, ex post facto, through a myriad of special and collective deals.[86]

As the Middle East's biggest customers, Europeans developed their own special economic and political ties. Europe's weapons were its wealth and technology, its rich market, and its varied and nimble diplomacy. Military weakness and political diversity carried certain compensatory advantages. European states could enter into various forms of partnership with developing Middle Eastern countries without the same intimidating political weight carried by the Americans. Europe's more ambivalent attitude toward Israel also served as a considerable political asset. Even those Middle Eastern countries who leaned heavily upon their special relations with the United States, like Iran, Egypt, and Saudi Arabia, were careful to cultivate European ties as an economic and political counterweight. The European strategy, of course, also leaned on American power not only to block the Russians, but to inhibit more extreme Middle Eastern forces and policies from pressing too close to vital Western interests.

In short, Europe and America's "partnership" in the Middle East mirrored their relations in general. European states depended upon American power for the overall security within which they pursued their separate and collective interests. American attempts to corral these "affluent allies" into a common policy, dictated by American perspectives, seldom achieved more than cosmetic success. Europeans remained not only America's geopolitical dependents but also its economic rivals, wary of American hegemony and fearful of seeing their dependence exploited. Europeans had no more intention of letting the Americans direct their policy in the Middle East than they had of letting the Americans control their relations with the Soviet Union.

But despite their adroit dodging of Kissinger's embrace, the allies remained locked into a common system with America. Whatever the weakness of American economic management, if the world system broke down, America was much better able to take care of itself than Japan or the separate states of Western Europe. Thus, as the allies grew more disenchanted, they also grew more dependent.

In essence, Nixon's policy was a contemporary form of mercantilism. Political power was used to gain economic advantage. The Nixon economic strategy did not so much strengthen the American role within the international system as derive greater national economic benefits from it. The United States defined its interest less as a systemic manager and more as a competitive national state. The expansionist policies followed at home and abroad required that the dollar depreciate regularly. Regular depreciation was possible because American monetary hegemony, and the geopolitical power that lay behind it, precluded effective foreign retaliation. The United States exacted a higher economic price for its imperial services at a time when the system's dislocations, even if caused by U.S. mismanagement, made those services more necessary than ever.

The Nixon policy has a variety of specific aspects, already touched on in passing but useful to review systematically. Along with the expansive fiscal and monetary management of the domestic economy were mercantilist offensives in trade, international finance, and development. There was also what might be described as America's "unilateralist" energy policy. True to their common Nixonian root, all were aggressively expansive policies depending upon periodic depreciations of the dollar.

Restoring America's declining trade balance was an open aim of the 1971 devaluation. Inflation, and the "over-valued" dollar, had greatly damaged the competitive position of domestic American heavy industry. Strong protectionist reactions began to threaten the whole international trading structure.[87] Nixon's strategy involved not only the devaluation of 1971, but a trade offen-

sive that lasted through the decade. In 1970, Congress passed a
new trade bill which provided the President with a fresh armory
of retaliatory measures.[88] A series of acrimonious bilateral negotiations followed with the Europeans and especially with the Japanese. A number of "gentlemen's agreements" ensued to protect
more vulnerable American domestic industries. The "Tokyo
Round" of GATT negotiations, concluded in 1977, brought considerable concessions.[89]

Repeated dollar depreciation combined with aggressive negotiating did improve the overall competitiveness of American
products at home and abroad.[90] From 1970 to 1975, U.S. exports
rose from 14.4 percent to 24.1 percent of all goods produced domestically. Around 1976, however, the rapid improvement slowed,
although the higher level was maintained. By 1977, the United
States was again running a large trade deficit, traceable more to
increasing oil imports as the recession ended than to declining
competitiveness of American products generally. The subsequent
sharp deterioration of the dollar from 1977 until 1980 helped U.S.
trade selectively in 1978 and 1979. By the late seventies, however,
American competitiveness was clearly beginning to suffer from
prolonged inflation's debilitating effects on investment. But without periodic dollar depreciation, the effects would have been far
worse.

Domestic-based manufacturing was not the only major seg-
ment of American business pleased by the Nixon revolution. The
Kennedy-Johnson policies involved defending an inflated dollar
with capital controls. Effective neither in saving the dollar's parity
nor in insulating domestic money markets from foreign high interest rates, they nevertheless seriously inhibited big American banks
in the huge offshore dollar market. As Nixon promised, a floating
dollar meant a gradual end to capital restrictions, removed completely by 1974.[91] Meanwhile, the oil crisis gave rise to an immense new business in "recycling" short-term capital. American
banks, assisted by American diplomacy, bid aggressively for the
OPEC petrodollars and for the loans of all who needed them.
America's domestic monetary base, plus the various mechanisms
of private credit-creation discussed earlier, opened an era of dizzy

international profit and power to American banking.[92] Maintaining these conditions of easy liquidity without controls required periodic depreciation of the dollar. Thus the fortunes of banking, like the competitiveness of heavy industry, were closely linked to the Nixon strategy.

OPEC's success helped spark a major economic revolt within the "developing" part of the *Pax Americana*. Third World countries, organized within the United Nations as the Group of 77, began a rhetorical offensive demanding redistribution of the world's economic wealth, a "New International Economic Order." The topic grew highly fashionable among American academics. Liberals acknowledged the moral justice of Third World claims, and the danger of ignoring them, while conservatives pointed out their absurd impracticality and potentially disastrous consequences for American prosperity. Secretary of State Kissinger, a pupil of Metternich rather than Jefferson, was clearly in the conservative camp. The Third World was nevertheless increasingly important for American enterprise. By 1975, for example, non-OPEC developing countries took a larger share of U.S. exports than the whole of the European Community and Soviet blocs combined.[93] American multinationals looked more and more to manufacturing and trading within the Third World.

America's national interest, as Kissinger defined it, required an open and congenial world economy, not a Third World of mercantilist states closed to American trade and investment.[94] Development to a more equal world would come not from despoiling rich countries, but from intelligently exploiting economic possibilities in poor countries. Overblown claims for sweeping world income redistribution would have to be met by a supple policy of constraints and blandishments designed to keep the Third World open to international private enterprise.

The view was hardly original but did receive added stress under the Nixon and Ford administrations. Third World countries seeking funds were exhorted to make themselves attractive to private investors.[95] As the unfortunate Allende illustrated in Chile, the United States was not above more direct encouragement. Carter's Third World policies, if more sensitive to liberal political

principles, nevertheless continued the penchant for domestic med-
dling, as well as the emphasis on private capital for development.

Private capital did indeed flow to the Third World in the
seventies as never before. Much of it, however, did not go for
development. Like the United States itself, many Third World
countries failed to adapt their economies to the new oil prices.
Huge balance-of-payments deficits resulted and debts accumulated rapidly. By the end of the decade funds required to keep the
Third World's debts afloat far exceeded the resources likely to be
available to the American government, or all the other Western
governments combined.[96] American banks, freed from capital controls, had obliged, and expanded spectacularly in the process.

America's response to the oil price explosion exhibits, in
bold relief, how the economy of the seventies came to orient itself
around the Nixon strategy. Nixon himself proposed an oil policy
aimed at eventual national self-sufficiency. But with Watergate in
the background, neither he nor Ford could persuade Congress to
enact the necessary measures.[97] As a practical matter, some mixture of conservation and substitution was needed to reduce America's appetite for imported oil. So long as Americans continued to
enjoy abundant gasoline and heating oil at a fraction of the international price, progress was unlikely. Congress, however, rejected
both rationing and decontrol, the free market alternative. To work,
decontrol required a sharp increase in the price of petroleum in
relation to the price of everything else, not merely a general inflation of all prices with petroleum the bellwether. This meant combining decontrol with policies of general economic restraint, including perhaps wage and price control. Most Western countries
had some such energy policy. But, thanks to congressional ob-
struction, the American energy market remained insulated from
the world and American fuel prices were kept well below the world
price. Federal policy continued to subsidize domestic consumption, with the perverse effect of discouraging both conservation
and substitution. The years went by. Not until OPEC pushed
through a second major hike in 1980 did Congress finally pass an
energy bill. Thereafter, the Reagan administration ignored the

painfully complex formulations of its precedessors, let domestic prices rise, and appeared to be dismantling the Energy Department as well as many of its subsidies and programs.[98]

Despite the absence of any coherent government energy policy in the seventies, the economy did, of course, adjust. During the recession of 1974 and 1975, the general decline in domestic demand not only cut U.S. oil imports but also encouraged a sharp rise in general exports. The newly rich OPEC countries furnished a vast new market, heavily oriented toward capital goods and armaments, two industries in which the United States remained highly competitive. The American government actively and effectively solicited Arab and Iranian business. As the world's leading food exporter, the United States had also been the principal beneficiary of the explosion in food prices. Thus, despite the oil price hike in 1974, U.S. trade enjoyed a considerable surplus in 1975, while the dollar actually strengthened.

The domestic reflation that began in 1976, however, soon returned trade to a deficit. As the domestic economy revived, petroleum imports jumped sharply. Rising domestic demand reduced export incentives. The government's stimulation soon rejuvenated inflation. Thereafter, the American adjustment to high oil prices took place mainly in the monetary rather than the real economy. As the inflating domestic economy went on importing oil without stint, a highly negative trade balance followed in 1976 and a large overall current account deficit in 1977. The dollar began to depreciate sharply.[99] Since international oil prices were factored in dollars, a depreciating dollar meant a falling real price for oil. By 1979, dollar depreciation and inflating industrial prices had brought real oil prices back to their 1973 level. To add insult to injury, most of OPEC's financial assets were held in the same depreciating dollars. As the dollar lost its value, oil producers were exchanging a real asset that appreciated in the ground for a monetary asset that depreciated in the bank. In short, America's adjustment to the oil crisis is a particular case study of that general Nixon strategy which informed American policy throughout the decade[100]

Most other industrial countries also benefited at OPEC's

expense. For those American competitors whose currencies were strongly appreciating against the dollar, like the Germans and Japanese, real oil prices fell even faster than in the United States. This helped keep down domestic costs and price inflation, and compensated their trade somewhat for the dollar's chronic depreciation. Europeans, however, were far from enthusiastic. Their scorn for America's apparent lack of an energy policy was a major part of their general condemnation of American inflation and grew increasingly vehement throughout the Carter administration.

Nixon's devaluation and general economic strategy permitted the boom of 1971–73. The subsequent inflation and recession lasted through the mid-seventies. By 1976, however, the Ford administration was able to help stimulate a reflationary boom that lasted until 1980. With the rest of the world still suffering from the shocks of inflation, recession, and exploding food and oil prices, the strong American recovery was remarkable. It was, of course, a recovery after the Nixon pattern. Unconcern about the dollar was its essential precondition. While the boom started under Ford, the political benefits fell to Carter. Carter's 1976 campaign called Ford's administration callously indifferent to unemployment and lagging growth. A "gap" of 10 percent was said to remain between the economy's potential and actual product. Rather disingenuously perhaps, Ford posed as the champion of stability against inflation.[101]

Once in power, Carter periodically grew concerned at the mounting inflation. Within the administration, however, forces opposing inflation were unable to prevail over the broad coalition favoring expansion. These latter naturally included labor and the poor, marginal businesses, and all overextended groups vulnerable to monetary stringency. Carter ran fiscal deficits of $49 billion, $27 billion, and nearly $60 billion for the boom years 1978, 1979, and 1980 respectively.

Thanks to mounting inflation and oil imports, the 1977 trade balance deteriorated to an unprecedented $31 billion deficit, which continued at roughly the same level throughout the decade.[102] The dollar continued to depreciate, thus regularly renewing the competitiveness of domestic-based industry and assuaging protectionist impulses. Meanwhile, easy liquidity helped the extraordinary rise in international lending by American banks, whose foreign profits more than doubled from 1977 to 1979.[103]

Unlike the United States, most other industrial nations were still trying to combat inflation while adjusting to the new oil prices. To European governments the dollar's renewed depreciation in 1977 not only reflected American inflation being pumped into the world, but represented a continually refreshed mercantilist advantage for American products. A heated ideological polemic resulted. America's official apologists unveiled the "locomotive" theory, the gist of which was that other rich economies should, like the United States, expand to pull the world out of its slump. Ranged on the American side were OECD economists who had encouraged domestic expansion as a response to the oil crisis, enthusiasts of Third World development, and indeed all others who had come to depend on an accelerating cycle of inflation and borrowing. Principal opposition spokesmen were the Germans, heavily dependent on foreign trade and determined to keep inflation under control in their own economy. The Americans, they argued, were confusing recovery with inflation. The world economy could hardly be restored by dragging its few remaining healthy economies into the maelstrom. The French strongly supported the Germans; Giscard d'Estaing and Schmidt united in notorious contempt for Carter.

Despite Franco-German disapproval, Carter's renewal of the Nixon strategy [104] appeared to serve American interests well. But this Nixon policy, however satisfactory in the medium term, was vulnerable in two crucial respects. First, because being able to depreciate the dollar regularly without foreign retaliation depended upon America's external predominance, any weakening of America's hegemony threatened its economic policy as well. Second, domestic prosperity based on continuing inflation was, in the end, economically self-defeating. Both these foreign and domestic vulnerabilities were apparent by the end of the Carter administration.

The external predominance that permitted the Nixon economic policy depended heavily upon America's relationship with

Europe, the Middle East, and, ultimately, the Soviet Union as well. Nixon and Kissinger carefully cultivated all three connections. Thanks to their success, the *Pax Americana* took a new lease on life.[105]

Europeans had been restive over American economic policy since de Gaulle's day. Disaffection took practical form in efforts to build a distinct monetary and trading bloc, a direction indicated not only by the progress of the European Community in general, but particularly by the recurrent attempts in the seventies to build a European Monetary Union.[106] From 1971 until 1979, American economic policy essentially rejected European protests. Transatlantic relations continued to deteriorate, but without arriving at some decisive mutation. The pattern of the sixties continued: as America's economic strength diminished, its hegemony grew more onerous. The Europeans and Japanese, nevertheless, remained unable to break from the hegemony and hence continued to tolerate the depreciating dollar.

America's renewed position in the Middle East after 1973 was possibly Kissinger's most striking diplomatic success. The Iranian and Saudi Arabian monarchies became America's regional surrogates. Kissinger's diplomacy finally captured even Egypt, the Arab world's major state, intellectual center, and, for two decades, the Soviet Union's principal regional ally.[107] Both Russians and Europeans were expelled from Arab-Israeli negotiations. As a practical consequence of its special relations, the United States became the region's arbiter, a position that discouraged any further raising of oil prices after 1973, despite America's demand, inflation, and dollar depreciation.

Soviet-American détente was a crucial indirect element in the Nixon-Kissinger version of the *Pax Americana*. As de Gaulle had often observed, détente between the superpowers was based on respect for each other's spheres of influence. Détente put a certain limit on Soviet willingness to encourage rebellion that might threaten American interests in Europe or the Middle East. Soviet diffidence over military support to Egypt was, for example, a major cause for Sadat's diplomatic revolution.[108]

The geopolitical conditions for the Nixon economic for-

mula were essentially precarious. Nixon and Kissinger's rejuvenated *Pax Americana* was never very stable. The Carter administration's tactical difficulties made the fragility of Kissinger's diplomatic
constructions more and more apparent. America's economic strategy and geopolitical position deteriorated together. Two major
events in 1979 dramatically illustrated the concomitant decline.

By the end of 1979, the United States was forced to stop
encouraging the dollar's depreciation. Europeans had grown increasingly outraged as the dollar resumed sliding in 1977. By November of 1978 their complaints had forced the Treasury and
Federal Reserve to announce a plan to bolster the dollar.[109] Within
a few months, however, monetary policy, troubled by signs of a
cyclical downturn, had returned to its habitual expansion. By the
summer of 1979, with European central banks flatly refusing their
support, the dollar was in a sinking spell so severe that many observers began to fear a major panic. The remarkable rise in gold
prices suggested a general flight from currencies altogether. [110] By
the end of 1979, the Federal Reserve, under Paul Volcker, its new
and unusually strong-minded chairman, was imposing unparal-
leled monetary severity, reinforced in early 1980 by direct credit
controls.[111] By March of 1980, a chastened Carter administration
began calling for a balanced fiscal budget—a bizarre goal for a
country entering a cyclical recession, already exaggerated by
Volcker's severe credit squeeze. The Volcker measures began a
sustained period of monetary restraint that was to endure into the
recession of the early eighties. His unprecedented defense of monetary stability, triggered by the revolt in international money markets, marked the end of the Nixon economic strategy.

Volcker's position was strongly reinforced by a second major event, 1979's sharp rise in oil prices. In one sharp jump, OPEC
regained the ground lost since 1973.[112] As OPEC's announce-
ments made clear, further oil price rises could be expected if accelerating American inflation and dollar depreciation were not
brought under control. OPEC's shift was closely linked to the fall
of the Iranian monarchy and the consequent damage to American
prestige in the Middle East. European and Arab disaffection rein-

forced each other, as Arabs were rumored to be dumping dollars and buying gold.

Deteriorating relations with the Soviet Union greatly complicated America's problems with Europe. Kissinger had apparently hoped that following a policy of détente would allow Russia to achieve strategic equality without increasing its influence beyond the traditional Soviet sphere. With a profusion of destabilizing regional problems, several new powers rising, and the steady relative growth of Soviet conventional reach, disillusion was inevitable. Russia's invasion of Afghanistan brought matters to a head. The Carter administration denounced détente and looked for ways to retaliate. With the larger part of American military resources committed to Western European defense, the administration hoped to use the Western alliance to pressure the Soviets. Instead, proposals for economic sanctions led to a further deterioration of transatlantic relations.

While Western European states had little enthusiasm for Russian incursions into the Third World, they had no intention of being used as a lever for American diplomacy against the Soviets. Europe's interest, as European governments saw it, lay in preserving the continent as a safe zone, its own regional détente insulated from superpower rivalries elsewhere. European détente, moreover, was intimately bound up with Western Europe's long-range economic, political, and human interest in the peaceful penetration of Eastern Europe. In immediate terms, Western Europe's economic stake in détente was vastly greater than that of the United States. Geographical proximity aside, U.S. Eastern European trade had been hobbled by congressional restrictions well before the Carter administration had itself sought further restraints. Not surprisingly, Europeans suspected Americans of commercial jealousy. For all these reasons, the allies resisted American demands for anti-Soviet economic and political sanctions within Europe itself. Americans read the European reaction as a growing "Finlandization." Rather than liberate the East, détente had suborned and divided the West. Commercial détente tied European manufacturing and banking to the Soviets. Proposals for a huge gas pipeline between Europe and the Soviet Union became an official American anathema.[113]

To offset what seemed an unfounded European complacency, American officials began stressing the formidable and growing Soviet conventional and nuclear forces aimed specifically at Western Europe. The United States began to demand a major NATO rearmament. The European response was diffident. Calls for enhanced conventional forces encountered the increasing budgetary difficulties of most European states. Plans for stationing more U.S. nuclear missiles on European soil, originally pressed by the Federal Republic itself, began in the early eighties to provoke a revival of militant European pacifism. Meanwhile, substantial increases in America's own defense spending clashed with the Carter administration's fitful efforts to control inflation by moving toward fiscal balance.[114]

This same linkage of contradictory policies and counteractive reactions became even more characteristic of the Reagan administration. Reagan's massive rearmament made nonsense of his economic strategy. Soaring defense budgets, combined with "supply-side" tax cuts and a deep recession, led toward very large fiscal deficits. Yet Reagan, determined to control inflation, also supported Volcker's tight monetary policy.[115] The combination of heavy spending and tight money meant unprecedented American interest rates and a strong appreciation of the dollar. Not only were deepening recession and a faltering trade balance the natural consequences, but the newly "overvalued" dollar considerably complicated Europe's management of its own unemployment, the worse since the war. The transatlantic economic irritation of the Carter era thus continued. Disputes over the Polish crisis and new deployments of American missiles reinforced economic disagreements with serious strategic and diplomatic differences.

In effect, the Reagan administration had inherited the breakdown of the Nixon policy, as the Nixon administration had inherited the breakdown of the Kennedy. But Reagan's new formula gave little promise of relieving America's economic malaise, even temporarily, let alone the tensions with the allies over economic policy. At heart, Reagan's problem was the same as the one that had bedevilled policy since Kennedy's day: the United States was unable to generate the resources necessary to cover its foreign and domestic ambitions. For nearly a decade, the Nixon formula had seemingly reconciled America's foreign role and domestic aspirations; but, it also increasingly offended the interests of the other major partners in the system. Thus, as American hegemony grew weaker, it also grew more onerous to its allies, an unstable combination of trends.

By Reagan's time, it also seemed clear that the Nixon strategy had brought few lasting advantages to the American domestic economy. An impressive number of new jobs had been created. Most, however, were jobs with low productivity in the service sector. America's industry, despite a decade of dollar depreciation, seemed no more competitive at the start of the 1980s than at the beginning of the 1970s.[116]

One cause for industrial weakness seemed obvious. Throughout the seventies, the United States had continued to lag well behind most other industrial states in its ratio of capital formation to GNP. America was not investing and hence not increasing its productivity. Americans were not saving either. America's ratio of savings to disposable personal income was generally a quarter of Japan's, a third of France's, and half of Germany's. Most shocking of all for a country supposedly at the forefront of technological progress, American investment in research and development had dwindled to the lowest rate among the major industrial countries.[117] Whatever special reasons might be imagined for such figures, low saving and investment were, in fact, familiar and predictable consequences of prolonged inflation.

The accelerating progress of that inflation was undeniable. The GNP price deflator had advanced from 1.6 percent in 1960 to 9.0 percent in 1980. In the 1970s, the Consumer Price Index oscillated from a low of 3.3 percent in 1972, to a high of nearly 20 percent in early 1980. More extreme oscillations of the cycles meant more violent swings of monetary policy. The prime rate had jumped from 4.82 percent in 1960, to a yearly average of 15.27 percent in 1980. Peaks of 20 percent were becoming commonplace.[118]

Seemingly inexorable inflation, accompanied by more and more violent policy shifts, could not but discourage real economic growth. Even if continual dollar depreciation offset many of inflation's effects on trade, it also slowly sapped the domestic economy of its real strength. While Volcker's tight money brought down price inflation dramatically, Reagan's huge deficits promised real interest rates too high to permit sustained recovery. The endemic gloom of the late seventies persisted into the eighties. Pessimism sprang from a sense that the economy's ills were cumulative, that underlying business cycles would grow more extreme, with perpetual stagflation the most likely outcome and either hyperinflation or depression the major alternatives. Any cure would await some miraculous explosion of new technology or some improbable resolution of America's domestic and international contradictions. In this cheerless perspective, in other words, the sixties and seventies seem a period when an overextended America ran down its economic and political capital.

It is difficult to judge the past without knowing the future. While the general trends of the past two decades seem clear enough, their ultimate outcome is another matter. America's frustrations may, in the end, come to be seen as part of a more benign historical pattern. The postwar liberal system based itself upon American hegemony. The striking success of that leadership rested, in turn, upon American domestic prosperity, containment of the Soviets, the successful recovery of the other major capitalist states, and the transformation of their colonial hinterland. By 1980, success was fading. The postwar liberal order, if still in place, was altered in a fashion that raised doubts about its continuing durability. Not only were superpower relations once more apparently growing unstable, but the system was severely troubled from within. In effect, the United States had become the victim of the success of its own strategy. Postwar Europe's rise to relative affluence and power was the natural consequence of America's own postwar foreign policy, as was the rise of Japan or those "Newly Industrialized Countries" whose development appears to have succeeded all too well. In short, that America's postwar empire should grow less "hegemonic" in its distribution of wealth, power, and aspiration was hardly unforeseeable. Equally predictable was the Soviet Union's demand for a larger voice in running the world's affairs.

In 1981, a new American administration came to power committed to reversing the decline from American primacy. As with the Kennedy administration, the perception of relative decline produced a determination to reaffirm strength. Growth, stimulated by enlightened economic policy, was to provide the added resources. The inflationary consequences of such a policy in the 1960s now seem clear. Kennedy, moreover, began with some leeway for experiment. He inherited Eisenhower's 1 percent inflation rate, whereas Reagan's legacy was a rate stretching toward 20 percent. As a result, Reagan has had to reconcile his ambitions within Volcker's monetary straitjacket.

What will Reagan's rearmament accomplish? Stopping the erosion of America's military position will, no doubt, be salutary. But, whether American primacy can be restored sufficiently to reverse the geopolitical trends of the past two decades seems doubtful. The basic problem will thus remain: Can the international system grow more plural without disintegrating? Can the demands of the rich allies, the Third World, and the American domestic society itself continue to be accommodated within the same integrated postwar system? Can the Russians be accommodated, or held at bay?

Since 1961, finding and reconciling solutions to these problems has posed an increasing challenge to American policy. The world owes the peace and prosperity of the past twenty years to that policy's continuing success. At the same time, much of the world economy's growing inflation and turbulence, as well as the American economy's own decline, can be traced to the failure to find the way to those basic system adjustments that seem required. Whether the past twenty years represent an inevitably troubled evolution toward more balanced integration, or simply disintegration, still remains to be seen.

Notes

1. *Economic Report of the President (ERP) 1981* (Washington, D.C.: GPO, 1981), p. 293. For a discussion of "Money illusion" see note 12.

2. For this and other parts of this essay, see Calleo, *The Imperious Economy* (Cambridge: Harvard University Press, 1982).

3. For recent Eisenhower studies, see Stephen E. Ambrose, "The Ike Age," *New Republic*, May 9, 1981, pp. 26–34; and Ronald Steel, "Two Cheers for Ike," *New York Review of Books*, Sept. 24, 1981, pp. 54–57.

4. For Eisenhower's economic policies, see Herbert Stein, *The Fiscal Revolution in America* (Chicago: University of Chicago Press, 1969), chs. 11–13.

5. The Library of Congress, *United States Defense Policies in 1961* (Washington, D.C.: GPO, 1962), pp. 115–17, and *United States Defense Policies in 1962* (Washington, D.C.: GPO, 1963), pp. 1–4, 50–52, 113–17.

6. For the logic of the investment tax credit, see George P. Shultz and Kenneth W. Dam, *Economic Policy Beyond the Headlines* (New York: Norton, 1977), pp. 200–3; and *ERP 1963*, pp. xvi–xviii and p. 47.

7. *ERP 1981*, pp. 233, 264.

8. For Kennedy and his economists, see Stein, *Fiscal Revolution*, pp. 379–81; James Tobin, *The New Economics One Decade Older* (Princeton: Princeton University Press, 1979), pp. 1–39; and Theodore Sorenson, *Kennedy* (New York: Bantam, 1966), pp. 447–49.

9. To apply the concept practically required some working definition of full employment. The Kennedy administration set a figure of 4 percent unemployed, raised by the end of the decade to 4.6 percent. In the 1970s the figure rose still higher, which underscored the elusive nature of the concept itself. For the evolution of the concept from its appearance in the New Deal to the 1960s, see Stein, *Fiscal Revolution*.

10. *ERP 1981*, p. 316. Kennedy's deficits in 1961, 1962, and 1963 were presumably justified by more conventional countercyclical practice. The double digit inflation of the late seventies brought balanced budgets back into rhetorical favor. Carter's administration could never achieve one and, by 1982, prospects for the Reagan administration did not seem better.

11. Stein, *The Fiscal Revolution in America*, pp. 241–80.

12. Money illusion is defined as a mistaken view that, as prices are changing, behavior "should be guided by money quantities, such as money income or money wealth, rather than real variables." C. P. Kindleberger, "Money Illusion and Foreign Exchange," in F. Bergsten and W. Tyler, eds., *Leading Issues in International Economic Policy* (Lexington, Mass.: Lexington Books, 1973), p. 51.

13. For the Phillips Curve, see A. W. Phillips, "Employment, Inflation and Growth," *Economica* (Feb. 1962), n.s. 29:1–16.

14. For wage and inflation rates, see *ERP 1980*, pp. 244 and 263. For Kennedy's "guideposts," see Robert A. Gordon, *Economic Instability and Growth: The American Record* (New York: Harper and Row, 1974), pp. 143–46; and Arthur Burns and Paul Samuelson, *Full-Employment, Guideposts and Economic Stability* (Washington, D.C.: American Enterprise Institute, 1967).

15. Spending for Vietnam seems to have had little to do with the early stages of inflation in 1965. Later, Vietnam appears only to have exacerbated an already established inflationary trend. Inflation went from 1.2 percent in 1963 to 1.3 percent in 1964. In the first six months of 1965 consumer prices jumped to an annual rate of approximately 2.5

percent, finishing at 1.7 percent over the entire year. By August 1966 the annual rate reached 5.4 percent. Rises in defense spending did not begin until the latter half of 1965, and even then by a relatively modest $3.3 billion. Federal spending in general stayed fairly level from the second quarter of 1962 to the second quarter of 1965. For inflation and unemployment rates see *ERP 1966*, pp. 65–67; *ERP 1967*, pp. 262, 239; for the evolution of military spending see *The Economic Impact of the Vietnam War* (Center for Strategic Studies, Georgetown University, Special Report Series no. 5, June 1976), pp. 22–24.

16. Johnson proposed and Congress passed the inadequate Tax Adjustment Act of 1966. In addition, in November 1966, the investment tax credit was temporarily suspended. *ERP 1966*, p. 11; and *Federal Reserve Bulletin* (September 1968), pp. 705–6. For 1966–68 monetary and fiscal policies and the politics behind them, see Arthur Okun, *The Political Economy of Prosperity* (Washington, D.C.: Brookings Institution, 1970), pp. 66–69; also James Tobin, *The New Economics One Decade Older*, pp. 34–35. For monetary policy, see also Philip Cagan, *Recent Monetary Policy and the Inflation* (Washington, D.C.: American Enterprise Institute, 1971), pp. 101–3.

17. Remarks by William C. Martin in the Joint Economic Committee of Congress, *Hearings on the 1968 Economic Report of the President*, 1:177–78; *Annual Report of the Board of Governors of the Federal Reserve*, 1969, p. 6. For interest rate and money supply figures, see statistical appendices to the *Federal Reserve Bulletin*. For annual inflation rates, see *ERP 1981*, p. 293.

18. For a balance-of-payments deficit as "exported inflation," see Jacques Rueff, *The Balance of Payments* (New York: Macmillan, 1967), and *The Monetary Sin of the West* (New York: Macmillan, 1972), pp. 159–67. Rueff defines inflation as excessive monetary growth, with rising domestic prices and a balance-of-payments deficit as its epiphenomena. By Rueff's definition it did not matter that the U.S. rate of domestic price increases was lower than in most countries in Europe, France included. The growth in the money supply was what mattered. Such growth is difficult to measure even in a single country, as the controversy over measurements of the U.S. money supply makes clear. Complications are compounded in comparing rates among countries, each with its distinct banking structure, statistical system, and rate of real GNP growth. Inflated growth exported through the balance of payments presumably does not show up in domestic price increases or even in measurements of the money supply. For all these reasons, comparing traditional national computations of rates of price inflation of monetary growth can be highly misleading. By Rueff's model, however, a country running a persistent balance-of-payments deficit in a relatively open international economy must be presumed more inflationary than the norm for the system as a whole.

19. From 1960 to 1970 federal defense spending increased by about one third from $73.8 billion to $90.3 billion while nondefense spending almost doubled from $76.8 to $130.3 billion. U.S. Department of Commerce, *Statistical Abstract of the United States* (1980), pp. 258–59. See also note 15.

20. *Public Welfare Expenditures in Selected OECD Countries As a Percentage of GNP*

	Early 60s	*Mid 70s*
France	17.0	20.9
Germany	16.5	20.6
Italy	13.6	19.6
U.K.	12.6	16.7
U.S.A.	10.3	15.7

SOURCE: OECD, *Public Expenditure Trends*, June 1978, p. 25.

21. Milton Friedman, "The Role of the Monetary Policy," *American Economic Review* (1968), 1:8.

22. For the figures, see U.S. Bureau of Labor Statistics, *Handbook of Labor Statistics 1973*, pp. 33–36. For an analysis of the inflationary consequences, see George Perry, "Changing Labor Markets and Inflation," *Brookings Papers on Economic Activity* (1970), no. 3, pp. 411–48; and Charles Schultze, "Has the Phillips Curve Shifted? Some Additional Evidence," *Brookings Papers on Economic Activity* (1971), no. 2, pp. 452–67.

23. *Unemployment Rates: 1960s*

	'60	'62	'64	'66	'68	'70
U.S.A.	5.5	5.5	5.2	3.8	3.6	4.9
F.R.G.	1.3	0.7	0.8	0.7	1.5	0.7
France	1.0	0.7	0.7	0.9	1.6	1.6
Italy	4.3	3.2	2.7	3.9	3.5	3.1
U.K.	1.5	1.8	1.6	1.4	2.3	2.5

SOURCE: De Nederlandsche Bank N.V. Annual Reports, cited in S. F. Frowen and A. S. Courakis, eds., *Monetary Policy and Economic Activity in West Germany* (New York: Halsted Press, 1977), p. x.

Also W. E. Kuhn, "Guest Workers as an Automatic Stabilizer of Cyclical Unemployment in Switzerland and Germany," *International Migration Review* (Summer 1978), 12:210–24.

24. *Federal Republic of Germany in the 1970s*

	Govt. Deficit [a] (DM billions)	Inflation [a] (%)	Discount [b] Rate	Growth in Money [b] Supply (% Change)	Call Money [b] Rate
1972	− 4.0		4.5	13.7	4.3
1973	+10.9	7.0	7.0	5.3	10.2
1974	−13.6	7.0	6.0	5.9	8.9
1975	−59.8	6.0	3.5	14.1	4.4
1976	−40.2	4.3	3.5	10.2	3.9
1977	−29.5	3.7	3.0	8.2	4.1
1978	−35.9	2.7	3.0	13.5	3.4
1979	−40.6	4.1	6.0	7.2	7.9

a. OECD *Economic Survey, Germany, 1980*
b. IMF *International Financial Statistics Yearbook*, 1980

25. For the Kennedy Round and its implications, see Ernest H. Preeg, *Traders and Diplomats* (Washington, D.C.: Brookings Institution, 1970); John W. Evans, *The Kennedy Round in American Trade Policy: The Twilight of GATT?* (Cambridge: Harvard University Press, 1971).

26. Both domestic expansion and liberal internationalism were traditional goals with powerful constituencies. Kennedy was not unaware of the difficulties in combining the two: "The President stressed increased investment, rising productivity, continuing cost and price stability and also faster growth," while at the same time hoping for "some inflation abroad." Seymour E. Harris, *Economics of Kennedy Years* (New York: Harper and Row, 1964), p. 151.

27. For an analysis of the effects on European agriculture of competition with the United States, see Food and Agricultural Organization of the United Nations, *Production Yearbook 1968*, 22:532, 534–36. Guy de Carmoy, *The Foreign Policies of France, 1944–1968* (Chicago: University of Chicago Press, 1970), pp. 416–29; and Edward L. Morse, *Foreign Policy and Interdependence in Gaullist France* (Princeton: Princeton University Press, 1973), pp. 77–83. For general political problems affecting the Kennedy Round, see Evans, *Kennedy Round*, pp. 265–79. For Britain's application and de Gaulle's 1963 veto, see Miriam Camps, *Britain and the European Community* (Princeton: Princeton University Press, 1964); and David P. Calleo, *Britain's Future* (New York: Horizon Press, 1968).

28. The Council of Economic Advisers in 1971 attributed the deterioration of the U.S. trade balance to "the relatively poor price-cost performance of the U.S. economy associated with the inflationary developments after 1965 . . ." *ERP 1972*, pp. 151–52. From 1964 to 1969, unit labor costs in manufacturing rose 2.5 percent per annum in the United States, twice as fast as the 1.2 percent among competitors. Some distinguished analysts believed the U.S. trade balance would deteriorate over time because the income elasticity of foreign demand for U.S. exports was abnormally low. See Hendrik S. Houthakker and Stephen P. Magee, "Income and Price Elasticities in World Trade," *Review of Economics and Statistics* (May 1969), pp. 111–25.

29. C. Fred Bergsten, "Crisis in U.S. Trade Policy," *Foreign Affairs* (July 1971), 49(4):619–35; see also Wilbur F. Monroe, *International Trade Policy in Transition* (Lexington, Mass.: Lexington Books, 1975), pp. 94–99.

30. For congressional opposition to East-West trade see Thomas A. Wolfe, *U.S. East-West Trade Policy* (Lexington, Mass.: Lexington Books, 1973), pp. 81–99; U.S. Dept. of Commerce, *The United States Role in East-West Trade: Problems and Prospects* (Washington, D.C.: GPO, 1975), pp. A-5 and A-6.

31. W. W. Rostow, *The Stages of Economic Growth: A Non-Communist Manifesto* (Cambridge: Cambridge University Press, 1960). For foreign aid policy, see Robert A. Packenham, *Liberal America and the Third World: Political Development Ideas in Foreign Aid and Social Science* (Princeton: Princeton University Press, 1973).

32.   *Value of U.S. Direct Investment in Foreign Countries (in billions of dollars)*

	Total	Europe	Canada	Latin America	Western Hemisph. Dependencies	Other
1958	27.4	4.6	9.4	7.8	0.7	4.9
1960	31.8	6.7	11.2	7.5	0.9	5.6
1962	37.3	8.9	12.1	8.5	1.0	6.7
1964	44.5	12.1	13.9	8.9	1.3	8.2
1966	54.8	16.2	17.0	9.9	1.6	10.0

SOURCE: U.S. Dept. of Commerce, *Historical Statistics of the U.S.* part 2, p. 870.

33. See, for example, Raymond Vernon, *Sovereignty at Bay* (New York: Basic Books, 1971); George Ball, "Cosmocorp: The Importance of Being Stateless," *Columbia Journal of World Business* (Nov.–Dec. 1967); Charles Kindleberger, *The International Corporation* (Cambridge: MIT Press, 1970); Sidney Rolfe *The International Corporation* (Paris: International Chamber of Commerce, 1969). For a critical view, see Robert Gilpin, *U.S. Power and the Multinational Corporation* (New York: Macmillan, 1975); Richard Barnet, *Global Reach* (New York: Simon and Schuster, 1974). For my own dissent, see David P. Calleo and Benjamin

M. Rowland, *American and the World Political Economy: Atlantic Dreams and National Realities* (Bloomington: Indiana University Press, 1973), ch. 7; and "Business Corporations and the National State," *Social Research* (Winter 1974). The functionalist approach is classically developed in Ernst Haas, *Beyond the Nation-State* (Stanford: Stanford University Press, 1964); and his *The Uniting of Europe* (Stanford: Stanford University Press, 1958). For a brief discussion of the differing perspectives of various schools see Leon Lindberg and Stuart Scheingold, *Europe's Would Be Policy* (New York: Prentice-Hall, 1970), pp. 6–8. For my own early critique, see *Europe's Future* (Englewood Cliffs, N.J.: Horizon Press, 1965), ch. 2.

34. See note 39.

35. For the gold-exchange standard, see Leland B. Yeager, *International Monetary Relations: Theory, History and Policy* (New York: Harper and Row, 1976); and Gerald M. Meier, *Problems of a World Monetary Order* (London: Oxford University Press, 1974). For the Gold Pool, see *1964 Annual Report of the Directors of the IMF*, pp. 131–32; Robert Solomon, *The International Monetary System, 1945–1976: An Insider's View* (New York: Harper and Row, 1977), pp. 114–27.

36. The Eurodollar market is a system by which dollar accounts, building up in banks outside the United States, are reloaned outside the United States without being converted into some currency other than dollars. Most of the loans are short-term. Considerable technical controversy exists over the actual size of the Eurodollar market and its relation to U.S. balance-of-payments deficits. Throughout the sixties and seventies, the Eurodollar market was unregulated by reserve requirements. Hence, the usual process of pyramiding credit was controlled only by bankers' notions of what constituted prudent reserves and margins. Though the initial credit base presumably consisted of dollar outflows from the United States, the unregulated system permitted rapid creation of additional credit. Money "leaked out" of the system only when it was actually spent in the United States or converted into a foreign currency. The scale of "creation" and "leakage" are both disputed among experts.

In due course, the Eurodollar market has become more and more integrated with the U.S. banking system. American bankers, remembering the 1929 crash, were still wary in the early sixties, but gradually lost their inhibitions. U.S. inflation also made domestic banking regulations and interest ceilings, like regulation Q, increasingly onerous. The Eurodollar market also offered relief from domestic tight money. In the 1969 credit crunch, for example, U.S. banks' holdings of Eurodollars increased from virtually nothing to $15 billion, and because of the pressure, Eurodollar interest rates climbed from 6.25 percent in September 1968 to 11.31 percent in September 1969. The change in the 1970s from fixed to floating exchange rates boosted the Eurodollar market tremendously, as banks evolved from hedging in the forward exchange markets to active speculation in exchange rate fluctuations. The Eurodollar market received a further giant boost by the "recycling" of oil profits to debtor countries after 1973. Ending U.S. capital controls in 1974 removed the last barriers between domestic and offshore dollar markets.

Literature on the Eurodollar market is vast. For a span of views from the vast literature, see Milton Friedman, "The Eurodollar Market: Some First Principles," *Morgan Guarantee Survey* (October 1969); Fritz Machlup, "Eurodollar Creation: A Mystery Story," *Banca Nationale del Lavoro, Quarterly Review* (September 1970); pp. 219–60; Helmut Myer, "Multiplier Effects and Credit Creation in the Eurodollar Market," *Banca Nationale del Lavoro, Quarterly Review* (September 1971), pp. 233–62; Carl H. Stem, John H. Makin, and Dennis E. Logue, eds., *Eurocurrencies and the International Monetary System* (Washington,

D.C.: American Enterprise Institute, 1976); Susan Strange, "International Monetary Relations," in Vol. II, Andrew Shonfield, ed., *International Economic Relations of the Western World, 1959–1971* (London: Oxford Univ. Press, 1976); Gunter Duffy, Ian H. Giddy, *The International Money Market* (Englewood Cliffs, N.J.: Prentice-Hall, 1978).

37. Strange, "International Monetary Relations," pp. 281–99.

38. DeGaulle's call for an end to the gold-exchange standard came in a declaration on Feb. 11, 1965. His arguments can be found in a press conference on Feb. 4, 1965. Gen. Charles de Gaulle, *Major Addresses, Statements and Press Conferences* (New York: French Embassy and Information Division, 1967), pp. 79–81.

39. The administration began in 1961 to manipulate the interest-rate structure according to a procedure dubbed "Operation Twist." Short-term rates were to be raised to discourage capital outflows, while long-term rates were to be kept easy to promote domestic investment in business and housing. *ERP 1964*, p. 47. Also in 1961, for the first time since the mid-1930s, the Treasury began cooperating with other central banks in foreign-exchange operations. *ERP 1962*, p. 164. President Kennedy also introduced an Interest Equalization Tax, effective July 1963, as a temporary measure to discourage the rapidly rising outflows of long-term capital from American purchases of foreign securities (from $523 million in 1961 to a seasonally adjusted $1.9 billion in the first half of 1963). Securities of underdeveloped nations as well as of Japan and Canada were generally exempt. In 1965, the IET was extended to apply, on a voluntary basis, to most long-term lending (one year or more) by banks and other financial corporations, such as insurance companies. Effective in closing off New York as a capital market accessible to foreigners, the IET boosted offshore dollar markets. *ERP 1964*, pp. 125–30; *ERP 1965*, pp. 76–77; *ERP 1966*, pp. 165–67; Sidney E. Rolfe and James Burtle, *The Great Wheel: The World Monetary System* (New York: Quadrangle, 1973), pp. 85–86, 95, 152–53.

40. Strange, "International Monetary Relations," pp. 263–78.

41. For Rueff's views in the context of the interwar period, see Judith L. Kooker, "French Financial Diplomacy: The Interwar Years," in *Balance of Power or Hegemony: The Interwar Monetary System*, Benjamin M. Rowland, ed., Lehrman Institute (New York: New York University Press, 1976). Rueff's initial critique of the gold-exchange standard was linked to Anglo-French political and financial rivalry in Eastern Europe during the twenties: "During the entire postwar period, Britain was able to loan to Central European countries funds that kept flowing back to Britain, since the moment they had entered the economy of the borrowing countries, they were deposited again in London. Thus, like soldiers marching across the stage in a musical comedy, they could reemerge indefinitely and enable their owners to continue making loans abroad, while, in fact, the inflow of foreign exchange, which in the past had made such loans possible, had dried up." Jacques Rueff, *Les Doctrines Monétaires à l'épreuve des faits* (Paris: Alcan, 1932); trans. in Jacques Rueff, *The Age of Inflation* (Chicago: Regnery, 1964), p. 30. For the weaknesses of the gold-exchange standard and the link to unsound domestic practices, see Rueff, *Balance of Payments*, J. Clement, trans. (New York: Macmillan, 1967); Rueff, *Monetary Sin of the West* (New York: Macmillan, 1972). See also the new edited version of his writings, E. M. Claassen and Georges Lane, *De l'aube au crépuscule* (1977); *Théorie monétaire* (1979); *Politique économique* (1980) and *L'ordre sociale* (Paris: Librairie Plon, forthcoming). For an English version, see W. H. Bruce Brittain and E. M. Claassen, *The Collected Works of Jacques Rueff* (Lehrman Institute, forthcoming).

42. Robert Triffin, *Gold and the Dollar Crisis* (New Haven: Yale University Press, 1960), and *The World Money Maze* (New Haven: Yale University Press, 1966).

450   David P. Calleo

43. *ERP 1968*, pp. 185–86. See also *Summary Proceedings, Annual Meeting 1967*, pp. 271–79; Stephen D. Cohen, *International Monetary Reform, 1964–1969, The Political Dimension* (New York: Praeger, 1970), pp. 50–69; Solomon, *The International Monetary System*, pp. 128–50; Strange, "International Monetary Relations," pp. 225–54; John Williamson, *The Failure of World Monetary Reform, 1971–1974* (New York: New York University Press, 1974).

44. *SDR Creation and World Liquidity (in millions of SDRs)*

Total Reserves	1970	1971	1972	1973
All Countries	93,247	123,235	146,519	152,240
Industrial Countries	65,806	88,793	97,461	95,750
SDRs	2,423	4,586	6,575	6,601

SOURCE: IMF, *International Financial Statistics*, December 1976, pp. 18, 20.

45. Liberal defenses of "benign neglect," are Gottfried Haberler and Thomas E. Willet, *A Strategy for U.S. Balance of Payments Policies* (Washington, D.C.: American Enterprise Institute, 1971); Lawrence B. Krause, "A Passive Balance of Payments Strategy," *Brookings Papers on Economic Activity* (1970), no. 3.

46. Economists use three broad analytical approaches to explain the balance of payments: the relative prices, absorption, and monetary approaches. The first approach focuses on relative prices and ignores the influence of important macro variables such as income flows and stocks of assets. To cure an imbalance, relative price adjustment through exchange rate changes or demand-management policies is recommended. The absorption approach sees payments balances characterized, if not caused, by differences, *ex ante*, between an economy's aggregate income and its aggregate domestic spending (absorption). In effect, this approach extends to an open economy the Keynesian model for a closed economy. Income and expenditure flows are emphasized and monetary variables and relative prices are ignored. Although the model's explanatory power is weak, linking the balance of payments to domestic income and expenditure is at least suggestive to policymakers. The third, monetary approach, is described in the text. D. G. Pierce and D. M. Shaw, *Monetary Economic Theories, Evidence and Policy* (London: Butterworth, 1976), pp. 337–55; William M. Corden, *Inflation, Exchange Rates, and the World Economy* (Chicago: University of Chicago Press, 1977), pp. 7–51.

47. Secretary of Defense McNamara; *U.S. Senate, Committees on Armed Services and Appropriations*, "Supplemental Military Procurement and Construction Authorizations, Fiscal Year 1967," Jan. 1967, pp. 96–97. But economic costs are made painfully clear in Robert Warren Stevens, *Vain Hopes, Grim Realities* (New York: New Viewpoints, 1976), pp. 103–20. For incomes, price, and trade effects see F. Gerard Adams and Helen B. Junz, "Effects of the Business Cycle on Trade Flows of the Industrialized Countries," *Journal of Finance* (May 1971).

48. See "Remarks of the Honorable John B. Connally, Secretary of the Treasury, at the International Banking Conference of the American Bankers Association, Munich, Germany," *Department of the Treasury News*, May 28, 1971. U.S. military exchange costs did, in fact, generally exceed the U.S. basic deficit.

49. See, e.g., Harold van B. Cleveland and W. H. Bruce Brittain, *The Great Inflation: A Monetarist View* (Washington, D.C.: National Planning Association 1976), from which much of the analysis is derived. For the internationalist-monetarist approach, see also Marina von N. Whitman, "Global Monetarism and the Monetary Approach to the Balance of Payments," *Brookings Papers on Economic Activity* (1975), no. 3, pp. 491–555;

Robert A. Mundell, *Monetary Theory: Inflation, Interest, and Growth in the World Economy* (Santa Monica, Calif.: Goodyear Publishing, 1971); and Harry Johnson, "The Monetary Approach to Balance of Payments Theory," *Journal of Financial and Quantitative Analysis* (March 1972); *Inflation and the Monetarist Controversy* (Amsterdam–London: North Holland, 1972).

50. Milton Friedman, Statement before the Joint Economic Committee, U.S. 88th Congress, 1st session, the U.S. Balance of Payments, Part 3, Nov. 14, pp. 452–59, cited in Meier, *Problems of a World Monetary Order*, pp. 236–42. See also Harry G. Johnson, "The Case for Flexible Exchange Rates," *Federal Reserve Bank of St. Louis, 1969 Report*, June 1969. For monetarist dissenters from the enthusiasm for floating rates, aside from Rueff, see F. A. von Hayek, *Full Employment at Any Price?* (London: Institute of Economic Affairs, 1975), Occasional Papers no. 45; Mundell's "Concluding Remarks," in *The New International Monetary System*, Robert A. Mundell and Jacques J. Polak, eds. (New York: Columbia University Press, 1977), pp. 237–44. See also *Oxford Economic Papers* (March 1976); 28:1–24.

51. See notes 20 and 23.

52. By 1973, four major changes in the work force had occurred: from 1947 through 1972, male participation went up from 42.7 million to 53.3 million, an increase of about 25 percent, whereas female participation nearly doubled, rising from 16.7 million to 33.3 million; the 16–17 and 18–19 male groups increased from 2.5 million to 4.5 million, nearly doubling, whereas the number of prime age workers, 20–64 years old, only increased from 38.2 million to 46.8 million, or 22.5 percent. From 1954 through 1972, nonwhite male participation rates went up from 4.2 million to 5.3 million, an increase of 26 percent, whereas white male participation went up around 20 percent from 39.8 million to 47.9 million; nonwhite females increased from 2.6 million to 4.2 million, about 75 percent, whereas white females increased from 17.0 million to 29.0 million, about 70 percent. U.S. Bureau of Labor Statistics, *Handbook of Labor Statistics 1973*, pp. 33–36. For the migration of blacks and its impact on unemployment, see Vivian W. Henderson, "Regions, Race, and Jobs," in *Employment, Race and Poverty*, A. M. Ross and Herbert Hill, eds. (New York: Harcourt Brace and World, 1967), pp. 90–97. For a later analysis of the changing work force and its consequences for productivity see Emma Rothschild "Reagan and the Real America," *New York Review of Books*, Feb. 5, 1981, pp. 12–18.

53. *Defense Expenditures as a Percentage of GNP*

	1963–64	1965	1966	1967	1968
U.S.A.	8.9	8.0	9.2	9.8	9.2
France	5.1	5.6	5.4	5.3	5.3
Germany	5.0	4.4	4.8	4.3	3.9
Italy	3.3	2.9	2.9	2.9	2.7
Japan	1.1	1.3	1.0	0.9	0.8
U.K.	6.7	6.3	6.0	5.7	5.3

SOURCE: ISS, *The Military Balance, 1963–64*, p. 43; *1969–70*, pp. 57–58.

For a critique on the productivity and growth consequences of defense spending see Lester C. Thurow, "How to Wreck the Economy," *New York Review of Books*, May 14, 1981, pp. 3–8.

54. For an excellent narrative of international monetary developments see Strange, "International Monetary Relations," pp. 263–99.

55. Charles E. McClure, Jr., "Gradualism and the New Economic Policy," in P. Cagan, ed., *A New Look at Inflation* (Washington, D.C.: American Enterprise Institute, 1973), pp. 46–47. See also *ERP 1970*, pp. 25–27.

56. For unemployment in December 1970, see *ERP 1971*, p. 225. For the Penn-Central bankruptcy, see *New York Times*, June 23, 1970, pp. 1 and 42. For monetary policy, see Cleveland and Brittain, *The Great Inflation: A Monetarist View*, pp. 34–35.

57. *ERP 1973*, p. 294; Harold van B. Cleveland, "How the Dollar Standard Died," *Foreign Policy* (1971–72), p. 45; Charles A. Coombes, "Treasury and Federal Reserve Foreign Exchange Operations," *Federal Reserve Bulletin* (October 1971), pp. 783–814.

58. "Transcript of President's Address on Moves to Deal with Economic Problems," *New York Times*, Aug. 16, 1971, p. 14.

59. Peter G. Peterson, *The United States in the Changing World Economy* (Washington, D.C.: GPO, 1971), 1:1–5, 12.

60. The U.S. market share of Eastern trade among Comecon countries went from 21 percent in 1948 to 7 percent in 1957–59 and 5 percent in 1967–69. Wolfe, *U.S. East-West Trade Policy*, p. 100. For the Nixon-Kissinger strategy in East-West trade see Henry Kissinger, "America's Permanent Interests," *Dept. of State Bulletin*, April 5, 1976, 74 (1919):428; and Kissinger, *Years of Upheaval* (Boston: Little, Brown, 1982), pp. 246–55.

61. For the theory of "free riders," see Kindleberger, *World in Depression, 1929–1939* (Los Angeles: University of California Press, 1973), pp. 301–8; Kindleberger, "Systems of International Economic Organization," in *Money and the Coming World Order*, David P. Calleo, ed., Lehrman Institute Book (New York: New York University Press, 1976).

62. See, for example, Corden, *Inflation, Exchange Rates and the World Economy*, pp. 31–32, 106–8.

63. For a mercantilist apology, see Hans O. Schmitt, "Mercantilism: A Modern Argument," *Manchester School* (June 1979), 47(2):93–111. For continuity between "benign neglect" of the late sixties and Nixon's devaluation, see H. Houthakker, *Wall Street Journal*, March 16, 1973.

64. For the 1971 dollar devaluation's impact on U.S. competitiveness, see James Riedel, "The Symptoms of Declining U.S. International Competitiveness: Causes and Consequences," Joint Economic Committee of the Congress of the United States, *The International Economy: U.S. Role in a World Market, Special Study on Economic Change* (Washington, D.C.: GPO, 1980), 9:230–50. See Robert E. Lawrence, "Toward a Better Understanding of Trade Balance Trends: The Cost Price Puzzle," *Brookings Papers on Economic Activity* (1979), no. 1, pp. 199–210.

65. U.S. Senate Committee on Foreign Relations, Subcommittee on International Economic Policy, *International Debt, the Banks, and U.S. Foreign Policy* (Washington, D.C.: GPO, August 1977), pp. 13–15.

66. See Edward Tufte, *Political Control of the Economy* (Princeton: Princeton University Press, 1978); M. Kalecki, "Political Aspects of Full Employment," *Political Quarterly* (October–December 1943), 14:322–31; William E. Nordhaus, "The Political Business Cycle," *Review of Economic Studies* (April 1975), 42:169–90; and Assar Lindbeck, "Stabilization Policy in Open Economies with Endogenous Politicians," *American Economic Review* (May 1976), 66:1–19. Otto Eckstein, *The Great Recession* (Amsterdam: North Holland, 1978), ch. 4, notes the singularity of Nixon's success in manipulating the economy for the election, a success that apparently eluded the incumbent party in 1960 and 1968 (not to mention 1976 and 1980).

67. *ERP 1981*, p. 293.

68. *ERP 1980*, p. 263. Otto Eckstein, *The Great Recession*, p. 52. Also "Commodities: Something Has to Give," *Fortune*, April 1974, p. 12; and "Trend of American Business," *U.S. News and World Report*, May 27, 1974, p. 70. Whereas the period from the Korean War to Vietnam was essentially free of exogenous shocks and consequently a time of stable economic growth, "since 1965, the shocks have come thick and fast, and have been the decisive movers of the economy." Eckstein, *The Great Recession*, p. 146.

69. *ERP 1975*, p. 143–44, 251, 277, 304.

70. Cited in Cleveland and Brittain, *The Great Inflation*, p. 26.

71. For French inflation and money supply, see IMF, *International Statistical Yearbook*, 1979, p. 55. Government expenditures and financing figures during this period are given in the various issues of the IMF's *International Financial Statistics*, 1968–74.

72. Michel Crozier, ed., *The Crisis of Democracy, Report on the Governability of Democracies to the Trilateral Commission* (New York: New York University Press, 1975). Also Ronald Inglehart, "The Silent Revolution in Europe: Intergenerational Change in Post-Industrial Societies," *American Political Science Review* (Dec. 1971), vol. 65. For welfare spending, social change, and inflation, see Morris Janowitz, *Social Control of the Welfare State* (Chicago: University of Chicago Press, 1976).

73. Cleveland and Brittain, *The Great Inflation*, p. 25–30.

74. Lewis Lehrman, "International Monetary Order," in *Money and the Coming World Order*, D.P. Calleo, ed., (New York: New York University Press, 1976), pp. 71–120. Whether the external monetary system acts to check a particular country's inflation depends essentially on the systemic norm. Even countries with strong domestic coalitions averse to inflation, like Germany or Switzerland, have had great difficulty in arresting their inflation at a level much below the systemic norm—despite willingness in recent years to appreciate their currencies.

75. See Paul Fabra, *Mutations dans la structure financière après Bretton Woods* (Madrid: Instituto de Cooperación Intercontinental; Amsterdam: Fondation Européenne de la Culture, 1980). See also Fabra's regular articles in *Le Monde*.

76.

	Net Size of Eurodollar Market (est.) (in billions of dollars)	U.S. Reserved	U.S. Basic Balance
1971	71.0	12.16	−10.478
1975	205.0	15.88	− 1.239
1976	475.0	20.20	−18.967

SOURCE: Bank of International Settlements, *Annual Reports*, nos. 40, 43, 47; *ERP 1973*, p. 299; *ERP 1976*, pp. 275, 278; *ERP 1980*, p. 324; IMF, *Balance of Payments Yearbook*, (1966–70), 23: 9; (1970–76), 28: 633; (1980), 31: 605.

77. Countries with current account and basic deficits and increasing national reserves financed through short-term capital flows appear to include Belgium, Sweden, Italy, Brazil, Israel, and Peru. IMF, *Balance of Payments Yearbook 1980*, vol. 31.

78. U.S. Senate Committee on Foreign Relations, Subcommittee on International Economic Policy, *International Debt, the Banks and U.S. Foreign Policy* (Washington, D.C.: GPO, 1977), pp. 59–68.

79. John M. Blair, *The Control of Oil* (New York: Pantheon Books, 1976), pp. 106–

204. For an international comparison of retail oil prices and of taxes as a percentage of the total price of oil, see *The Economist*, March 1, 1980, p. 73.

80. Walt W. Rostow gives an exhaustive and fascinating analysis of the Kondratieff cycle's implications for the world economy. Rostow, *The World Economy: History and Prospect* (Austin: University of Texas Press, 1978). The 1973–77 price rise is seen as the upswing of the fifth Kondratieff cycle. Previous cycles peaked in the 1790s, 1860s, 1910s, and late 1940s, as Malthusian shortages and anxieties effected a shift in terms of trade against manufactured goods; pp. 578, 626–43. See also N. D. Kondratieff, "The Long Waves in Economic Life," *Review of Economic Statistics*, (November 1935), 17(6):105–15.

81. *ERP 1980*, p. 263. Also Eckstein, *The Great Recession*, p. 52, see also "Commodities: Something Has to Give," *Fortune*, April 1974, p. 12; and "Trend of American Business," *U.S. News and World Report*, May 27, 1974, p. 70. For prices, see Rostow, *The World Economy*, pp. 248–49.

82. John M. Blair, *The Control of Oil*, pp. 159–86.

83. *Consumption of Commercial Energy per Capita (in kilograms of coal equivalent)*

	U.S.A.	European Market Economies
1955	7,889	3,504
1960	8,172	3,810
1965	9,176	4,521
1970	10,870	5,739
1975	10,693	5,836
1979	11,361	6,317

SOURCE: United Nations, *World Energy Supplies* 1950–74; United Nations, *Yearbook of World Energy Statistics, 1979*.

84. From 1947 to 1965, U.S. energy consumption grew at 2.8 percent annually; from 1965 to 1973, at 4.2 percent per year. With domestic production almost at peak capacity in 1972, the mandatory oil import quotas were removed. By 1973, the United States received one-third of its oil imports from the Arab nations. Eckstein, *The Great Recession*, pp. 114–15; Blair, *The Control of Oil*, pp. 159–88.

85. David P. Calleo, "The European Coalition in a Fragmenting World," *Foreign Affairs* (October 1975), 54:103–12. For U.S proposals on the safety net, see Thomas O. Enders, "The Role of Financial Mechanisms in the Overall Oil Strategy," *Department of State Bulletin*, March 10, 1975, pp. 312–17. For the French stance at the Washington Conference and Kissinger's response, see "Text of Communique to Washington Energy Conference and Summary Statement," and "Secretary Kissinger's News Conference of February 13," *Department of State Bulletin*, March 4, 1974, pp. 220–30.

86. For European energy policies after the 1973 crisis see Guy de Carmoy, *Energy for Europe: Economic and Political Implications* (Washington, D.C.: American Enterprise Institute for Public Policy Research, 1977); R. Prodi and A. Cio, "The Oil Crisis: Europe" *Daedelus* (Fall 1975), pp. 91–112. For recent European energy policies see Wilfrid L. Kohl, ed., *After the Second Oil Crisis: Energy Policies in Europe, America and Japan* (Lexington, Mass.: Lexington Books, 1982).

87. "The Raging Fight over Burke Hartke," *Business Week*, Feb. 12, 1972, p. 14; *ERP 1969*, pp. 4–126.

88. The bill also liberalized adjustment assistance "to workers and businesses adversely affected by imports," *ERP 1971*, pp. 154–58.

89. For an assessment of the Tokyo round negotiations see William R. Cline, *Trade Negotiations in the Tokyo Round: A Quantitative Assessment* (Washington, D.C.: Brookings Institution, 1978).

90. Riedel, "The Symptoms of Declining U.S. International Competitiveness," p. 23–250.

91. Shultz and Dam, *Economic Policy Beyond the Headlines*, pp. 18–19.

92. For petro-dollar recycling by U.S. banks in the years immediately after 1974, see Paul A. Volcker, "The Recycling Problem Revisited," *Challenge* (July/August 1980), pp. 3–14. See also, Fabra, *Mutations dans la structure financière.* Technical innovations in banking, like Electronic Funds Transfer and Negotiable Order of Withdrawal accounts changed the character and velocity of the money supply and made the Fed's control even more tenuous. See "More Bang for the Buck," *Fortune*, May 1977, pp. 202–28; *Fortune*, April 24, 1978, p. 82; *ERP 1979*, pp. 47–53; *ERP 1980*, pp. 51–58. For a radical critique of the Fed's pretension to control the money supply, see Lewis E. Lehrman, *Monetary Policy, the Federal Reserve System, and Gold*, Morgan Stanley, Investment Research Memorandum, Jan. 25, 1980.

93. In 1979, roughly one quarter of U.S. exports went to non-OPEC developing countries, a share close to that taken by Western Europe. The dependence of Japan and the EEC on trade with the Third World was substantially greater. Geoffrey Barraclough, "The Struggle for the Third World," *New York Review of Books*, Nov. 9, 1978, pp. 47–48. For a discussion, see *ERP 1981*, p. 347.

94. For Kissinger's views, see his speech "Energy, Raw Materials and Development: The Search for Common Ground," *Department of State Bulletin*, Jan. 12, 1976, pp. 37–48.

95. Benjamin M. Rowland, "Economic Policy and Development: The Case of Latin America," in *Retreat from Empire?* Robert E. Osgood, ed., (Baltimore: Johns Hopkins University Press, 1973), pp. 241–77.

96. U.S. Senate Committee on Foreign Relations, Subcommittee on International Economic Policy, *International Debt, the Banks and U.S. Foreign Policy*, pp. 9–12, 43. Also Volcker, "The Recycling Problem Revisited"; Robert N. Dunn, Jr., "Exchange Rates, Payments Adjustment, and OPEC: Why Oil Deficits Persist," *Princeton Essays in International Finance*, (Dec. 1979), no. 137.

97. For the Nixon administration's "Project Independence," see *ERP 1974*, pp. 122–25. For Ford's program, see *ERP 1975*, pp. 20–24. For the much diluted "Energy Policy and Conservation Act" of 1975, see *ERP 1976*, pp. 23–24; *New York Times*, Dec. 23, 1975, p. 1. See also Craufurd D. Goodwin, ed., *Energy Policy in Perspective: Today's Problems, Yesterday's Solutions* (Washington, D.C.: Brookings Institution, 1981).

98. For Carter's original energy proposals, see *OECD Economic Survey: United States*, July 1978, pp. 53–54. To contrast them with the final product, see "Seven Years after the Embargo, U.S. Has an Energy Policy," *Congressional Quarterly Weekly Report*, Oct. 25, 1980, pp. 3207–12. For Reagan's position on decontrol and his view toward the U.S. Energy Dept., see "President Reagan's Oil Decontrol Statement," *New York Times*, Jan. 29, 1981, p. D6; "Reagan Adopts Plan to End Energy Dept. and Shift Its Duties," *New York Times*, Dec. 17, 1981, pp. A1 and D23.

99. For figures, see U.S. Department of Commerce, *International Economic Indicators* (Sept. 1979), pp. 26, 46, 62, 63, 78.

100. *Relative Price of Oil (percent changes from prior periods)*

	U.S. Consumer Price Index	Price of Oil Per Barrel[a]	Dollar Depreciation	
			SDR	DM
1970	31.0	− 15.4	−	−12.5
1971	4.3	21.2	−0.4	−10.4
1972	3.5	15.2	−7.7	− 1.8
1973	6.2	42.1	−8.9	−15.6
1974	11.0	261.5	−0.9	−10.9
1975	9.1	9.8	−0.9	8.9
1976	5.8	7.4	5.2	− 9.9
1977	6.5	7.7	−1.1	−10.9
1978	7.7	2.4	−6.7	−13.2
1979	11.3	33.6	−3.1	− 5.3
1980	12.5	65.4	−0.9	10.9 (November)

SOURCE: *ERP 1981*, P. 289; IMF, *International Financial Statistics*, November 1960, pp. 130–31; September 1977, pp. 148–49; January 1981, pp. 10, 52, 133–34.

a. Saudi Arabian Light Crude (34–34.9°) in 1975 dollars

101. "The Final Stretch—and Both Men are Behind," *The Economist*, Oct. 30, 1976, pp. 45–46.

102. *ERP 1982*, pp. 318, 346.

103. Subcommittee on Foreign Economic Policy, U.S. Senate Committee on Foreign Relations, *International Debt, the Banks, and U.S. Foreign Policy*, p. 9.

104. For an influential OECD perspective, see Paul McCracken, ed., *Towards Full Employment and Price Stability* (Paris: OECD, 1977). For an American critique of the "locomotive" theory, see Geoffrey E. Wood and Nancy Ammon Jianakoplos, "Coordinated International Expansion: Are Convoys of Locomotives the Answer?" *Federal Reserve Bank of St. Louis*, (July 1978), 60(7). For the German critique, see the *Annual Report of the Deutsche Bundesbank, 1976*, p. 48. See also, "The Spirit of Rambouillet," *The Economist*, Nov. 22, 1975, pp. 77–78; "Jawing in Jamaica," *The Economist*, Jan. 1976, p. 81.

105. For a fuller development, see my "Inflation and American Power," *Foreign Affairs* (Spring 1981), 59:781–812.

106. See Loukas Tsoukalis, *The Politics and Economics of European Monetary Integration* (London: Allen and Unwin, 1977), and Tom De Vries, "On the Meaning and Future of the European Monetary System," *Princeton Essays in International Finance*, (Sept. 1980), no. 138.

107. See Malcolm MacKintosh, "The Impact of the Middle East Crisis on Super-Power Relations," *Adelphi Papers* (London: International Institute for Strategic Studies, Spring 1975) no. 114, pp. 1–19; Leslie M. Pryor, "Arms and the Shah," *Foreign Policy* (Summer 1978), 31:56–71; Geoffrey Kemp, "The Military Build-up: Arms Control or Arms Trade?" *Adelphi Papers* (London: International Institute for Strategic Studies, Spring 1975), no. 114, pp. 31–37.

108. See Raymond William Baker, *Egypt's Uncertain Revolution under Nasser and Sadat* (Cambridge: Harvard University Press, 1978) pp. 127–29, 138–43.

109. *ERP 1979*, pp. 153–56.

110. "Manic Gold Trading Poses a Global Threat," *Business Week*, Oct. 1, 1979, p. 56; "More Shocks for the Monetary System," *Business Week*, Jan. 21, 1980, pp. 86–89.

111. *ERP 1980*, pp. 54–55; Paul Volcker, "Statements to Congress on October 17, 1979," *Federal Reserve Bulletin* (Nov. 1979), vol. 65:888–89; *New York Times Magazine*, Dec. 2, 1979, pp. 59, 62. For interest rates and the recovery of the dollar during this period see *ERP 1981*, pp. 309–43.

112. IMF, *International Financial Statistics* (March 1980), p. 52; (June 1981), p. 52.

113. See, for example, Leslie Gelb, "NATO Is Facing Paralysis of Will, Experts Contend," *New York Times*, July 12, 1981, pp. 1, 14; Richard Halloran, "Weinberger, in London, Cautions Against Appeasement of Moscow," *New York Times*, Oct. 23, 1981, p. 6. The "Finlandization" scenario is most eloquently argued by Walter Laqueur, *A Continent Astray: Europe, 1970–1978* (New York: Oxford University Press, 1979) pp. 180–283. For the gas pipeline controversy see John Schutte, Jr. "Pipeline Politics," *SAIS Review* (Summer, 1982), no. 4, pp. 137–47.

114. U.S. defense spending increases were especially heavy in fiscal years 1979 ($12.5 billion), 1980 ($18.2 billion), and 1981 ($23.9 billion). In the same years, overall fiscal deficits were $27.7 billion, $59.6 billion, and $57.9 billion respectively. In a downswing, of course, deficits are swollen by antirecession stabilizers as well as a relative decline in revenue. *ERP 1982*, pp. 316–19.

115. For Reagan's policies see *America's New Beginning: A Program for Economic Recovery*, The White House, Office of the Press Secretary, Feb. 18, 1981; *Budget of the United States Government*, Executive Office of the President, Office of Management and Budget, FY 1982 and FY 1983 (Washington, D.C.: GPO); *ERP 1982*, pp. 21–191.

116. Robert E. Lawrence, "An Analysis of the 1977 U.S. Trade Deficit," *Brookings Papers on Economic Activity* (1978), no. 1, p. 182; and Rothschild, "Reagan and the Real America." See also note 64.

117. See, for example, "Reindustrialization of America," *Business Week*, June 30, 1980, pp. 55–61.

118. *ERP 1982*, pp. 239, 295, 310.

Epilogue
An Assessment

ECONOMIC ISSUES HAVE critically influenced the ways in which American diplomats have perceived and implemented foreign policy. This study was prompted in large part by the attention that revisionist historians brought to the role of economic change and ideology in American diplomacy. Fundamentally, our findings on the interaction of economics and diplomacy do not support their interpretation, which emphasizes an ideologically based consensus in the United States on the need for foreign economic expansion to solve domestic economic and social problems. Nevertheless, revisionist scholarship has made an important contribution by drawing attention to the domestic sources of foreign policy, and in this sense we see our efforts as a vindication of their work. With this volume, we wanted to move beyond the debate engendered by the economic determinism of the revisionists' work and develop a more comprehensive framework for understanding the role of economic factors in American foreign policy.

In the future, we believe that scholars interested in the interaction of economics and diplomacy will have to ground their work securely in an understanding of the broad international economic setting in which the United States acted. Among the key variables shaping the nature of the global economic system for any given period were the relative power of the major states, the compatibility of their economic strategies, and the extent to which any nation's economy influenced the behavior of other states. At times, economics provided the primary context within which American diplomacy developed. The foregoing essays demonstrate, however, that broad structural changes in the domestic and world economies and in the international political environment usually shaped American diplomacy more than the pressures of particular domestic interest groups or the ideological predispositions of elite groups and policymakers. In other words, American businessmen and statesmen often found themselves facing limited options that did not live up to their desires and expectations in the foreign sphere.

The fundamental change in the American economy over the last two centuries, from a system based on agriculture to one based on industry, *lessened* the impact of economic considerations on U.S. foreign policy, at least until recently. Diplomacy before the Civil War was influenced by the American economy's heavy reliance on foreign capital and trade in agricultural commodities. In contrast, the increasingly industrial and urban economy of the late nineteenth and early twentieth centuries was much less susceptible to the vicissitudes of the international marketplace. The domestic market itself became the great prize, and businessmen, politicians, and diplomats understood the shift and its implications. Moreover, foreign trade in manufactured goods was less than the trade in agricultural products and never assumed the economic importance in the United States that it did in the other major industrial countries. In such circumstances, domestic politics tended to override diplomacy in American public life.

Changes in the international economic and political structure brought about a corresponding rise or decline of economic considerations in American foreign policy. In the early days of the republic, when Great Britain and France struggled over the spread of revolution in Europe and beyond, the United States found itself buffeted by the competing military and economic strategies of the two stronger powers and ultimately driven to war with England in 1812. While the United States repeatedly had to contend with the overwhelming naval and commercial power of Great Britain after 1815, it benefitted from the relative security brought to international affairs by the stable European balance of power. The free trade policies promoted by Britain through most of the nineteenth century also boosted American exports of agricultural commodities, such as cotton, which were of great importance to the national economy. Similarly, American exports and imports, as well as investments made by Europeans in this country and by Americans abroad, flowed through channels of an international economic system dominated and efficiently served by London bankers, shippers, and insurance agents. By the late nineteenth century, rapid industrialization made the United States more self-sufficient in manufactured goods, thereby setting the stage for dramatic export growth at the turn of the century.

While the British-dominated international economy of the pre–World War I period served American foreign economic interests quite well, the United States had numerous, far-flung territories to protect after the Spanish-American War. Strategic issues, especially in the Caribbean, preoccupied American Presidents to a greater extent than at any time after the early days of independence. The United States used its economic power quite effectively in the Caribbean before the First World War, but enjoyed less success in the Far East. The government also used investment and trade inducements before and after the war, albeit often in a clumsy and unsystematic fashion, to attain larger foreign policy goals in Latin America. For the first time, American policymakers were able to mobilize economic power to serve important strategic and political ends.

World War I was a pivotal event in American foreign relations. Economic issues assumed a greater place in American diplomacy than they had in the first half of the nineteenth century when agricultural exports had driven foreign economic policy choices. But by 1920 both the structure of the international economy and the role of the United States were very different from a century before. At this point the United States had become a major creditor nation, and its bankers, merchants, shippers, and manufacturers filled the vacuum left by the decline of the international monetary and trading system built by the British. At the same time, the war brought greater political and military security to the United States, for potential enemies were weakened. Yet foreign policy remained subordinated to domestic politics during the 1920s and 1930s. The United States government squandered its considerable leverage in the interwar period by relegating international economic problems to the private sector, which, however effective it was in managing short-term problems, could not manage the international panic and depression that followed the collapse of financial institutions and of world trade in the late 1920s and early 1930s. The indifference or hostility of Presidents Hoover and Roosevelt toward international economic institutions probably compounded the depression. When Secretary of State Cordell Hull finally won Roosevelt's blessing to begin reducing barriers to trade and currency convertibility, the damage was already done.

Economic issues and interests again assumed a major role in American diplomacy after World War II. The United States sought to reshape the international economic system on a multilateral and interdependent basis and, where that proved impossible, to use economic instruments to strengthen the West against the threat posed by the Soviet Union. In this period, foreign policy goals, not the least of which was the maintenance of an international economic order that would promote peace and prosperity, usually superseded domestic politics. Having implemented its liberal economic and political program with the Bretton Woods agreements, the Marshall Plan, the General Agreement on Trade and Tariffs, and the integration of Germany and Japan into a multilateral economic order, the United States dominated the world economy for the first two decades after World War II. In part, this extraordinary influence flowed from America's predominant economic and military power within the international system. In a world struggling to rebuild after the devastation of the war, an unscathed America could expand its influence and spread its ideas and institutions through the non-Communist world essentially without challenge. But the multilateral economic institutions, which the United States inspired and directed, also helped maintain American power by providing reliable foreign sources of raw materials and outlets for American exports and investment.

With the recovery of America's Western allies and former

Axis adversaries, the relative power and influence of the United States within the international structure declined. The multilateral institutions remained in place, but the United States was no longer preeminent, as its allies were less likely to defer automatically to American wishes. European and Japanese policymakers have held the United States responsible for the troubling inflation that has plagued the world since the late 1970s, and protectionist tendencies in the United States and abroad threaten the multilateral world order. Facing a number of seemingly intractable domestic economic problems, Americans are less willing to pay the price—foreign economic aid, liberal commercial policies, and a global military presence—necessary to maintain the postwar multilateral order.

As important as the broad context of international power is to an understanding of the impact of economics on diplomacy, it is not in itself a sufficient explanation. If the first prescription of this study is to keep in mind the broad international economic and political context, our second recommendation is not to forget the complexity of the domestic context, especially the role of ideology and economic interest groups. Like the revisionists, we find in the American experience an ideological consensus for a world open to trade and investment, free enterprise, and liberal political institutions. Yet throughout most of the nation's two hundred years, other factors exercised greater influence than ideology in the formation of policy.

Ideology played an important role in American diplomacy in shaping the diplomatists' image of a desirable world order. It was a consistent and humane body of doctrine. During most of the national experience, however, the United States did not have the power to impose its values on an inhospitable international system. Strategic needs often overrode ideological preferences. Most importantly, foreign policy goals remained subordinated to domestic economic and political considerations for much of the American experience. Throughout American history, and especially since the Civil War, the domestic market has been far more important than the foreign one. Businessmen, congressmen, and policymakers knew that and shared a belief in limited government at home and abroad, even after World War I when some policymakers began to grasp the growing interdependence of the major industrial states. Then, too, protectionist business opinion in the United States was often at odds with the liberal ideology of free trade and investment. The Congress' predisposition toward limited government at home and abroad, at least before 1945, made the United States miss opportunities, especially in the 1920s, to implement its own ideas. Thus, even if liberal ideology had been universally shared throughout the American national experience, it did not necessarily prescribe an activist and expansive foreign economic policy.

Domestic economic interests exercised an important, but seldom predominant, influence in the making of American foreign policy. Economic interests at home played an uneven and often negative role in policy choices, and they rarely prevailed without being closely tied to other factors such as strategic advantage or prevailing ideology. None of us found a sustained and coherent effort by domestic interest groups to press governmental officials to solve domestic problems by economic expansion. The influence of domestic interest groups was limited by their number and their general lack of consensus. Private groups did at times play an important part in American diplomacy. But we failed to find a distinct pattern in the role of private economic interests in American diplomacy.

In short, scholars need to devote greater effort to examining the complex interrelationships among economic aspirations, ideological tenets, and national security imperatives. For studies of the twentieth century, this involves identifying key policymaking bodies and analyzing the interaction of these bureaucracies with interest groups and the Congress. In every case, understanding the political context is essential; one cannot understand an official's public statement without relating it to his audience and his actual behavior.

We asked at the beginning of this study whether or not economics constitutes the primary context by which one can understand American foreign policy. Our general conclusion is that international economic conditions were on occasion the dominant feature of American foreign policy. In the early decades of the republic, America's foreign trade and economic relations with Great Britain were central to foreign policy, but during most of the nineteenth century the challenge of settling the frontier and other domestic problems relegated all foreign policy issues to a secondary status. In the 1920s, economic considerations played a central role in American diplomacy, but mostly because the United States did not face serious challenges to its security from abroad. The experience of the 1930s was a powerful lesson on the dangers of economic nationalism and the need for American leadership of the world economy. In the post–World War II period, when the security challenge to the United States was perceived as greater, a rough consensus reemerged among policymakers that American security required the creation of an international economic system that could contribute to the prosperity of the United States and other countries.

By the 1970s, both the Western allies and the developing countries were seriously challenging American domination of the postwar international system. For the foreseeable future, economic issues may well become the primary context of American foreign policy. Given the increasing interdependence of the world economy, the performance of foreign economies is likely to have a greater impact upon the United States than at any time in the last 150 years. Security issues, too, are increasingly tied to international and domestic economic developments. The decline of America's productivity and competitiveness in international markets will undoubtedly erode its capability to sustain a major rearmament and a substantial overseas military presence at the same time. The interdependent economic order which the United States fostered after the Second World War has generated unprecedented prosperity for its citizens and unrivaled military power through most of the postwar era, but these benefits have come at the price of increasing vulnerability to perhaps uncontrollable changes in the world economic and political structure.

Index

American War, 174; growth during World War II, 313; improved consular service, 128; and promoting economic interests, 175, 181–84; and trade assistance, 129–32; and trade before *1898*, 188
Department of War, 174
Depew, Chauncey M., 125, 166
Dingley, Nelson, 140
Dingley Tariff, 136
Dodge, Joseph, 363
"Dollar Diplomacy," 194–95, 203; *see also* Philander Knox; William Howard Taft
Dominican Republic, 193–94, 204–5
Dulles, Allen, 375
Dulles, John Foster, 368–69, 375
Dupont Company, 261
Dwight, Timothy, 52

Economic determinism, xi, xiii; *see also* Revisionism
Edge Banks, 218, 229, 250
Edison, Thomas A., 131
Elliot, Jonathan, 50
Embargo, 24, 25, 32, 34; *see also* Thomas Jefferson
Eisenhower, Dwight D.: and balance of payments, 379–81; and Cuba, 377–79; Eisenhower Doctrine, 370; and foreign economic policy, 358–63; and foreign investment, 354; and inflation, 399, 402; and Latin America, 374–79; on oil and national security, 365–66; and Suez crisis, 368–71; and USSR in Third World, 364
England, *see* Great Britain
Eppes Bill, 37
Erie Canal, 43
Erskine Agreement, 34–35
Essex case, 30
Essex Junto, 24
European Coal Organization, 346
European Common Market, 367
Evarts, William M., 124
Everett, Edward, 87, 100
Eximbank, 288–89, 292–93, 305, 310, 328, 337, 340, 344, 352, 362, 372–74, 384
Expansionists, *see* Commercial expansionists
Exports, *see* Commercial expansionists; Foreign economic policy; Foreign trade

Farrell, James, 260
Federal Reserve System, 180, 213, 218, 229, 240, 251
Federal Trade Commission, 175
Federalists, 17, 23, 24
Feis, Herbert, 300, 323
Fillmore, Millard, 89
Firestone, Harvey, 290
Firestone Tire and Rubber Company, 326
Fish, Hamilton, 130, 145
Florida(s), 36, 37
Florida Treaty of 1819, 43
Forbes, James Murray, 69, 112
Forbes, Ralph, 68
Ford, Gerald R., 433
Ford, Worthington C., 134
Ford Motor Company, 326
Fordney-McComber Tariff, 249, 255
Foreign Economic Administration, 314
Foreign economic policy: between 1861 and 1898, 127; and Eisenhower, 358, 379–81; and Truman, 357; after War of *1812*, 40; and World War II, 313–15; after World War II, 334–36; *see also* Foreign investment; Foreign trade
Foreign investment, 122, 246–51, 258–59, 352, 354, 359
Foreign trade: and American diplomacy, 460; and Blaine, 124; after *1820*, 55–61; and Jefferson, 30–32; in 1920s, 246–51, 258–59; in 1930s, 277–78, 296–97, 301; significance of cotton in, 57–58; standing of U.S. before 1900 in, 121–23, 146–47; of U.S. by *1913*, 176–77; after World War II, 333–34, 345, 349
Foster, John W., 129, 145, 152
Free trade, *see* Protectionism; Tariffs
Frelinghuysen, Frederick T., 130, 156
Freneau, Philip, 52
Friedman, Milton, 404, 414
Frye, William P., 140
Fulton, Robert, 22

Gadsden Purchase, 43
Gallatin, Albert, 25, 35, 41
Gardner, Lloyd, 289

THE POLITICAL ECONOMY
OF INTERNATIONAL CHANGE
John Gerard Ruggie, General Editor